CW01160108
THIS BOOK BELONGS TO
Mansoor ullah Khan
Notes

CONTENTS

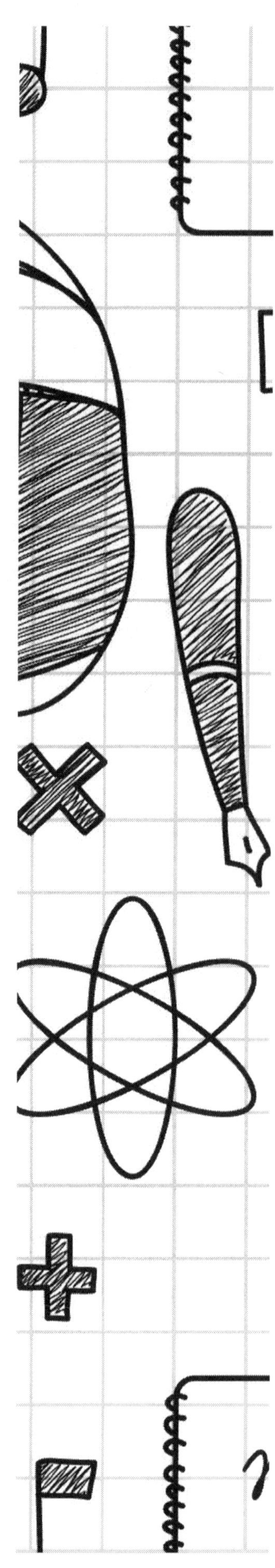

Addition, Subtraction & Multiplication

Puzzle 1
Junior
+ = 12
- = 0
+ = 9
+ =

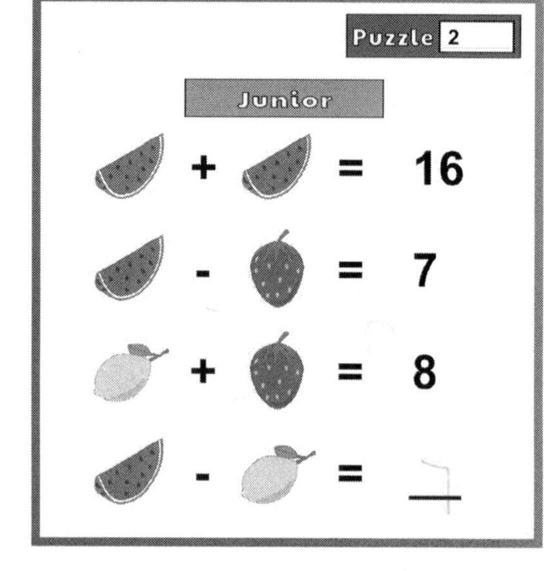
Puzzle 2
Junior
+ = 16
- = 7
+ = 8
- =

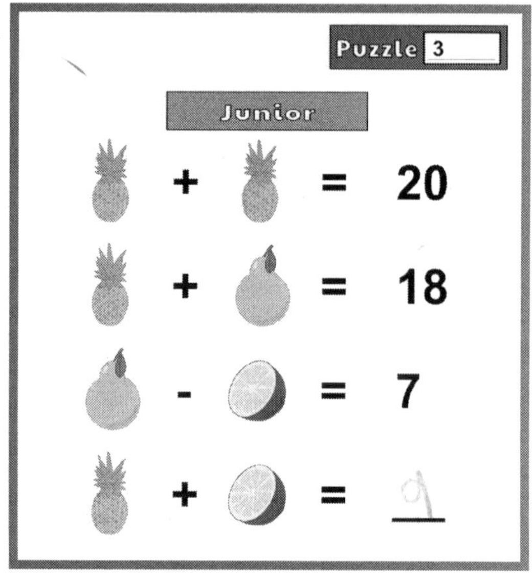
Puzzle 3
Junior
+ = 20
+ = 18
- = 7
+ =

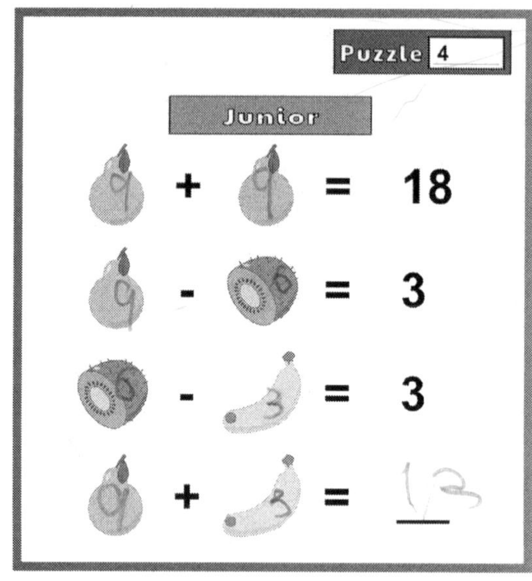
Puzzle 4
Junior
+ = 18
- = 3
- = 3
+ =

Puzzle 5
Junior
+ = 12
- = 5
+ = 11
+ =

Puzzle 6
Junior
+ = 2
+ = 11
+ = 14
- =

Puzzle 7
Junior
+ = 14
+ = 11
+ = 13
- =

Puzzle 8
Junior
+ = 2
+ = 8
- = 1
+ =

Puzzle 9
Junior
+ = 18
+ = 14
- = 1
- =

Puzzle 10
Junior
+ = 20
- = 4
+ = 9
+ =

Puzzle 11
Junior
+ = 14
+ = 10
+ = 5
- =

Puzzle 12
Junior
+ = 12
+ = 16
+ = 14
- =

Puzzle 13
Junior
+ = 2
+ = 10
- = 5
+ =

Puzzle 14
Junior
+ = 4
- = 1
+ = 7
+ =

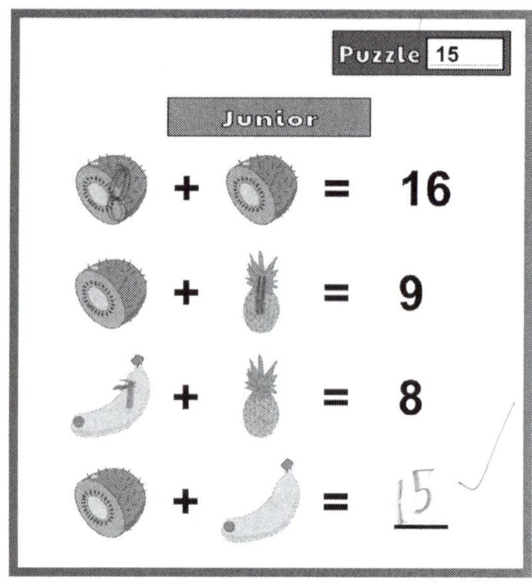

Puzzle 15
Junior
+ = 16
+ = 9
+ = 8
+ =

Puzzle 16
Junior
+ = 2
- = 9
+ = 19
+ =

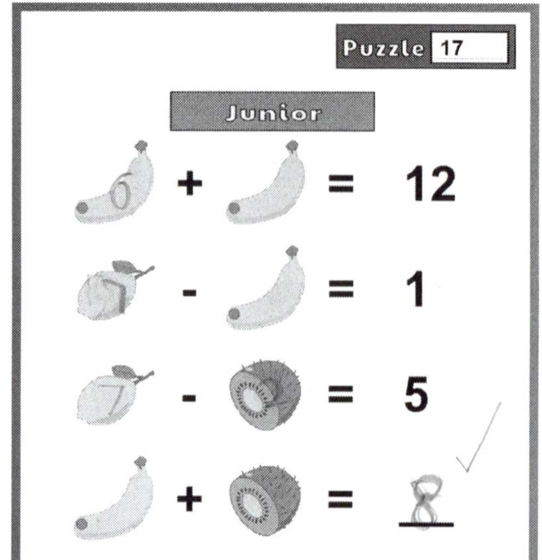

Puzzle 17
Junior
+ = 12
- = 1
- = 5
+ =

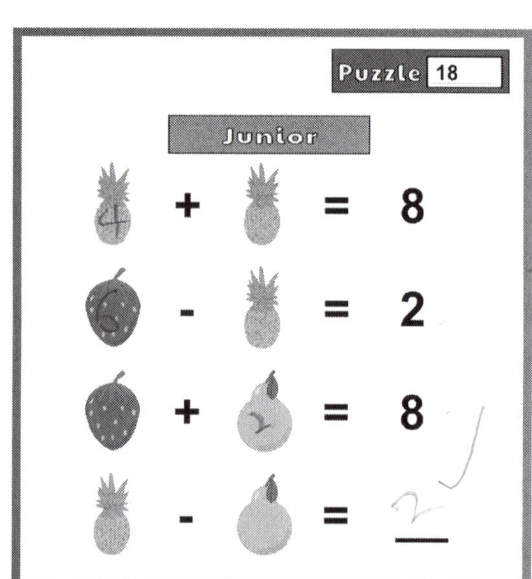

Puzzle 18
Junior
+ = 8
- = 2
+ = 8
- =

Puzzle 19
Junior
+ = 16
- = 1
+ = 16
- =

Puzzle 20
Junior
+ = 4
- = 4
- = 1
- =

Puzzle 21
Junior
+ = 12
+ = 16
+ = 13
- =

Puzzle 22
Junior
+ = 4
- = 4
- = 1
- =

Puzzle 23
Junior
+ = 18
+ = 11
- = 5
+ =

Puzzle 24
Junior
+ = 20
- = 2
- = 1
+ =

Puzzle 25
Junior
+ = 2
+ = 6
+ = 12
- = __

Puzzle 26
Junior
+ = 6
+ = 8
- = 3
+ = __

Puzzle 27
Junior
+ = 16
- = 0
+ = 11
+ = __

Puzzle 28
Junior
+ = 6
+ = 4
- = 9
- = __

Puzzle 29
Junior
+ = 16
- = 2
+ = 14
- = __

Puzzle 30
Junior
+ = 12
+ = 15
+ = 16
+ = __

Puzzle 31
Medium
+ = 10
- = -15
+ = 25
x = __

Puzzle 32
Medium
+ = 4
+ = 12
+ = 13
x = __

Puzzle 33
Medium
+ = 4
+ = 5
- = -5
+ = __

Puzzle 34
Medium
+ = 18
+ = 11
+ = 9
+ = __

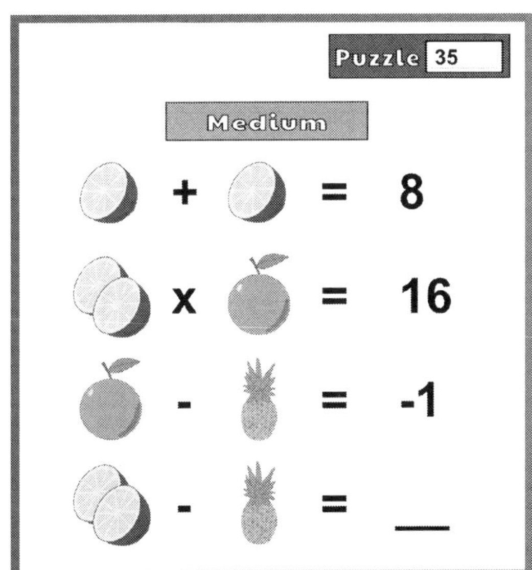
Puzzle 35
Medium
+ = 8
x = 16
- = -1
- = __

Puzzle 36
Medium
+ = 24
x = 48
- = -2
+ = __

Puzzle 37
Medium
+ = 10
+ = 7
- = -1
x = __

Puzzle 38
Medium
+ = 30
- = 8
x = 10
+ = __

Puzzle 39
Medium
+ = 4
- = -7
+ = 16
+ = __

Puzzle 40
Medium
+ = 30
x = 60
- = -3
+ = __

Puzzle 41
Medium
+ = 18
- = 5
+ = 12
x = __

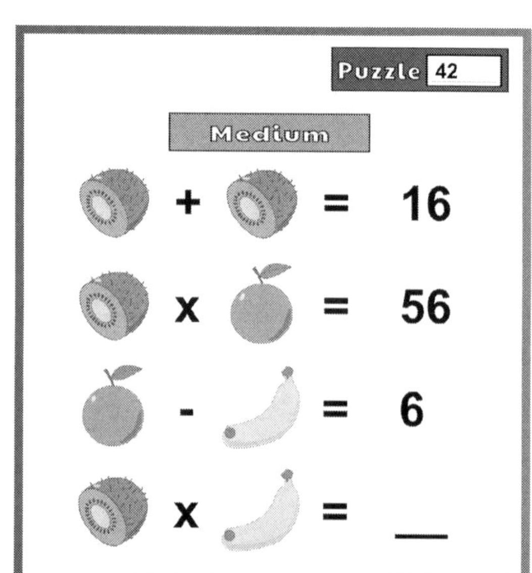
Puzzle 42
Medium
+ = 16
x = 56
- = 6
x = __

Puzzle 43
Medium
+ = 6
x = 60
- = 1
x = ___

Puzzle 44
Medium
+ = 6
- = 0
x = 30
- = ___

Puzzle 45
Medium
+ = 12
x = 54
- = -1
- = ___

Puzzle 46
Medium
+ = 12
- = -6
+ = 18
- = ___

Puzzle 47
Medium
+ = 8
x = 28
+ = 15
x = ___

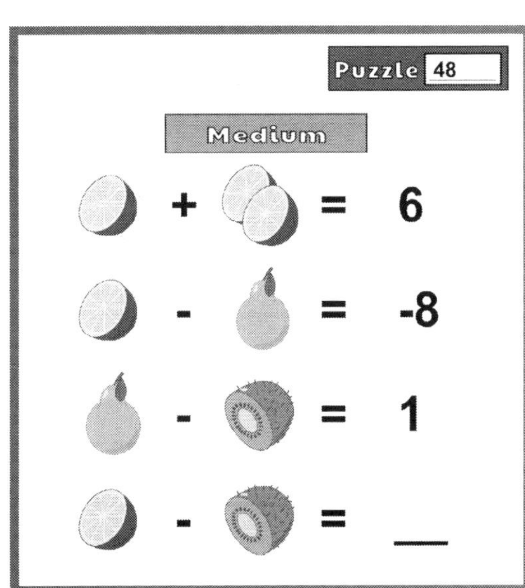
Puzzle 48
Medium
+ = 6
- = -8
- = 1
- = ___

Puzzle 49
Medium
+ = 10
x = 15
x = 15
- =

Puzzle 50
Medium
+ = 6
- = 1
- = -8
- =
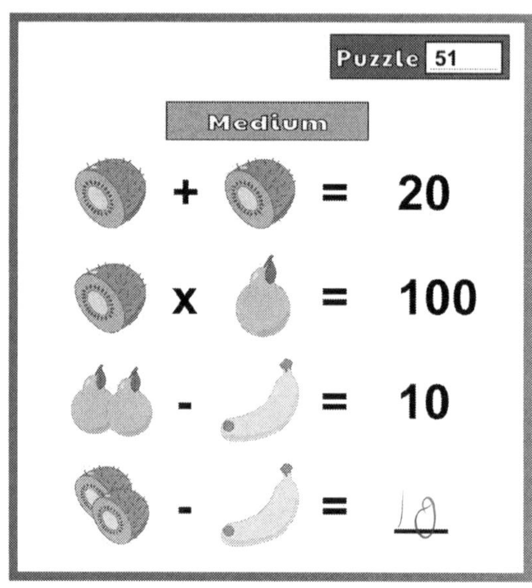
Puzzle 51
Medium
+ = 20
x = 100
- = 10
- =

Puzzle 52
Medium
+ = 18
+ = 10
x = 40
- =

Puzzle 53
Medium
+ = 6
- = -9
x = 12
+ =

Puzzle 54
Medium
+ = 4
+ = 12
+ = 14
- =

Puzzle 55
Medium
+ = 18
- = 2
- = -2
- = __

Puzzle 56
Medium
+ = 12
- = -6
- = 8
- = __

Puzzle 57
Medium
+ = 14
x = 98
+ = 15
- = __

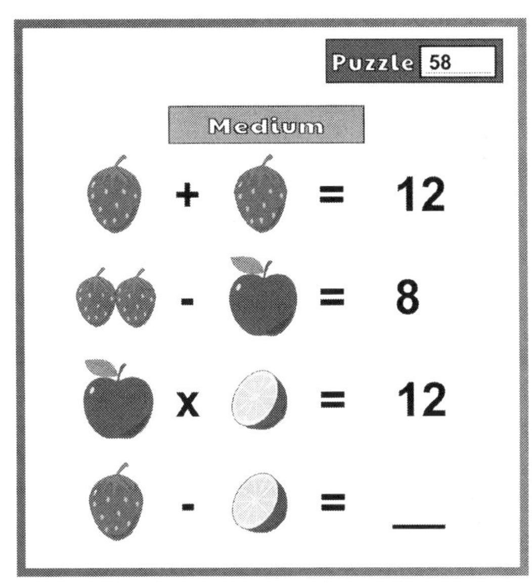
Puzzle 58
Medium
+ = 12
- = 8
x = 12
- = __

Puzzle 59
Medium
+ = 14
+ = 10
+ = 13
- = __

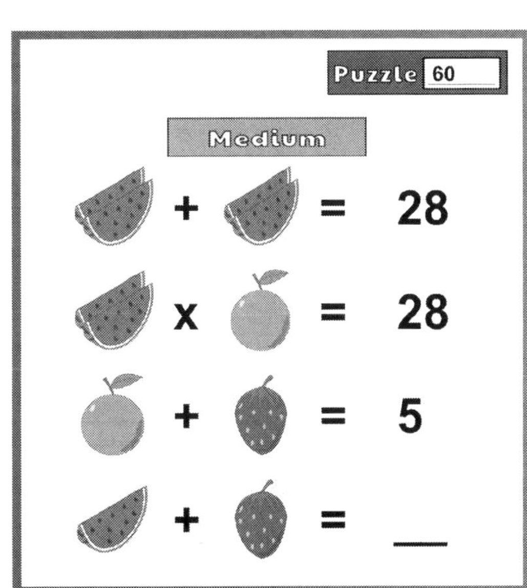
Puzzle 60
Medium
+ = 28
x = 28
+ = 5
+ = __

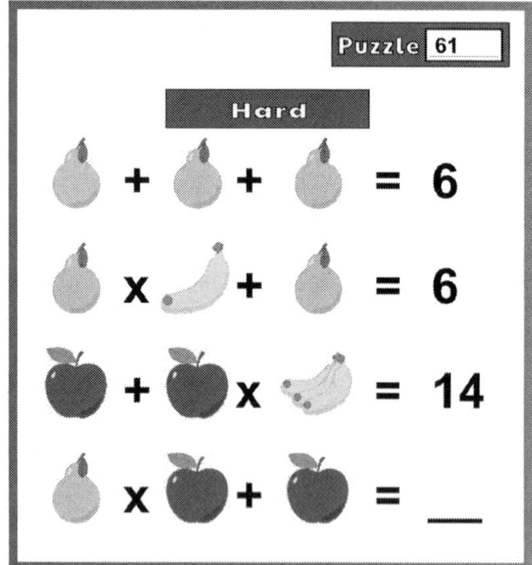
Puzzle 61
Hard
+ + = 6
x + = 6
+ x = 14
x + = __

Puzzle 62
Hard
+ + = 12
+ x = 48
+ x = 10
- + = __
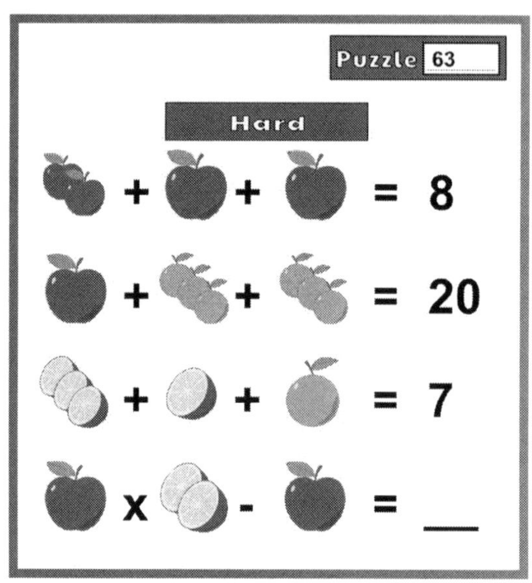
Puzzle 63
Hard
+ + = 8
+ + = 20
+ + = 7
x - = __

Puzzle 64
Hard
+ + = 30
+ + = 23
+ + = 10
x - = __
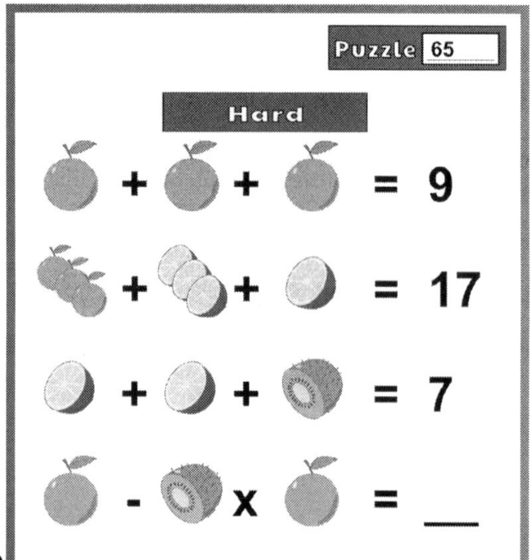
Puzzle 65
Hard
+ + = 9
+ + = 17
+ + = 7
- x = __
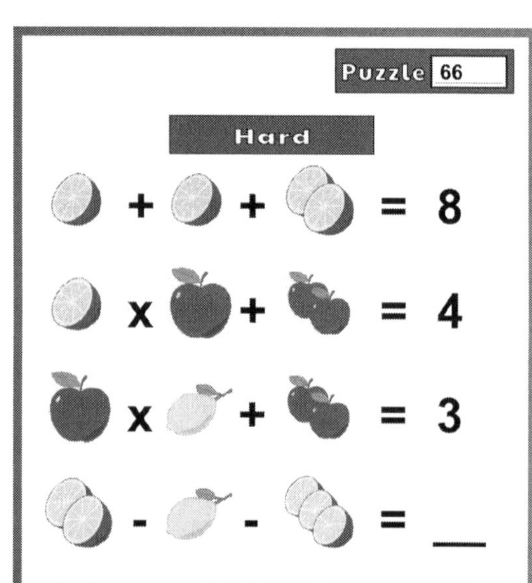
Puzzle 66
Hard
+ + = 8
x + = 4
x + = 3
- - = __

Puzzle 67
Hard
+ + = 15
+ x = 7
+ + = 13
x + = __

Puzzle 68
Hard
+ + = 24
+ x = 56
+ + = 20
- x = __

Puzzle 69
Hard
+ + = 10
x + = 3
+ x = 17
+ x = __

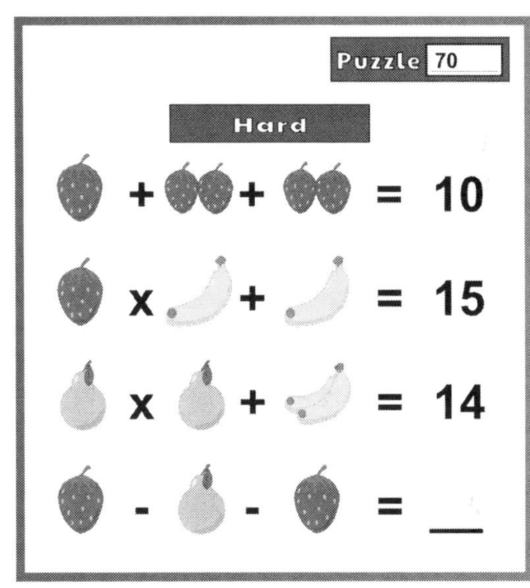
Puzzle 70
Hard
+ + = 10
x + = 15
x + = 14
- - = __

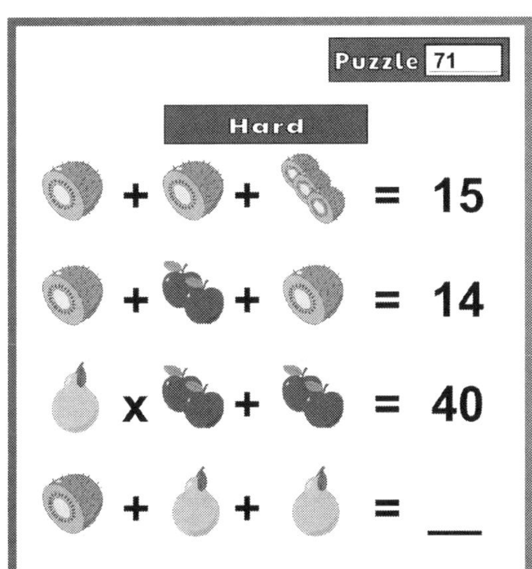
Puzzle 71
Hard
+ + = 15
+ + = 14
x + = 40
+ + = __

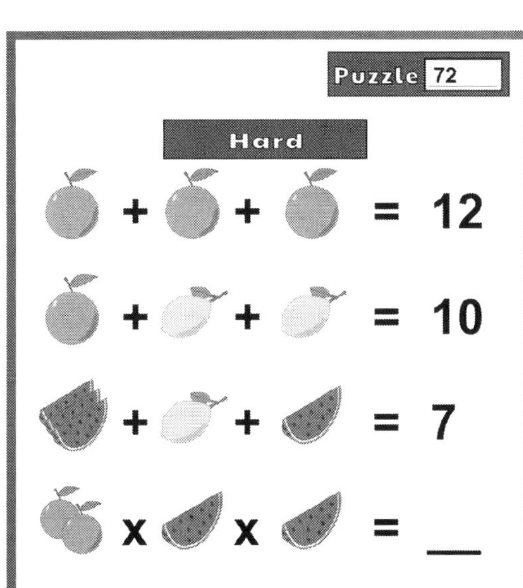
Puzzle 72
Hard
+ + = 12
+ + = 10
+ + = 7
x x = __

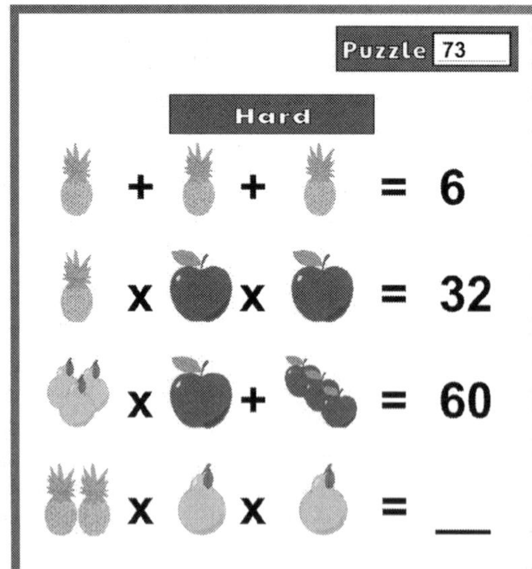
Puzzle 73
Hard
+ + = 6
x x = 32
x + = 60
x x = __

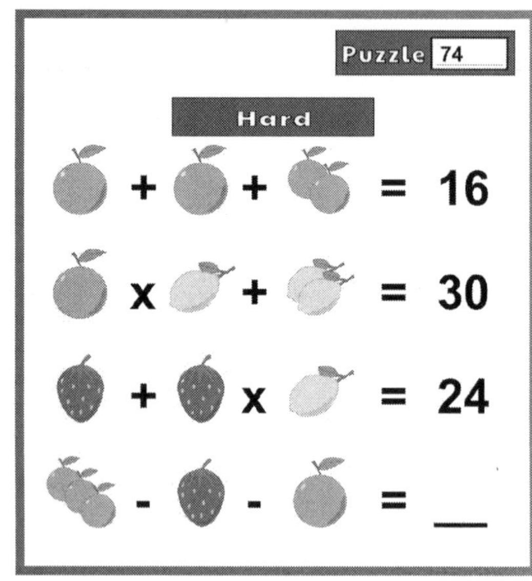
Puzzle 74
Hard
+ + = 16
x + = 30
+ x = 24
- - = __

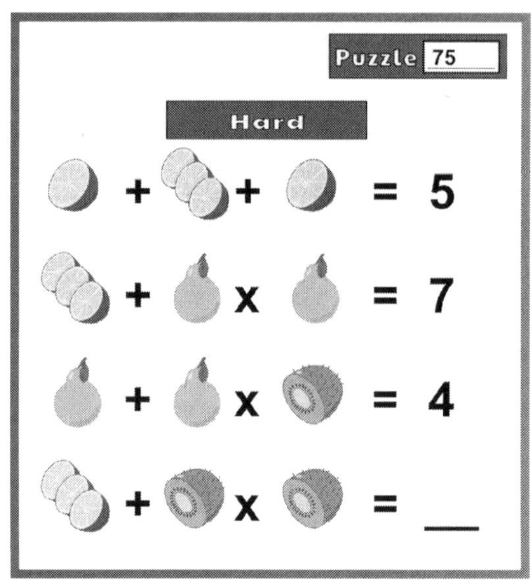
Puzzle 75
Hard
+ + = 5
+ x = 7
+ x = 4
+ x = __

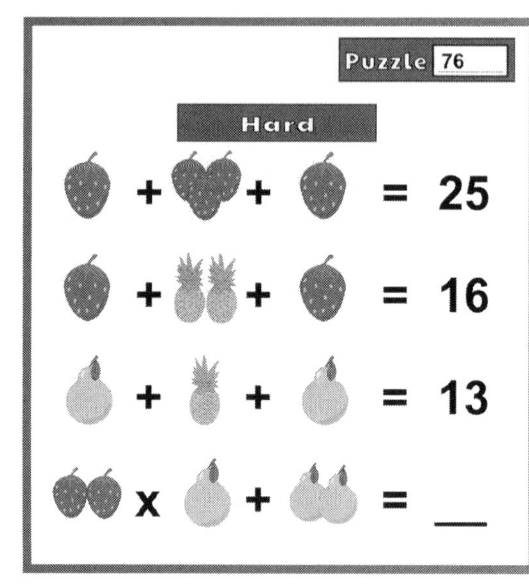
Puzzle 76
Hard
+ + = 25
+ + = 16
+ + = 13
x + = __

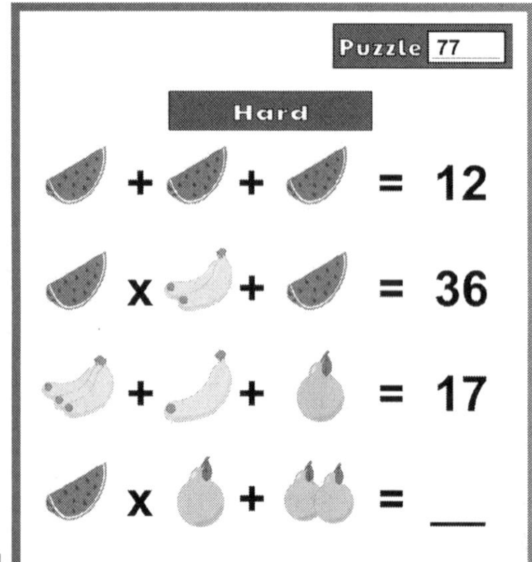
Puzzle 77
Hard
+ + = 12
x + = 36
+ + = 17
x + = __

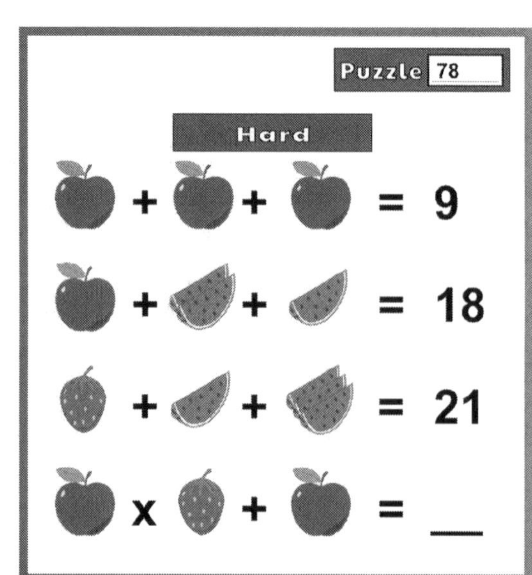
Puzzle 78
Hard
+ + = 9
+ + = 18
+ + = 21
x + = __

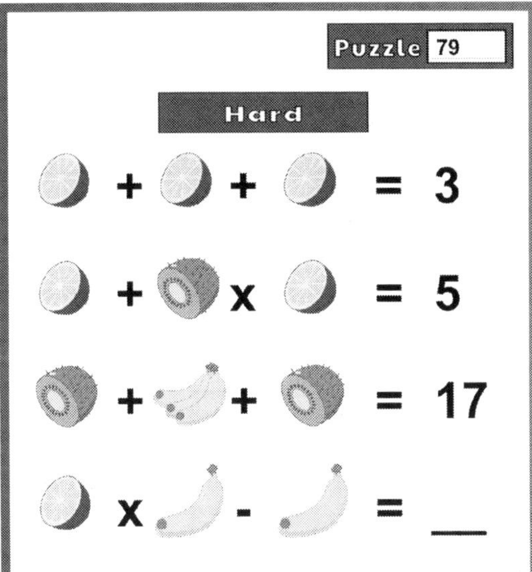
Puzzle 79
Hard
+ + = 3
+ x = 5
+ + = 17
x - = __

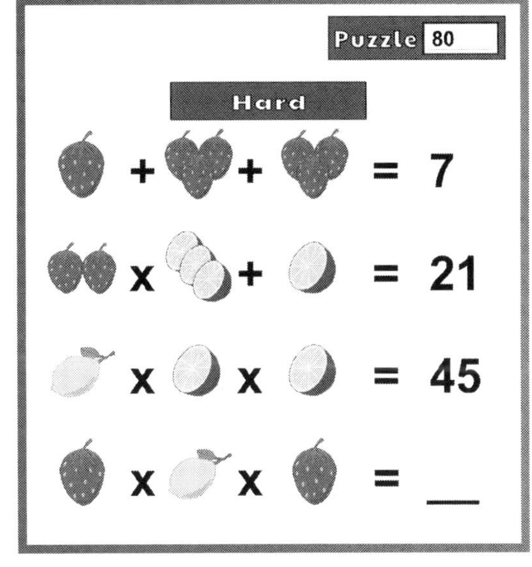
Puzzle 80
Hard
+ + = 7
x + = 21
x x = 45
x x = __

Puzzle 81
Hard
+ + = 6
+ + = 4
+ x = 27
x + = __

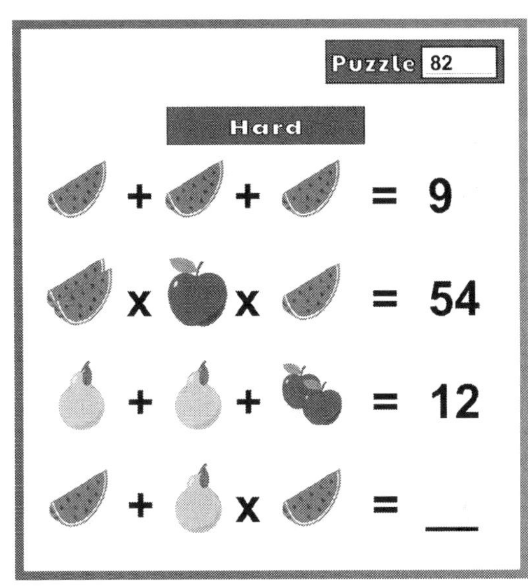
Puzzle 82
Hard
+ + = 9
x x = 54
+ + = 12
+ x = __

Puzzle 83
Hard
+ + = 9
x + = 9
x + = 18
x + = __

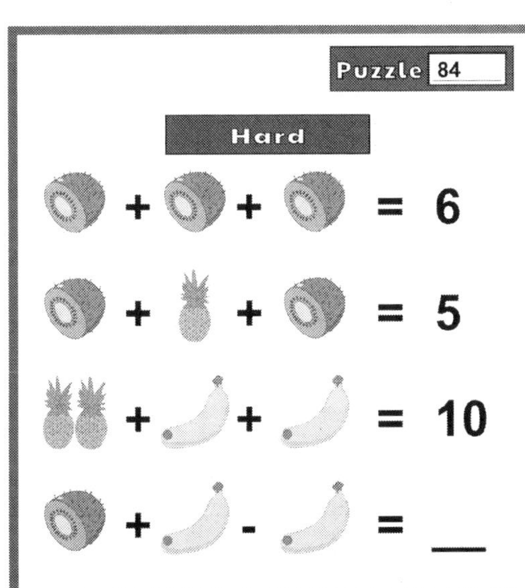
Puzzle 84
Hard
+ + = 6
+ + = 5
+ + = 10
+ - = __

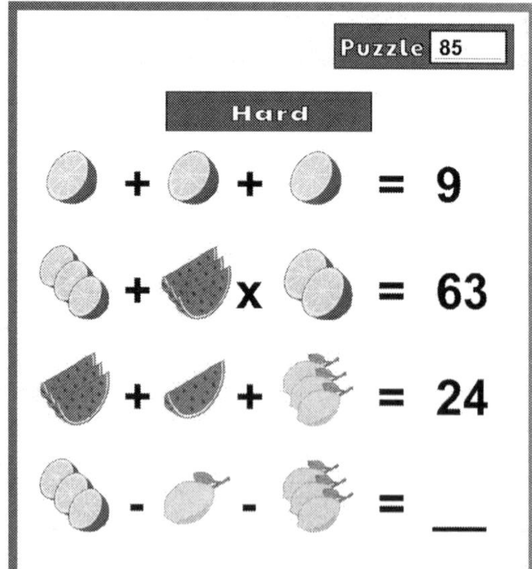
Puzzle 85
Hard
+ + = 9
+ x = 63
+ + = 24
- - = __

Puzzle 86
Hard
+ + = 15
+ x = 35
x + = 25
x x = __

Puzzle 87
Hard
+ + = 7
+ x = 3
+ x = 9
- x = __

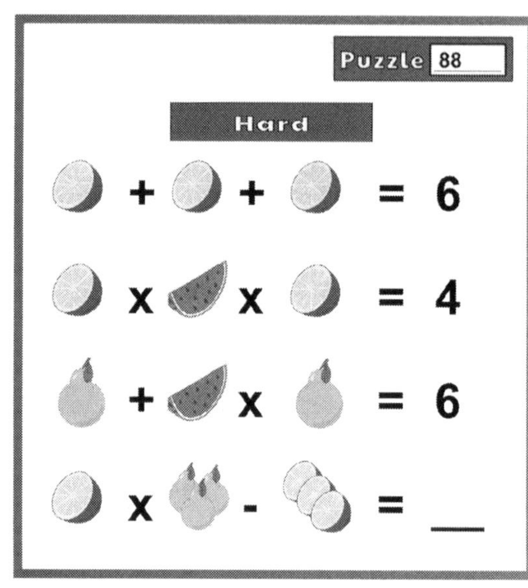
Puzzle 88
Hard
+ + = 6
x x = 4
+ x = 6
x - = __

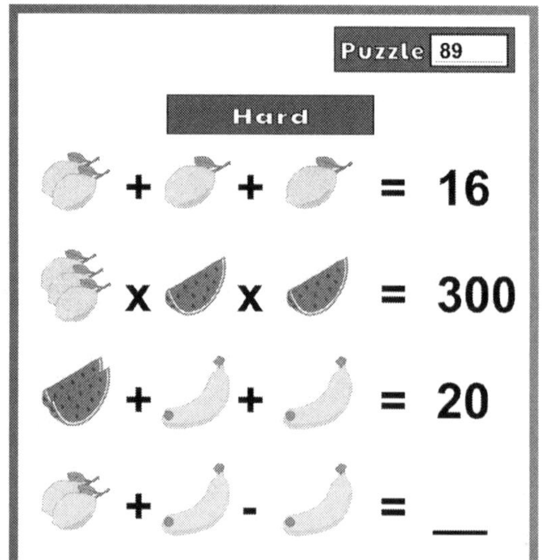
Puzzle 89
Hard
+ + = 16
x x = 300
+ + = 20
+ - = __

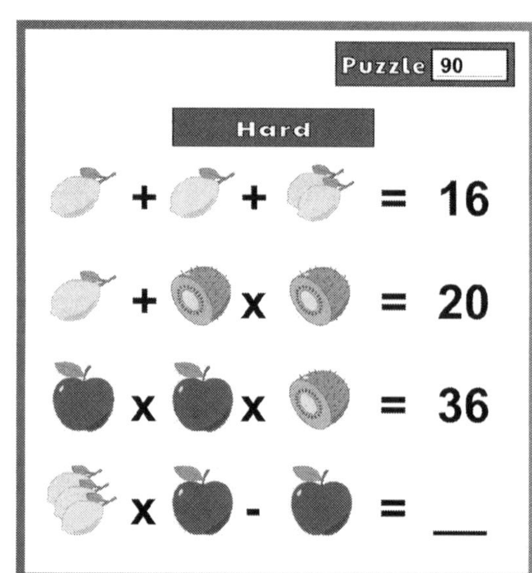
Puzzle 90
Hard
+ + = 16
+ x = 20
x x = 36
x - = __

SINGLE ADDITION SHEET 1

2 + 1 =	3 + 8 =	2 + 2 =	8 + 2 =	8 + 7 =	6 + 5 =
0 + 4 =	2 + 6 =	5 + 0 =	8 + 3 =	1 + 4 =	8 + 7 =
7 + 8 =	0 + 2 =	1 + 2 =	4 + 8 =	0 + 7 =	8 + 7 =
2 + 8 =	0 + 2 =	2 + 7 =	6 + 7 =	1 + 5 =	7 + 8 =
6 + 3 =	5 + 0 =	5 + 2 =	6 + 4 =	8 + 5 =	8 + 5 =
1 + 6 =	1 + 8 =	8 + 3 =	6 + 8 =	7 + 4 =	6 + 7 =
3 + 6 =	8 + 2 =	2 + 2 =	7 + 1 =	0 + 0 =	5 + 8 =

SINGLE ADDITION SHEET 2

6 + 0	4 + 5	1 + 6	1 + 6	0 + 4	8 + 1
4 + 5	2 + 3	8 + 6	0 + 2	7 + 7	0 + 6
8 + 4	0 + 3	0 + 2	7 + 0	8 + 8	6 + 7
3 + 0	8 + 3	2 + 1	0 + 0	0 + 6	8 + 8
1 + 4	1 + 2	4 + 6	5 + 1	5 + 0	5 + 4
4 + 4	6 + 6	4 + 6	1 + 4	0 + 5	6 + 4
1 + 1	6 + 6	7 + 5	1 + 4	5 + 2	3 + 8

SINGLE ADDITION SHEET 3

2 + 0	0 + 6	5 + 0	1 + 5	3 + 4	8 + 4
0 + 5	4 + 3	6 + 5	8 + 1	6 + 4	0 + 5
2 + 7	1 + 6	5 + 3	8 + 7	6 + 3	1 + 6
6 + 3	0 + 5	8 + 4	1 + 1	2 + 7	5 + 0
5 + 7	7 + 7	8 + 3	1 + 6	2 + 8	4 + 1
2 + 2	8 + 6	5 + 8	6 + 5	5 + 6	7 + 3
5 + 6	3 + 8	2 + 2	0 + 2	6 + 1	1 + 1

SINGLE ADDITION SHEET 4

$3 + 0 =$ ___ ; $3 + 3 =$ ___ ; $4 + 3 =$ ___ ; $5 + 8 =$ ___ ; $8 + 0 =$ ___ ; $5 + 6 =$ ___

$2 + 1 =$ ___ ; $1 + 7 =$ ___ ; $3 + 3 =$ ___ ; $3 + 1 =$ ___ ; $2 + 5 =$ ___ ; $6 + 0 =$ ___

$8 + 7 =$ ___ ; $0 + 6 =$ ___ ; $3 + 4 =$ ___ ; $8 + 0 =$ ___ ; $2 + 1 =$ ___ ; $1 + 2 =$ ___

$8 + 7 =$ ___ ; $2 + 0 =$ ___ ; $6 + 6 =$ ___ ; $7 + 3 =$ ___ ; $7 + 6 =$ ___ ; $1 + 3 =$ ___

$8 + 5 =$ ___ ; $4 + 8 =$ ___ ; $1 + 5 =$ ___ ; $7 + 4 =$ ___ ; $1 + 8 =$ ___ ; $6 + 1 =$ ___

$0 + 0 =$ ___ ; $6 + 2 =$ ___ ; $3 + 8 =$ ___ ; $3 + 8 =$ ___ ; $5 + 5 =$ ___ ; $5 + 3 =$ ___

$5 + 4 =$ ___ ; $4 + 8 =$ ___ ; $7 + 6 =$ ___ ; $8 + 1 =$ ___ ; $8 + 5 =$ ___ ; $7 + 4 =$ ___

DOUBLE ADDITION SHEET 1

30	57	46	23	48	61
+ 22	+ 50	+ 52	+ 58	+ 25	+ 38
19	25	73	92	93	50
+ 21	+ 66	+ 61	+ 72	+ 94	+ 92
92	67	77	20	49	15
+ 98	+ 80	+ 82	+ 69	+ 36	+ 42
95	14	16	51	83	31
+ 51	+ 67	+ 46	+ 15	+ 35	+ 79
15	10	61	65	27	93
+ 51	+ 52	+ 15	+ 60	+ 23	+ 61
32	40	15	69	43	92
+ 87	+ 96	+ 50	+ 98	+ 28	+ 14
30	86	85	42	51	27
+ 94	+ 22	+ 33	+ 61	+ 86	+ 43

DOUBLE ADDITION SHEET 2

75 + 92 = ___	59 + 15 = ___	99 + 13 = ___	46 + 12 = ___	49 + 17 = ___	10 + 60 = ___
96 + 22 = ___	69 + 60 = ___	37 + 28 = ___	35 + 23 = ___	52 + 59 = ___	62 + 63 = ___
19 + 68 = ___	82 + 81 = ___	76 + 74 = ___	88 + 27 = ___	19 + 20 = ___	36 + 48 = ___
37 + 35 = ___	70 + 20 = ___	69 + 33 = ___	97 + 89 = ___	49 + 89 = ___	90 + 39 = ___
58 + 77 = ___	34 + 97 = ___	61 + 67 = ___	17 + 46 = ___	89 + 86 = ___	95 + 29 = ___
49 + 99 = ___	42 + 92 = ___	22 + 18 = ___	88 + 67 = ___	47 + 10 = ___	40 + 23 = ___
86 + 53 = ___	27 + 50 = ___	22 + 28 = ___	39 + 42 = ___	83 + 32 = ___	98 + 33 = ___

DOUBLE ADDITION SHEET 3

80 + 16	37 + 32	32 + 19	30 + 26	32 + 94	21 + 99
55 + 72	27 + 61	14 + 26	76 + 76	53 + 66	43 + 92
23 + 19	70 + 66	31 + 87	30 + 63	32 + 92	10 + 55
84 + 54	71 + 57	47 + 86	12 + 36	99 + 43	46 + 52
75 + 56	98 + 58	41 + 62	78 + 87	35 + 25	20 + 62
40 + 63	77 + 79	11 + 72	43 + 51	47 + 60	96 + 12
59 + 55	64 + 58	63 + 40	45 + 45	57 + 52	60 + 23

DOUBLE ADDITION SHEET 4

77 + 24 =	40 + 14 =	11 + 82 =	40 + 15 =	10 + 61 =	98 + 47 =
34 + 72 =	19 + 52 =	48 + 54 =	46 + 98 =	33 + 42 =	80 + 13 =
74 + 48 =	38 + 23 =	64 + 82 =	99 + 98 =	18 + 11 =	49 + 99 =
71 + 16 =	37 + 31 =	93 + 87 =	61 + 50 =	69 + 37 =	69 + 67 =
32 + 66 =	94 + 90 =	33 + 57 =	73 + 82 =	19 + 83 =	88 + 64 =
38 + 60 =	15 + 85 =	61 + 83 =	73 + 17 =	36 + 92 =	83 + 52 =
80 + 33 =	51 + 11 =	51 + 47 =	67 + 29 =	98 + 28 =	13 + 70 =

TRIPLE ADDITION SHEET 1

277 + 860	435 + 793	229 + 662	606 + 892	121 + 929	773 + 238
317 + 501	664 + 802	337 + 331	401 + 447	933 + 469	406 + 179
907 + 255	148 + 171	662 + 935	362 + 990	583 + 950	823 + 650
445 + 209	822 + 364	928 + 874	188 + 922	539 + 692	333 + 117
380 + 507	514 + 532	148 + 972	979 + 877	154 + 480	534 + 896
937 + 614	485 + 485	265 + 138	216 + 690	654 + 439	945 + 734
658 + 263	764 + 428	353 + 639	502 + 734	655 + 605	937 + 451

TRIPLE ADDITION SHEET 2

680 + 894	975 + 431	229 + 913	182 + 660	800 + 365	208 + 570
816 + 269	169 + 851	183 + 454	448 + 722	227 + 834	957 + 770
150 + 813	453 + 717	224 + 426	675 + 990	797 + 938	936 + 235
850 + 881	554 + 194	402 + 605	342 + 431	633 + 606	460 + 420
936 + 681	316 + 717	775 + 726	975 + 832	422 + 849	366 + 852
488 + 599	747 + 233	628 + 751	208 + 273	978 + 356	774 + 750
651 + 339	209 + 219	246 + 901	518 + 832	670 + 488	600 + 179

TRIPLE ADDITION SHEET 3

254 + 389	366 + 944	189 + 588	933 + 400	793 + 889	790 + 284
977 + 531	595 + 290	338 + 775	598 + 252	449 + 682	436 + 671
110 + 226	525 + 794	883 + 852	322 + 125	302 + 544	991 + 123
867 + 881	935 + 831	393 + 555	688 + 305	469 + 124	822 + 270
738 + 342	390 + 678	983 + 367	178 + 538	629 + 464	571 + 388
770 + 204	683 + 675	273 + 538	180 + 358	147 + 438	577 + 130
226 + 116	722 + 720	250 + 166	854 + 560	461 + 444	906 + 408

TRIPLE ADDITION SHEET 4

578 + 433 =	415 + 619 =	224 + 934 =	655 + 610 =	256 + 962 =	268 + 525 =
760 + 701 =	659 + 412 =	217 + 720 =	313 + 637 =	797 + 565 =	109 + 453 =
615 + 709 =	841 + 234 =	620 + 883 =	776 + 433 =	500 + 137 =	705 + 793 =
707 + 543 =	790 + 354 =	500 + 503 =	542 + 588 =	411 + 824 =	956 + 967 =
547 + 458 =	790 + 748 =	352 + 822 =	566 + 558 =	951 + 988 =	231 + 248 =
213 + 716 =	200 + 887 =	899 + 243 =	154 + 948 =	128 + 288 =	737 + 954 =
763 + 748 =	736 + 335 =	166 + 659 =	996 + 989 =	587 + 755 =	988 + 735 =

SINGLE SUBTRACTION SHEET 1

8 - 6	5 - 4	8 - 6	7 - 4	5 - 2	4 - 3
7 - 6	4 - 0	2 - 1	5 - 0	5 - 3	3 - 1
8 - 5	8 - 1	6 - 1	7 - 1	6 - 1	3 - 1
7 - 4	1 - 1	5 - 0	7 - 0	8 - 0	5 - 1
8 - 7	8 - 2	8 - 7	3 - 2	6 - 1	8 - 2
8 - 5	8 - 1	2 - 1	8 - 0	8 - 4	5 - 5
6 - 0	6 - 0	4 - 3	7 - 7	1 - 1	7 - 1

SINGLE SUBTRACTION SHEET 2

6 - 3	6 - 3	7 - 2	8 - 1	3 - 2	7 - 0
6 - 0	6 - 1	6 - 3	6 - 1	8 - 1	7 - 6
7 - 1	7 - 0	8 - 6	1 - 0	5 - 0	8 - 1
6 - 0	3 - 0	5 - 4	3 - 0	4 - 2	5 - 5
4 - 2	2 - 0	8 - 7	3 - 2	8 - 4	6 - 1
2 - 2	0 - 0	8 - 7	4 - 2	2 - 1	6 - 0
6 - 0	4 - 0	4 - 4	6 - 0	7 - 6	4 - 1

SINGLE SUBTRACTION SHEET 3

$8 - 2$	$7 - 0$	$8 - 0$	$8 - 5$	$5 - 0$	$2 - 0$
$0 - 0$	$6 - 1$	$8 - 4$	$8 - 5$	$7 - 1$	$3 - 2$
$6 - 4$	$5 - 2$	$8 - 0$	$5 - 0$	$2 - 1$	$7 - 1$
$8 - 5$	$3 - 1$	$5 - 2$	$7 - 4$	$5 - 0$	$3 - 2$
$6 - 0$	$7 - 5$	$5 - 3$	$4 - 3$	$6 - 2$	$2 - 2$
$7 - 5$	$6 - 5$	$7 - 7$	$5 - 4$	$4 - 3$	$4 - 0$
$8 - 4$	$4 - 4$	$8 - 7$	$1 - 1$	$4 - 4$	$7 - 6$

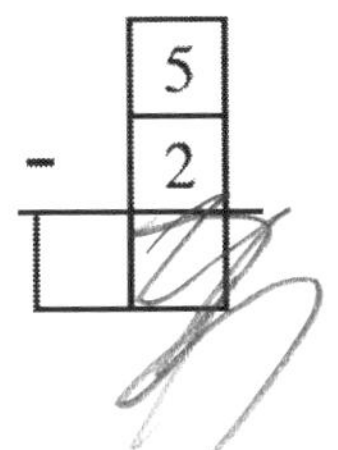

SINGLE SUBTRACTION SHEET 4

8 − 6 = ☐☐	6 − 6 = ☐☐	8 − 7 = ☐☐	7 − 4 = ☐☐	5 − 2 = ☐☐	8 − 8 = ☐☐
8 − 3 = ☐☐	8 − 5 = ☐☐	8 − 3 = ☐☐	8 − 4 = ☐☐	4 − 3 = ☐☐	6 − 6 = ☐☐
4 − 2 = ☐☐	8 − 0 = ☐☐	3 − 3 = ☐☐	5 − 2 = ☐☐	5 − 2 = ☐☐	7 − 6 = ☐☐
8 − 1 = ☐☐	8 − 0 = ☐☐	1 − 1 = ☐☐	8 − 5 = ☐☐	7 − 5 = ☐☐	4 − 2 = ☐☐
7 − 7 = ☐☐	3 − 2 = ☐☐	8 − 5 = ☐☐	2 − 2 = ☐☐	8 − 7 = ☐☐	7 − 3 = ☐☐
7 − 2 = ☐☐	8 − 6 = ☐☐	7 − 6 = ☐☐	8 − 4 = ☐☐	3 − 1 = ☐☐	8 − 5 = ☐☐
6 − 3 = ☐☐	5 − 4 = ☐☐	7 − 3 = ☐☐	3 − 3 = ☐☐	6 − 3 = ☐☐	8 − 7 = ☐☐

DOUBLE SUBTRACTION SHEET 1

98 − 79	90 − 15	99 − 95	65 − 60	65 − 62	88 − 45
94 − 59	85 − 79	74 − 55	94 − 59	68 − 32	87 − 83
81 − 63	93 − 56	52 − 34	95 − 86	85 − 80	48 − 34
69 − 60	53 − 11	58 − 22	69 − 21	78 − 59	66 − 58
79 − 25	92 − 79	65 − 11	84 − 30	68 − 67	78 − 78
53 − 23	88 − 25	98 − 77	85 − 84	34 − 26	60 − 38
88 − 48	87 − 64	44 − 42	48 − 14	65 − 18	72 − 18

DOUBLE SUBTRACTION SHEET 2

93 − 24	92 − 87	92 − 89	84 − 43	88 − 59	44 − 25
63 − 57	84 − 29	84 − 29	70 − 17	98 − 15	99 − 93
62 − 37	66 − 37	68 − 24	66 − 65	81 − 46	51 − 31
57 − 11	96 − 54	18 − 13	89 − 79	30 − 25	45 − 44
89 − 23	88 − 73	84 − 67	97 − 32	99 − 53	67 − 22
60 − 55	31 − 11	75 − 10	63 − 45	94 − 89	85 − 35
72 − 71	92 − 21	69 − 54	49 − 38	66 − 38	84 − 26

DOUBLE SUBTRACTION SHEET 3

83	91	95	90	88	69
- 56	- 34	- 44	- 39	- 42	- 17

84	85	85	72	88	84
- 53	- 54	- 52	- 63	- 85	- 28

72	83	53	69	82	36
- 16	- 24	- 32	- 68	- 52	- 12

94	52	69	28	93	51
- 89	- 39	- 47	- 13	- 40	- 31

85	85	23	39	53	95
- 17	- 13	- 21	- 18	- 33	- 38

97	87	19	65	34	73
- 86	- 76	- 19	- 33	- 20	- 65

43	74	80	95	44	97
- 12	- 73	- 39	- 70	- 25	- 84

DOUBLE SUBTRACTION SHEET 4

61 − 53	89 − 75	92 − 32	33 − 30	78 − 65	40 − 38
90 − 73	77 − 49	91 − 87	70 − 44	24 − 22	50 − 33
86 − 37	90 − 30	99 − 48	74 − 66	91 − 42	97 − 43
71 − 57	77 − 41	58 − 34	93 − 65	65 − 14	84 − 82
65 − 13	92 − 23	33 − 19	43 − 29	98 − 92	79 − 14
65 − 62	45 − 40	83 − 38	65 − 60	76 − 72	28 − 22
95 − 43	87 − 45	79 − 49	89 − 31	63 − 57	51 − 30

TRIPLE SUBTRACTION SHEET 1

569 - 229	757 - 369	815 - 326	243 - 194	809 - 271	596 - 487
247 - 131	713 - 175	658 - 623	578 - 135	891 - 111	477 - 372
313 - 190	525 - 297	451 - 341	395 - 143	782 - 477	630 - 590
379 - 220	979 - 422	513 - 205	998 - 736	855 - 656	874 - 506
571 - 305	853 - 479	696 - 543	921 - 183	831 - 690	703 - 329
891 - 418	491 - 387	459 - 356	860 - 320	891 - 184	248 - 112
986 - 971	333 - 169	715 - 416	824 - 499	720 - 139	835 - 154

TRIPLE SUBTRACTION SHEET 2

316 − 229	459 − 285	761 − 423	739 − 214	835 − 626	450 − 449
847 − 303	724 − 351	725 − 521	423 − 256	958 − 340	261 − 200
754 − 709	154 − 103	793 − 152	604 − 459	671 − 612	804 − 281
966 − 552	955 − 686	622 − 225	382 − 330	677 − 385	952 − 144
980 − 248	754 − 450	768 − 312	614 − 243	460 − 201	784 − 266
671 − 496	272 − 253	284 − 138	643 − 172	362 − 204	570 − 560
482 − 260	499 − 297	648 − 337	742 − 728	620 − 483	743 − 358

TRIPLE SUBTRACTION SHEET 3

756 − 682	387 − 292	284 − 244	809 − 370	535 − 330	514 − 176
988 − 883	719 − 304	923 − 253	332 − 310	718 − 615	699 − 258
321 − 191	797 − 459	768 − 537	598 − 392	717 − 485	745 − 438
728 − 461	360 − 117	810 − 217	333 − 103	243 − 220	874 − 578
510 − 303	919 − 824	634 − 403	881 − 298	870 − 732	843 − 552
762 − 239	623 − 360	254 − 162	891 − 680	657 − 428	916 − 896
668 − 120	835 − 793	684 − 562	399 − 257	578 − 280	674 − 423

TRIPLE SUBTRACTION SHEET 4

782 − 128	873 − 815	840 − 692	566 − 125	638 − 465	849 − 745
634 − 351	988 − 487	907 − 496	792 − 347	580 − 185	976 − 828
615 − 265	520 − 214	515 − 132	440 − 244	950 − 743	715 − 641
992 − 950	888 − 841	682 − 266	901 − 529	859 − 809	521 − 162
881 − 250	562 − 559	933 − 383	841 − 419	980 − 463	703 − 378
894 − 726	633 − 236	780 − 448	911 − 263	777 − 706	871 − 596
587 − 314	466 − 142	536 − 445	710 − 479	739 − 423	889 − 800

SINGLE MULTIPLICATION SHEET 1

		2	0
x			7

		8	8
x			1

	9	8	0
x			4

		1	0
x			0

			1
x			6

			1
x			5

		2	4
x			3

	8	7	9
x			4

	5	4	2
x			2

	4	2	4
x			5

	2	0	5
x			7

		7	4
x			5

			1
x			7

		8	1
x			0

		7	2
x			2

		9	8
x			4

			3
x			6

			1
x			4

	3	6	8
x			6

			7
x			0

		7	7
x			7

			4
x			1

		5	4
x			0

	9	4	3
x			3

	6	4	2
x			7

	8	8	2
x			2

			6
x			1

			4
x			0

			7
x			8

		5	9
x			8

			6
x			3

			3
x			4

	9	7	1
x			2

			3
x			1

	2	5	7
x			5

SINGLE MULTIPLICATION SHEET 2

884 x 0	848 x 4	78 x 2	8 x 3	7 x 4
443 x 0	290 x 6	7 x 8	41 x 7	54 x 7
62 x 3	199 x 0	77 x 7	7 x 8	729 x 4
0 x 7	3 x 8	396 x 5	39 x 6	389 x 2
900 x 4	48 x 1	947 x 0	669 x 7	815 x 2
44 x 5	2 x 0	88 x 8	773 x 7	4 x 8
4 x 1	6 x 0	78 x 7	51 x 1	2 x 4

SINGLE MULTIPLICATION SHEET 3

13 x 7 = ___	64 x 0 = ___	105 x 3 = ___	7 x 5 = ___	69 x 5 = ___
809 x 3 = ___	517 x 7 = ___	41 x 5 = ___	8 x 0 = ___	8 x 8 = ___
96 x 0 = ___	4 x 0 = ___	38 x 0 = ___	0 x 2 = ___	61 x 4 = ___
67 x 2 = ___	61 x 2 = ___	10 x 6 = ___	109 x 1 = ___	107 x 4 = ___
6 x 3 = ___	747 x 8 = ___	4 x 4 = ___	783 x 8 = ___	31 x 3 = ___
0 x 7 = ___	43 x 5 = ___	4 x 6 = ___	245 x 5 = ___	668 x 2 = ___
14 x 8 = ___	5 x 6 = ___	5 x 4 = ___	48 x 3 = ___	96 x 5 = ___

SINGLE MULTIPLICATION SHEET 4

19 x 2	66 x 2	8 x 4	7 x 2	248 x 8
610 x 6	701 x 7	7 x 5	8 x 0	92 x 3
6 x 7	580 x 1	566 x 4	8 x 7	823 x 6
51 x 1	4 x 8	396 x 6	79 x 8	266 x 3
76 x 7	684 x 3	257 x 1	578 x 0	12 x 6
8 x 7	28 x 4	543 x 1	524 x 4	1 x 8
99 x 3	562 x 1	686 x 5	7 x 2	115 x 3

DOUBLE MULTIPLICATION SHEET 1

51 × 49	84 × 91	51 × 89	35 × 12	86 × 19
40 × 41	85 × 29	67 × 14	42 × 14	22 × 82
54 × 40	51 × 11	78 × 53	98 × 47	41 × 66
61 × 52	90 × 16	26 × 46	71 × 89	36 × 60
39 × 14	68 × 96	47 × 16	67 × 67	75 × 29
58 × 67	39 × 52	30 × 41	40 × 23	31 × 83

DOUBLE MULTIPLICATION SHEET 2

76 x 55	61 x 48	49 x 50	86 x 90	95 x 45
56 x 83	71 x 10	17 x 60	72 x 55	98 x 56
57 x 51	69 x 68	79 x 44	95 x 32	99 x 53
12 x 66	65 x 62	71 x 20	26 x 54	58 x 67
82 x 81	17 x 56	16 x 24	56 x 42	81 x 80
41 x 40	62 x 80	56 x 53	57 x 71	10 x 55

DOUBLE MULTIPLICATION SHEET 3

95 x 87	41 x 77	77 x 71	76 x 54	16 x 71
93 x 44	36 x 61	35 x 90	75 x 41	74 x 95
37 x 99	18 x 72	78 x 88	46 x 99	56 x 67
68 x 73	26 x 49	29 x 92	29 x 77	88 x 94
69 x 78	30 x 81	48 x 78	58 x 80	17 x 67
56 x 21	55 x 58	24 x 13	60 x 34	89 x 44

DOUBLE MULTIPLICATION SHEET 4

44 x 69	48 x 34	26 x 95	44 x 30	86 x 10
34 x 46	85 x 96	76 x 82	93 x 13	58 x 96
75 x 82	42 x 79	15 x 81	44 x 64	30 x 94
78 x 84	96 x 37	33 x 25	70 x 31	66 x 31
85 x 22	43 x 50	70 x 64	81 x 22	39 x 95
23 x 74	90 x 90	39 x 31	89 x 20	47 x 65

TRIPLE MULTIPLICATION SHEET 1

674 x 84	127 x 60	775 x 82	853 x 67
191 x 84	579 x 61	284 x 49	893 x 61
605 x 91	331 x 40	625 x 12	971 x 86
722 x 95	802 x 89	126 x 74	127 x 24
627 x 56	776 x 88	579 x 84	969 x 13
149 x 65	617 x 75	358 x 78	769 x 79

TRIPLE MULTIPLICATION SHEET 2

	2	6	5
x		8	3

	9	9	8
x		1	9

	8	6	4
x		6	7

	9	3	4
x		4	8

	6	9	5
x		1	5

	1	4	1
x		9	9

	6	0	7
x		8	0

	3	7	2
x		3	8

	8	2	0
x		3	4

	9	0	6
x		5	4

	1	2	8
x		1	9

	1	4	2
x		7	0

	3	7	2
x		3	7

	7	1	5
x		2	7

	1	1	7
x		9	2

	6	5	4
x		7	8

	2	3	7
x		5	8

	7	4	2
x		3	7

	2	9	6
x		2	5

	5	5	7
x		8	2

	8	9	2
x		1	7

	2	5	9
x		7	3

	2	8	0
x		1	1

	2	4	1
x		9	5

TRIPLE MULTIPLICATION SHEET 3

334 × 82

781 × 20

975 × 83

487 × 51

944 × 21

716 × 24

612 × 50

876 × 37

147 × 89

371 × 27

746 × 78

837 × 27

206 × 32

701 × 25

794 × 89

706 × 28

508 × 86

268 × 56

911 × 38

380 × 33

289 × 27

384 × 50

520 × 74

461 × 51

TRIPLE MULTIPLICATION SHEET 4

727 × 86	791 × 77	811 × 70	881 × 12
409 × 66	940 × 35	557 × 50	750 × 17
322 × 39	815 × 32	414 × 19	921 × 31
179 × 74	121 × 78	447 × 91	643 × 90
250 × 52	733 × 20	523 × 38	458 × 51
523 × 54	295 × 71	523 × 70	818 × 15

Fractions

FRACTIONS CHEAT SHEET

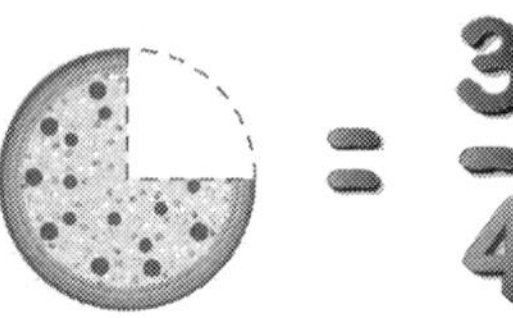 $= \frac{3}{4} =$ A Fraction represents a part of a whole

The **top** number is called the 'NUMERATOR', this tells you how pieces you have from the whole.

The **bottom** number is called the 'DENOMINATOR', this tells you how pieces you have from the whole.

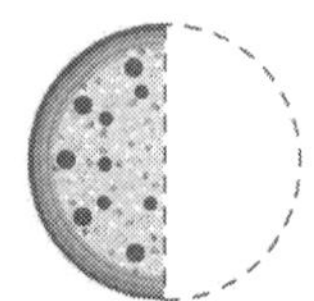

IMPROPER FRACTION

$\frac{5}{4}$

An improper fraction is one where the top number is larger than (or equal to) the bottom number

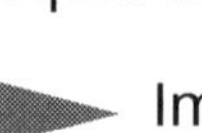 Improper fractions are easier to use in calculations

PROPER FRACTION

A proper fraction is one where the top number is less than the bottom number, and the fraction is less than 1

MIXED NUMBER

A mixed number is made up of a whole number and a proper fraction $= 1\frac{3}{4} =$

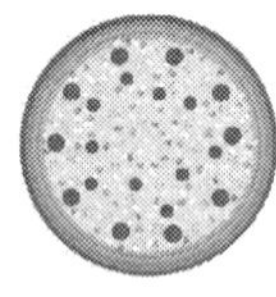

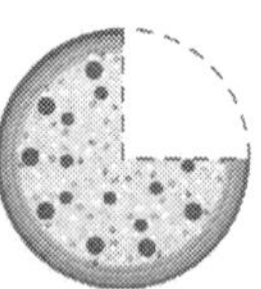

CONVERTING MIXED NUMBERS TO IMPROPER FRACTIONS

$1\frac{3}{4}$

Step 1: Carry the bottom number $= \frac{}{4}$

Step 2: Multiply the whole number with the bottom number of fraction (1 x 4), then add the top number (+3)

$1\frac{3}{4} = \frac{7}{4}$

CONVERTING IMPROPER FRACTIONS TO MIXED NUMBERS

$\frac{23}{6}$

Step 1: How many times can the bottom number go into the top number? Write it down as the whole number. $= 3$

Step 2: Write the remainder as the top number of the fraction $= 3\frac{5}{}$

$\frac{23}{6} = 3\frac{5}{6}$

Step 3: Carry the bottom number of fraction

FRACTIONS CHEAT SHEET

ADDING FRACTIONS WITH THE SAME DENOMINATORS

$\frac{1}{5} + \frac{3}{5}$

Step 1: Carry the denominator across $= \frac{\ }{5}$

Step 2: Add the numerators together $= \frac{1+3}{5} = \frac{4}{5}$

Step 3: Can it be simplified? Find a number that both the nominator and denominator can be divided by

$\frac{4}{5}$ 4/5 cannot be simplified any further

ADDING FRACTIONS WITH DIFFERENT DENOMINATORS

$\frac{1}{2} + \frac{3}{4}$

Step 1: Multiply the denominators so both fractions share the same denominator.

$\frac{1}{2} + \frac{3}{4} = \frac{1}{8} + \frac{3}{8}$

Step 2: Multiply the diagonals (starting top left -> bottom right, to ensure the fractions hold the same value as before.

$\frac{1}{2} \times \frac{3}{4} = \frac{4}{8} + \frac{6}{8}$

Step 3: Add the numerators together

Step 4: Can it be simplified further?

$\frac{10}{8}$ Improper fractions can be simplified further by converting them to Mixed Numbers $= 1\frac{2}{8}$

SUBTRACTING FRACTIONS WITH THE SAME DEMONIMATORS

Step 1: Carry the denominator across

Step 2: Subtract the numerators

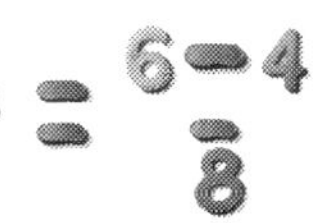

Step 3: Can it be simplified? Find a number that both the nominator and denominator can be divided by

2/8 can be simplified further by dividing by 2. The result is 1/4

$= \frac{1}{4}$

FRACTIONS CHEAT SHEET

SUBTRACTING FRACTIONS WITH DIFFERENT DENOMINATORS

$\frac{6}{7} - \frac{1}{2}$

Step 1: Multiply the denominators so both fractions share the same denominator.

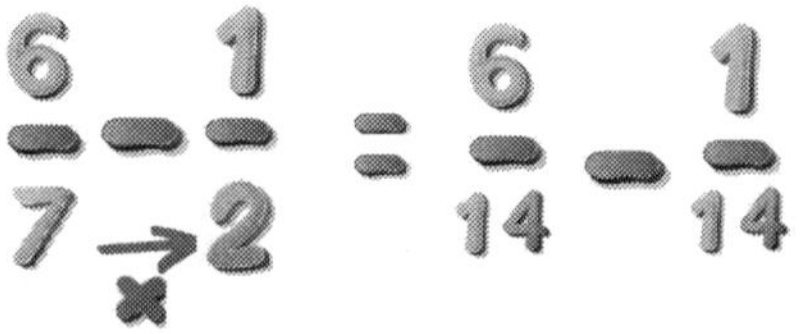

$\frac{6}{7} - \frac{1}{2} = \frac{6}{14} - \frac{1}{14}$

Step 2: Multiply the diagonals (starting top left -> bottom right, to ensure the fractions hold the same value as before.

$\frac{6}{7} - \frac{1}{2} = \frac{12}{14} - \frac{7}{14}$

Step 3: Subtract the numerators

$= \frac{5}{14}$

Step 4: Can it be simplified further? (in this case 5/14 is already in it's simplest form as there are no numbers that both 5 and 14 are divisible by).

SUBTRACTING MIXED FRACTIONS

$3\frac{3}{4} - 2\frac{1}{7}$

Step 1: Convert to improper fractions

$3\frac{3}{4} - 2\frac{1}{7} = \frac{15}{4} - \frac{15}{7}$

Step 2: Multiply the denominators so both fractions share the same denominator.

$= \frac{15}{28} - \frac{15}{28}$

Step 3: Multiply the diagonals (starting top left -> bottom right, to ensure the fractions hold the same value as before.

$\frac{15}{4} \times \frac{15}{7} = \frac{105}{28} - \frac{60}{28}$

Step 4: Subtract the numerators

$= \frac{45}{28}$

Step 5: Can it be simplified? (Yes, improper fractions are better displayed as mixed numbers)

$= 1\frac{17}{28}$

FRACTIONS CHEAT SHEET

MULTIPLYING PROPER FRACTIONS

Step 1: Multiply both **numerators** with eachother

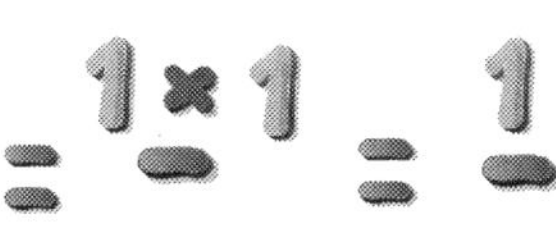

Step 2: Multiply both **denominators** with eachother

Step 2: Can it be **simplified**?  1/4 cannot be simplified any further

Another way of looking at this question is:
How much is one half of one half.

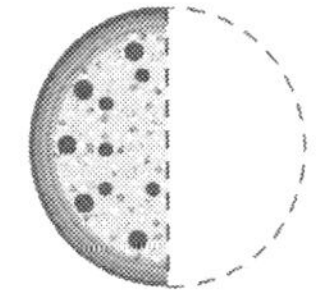

One Half

One Half of One Half

MULTIPLYING WHOLE NUMBERS WITH FRACTIONS

Step 1: Convert whole number to an improper fraction

Step 2: Multiply both **numerators** with eachother

Step 3: Multiply both **denominators** with eachother

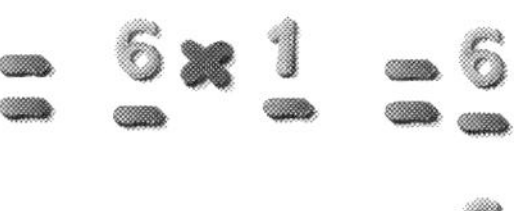

Step 4: Can it be **simplified** further? $\frac{6}{2}$ 6 can be divided by 2 3 times so the simplified answer is 3

MULTIPLYING MIXED NUMBERS WITH MIXED NUMBERS

Step 1: Convert mixed numbers to improper fractions $= \frac{9}{4} \times \frac{7}{2}$

Step 2: Multiply **numerators**

Step 3: Multiply **denominators** $= \frac{}{4} \times \frac{}{2} = \frac{63}{8}$

Step 4: Can it be **simplified** further?

63 can be simplified into a mixed number.
63 can by divided by 8, 7 times with a remainder of 6:

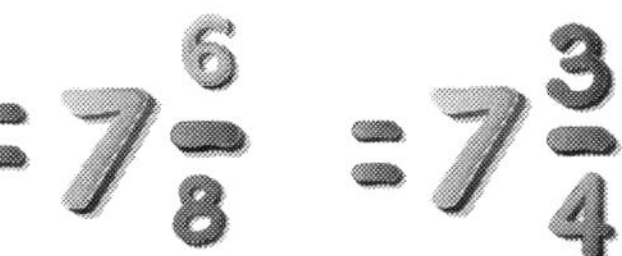

FRACTIONS CHEAT SHEET

DIVIDING PROPER FRACTIONS

$\frac{1}{2} \div \frac{4}{9}$

Step 1: Multiply the **top left** numerator with **bottom right** denominator to find the numerator. $= \frac{1}{2} \times \frac{4}{9} = \frac{9}{\ }$

Step 2: Multiply the **bottom left** denominator with the **top right** numerator to find the denominator. $= \frac{1}{2} \times \frac{4}{9} = \frac{9}{8}$

Step 3: Can it be **simplified** further? (Yes, an improper fraction is better displayed as a mixed fraction!). $\frac{9}{8} = 1\frac{1}{8}$

DIVIDING IMPROPER FRACTIONS

$\frac{5}{2} \div \frac{6}{4}$

Step 1: Multiply the **top left** numerator with **bottom right** denominator to find the numerator. $= \frac{5}{2} \times \frac{6}{4} = \frac{20}{\ }$

Step 2: Multiply the **bottom left** denominator with the **top right** numerator to find the denominator. $= \frac{5}{2} \times \frac{6}{4} = \frac{20}{12}$

Step 3: Can it be **simplified** further? (Yes, an improper fraction is better displayed as a mixed fraction!). $\frac{20}{12} = 1\frac{8}{12} = 1\frac{2}{3}$

DIVIDING MIXED FRACTIONS

Step 1: Convert mixed numbers to improper fractions. $= \frac{5}{2} \div \frac{7}{5}$

Step 2: Multiply the **top left** numerator with **bottom right** denominator to find the numerator. $= \frac{5}{2} \times \frac{7}{5} = \frac{25}{\ }$

Step 3: Multiply the **bottom left** denominator with the **top right** numerator to find the denominator. $= \frac{5}{2} \times \frac{7}{5} = \frac{25}{14}$

Step 4: Can it be simplified? $\frac{25}{14} = 1\frac{11}{14}$

FRACTIONS PUZZLE 1

ADDING PROPER FRACTIONS

"Help the miner find the coordinates of hidden treasures by solving equations.
Calculate the total value of mined treasures."

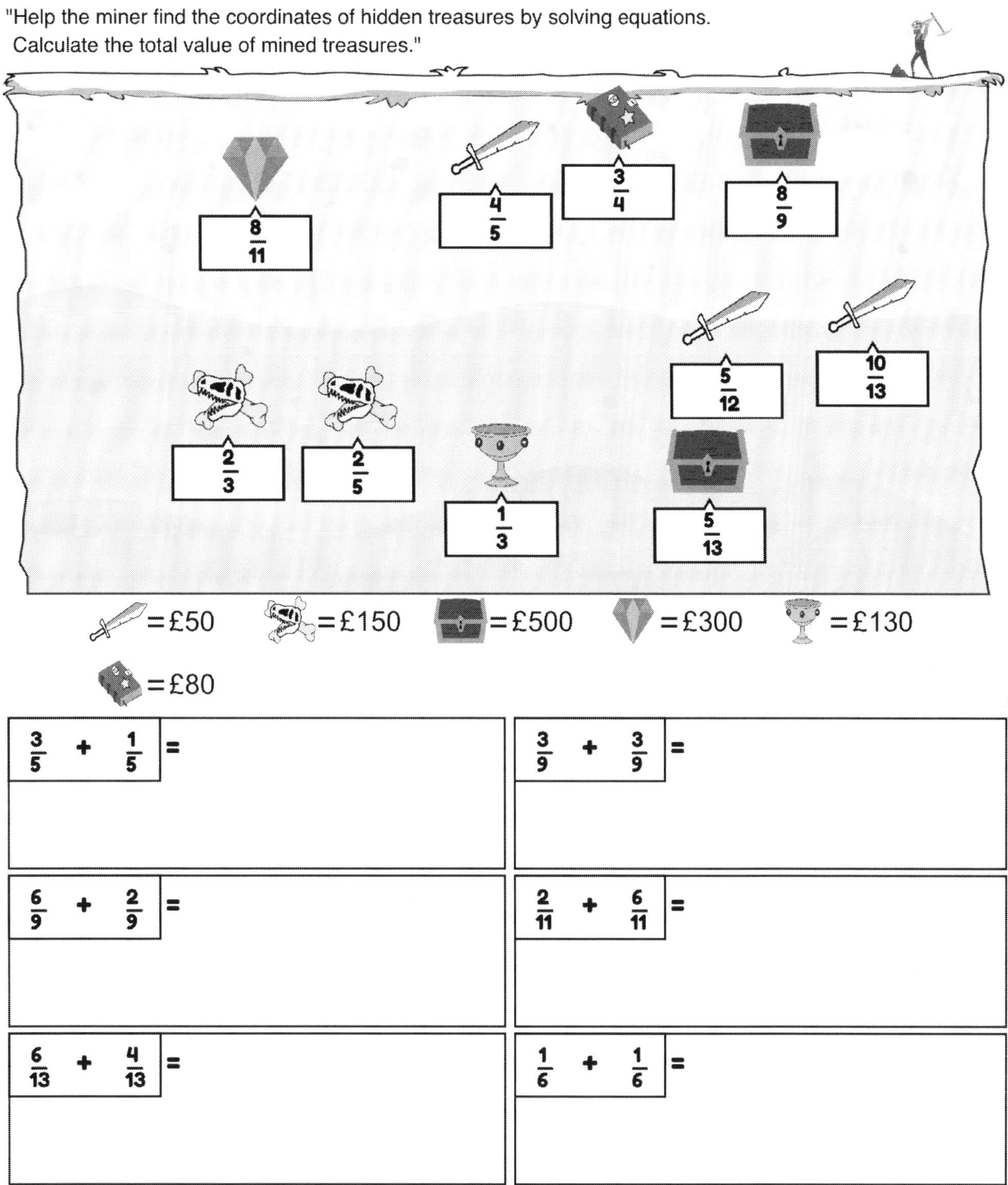

$\frac{3}{5} + \frac{1}{5} =$	$\frac{3}{9} + \frac{3}{9} =$
$\frac{6}{9} + \frac{2}{9} =$	$\frac{2}{11} + \frac{6}{11} =$
$\frac{6}{13} + \frac{4}{13} =$	$\frac{1}{6} + \frac{1}{6} =$

The total value of mined treasures = £

FRACTIONS PUZZLE 2

ADDING PROPER FRACTIONS

"Help the miner find the coordinates of hidden treasures by solving equations. Calculate the total value of mined treasures."

$\frac{2}{7}$ $\frac{6}{7}$ $\frac{1}{4}$ $\frac{8}{9}$ $\frac{4}{7}$ $\frac{1}{2}$ $\frac{12}{13}$ $\frac{10}{11}$ $\frac{3}{4}$ $\frac{3}{7}$

=£280 =£120 =£150 =£130 =£300

$\frac{3}{14} + \frac{5}{14} =$	$\frac{1}{14} + \frac{3}{14} =$
$\frac{2}{9} + \frac{6}{9} =$	$\frac{7}{13} + \frac{5}{13} =$
$\frac{1}{4} + \frac{1}{4} =$	$\frac{7}{11} + \frac{3}{11} =$

The total value of mined treasures = £

FRACTIONS PUZZLE 3

ADDING PROPER FRACTIONS

Fix the leaking pipes by solving equations.

Find which pipes still have leakages after all possible leaks are fixed

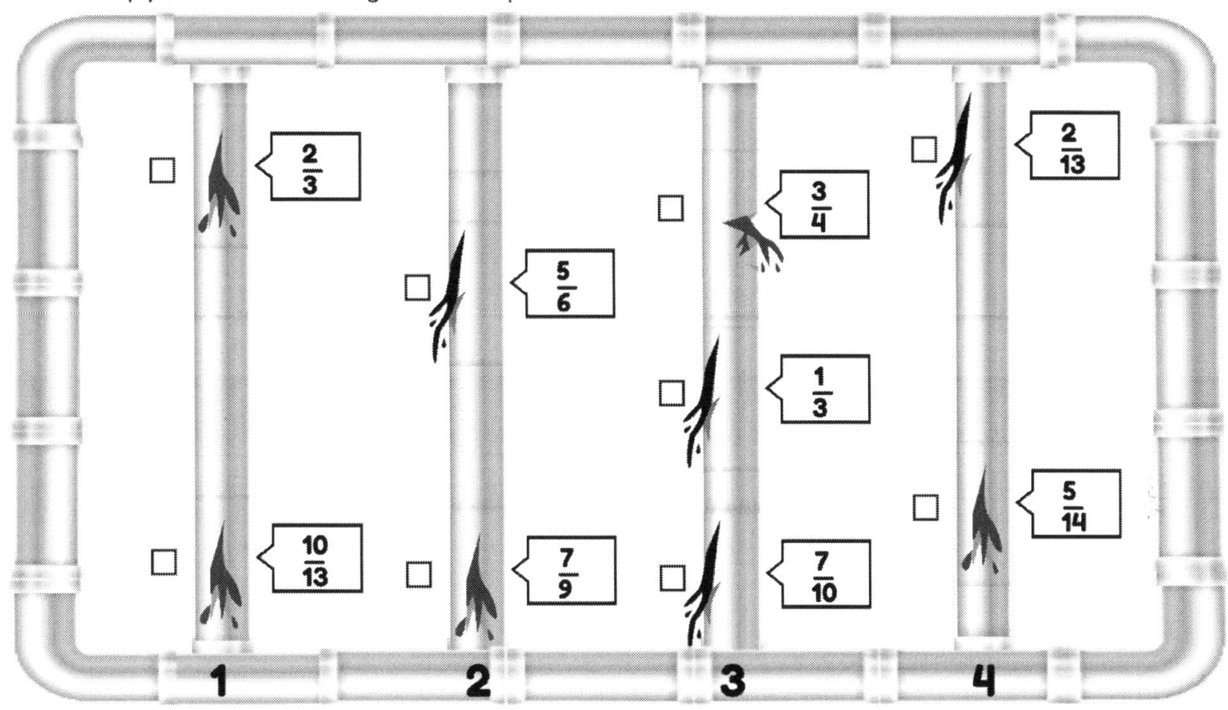

$\frac{4}{6} + \frac{1}{6} =$	$\frac{1}{14} + \frac{4}{14} =$
$\frac{1}{3} + \frac{1}{3} =$	$\frac{1}{13} + \frac{1}{13} =$
$\frac{6}{13} + \frac{4}{13} =$	$\frac{2}{4} + \frac{1}{4} =$

The numbers of the pipes which still have leaks are:

FRACTIONS PUZZLE 4

ADDING PROPER FRACTIONS

Fix the leaking pipes by solving equations.
Find which pipes still have leakages after all possible leaks are fixed

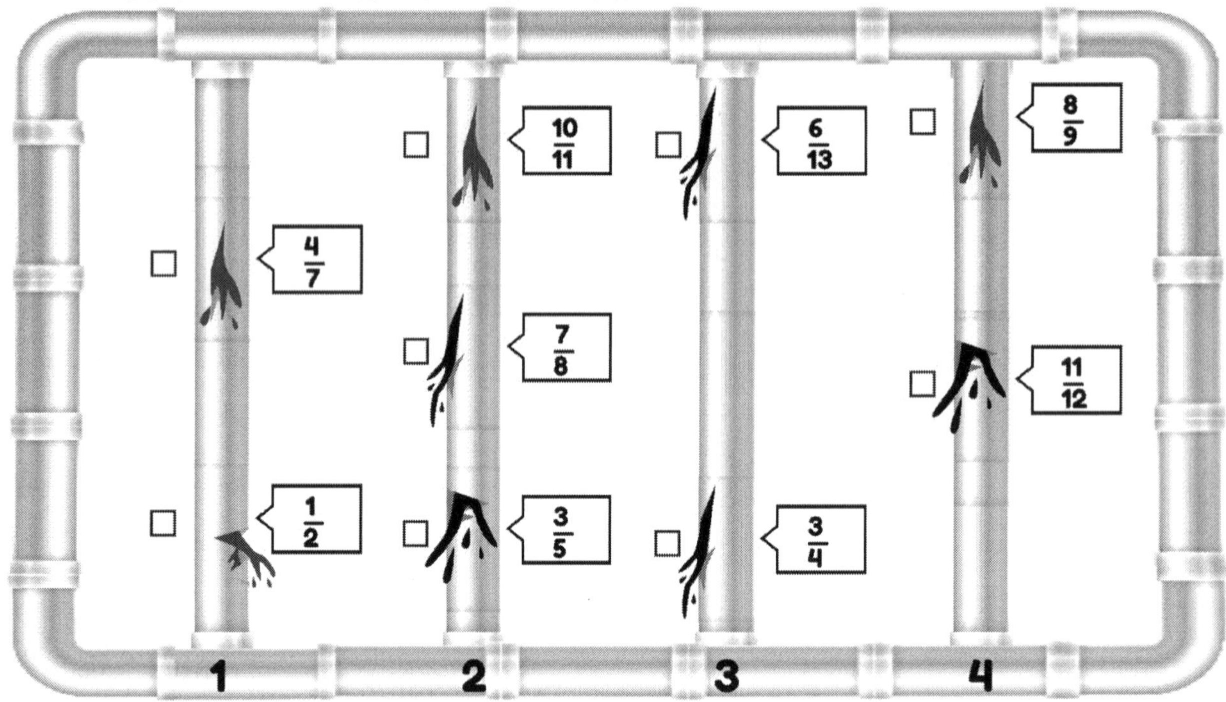

$\frac{4}{12} + \frac{7}{12} =$	$\frac{2}{13} + \frac{4}{13} =$
$\frac{3}{7} + \frac{1}{7} =$	$\frac{1}{4} + \frac{2}{4} =$
$\frac{1}{6} + \frac{2}{6} =$	$\frac{3}{8} + \frac{4}{8} =$

The numbers of the pipes which still have leaks are:

FRACTIONS PUZZLE 5

ADDING IMPROPER FRACTIONS

"Help the miner find the coordinates of hidden treasures by solving equations.
Calculate the total value of mined treasures."

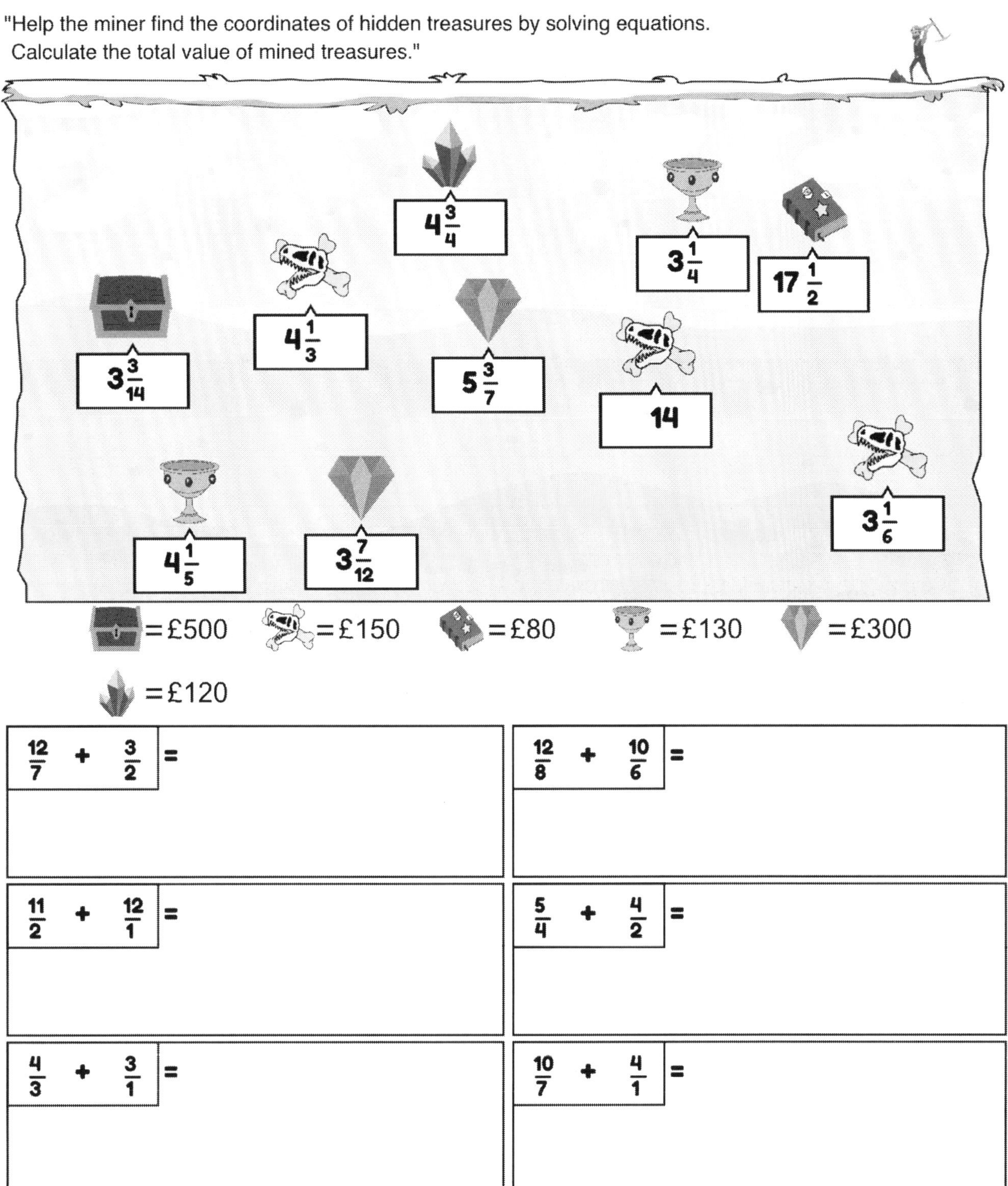

$\frac{12}{7} + \frac{3}{2} =$	$\frac{12}{8} + \frac{10}{6} =$
$\frac{11}{2} + \frac{12}{1} =$	$\frac{5}{4} + \frac{4}{2} =$
$\frac{4}{3} + \frac{3}{1} =$	$\frac{10}{7} + \frac{4}{1} =$

The total value of mined treasures = £

FRACTIONS PUZZLE 6

ADDING IMPROPER FRACTIONS

"Help the miner find the coordinates of hidden treasures by solving equations.
Calculate the total value of mined treasures."

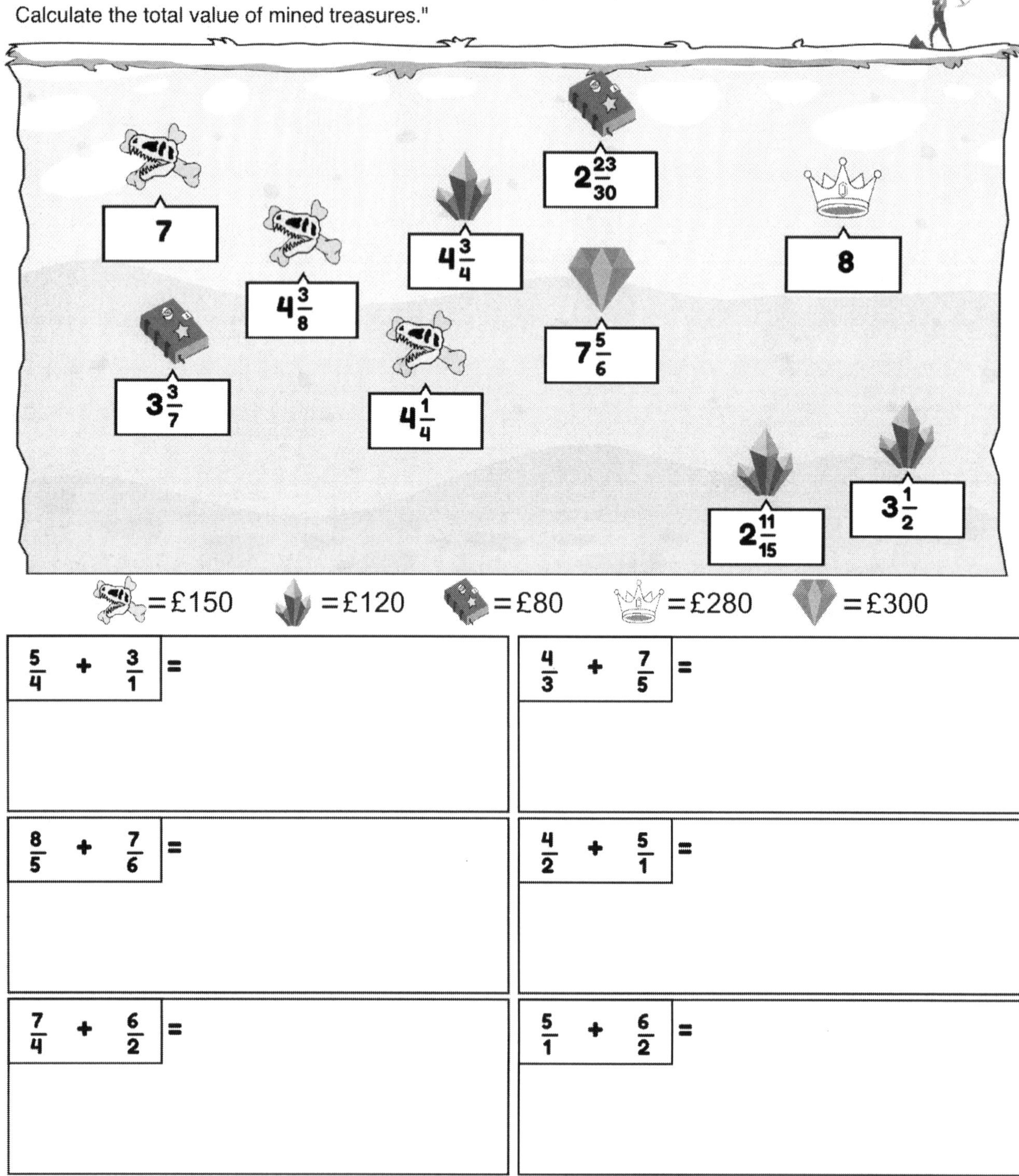

$\frac{5}{4} + \frac{3}{1} =$

$\frac{4}{3} + \frac{7}{5} =$

$\frac{8}{5} + \frac{7}{6} =$

$\frac{4}{2} + \frac{5}{1} =$

$\frac{7}{4} + \frac{6}{2} =$

$\frac{5}{1} + \frac{6}{2} =$

The total value of mined treasures = £

FRACTIONS PUZZLE 7

ADDING IMPROPER FRACTIONS

Fix the leaking pipes by solving equations.
Find which pipes still have leakages after all possible leaks are fixed

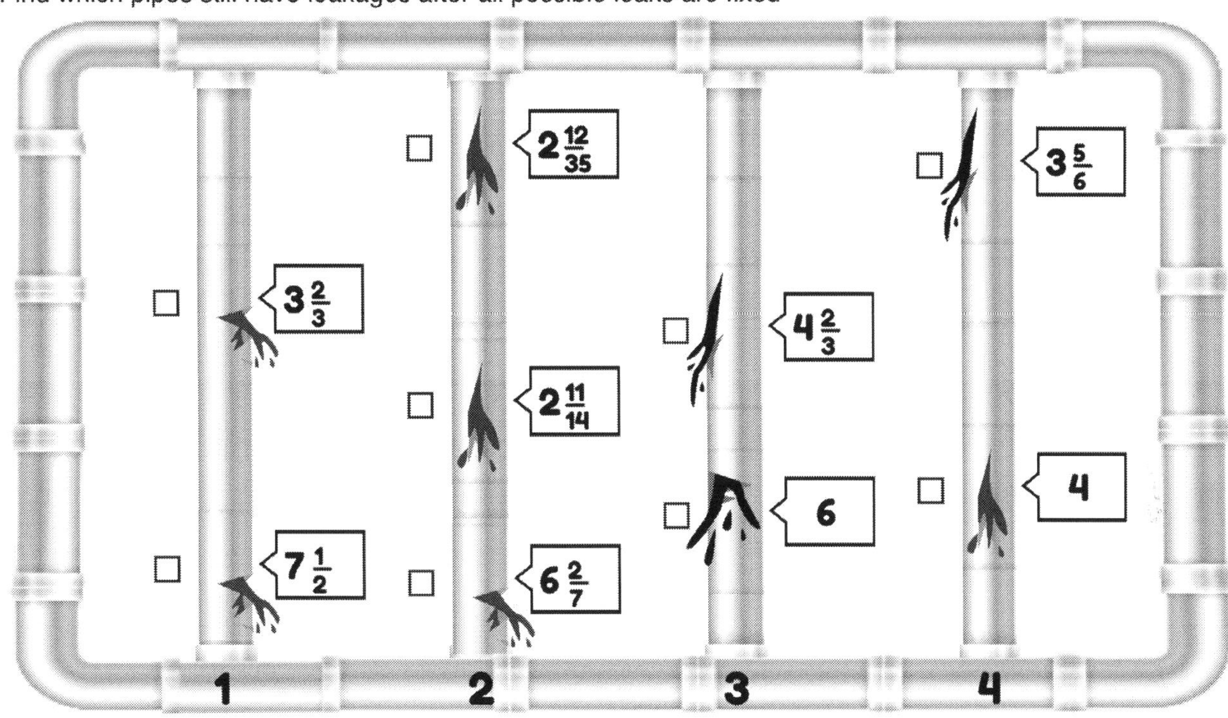

$\frac{12}{9} + \frac{10}{3} =$	$\frac{6}{4} + \frac{9}{7} =$
$\frac{3}{2} + \frac{10}{4} =$	$\frac{8}{6} + \frac{7}{3} =$
$\frac{8}{4} + \frac{11}{2} =$	$\frac{7}{3} + \frac{9}{6} =$

The numbers of the pipes which still have leaks are:

FRACTIONS PUZZLE 8

ADDING IMPROPER FRACTIONS

Fix the leaking pipes by solving equations.
Find which pipes still have leakages after all possible leaks are fixed

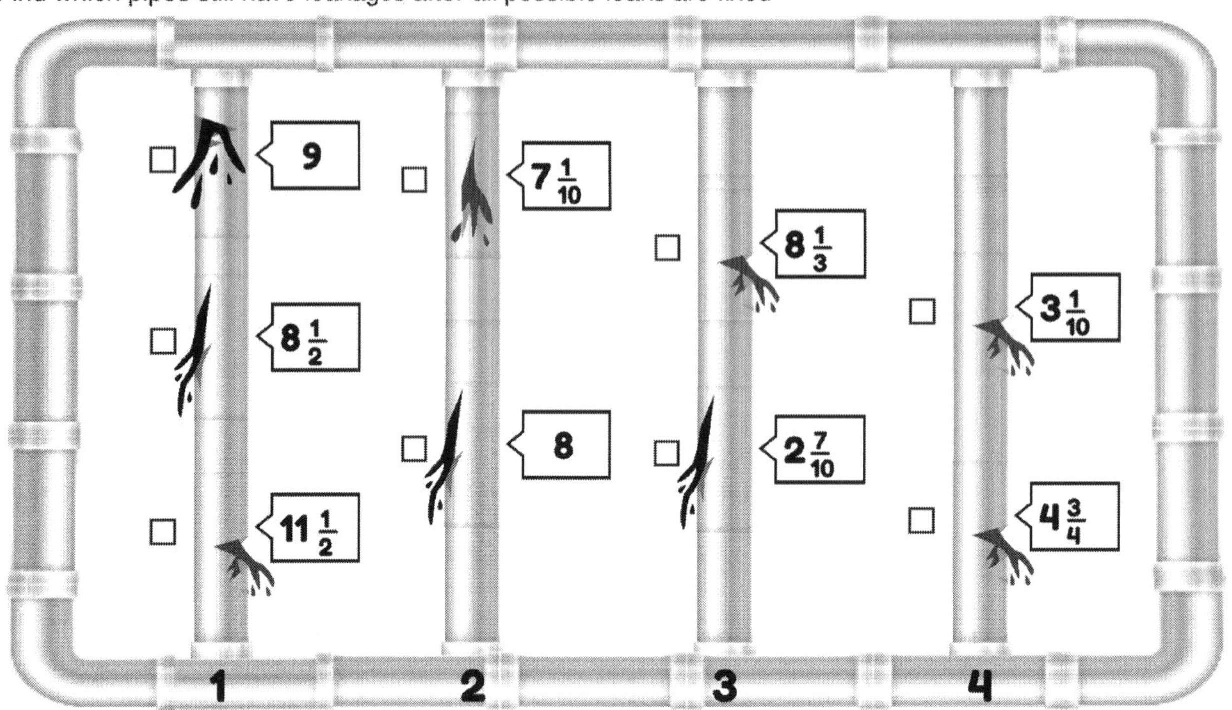

$\frac{3}{1} + \frac{7}{4} =$	$\frac{3}{2} + \frac{7}{1} =$
$\frac{8}{5} + \frac{3}{2} =$	$\frac{11}{2} + \frac{8}{5} =$
$\frac{6}{5} + \frac{6}{4} =$	$\frac{7}{2} + \frac{8}{1} =$

The numbers of the pipes which still have leaks are:

FRACTIONS PUZZLE 9

ADDING MIXED FRACTIONS

"Help the miner find the coordinates of hidden treasures by solving equations.
Calculate the total value of mined treasures."

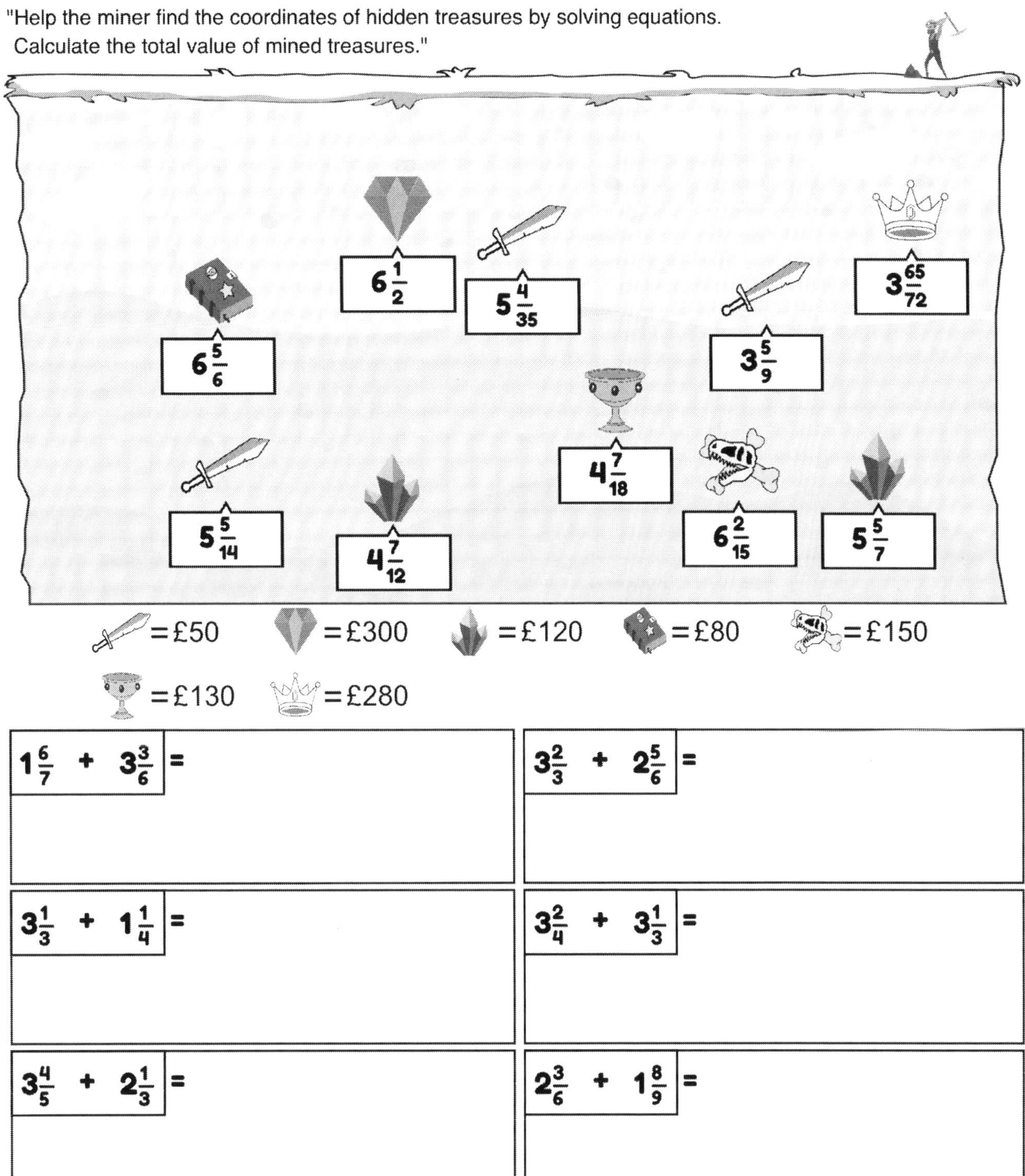

$1\frac{6}{7} + 3\frac{3}{6} =$

$3\frac{2}{3} + 2\frac{5}{6} =$

$3\frac{1}{3} + 1\frac{1}{4} =$

$3\frac{2}{4} + 3\frac{1}{3} =$

$3\frac{4}{5} + 2\frac{1}{3} =$

$2\frac{3}{6} + 1\frac{8}{9} =$

The total value of mined treasures = £

FRACTIONS PUZZLE 10

ADDING MIXED FRACTIONS

"Help the miner find the coordinates of hidden treasures by solving equations. Calculate the total value of mined treasures."

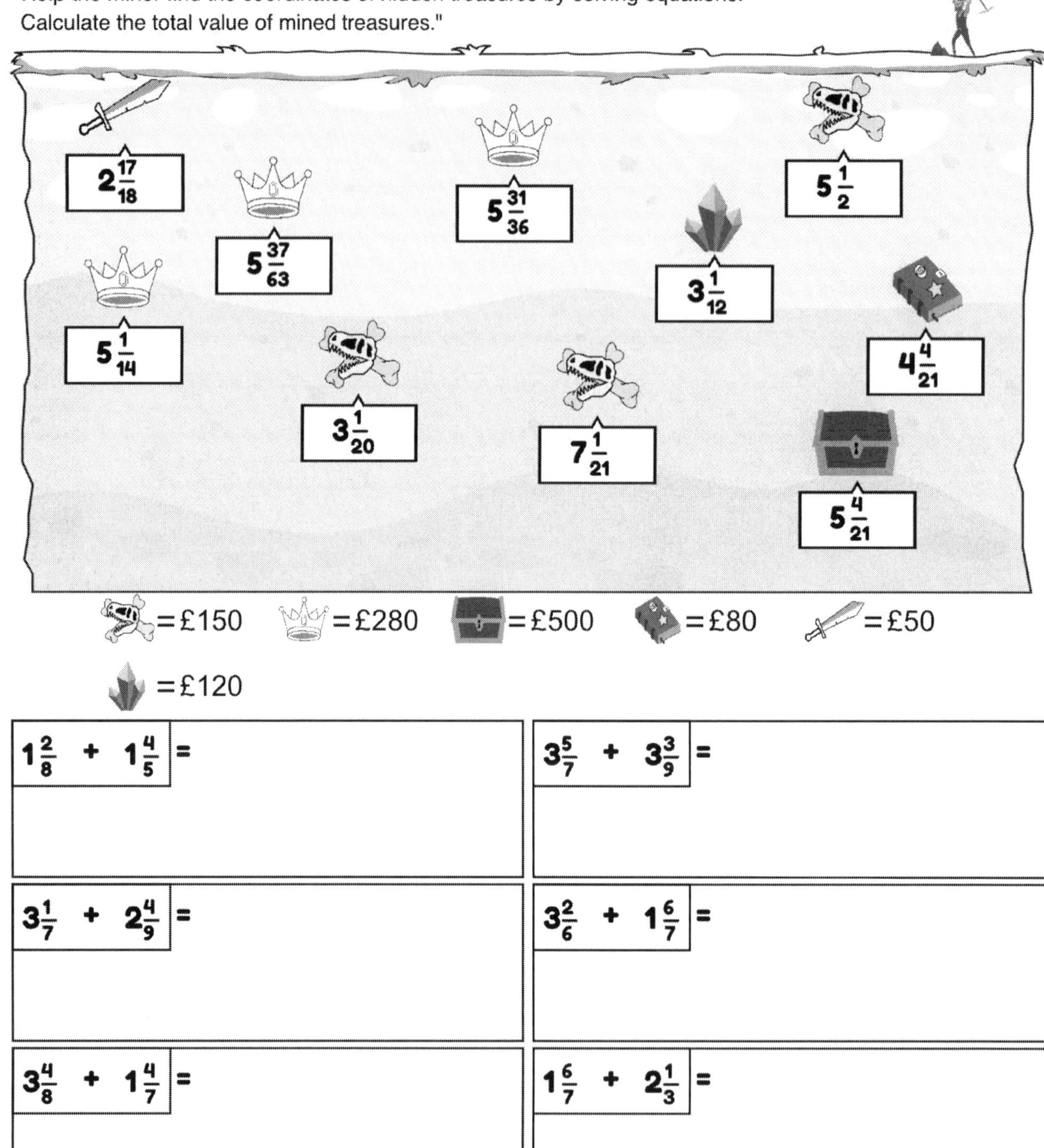

$1\frac{2}{8} + 1\frac{4}{5} =$	$3\frac{5}{7} + 3\frac{3}{9} =$
$3\frac{1}{7} + 2\frac{4}{9} =$	$3\frac{2}{6} + 1\frac{6}{7} =$
$3\frac{4}{8} + 1\frac{4}{7} =$	$1\frac{6}{7} + 2\frac{1}{3} =$

The total value of mined treasures = £

FRACTIONS PUZZLE 11

ADDING MIXED FRACTIONS

Fix the leaking pipes by solving equations.
Find which pipes still have leakages after all possible leaks are fixed

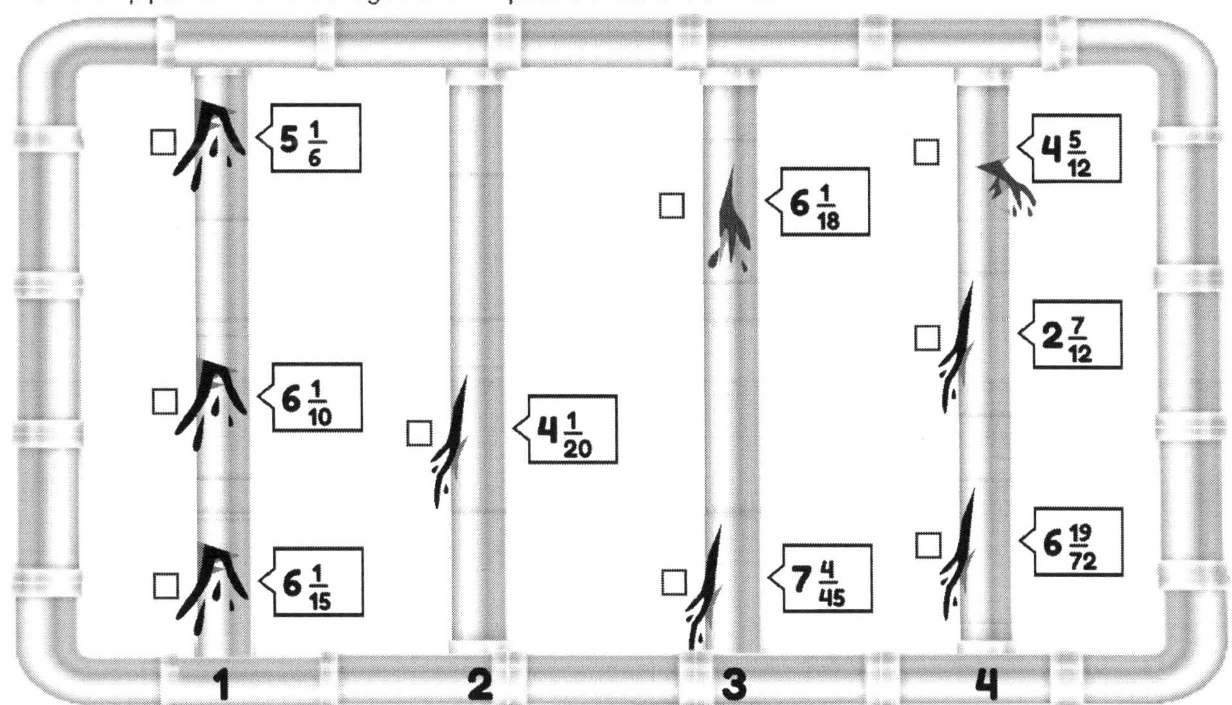

$3\frac{4}{8} + 1\frac{4}{6} =$	$3\frac{8}{9} + 3\frac{1}{5} =$
$1\frac{1}{4} + 1\frac{1}{3} =$	$3\frac{4}{6} + 2\frac{2}{5} =$
$3\frac{2}{4} + 2\frac{5}{9} =$	$1\frac{4}{5} + 2\frac{1}{4} =$

The numbers of the pipes which still have leaks are:

FRACTIONS PUZZLE 12

ADDING MIXED FRACTIONS

Fix the leaking pipes by solving equations.
Find which pipes still have leakages after all possible leaks are fixed

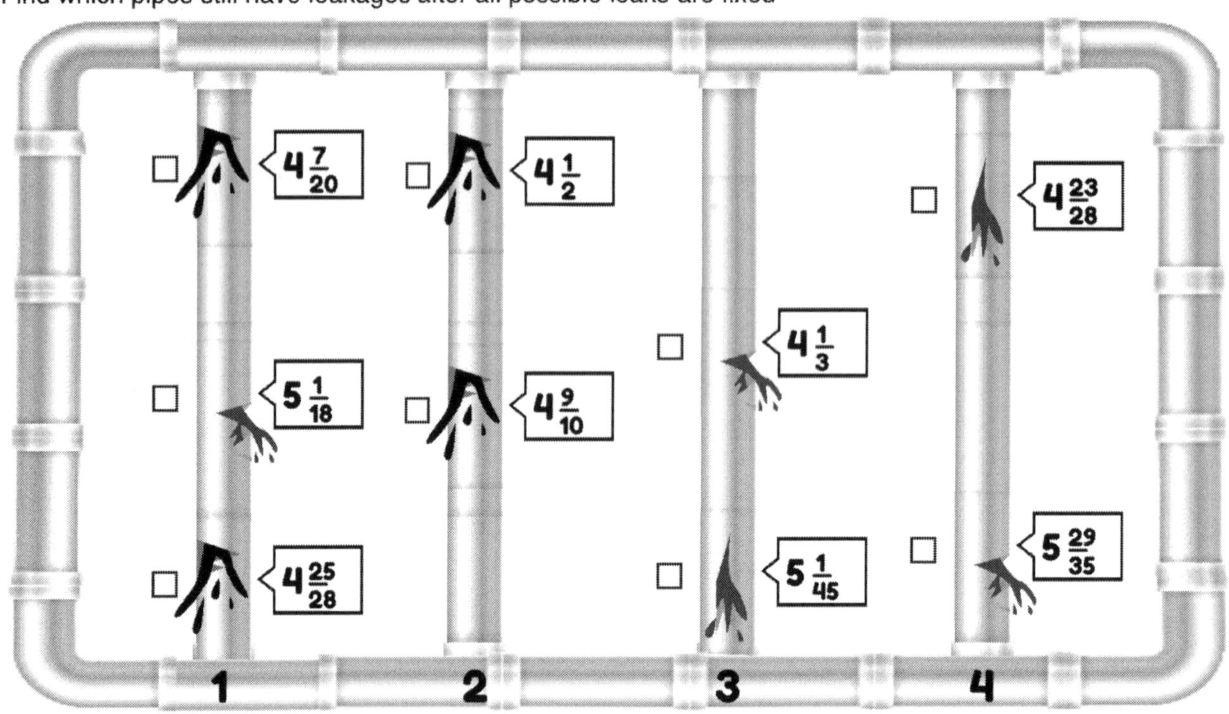

$1\frac{2}{9} + 3\frac{5}{6} =$	$3\frac{2}{4} + 1\frac{2}{5} =$
$2\frac{3}{7} + 3\frac{2}{5} =$	$3\frac{2}{9} + 1\frac{4}{5} =$
$3\frac{2}{8} + 1\frac{1}{4} =$	$2\frac{3}{6} + 1\frac{5}{6} =$

The numbers of the pipes which still have leaks are:

FRACTIONS PUZZLE 13

SUBTRACTING PROPER FRACTIONS

"Help the miner find the coordinates of hidden treasures by solving equations.
Calculate the total value of mined treasures."

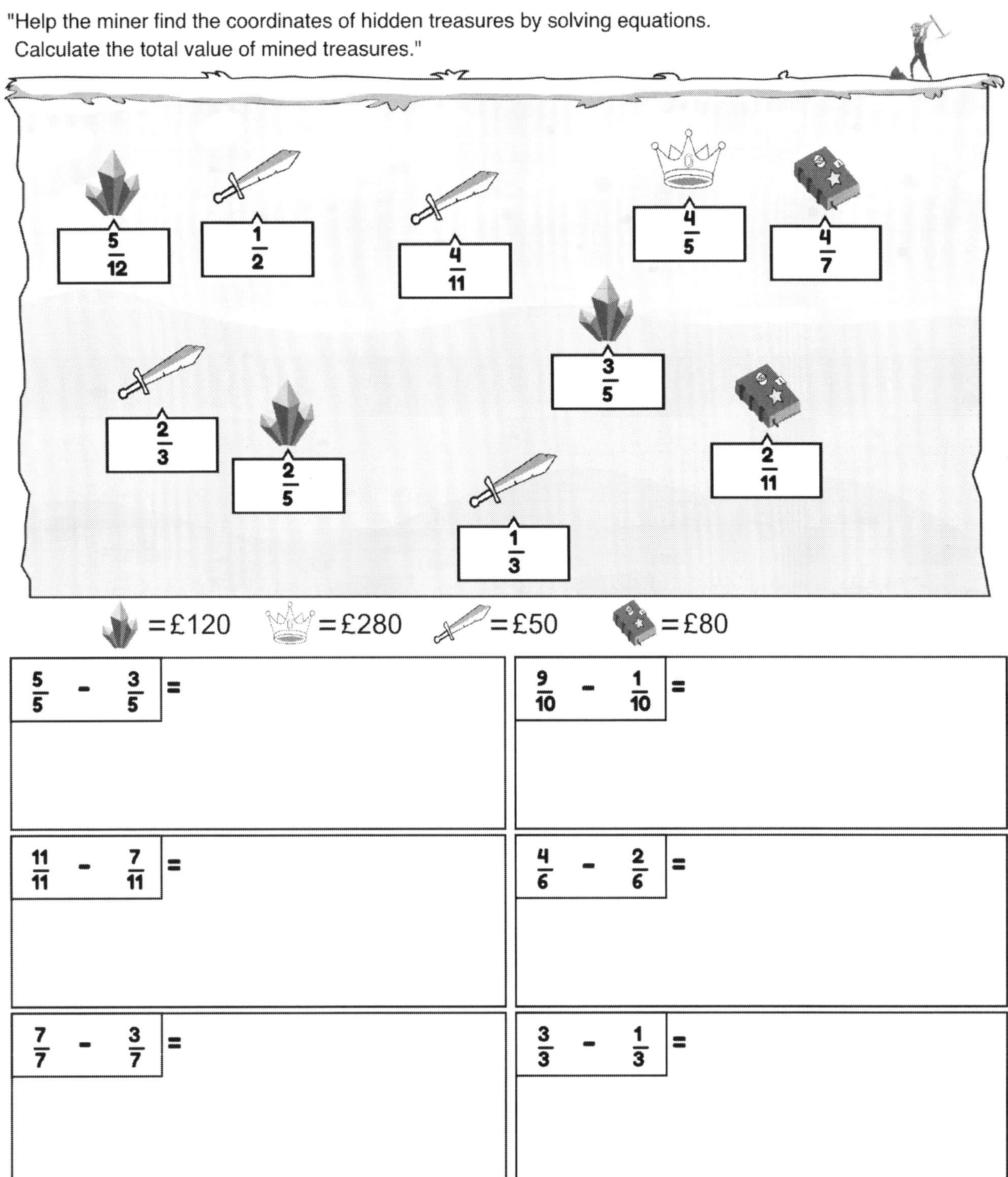

The total value of mined treasures = £

FRACTIONS PUZZLE 14

SUBTRACTING PROPER FRACTIONS

"Help the miner find the coordinates of hidden treasures by solving equations. Calculate the total value of mined treasures."

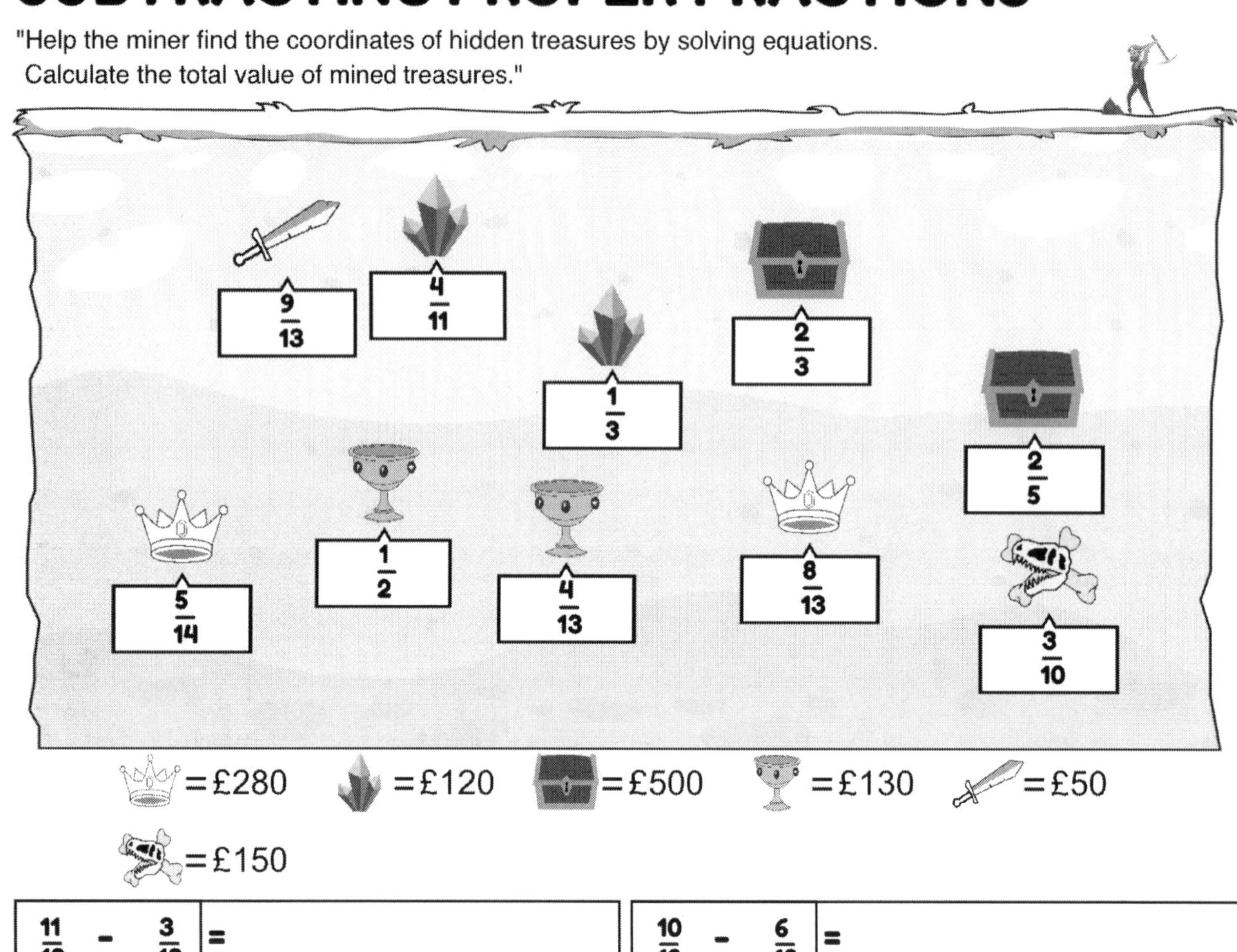

=£280 =£120 =£500 =£130 =£50

=£150

$\frac{11}{13} - \frac{3}{13} =$	$\frac{10}{12} - \frac{6}{12} =$
$\frac{3}{5} - \frac{1}{5} =$	$\frac{4}{4} - \frac{2}{4} =$
$\frac{3}{3} - \frac{1}{3} =$	$\frac{11}{13} - \frac{2}{13} =$

The total value of mined treasures = £

FRACTIONS PUZZLE 15

SUBTRACTING PROPER FRACTIONS

Fix the leaking pipes by solving equations.
Find which pipes still have leakages after all possible leaks are fixed

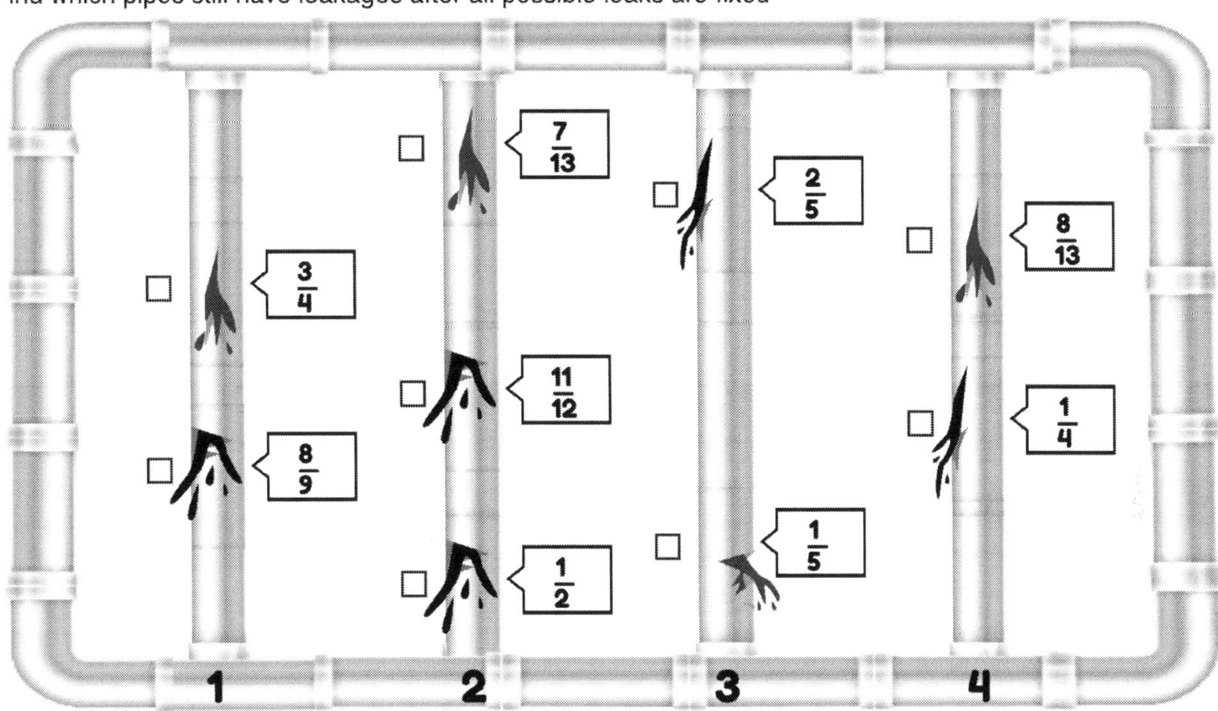

$\frac{12}{12} - \frac{1}{12} =$	$\frac{5}{10} - \frac{3}{10} =$
$\frac{10}{12} - \frac{1}{12} =$	$\frac{13}{13} - \frac{5}{13} =$
$\frac{7}{12} - \frac{4}{12} =$	$\frac{3}{5} - \frac{1}{5} =$

The numbers of the pipes which still have leaks are:

FRACTIONS PUZZLE 16

SUBTRACTING PROPER FRACTIONS

Fix the leaking pipes by solving equations.

Find which pipes still have leakages after all possible leaks are fixed

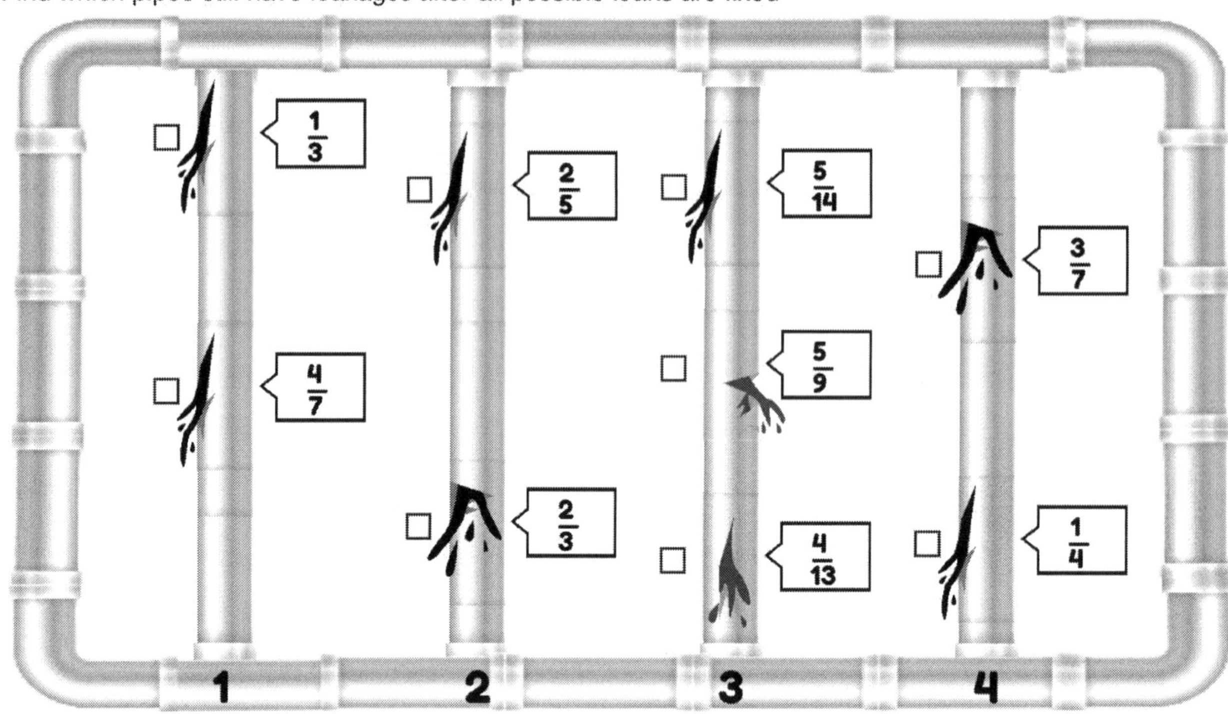

$\frac{7}{9} - \frac{2}{9} =$	$\frac{3}{3} - \frac{1}{3} =$
$\frac{5}{5} - \frac{3}{5} =$	$\frac{6}{7} - \frac{2}{7} =$
$\frac{10}{13} - \frac{6}{13} =$	$\frac{7}{7} - \frac{4}{7} =$

The numbers of the pipes which still have leaks are:

FRACTIONS PUZZLE 17

SUBTRACTING IMPROPER FRACTIONS

"Help the miner find the coordinates of hidden treasures by solving equations.
Calculate the total value of mined treasures."

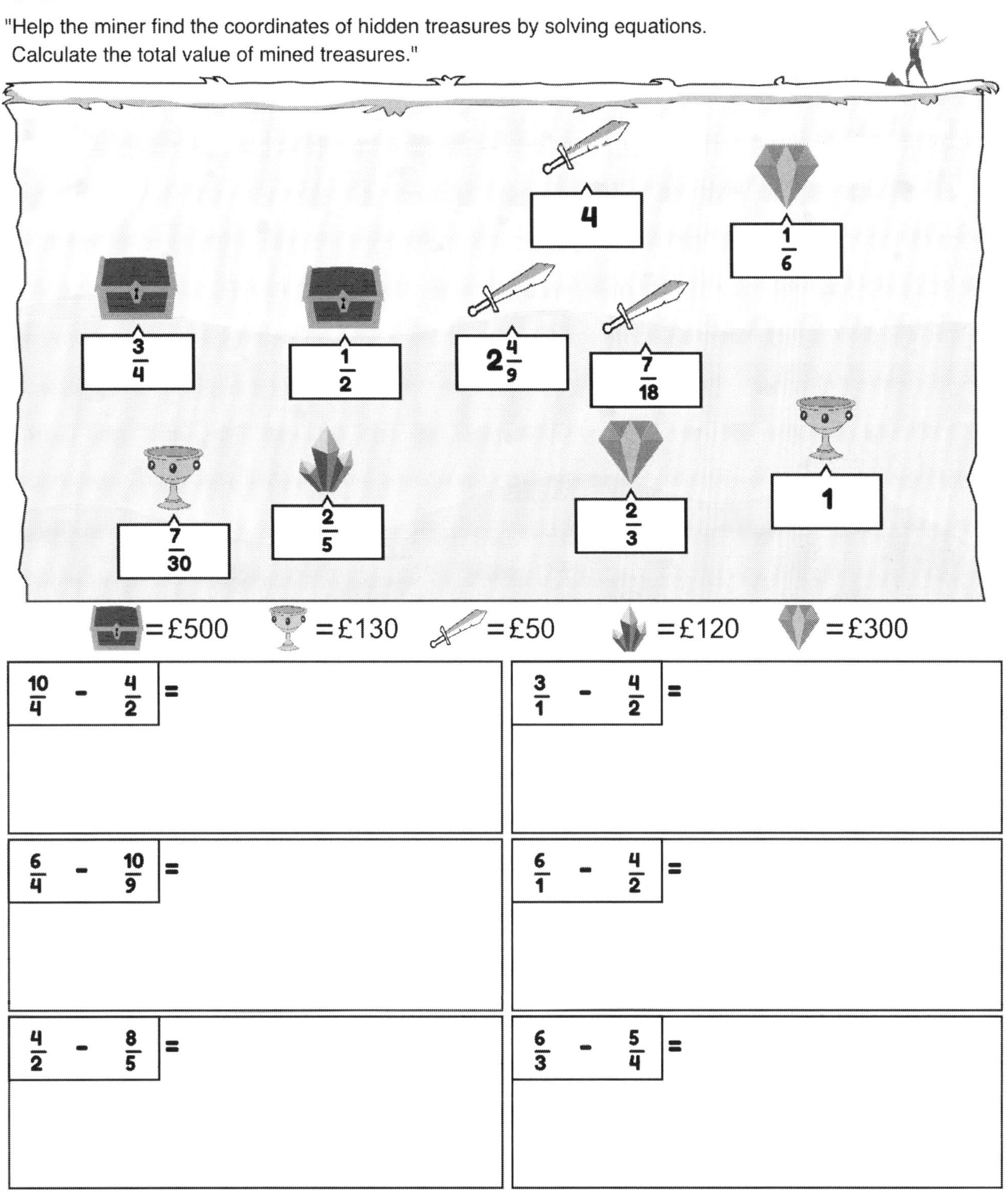

$\frac{10}{4} - \frac{4}{2} =$

$\frac{3}{1} - \frac{4}{2} =$

$\frac{6}{4} - \frac{10}{9} =$

$\frac{6}{1} - \frac{4}{2} =$

$\frac{4}{2} - \frac{8}{5} =$

$\frac{6}{3} - \frac{5}{4} =$

The total value of mined treasures = £

FRACTIONS PUZZLE 18

SUBTRACTING IMPROPER FRACTIONS

"Help the miner find the coordinates of hidden treasures by solving equations.
Calculate the total value of mined treasures."

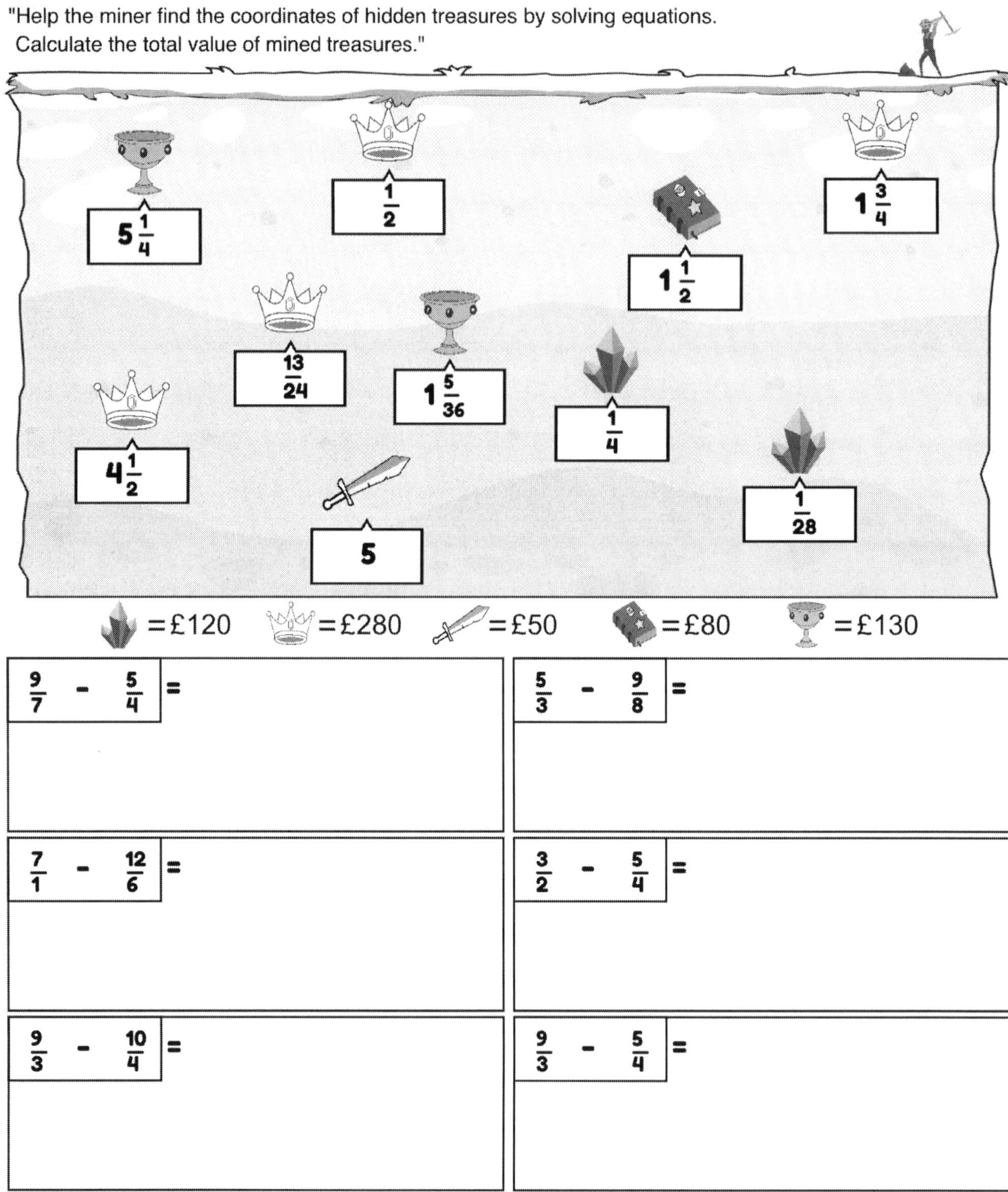

$\frac{9}{7} - \frac{5}{4} =$	$\frac{5}{3} - \frac{9}{8} =$
$\frac{7}{1} - \frac{12}{6} =$	$\frac{3}{2} - \frac{5}{4} =$
$\frac{9}{3} - \frac{10}{4} =$	$\frac{9}{3} - \frac{5}{4} =$

The total value of mined treasures = £

FRACTIONS PUZZLE 19

SUBTRACTING IMPROPER FRACTIONS

Fix the leaking pipes by solving equations.

Find which pipes still have leakages after all possible leaks are fixed

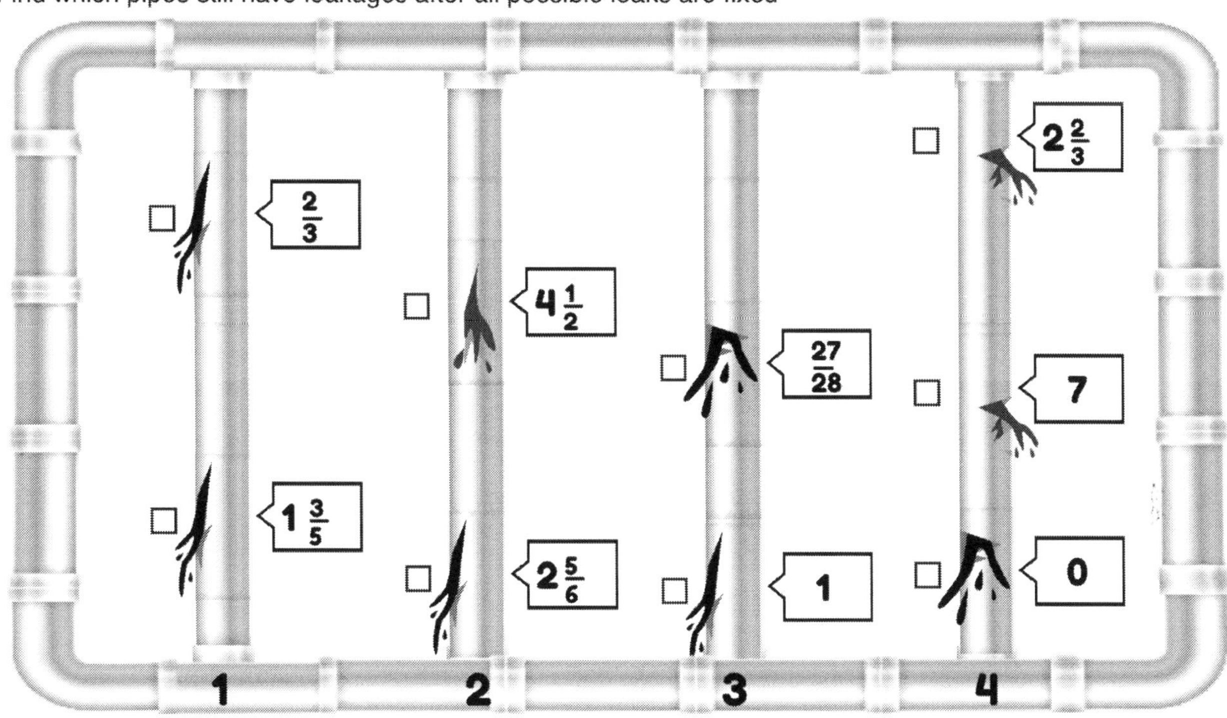

$\frac{3}{1} - \frac{7}{5} =$	$\frac{8}{6} - \frac{12}{9} =$
$\frac{4}{1} - \frac{4}{3} =$	$\frac{3}{1} - \frac{4}{2} =$
$\frac{8}{3} - \frac{4}{2} =$	$\frac{9}{4} - \frac{9}{7} =$

The numbers of the pipes which still have leaks are:

FRACTIONS PUZZLE 20

SUBTRACTING IMPROPER FRACTIONS

Fix the leaking pipes by solving equations.

Find which pipes still have leakages after all possible leaks are fixed

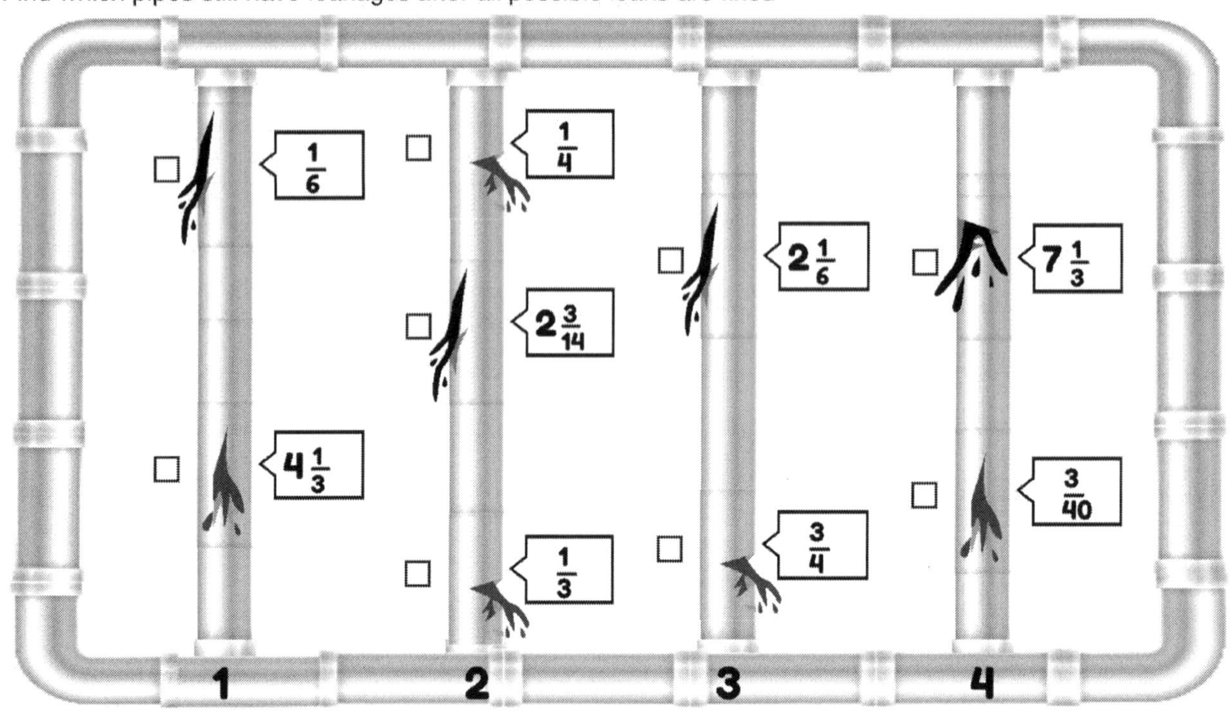

$\frac{5}{3} - \frac{3}{2} =$	$\frac{7}{2} - \frac{9}{7} =$
$\frac{12}{2} - \frac{5}{3} =$	$\frac{3}{2} - \frac{7}{6} =$
$\frac{12}{10} - \frac{9}{8} =$	$\frac{11}{3} - \frac{3}{2} =$

The numbers of the pipes which still have leaks are:

FRACTIONS PUZZLE 21

SUBTRACTING MIXED FRACTIONS

"Help the miner find the coordinates of hidden treasures by solving equations.
Calculate the total value of mined treasures."

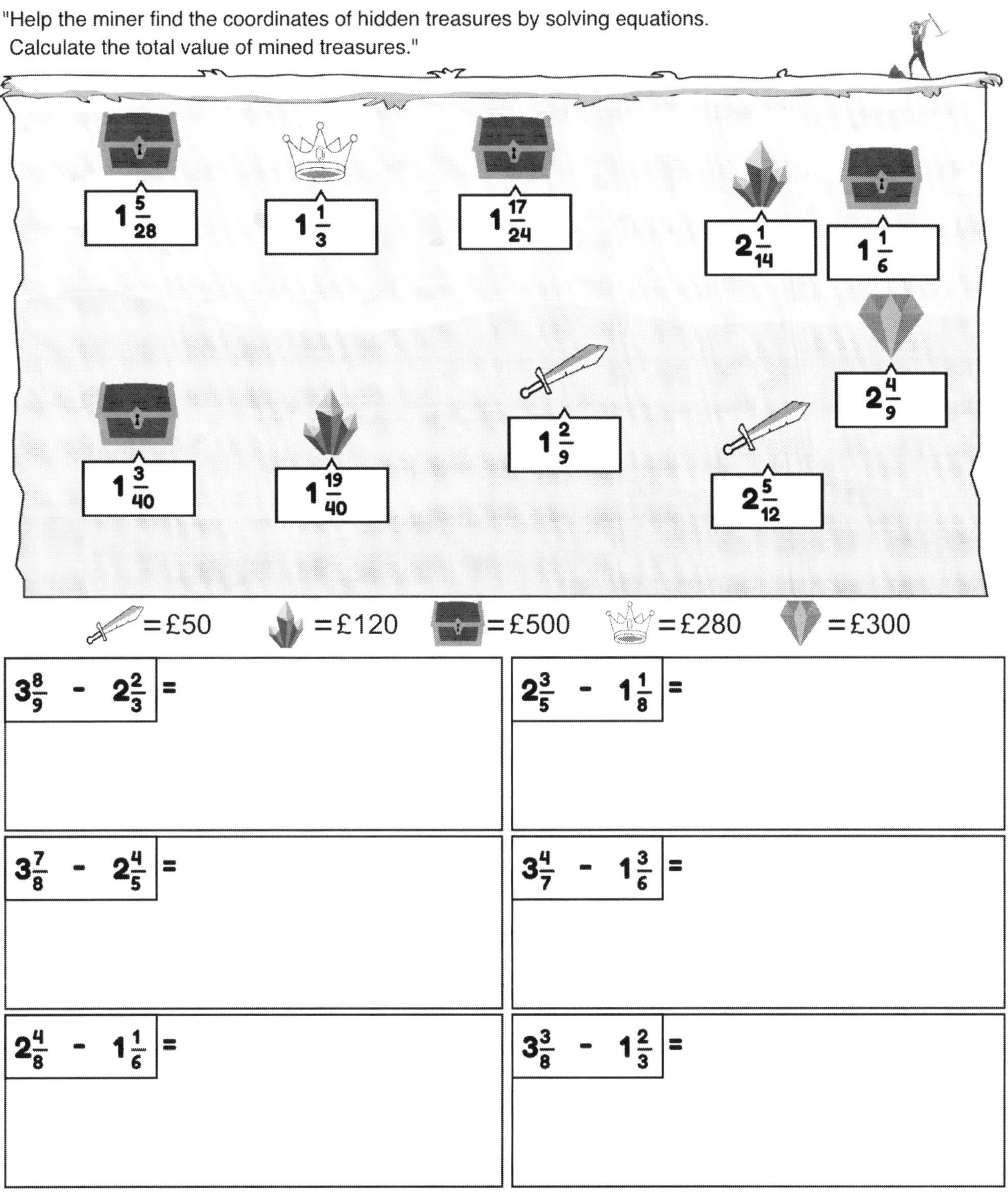

$3\frac{8}{9} - 2\frac{2}{3} =$

$2\frac{3}{5} - 1\frac{1}{8} =$

$3\frac{7}{8} - 2\frac{4}{5} =$

$3\frac{4}{7} - 1\frac{3}{6} =$

$2\frac{4}{8} - 1\frac{1}{6} =$

$3\frac{3}{8} - 1\frac{2}{3} =$

The total value of mined treasures = £

FRACTIONS PUZZLE 22

SUBTRACTING MIXED FRACTIONS

"Help the miner find the coordinates of hidden treasures by solving equations.
Calculate the total value of mined treasures."

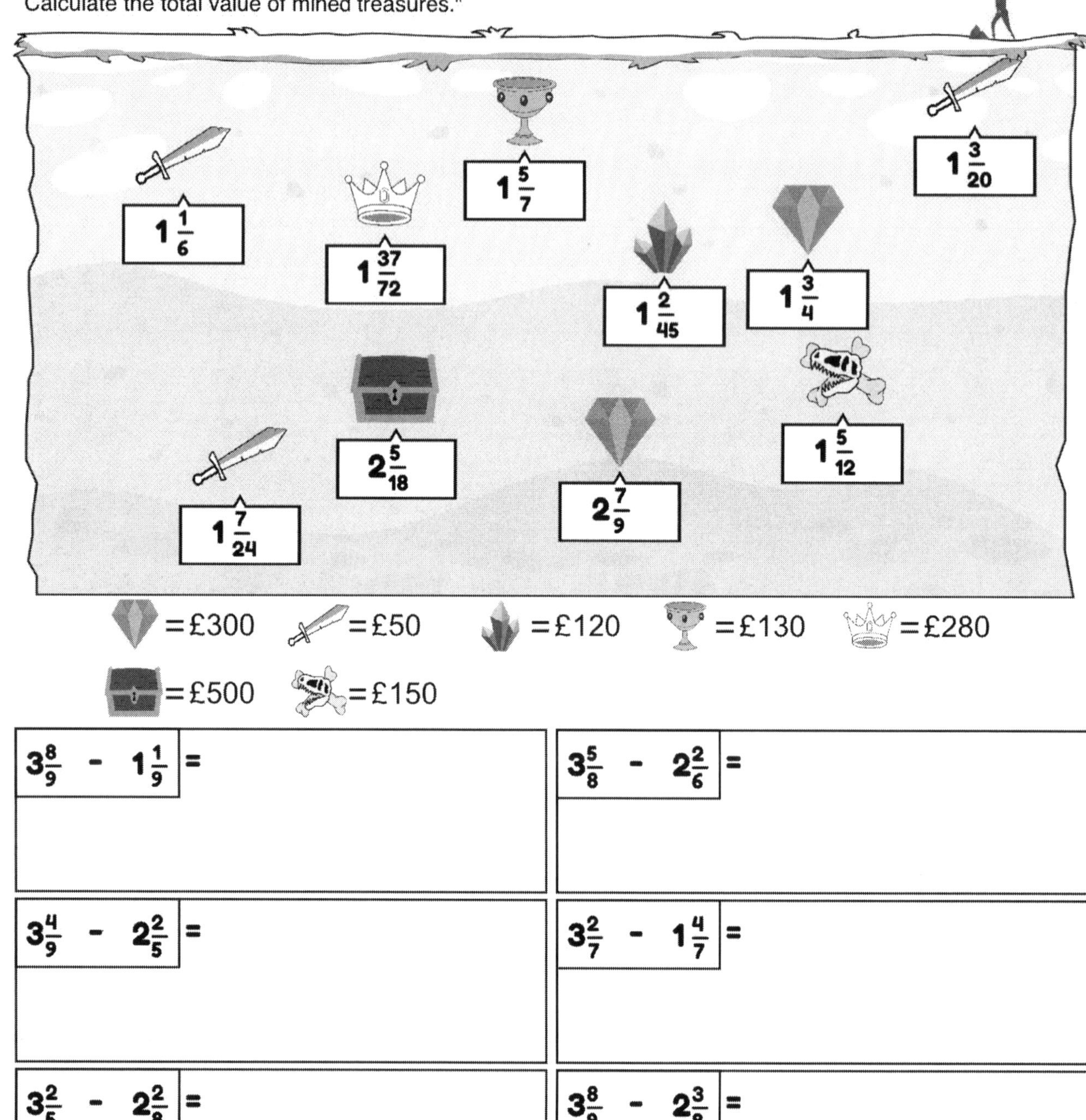

$3\frac{8}{9} - 1\frac{1}{9} =$	$3\frac{5}{8} - 2\frac{2}{6} =$
$3\frac{4}{9} - 2\frac{2}{5} =$	$3\frac{2}{7} - 1\frac{4}{7} =$
$3\frac{2}{5} - 2\frac{2}{8} =$	$3\frac{8}{9} - 2\frac{3}{8} =$

The total value of mined treasures = £

FRACTIONS PUZZLE 23

SUBTRACTING MIXED FRACTIONS

Fix the leaking pipes by solving equations.

Find which pipes still have leakages after all possible leaks are fixed

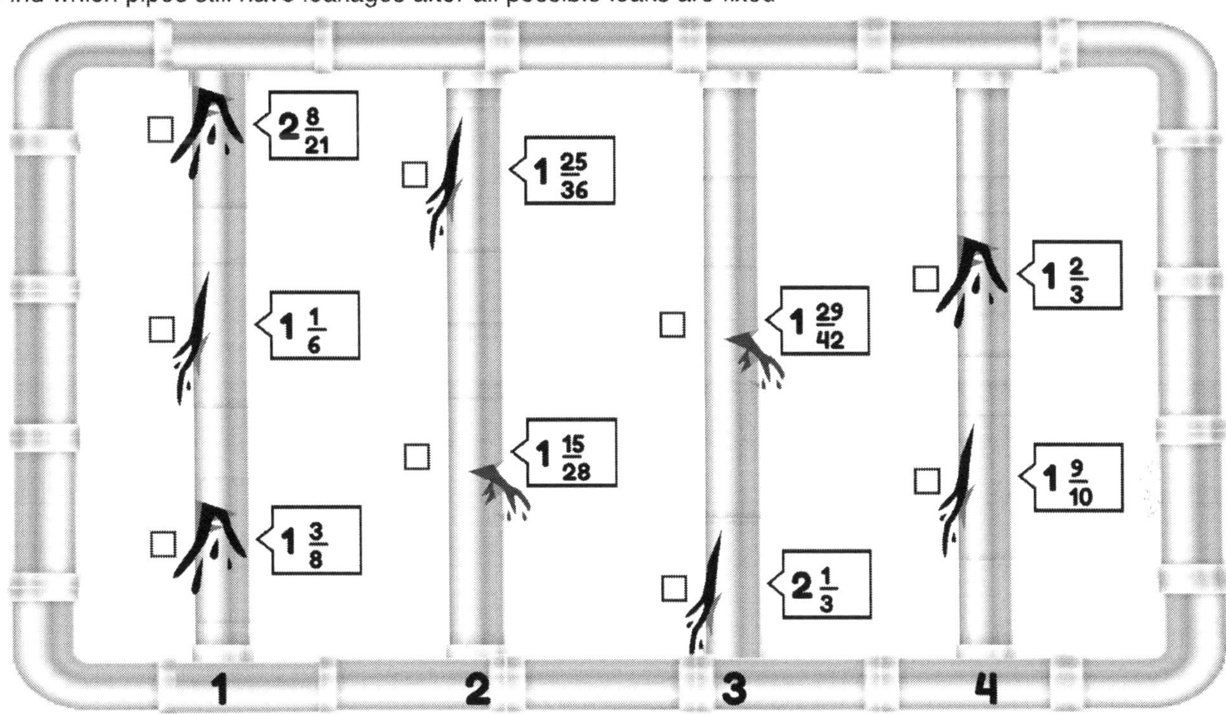

$3\frac{2}{7} - 1\frac{6}{8} =$	$3\frac{2}{5} - 1\frac{2}{4} =$
$2\frac{2}{3} - 1\frac{2}{4} =$	$2\frac{5}{6} - 1\frac{1}{7} =$
$3\frac{4}{9} - 1\frac{3}{4} =$	$3\frac{5}{8} - 2\frac{1}{4} =$

The numbers of the pipes which still have leaks are:

FRACTIONS PUZZLE 24

SUBTRACTING MIXED FRACTIONS

Fix the leaking pipes by solving equations.

Find which pipes still have leakages after all possible leaks are fixed

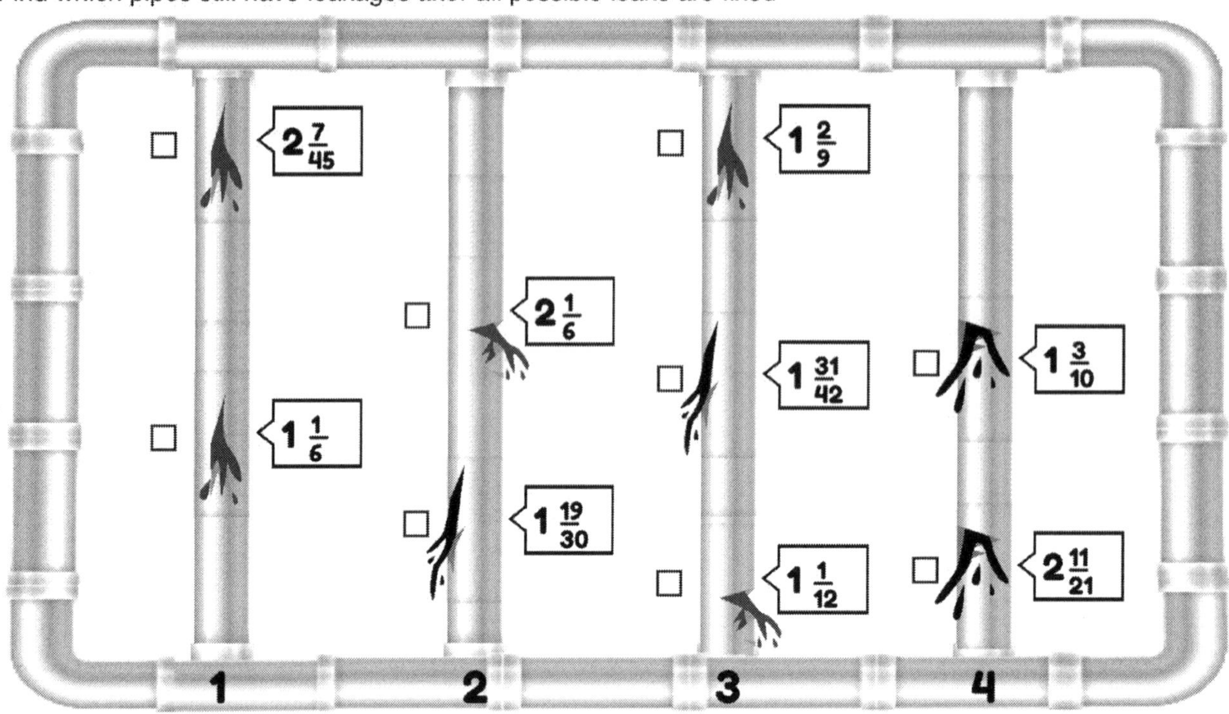

$3\frac{3}{5} - 1\frac{4}{9} =$	$2\frac{2}{4} - 1\frac{1}{5} =$
$2\frac{4}{5} - 1\frac{1}{6} =$	$3\frac{6}{9} - 1\frac{4}{8} =$
$3\frac{1}{3} - 2\frac{1}{4} =$	$3\frac{5}{9} - 2\frac{3}{9} =$

The numbers of the pipes which still have leaks are:

FRACTIONS PUZZLE 25

DIVIDING PROPER FRACTIONS

"Help the miner find the coordinates of hidden treasures by solving equations.
Calculate the total value of mined treasures."

$1\frac{1}{8}$ $2\frac{3}{16}$ 1 $\frac{5}{8}$ $\frac{9}{35}$

$1\frac{3}{7}$ $1\frac{1}{9}$ $1\frac{1}{3}$ $\frac{2}{3}$ $\frac{20}{21}$

=£500 =£150 =£280 =£130 =£120

$\frac{4}{9} \div \frac{2}{5} =$	$\frac{3}{6} \div \frac{4}{5} =$
$\frac{2}{3} \div \frac{6}{9} =$	$\frac{4}{9} \div \frac{2}{3} =$
$\frac{6}{7} \div \frac{3}{5} =$	$\frac{1}{4} \div \frac{2}{9} =$

The total value of mined treasures = £

FRACTIONS PUZZLE 26

DIVIDING PROPER FRACTIONS

"Help the miner find the coordinates of hidden treasures by solving equations. Calculate the total value of mined treasures."

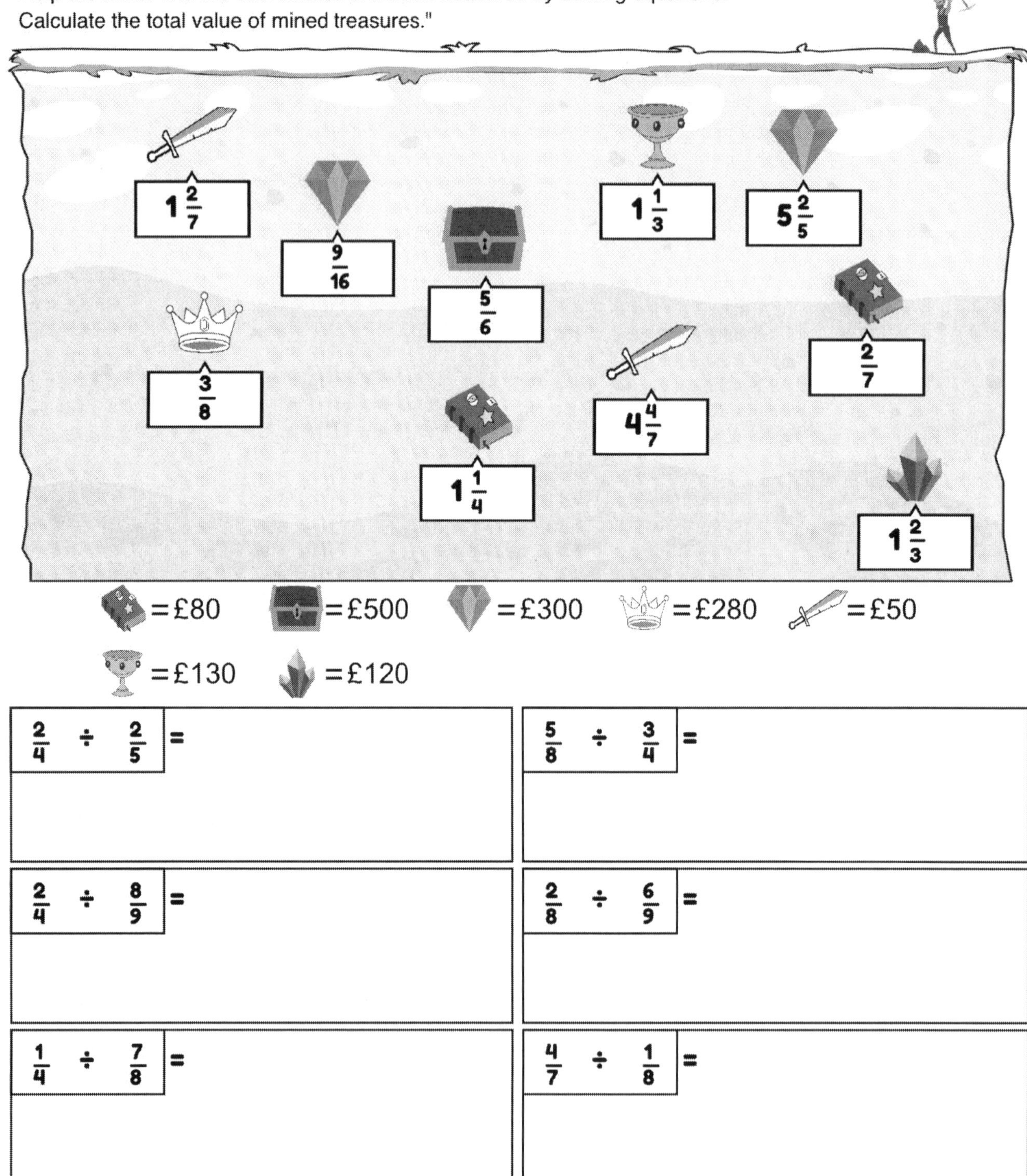

$\frac{2}{4} \div \frac{2}{5} =$

$\frac{5}{8} \div \frac{3}{4} =$

$\frac{2}{4} \div \frac{8}{9} =$

$\frac{2}{8} \div \frac{6}{9} =$

$\frac{1}{4} \div \frac{7}{8} =$

$\frac{4}{7} \div \frac{1}{8} =$

The total value of mined treasures = £

FRACTIONS PUZZLE 27

DIVIDING PROPER FRACTIONS

Fix the leaking pipes by solving equations.
Find which pipes still have leakages after all possible leaks are fixed

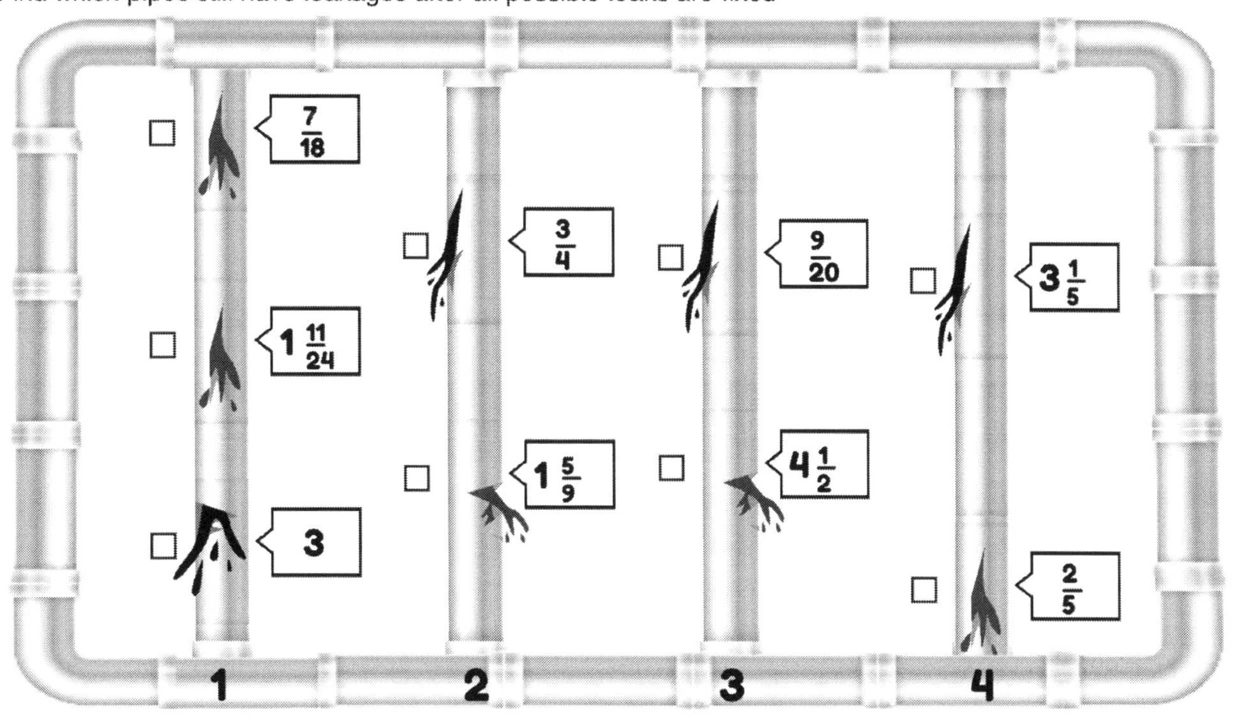

$\frac{3}{4} \div \frac{1}{6} =$	$\frac{5}{8} \div \frac{3}{7} =$
$\frac{4}{5} \div \frac{1}{4} =$	$\frac{3}{9} \div \frac{6}{7} =$
$\frac{1}{4} \div \frac{5}{9} =$	$\frac{3}{9} \div \frac{5}{6} =$

The numbers of the pipes which still have leaks are:

FRACTIONS PUZZLE 28

DIVIDING PROPER FRACTIONS

Fix the leaking pipes by solving equations.

Find which pipes still have leakages after all possible leaks are fixed

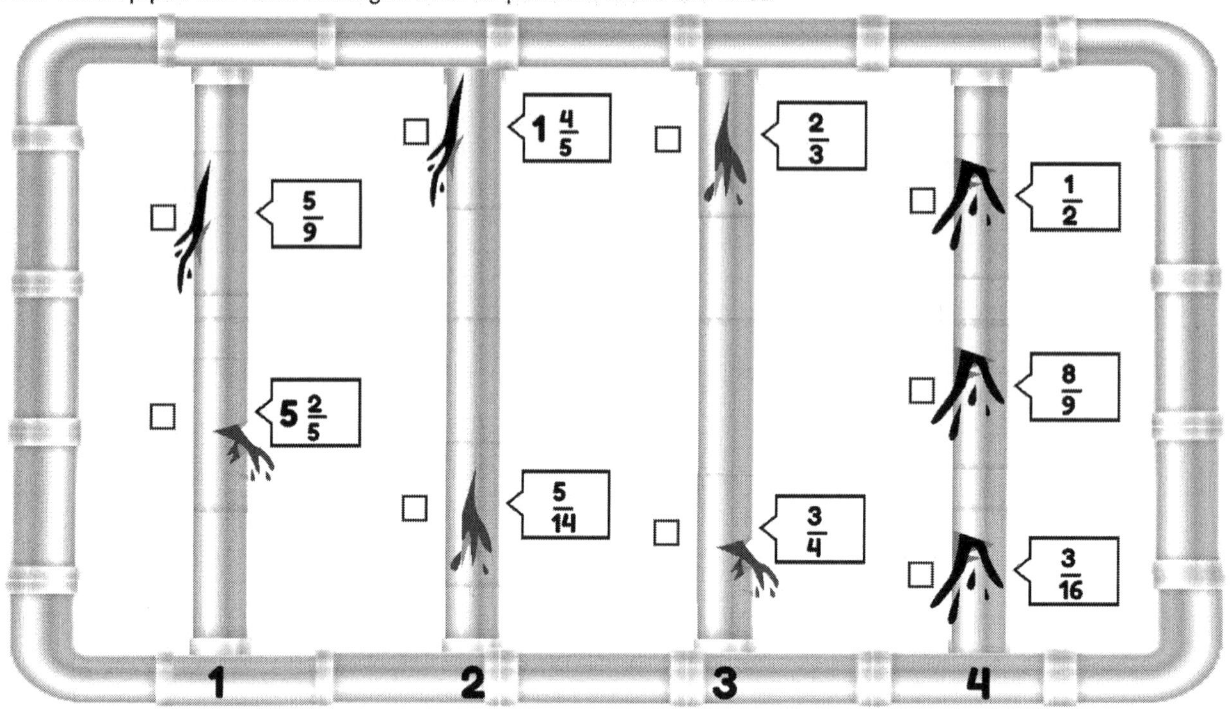

$\frac{3}{5} \div \frac{1}{9} =$	$\frac{1}{3} \div \frac{2}{3} =$
$\frac{4}{6} \div \frac{8}{9} =$	$\frac{1}{8} \div \frac{4}{6} =$
$\frac{2}{8} \div \frac{3}{8} =$	$\frac{2}{7} \div \frac{4}{5} =$

The numbers of the pipes which still have leaks are:

FRACTIONS PUZZLE 29

DIVIDING IMPROPER FRACTIONS

"Help the miner find the coordinates of hidden treasures by solving equations.
Calculate the total value of mined treasures."

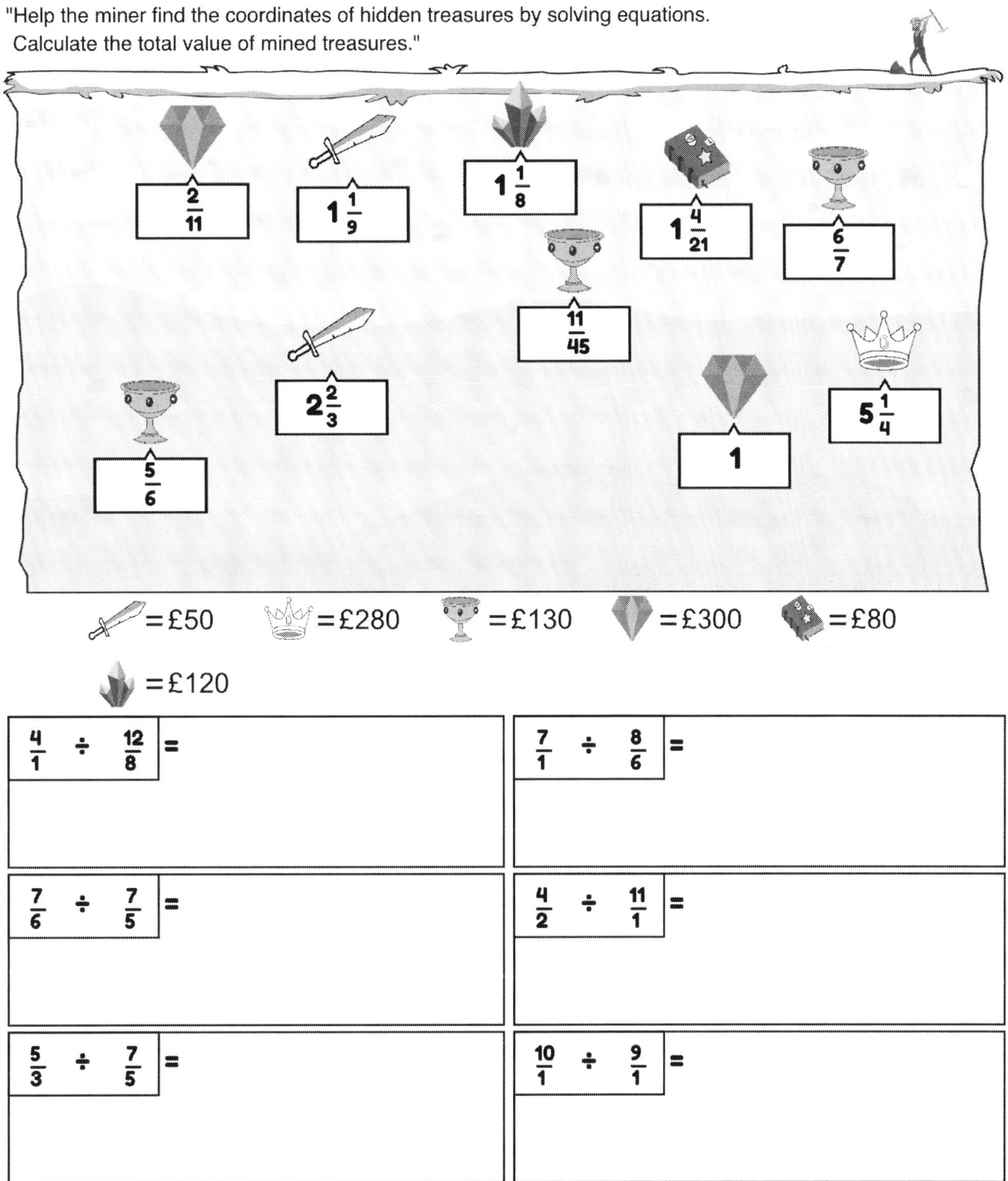

$\frac{4}{1} \div \frac{12}{8} =$	$\frac{7}{1} \div \frac{8}{6} =$
$\frac{7}{6} \div \frac{7}{5} =$	$\frac{4}{2} \div \frac{11}{1} =$
$\frac{5}{3} \div \frac{7}{5} =$	$\frac{10}{1} \div \frac{9}{1} =$

The total value of mined treasures = £

FRACTIONS PUZZLE 30

DIVIDING IMPROPER FRACTIONS

"Help the miner find the coordinates of hidden treasures by solving equations.
Calculate the total value of mined treasures."

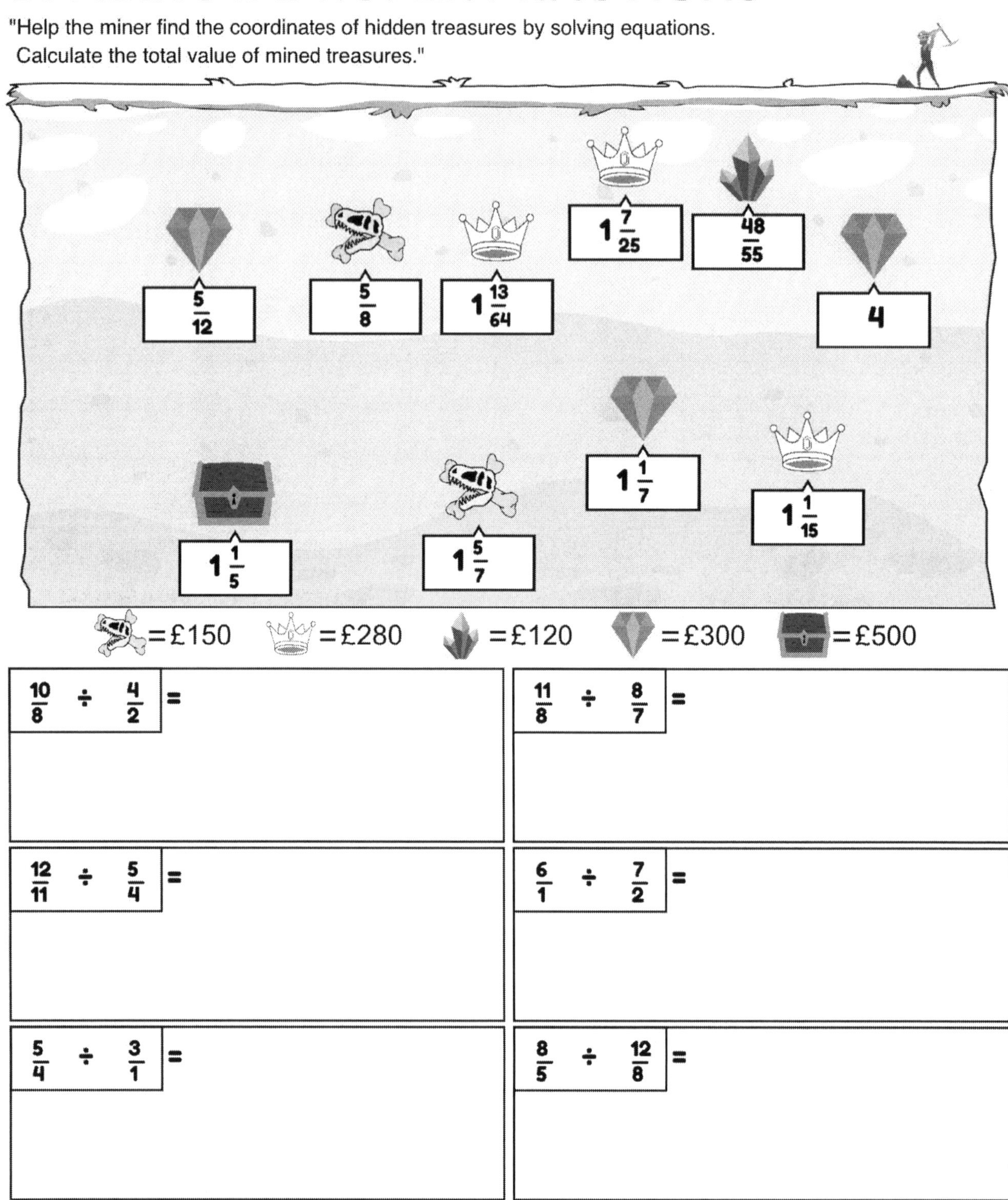

$\frac{10}{8} \div \frac{4}{2} =$	$\frac{11}{8} \div \frac{8}{7} =$
$\frac{12}{11} \div \frac{5}{4} =$	$\frac{6}{1} \div \frac{7}{2} =$
$\frac{5}{4} \div \frac{3}{1} =$	$\frac{8}{5} \div \frac{12}{8} =$

The total value of mined treasures = £

FRACTIONS PUZZLE 31

DIVIDING IMPROPER FRACTIONS

Fix the leaking pipes by solving equations.

Find which pipes still have leakages after all possible leaks are fixed

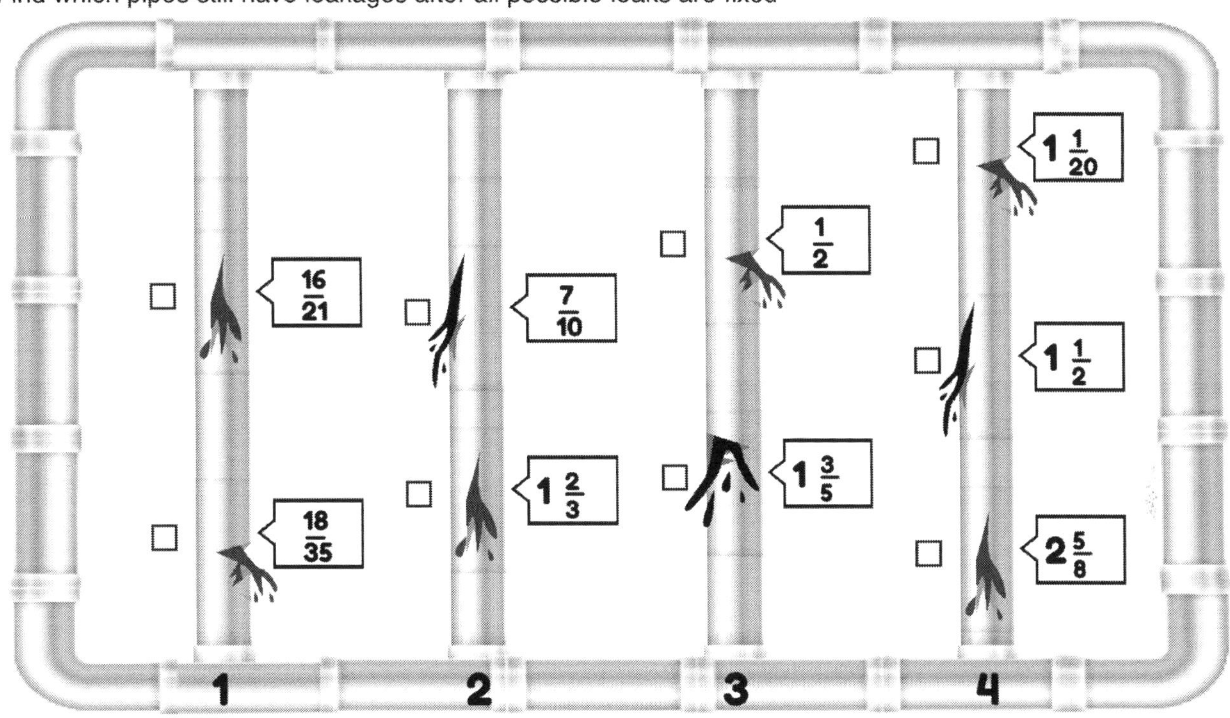

$\frac{4}{2} \div \frac{4}{3} =$	$\frac{4}{2} \div \frac{4}{1} =$
$\frac{5}{2} \div \frac{9}{6} =$	$\frac{8}{7} \div \frac{3}{2} =$
$\frac{7}{2} \div \frac{8}{6} =$	$\frac{4}{2} \div \frac{5}{4} =$

The numbers of the pipes which still have leaks are:

FRACTIONS PUZZLE 32

DIVIDING IMPROPER FRACTIONS

Fix the leaking pipes by solving equations.
Find which pipes still have leakages after all possible leaks are fixed

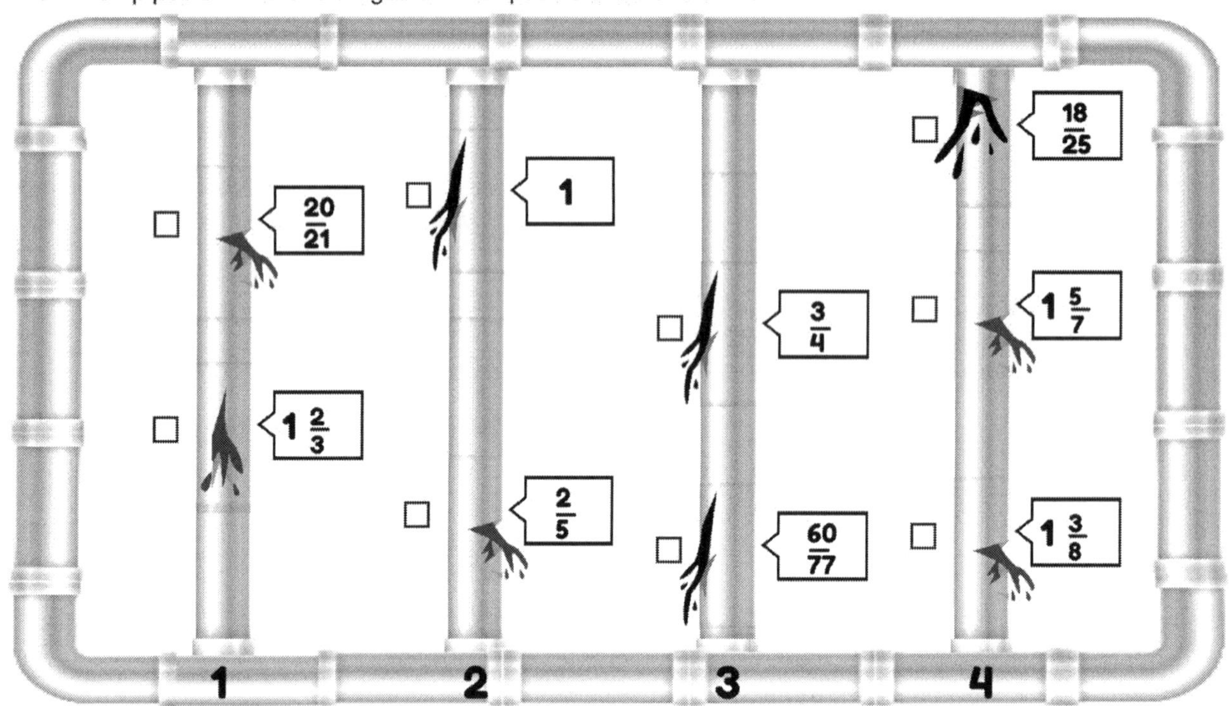

$\frac{8}{1} \div \frac{8}{1} =$	$\frac{10}{7} \div \frac{11}{6} =$
$\frac{3}{1} \div \frac{7}{4} =$	$\frac{4}{2} \div \frac{5}{1} =$
$\frac{10}{8} \div \frac{5}{3} =$	$\frac{3}{1} \div \frac{9}{5} =$

The numbers of the pipes which still have leaks are:

FRACTIONS PUZZLE 33

DIVIDING MIXED FRACTIONS

"Help the miner find the coordinates of hidden treasures by solving equations.
Calculate the total value of mined treasures."

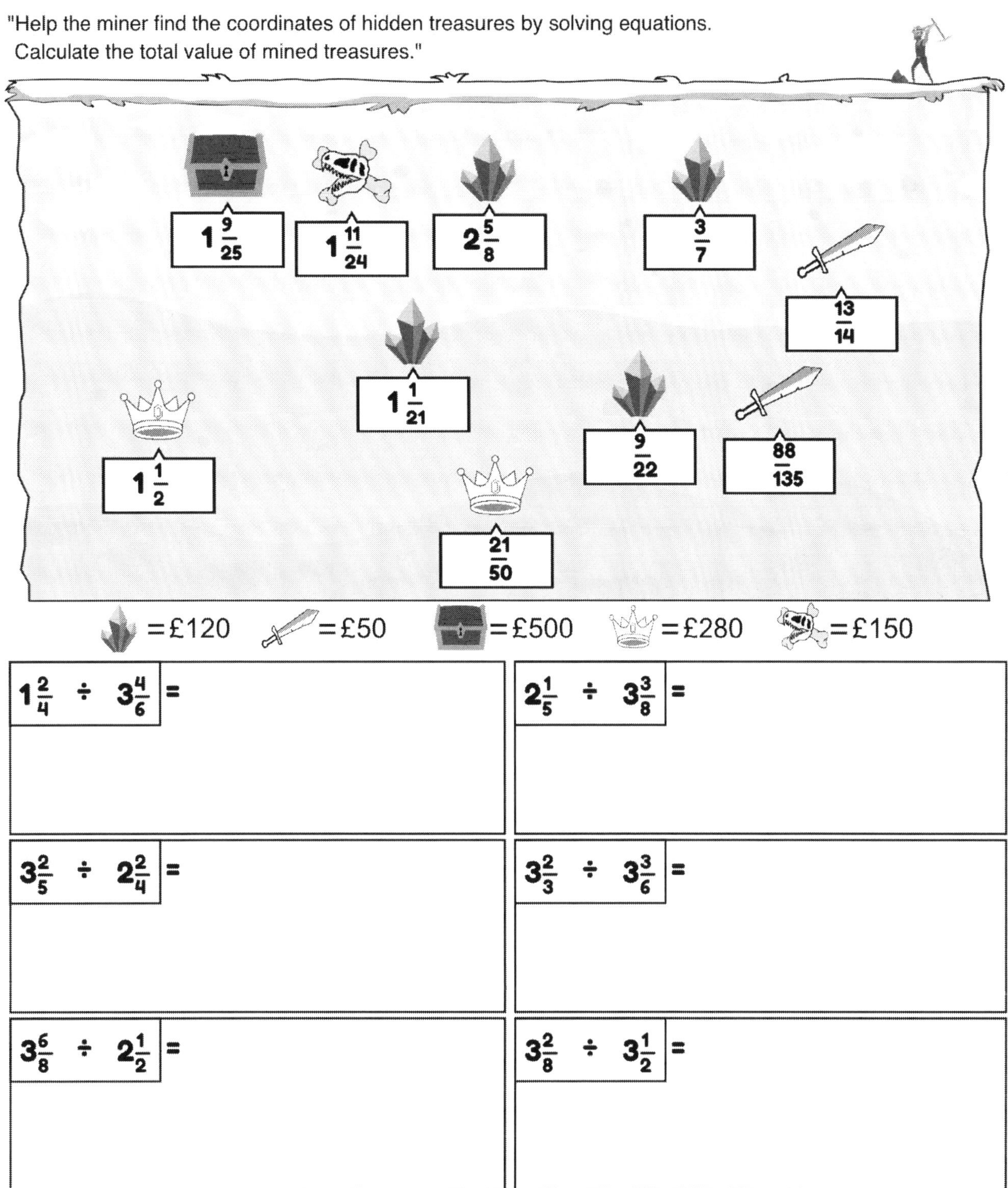

$1\frac{2}{4} \div 3\frac{4}{6} =$	$2\frac{1}{5} \div 3\frac{3}{8} =$
$3\frac{2}{5} \div 2\frac{2}{4} =$	$3\frac{2}{3} \div 3\frac{3}{6} =$
$3\frac{6}{8} \div 2\frac{1}{2} =$	$3\frac{2}{8} \div 3\frac{1}{2} =$

The total value of mined treasures = £

FRACTIONS PUZZLE 34

DIVIDING MIXED FRACTIONS

"Help the miner find the coordinates of hidden treasures by solving equations.
Calculate the total value of mined treasures."

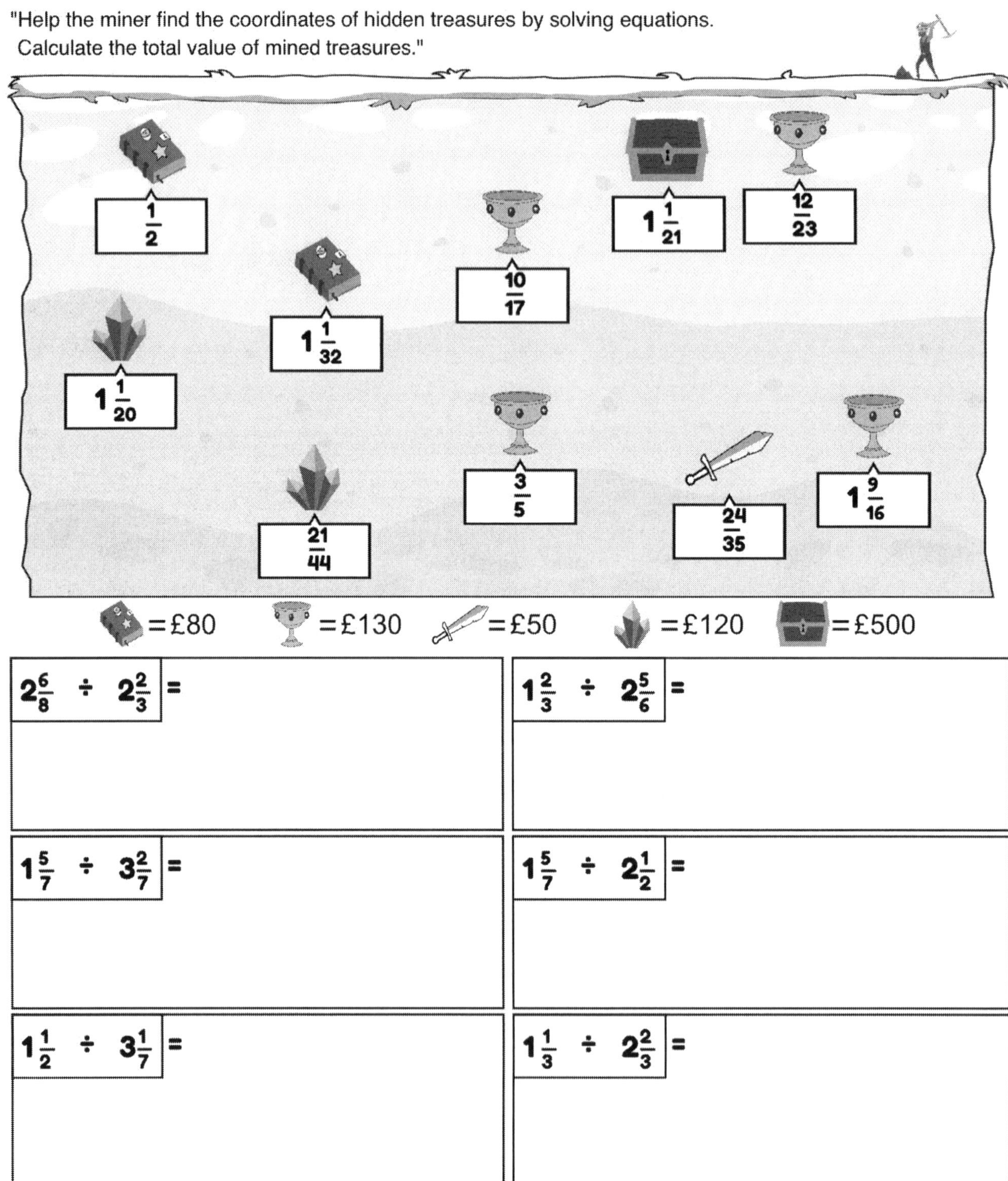

$2\frac{6}{8} \div 2\frac{2}{3} =$

$1\frac{2}{3} \div 2\frac{5}{6} =$

$1\frac{5}{7} \div 3\frac{2}{7} =$

$1\frac{5}{7} \div 2\frac{1}{2} =$

$1\frac{1}{2} \div 3\frac{1}{7} =$

$1\frac{1}{3} \div 2\frac{2}{3} =$

The total value of mined treasures = £

FRACTIONS PUZZLE 35

DIVIDING MIXED FRACTIONS

Fix the leaking pipes by solving equations.
Find which pipes still have leakages after all possible leaks are fixed

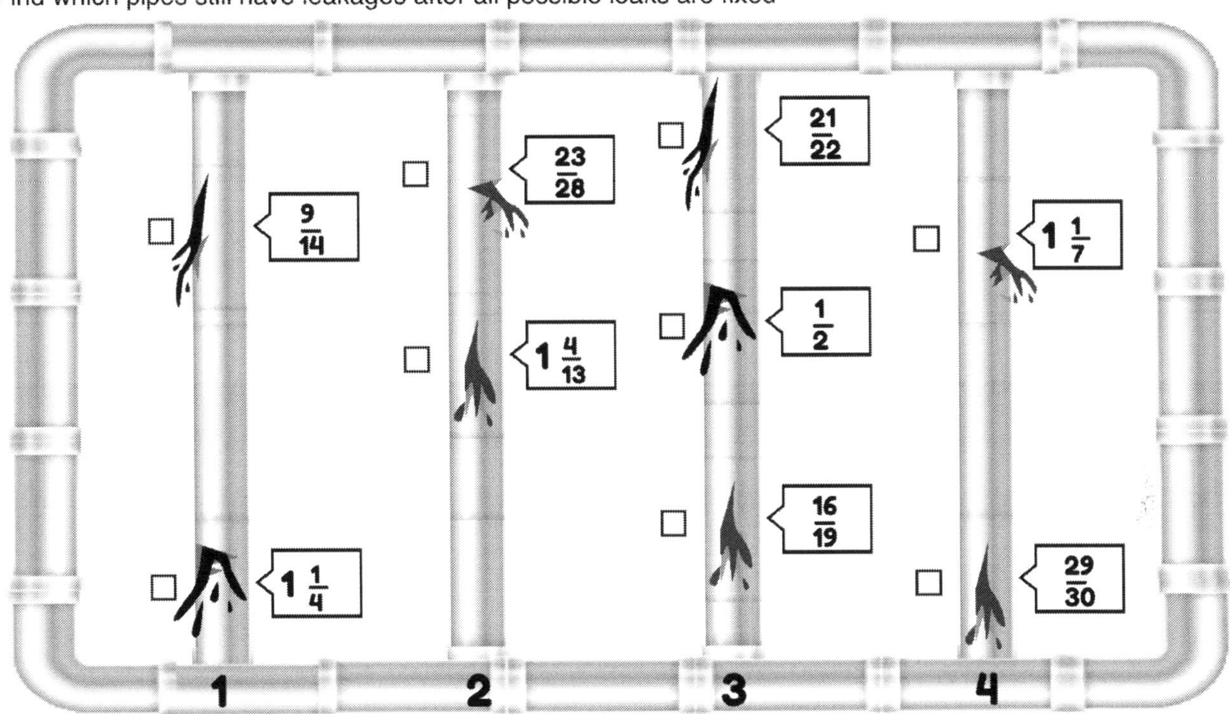

$1\frac{6}{8} \div 3\frac{1}{2} =$	$3\frac{5}{8} \div 3\frac{6}{8} =$
$3\frac{2}{5} \div 2\frac{3}{5} =$	$1\frac{5}{7} \div 1\frac{2}{4} =$
$2\frac{2}{3} \div 3\frac{1}{6} =$	$1\frac{3}{6} \div 2\frac{1}{3} =$

The numbers of the pipes which still have leaks are:

FRACTIONS PUZZLE 36

DIVIDING MIXED FRACTIONS

Fix the leaking pipes by solving equations.

Find which pipes still have leakages after all possible leaks are fixed

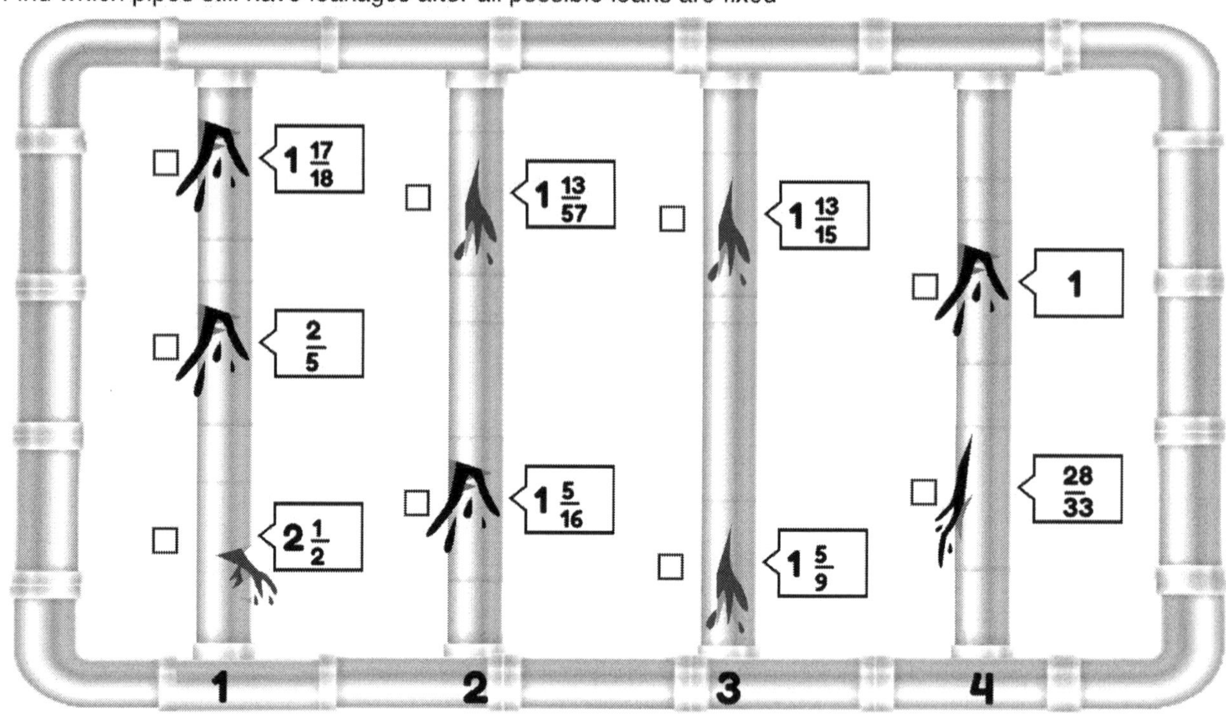

$2\frac{2}{6} \div 2\frac{6}{8} =$	$3\frac{2}{4} \div 2\frac{1}{4} =$
$2\frac{4}{5} \div 1\frac{2}{4} =$	$1\frac{2}{3} \div 1\frac{4}{6} =$
$3\frac{1}{2} \div 2\frac{2}{3} =$	$1\frac{1}{2} \div 3\frac{6}{8} =$

The numbers of the pipes which still have leaks are:

FRACTIONS PUZZLE 37

MULTIPLYING PROPER FRACTIONS

"Help the miner find the coordinates of hidden treasures by solving equations.
Calculate the total value of mined treasures."

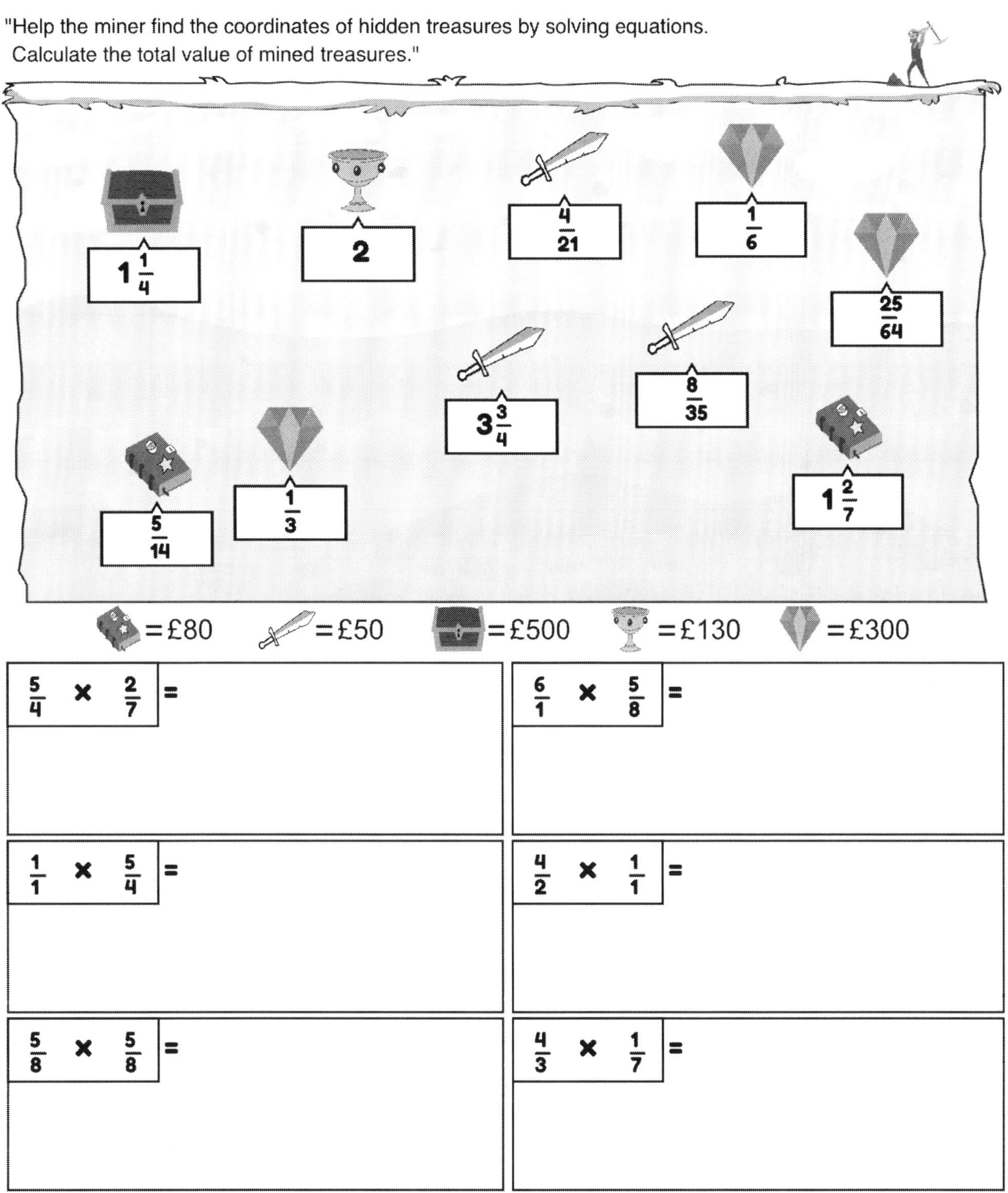

$\frac{5}{4} \times \frac{2}{7} =$	$\frac{6}{1} \times \frac{5}{8} =$
$\frac{1}{1} \times \frac{5}{4} =$	$\frac{4}{2} \times \frac{1}{1} =$
$\frac{5}{8} \times \frac{5}{8} =$	$\frac{4}{3} \times \frac{1}{7} =$

The total value of mined treasures = £

FRACTIONS PUZZLE 38

MULTIPLYING PROPER FRACTIONS

"Help the miner find the coordinates of hidden treasures by solving equations.
Calculate the total value of mined treasures."

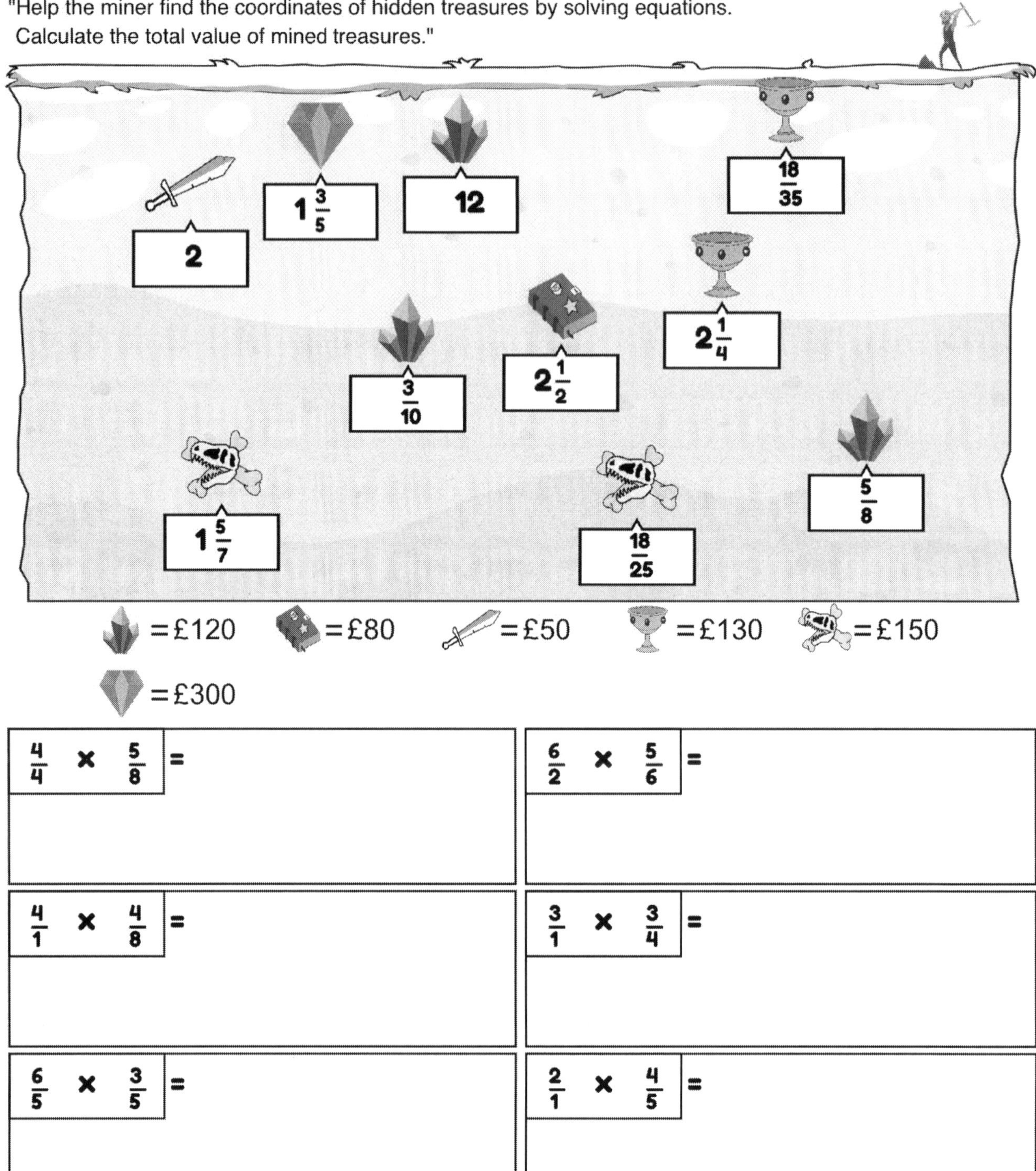

$\frac{4}{4} \times \frac{5}{8} =$	$\frac{6}{2} \times \frac{5}{6} =$
$\frac{4}{1} \times \frac{4}{8} =$	$\frac{3}{1} \times \frac{3}{4} =$
$\frac{6}{5} \times \frac{3}{5} =$	$\frac{2}{1} \times \frac{4}{5} =$

The total value of mined treasures = £

FRACTIONS PUZZLE 39

MULTIPLYING PROPER FRACTIONS

Fix the leaking pipes by solving equations.

Find which pipes still have leakages after all possible leaks are fixed

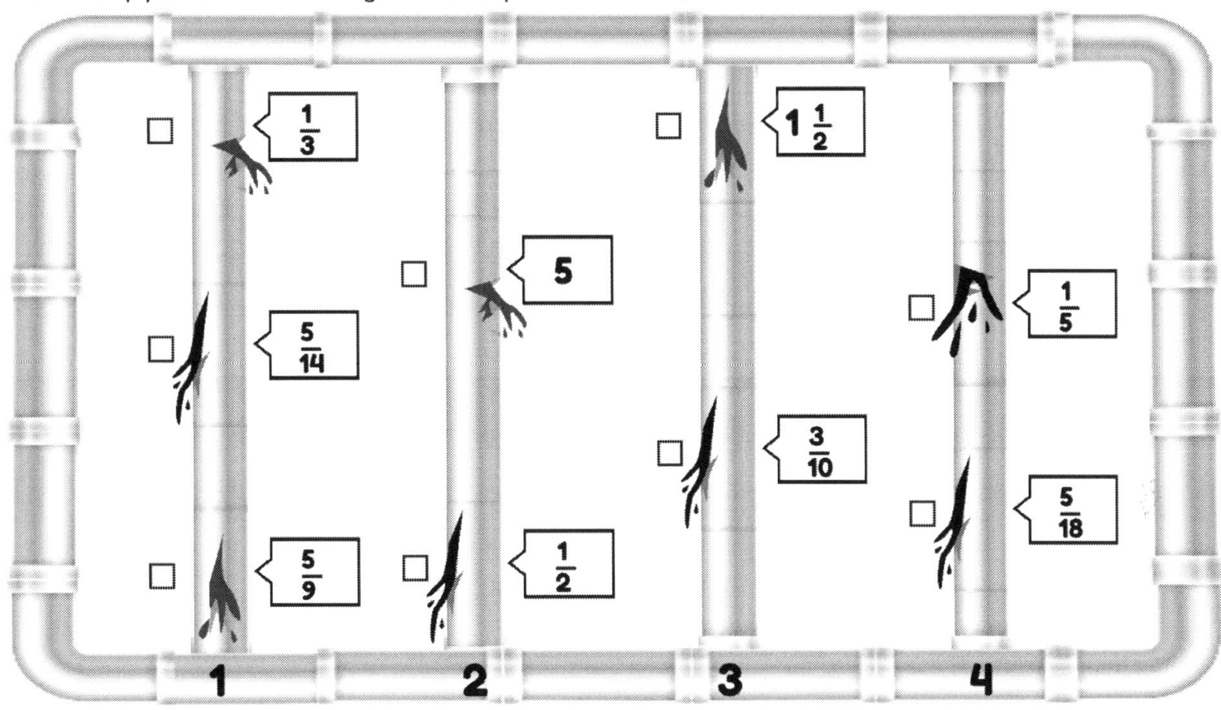

$\frac{1}{5} \times \frac{5}{5} =$

$\frac{5}{3} \times \frac{1}{5} =$

$\frac{5}{2} \times \frac{1}{7} =$

$\frac{3}{5} \times \frac{3}{6} =$

$\frac{5}{3} \times \frac{1}{6} =$

$\frac{3}{1} \times \frac{4}{8} =$

The numbers of the pipes which still have leaks are:

FRACTIONS PUZZLE 40

MULTIPLYING PROPER FRACTIONS

Fix the leaking pipes by solving equations.
Find which pipes still have leakages after all possible leaks are fixed

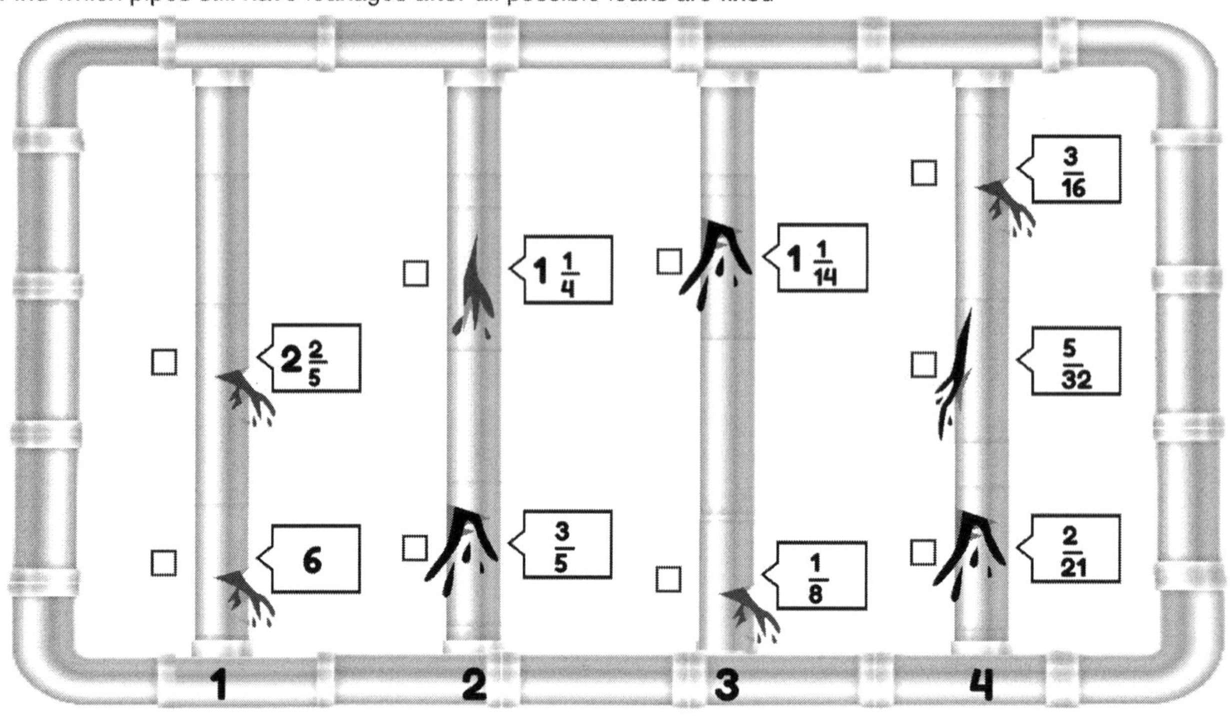

$\frac{2}{5} \times \frac{6}{1} =$	$\frac{3}{4} \times \frac{4}{5} =$
$\frac{6}{3} \times \frac{5}{8} =$	$\frac{2}{7} \times \frac{2}{6} =$
$\frac{2}{8} \times \frac{3}{4} =$	$\frac{1}{8} \times \frac{3}{3} =$

The numbers of the pipes which still have leaks are:

FRACTIONS PUZZLE 41

MULTIPLYING IMPROPER FRACTIONS

"Help the miner find the coordinates of hidden treasures by solving equations.
Calculate the total value of mined treasures."

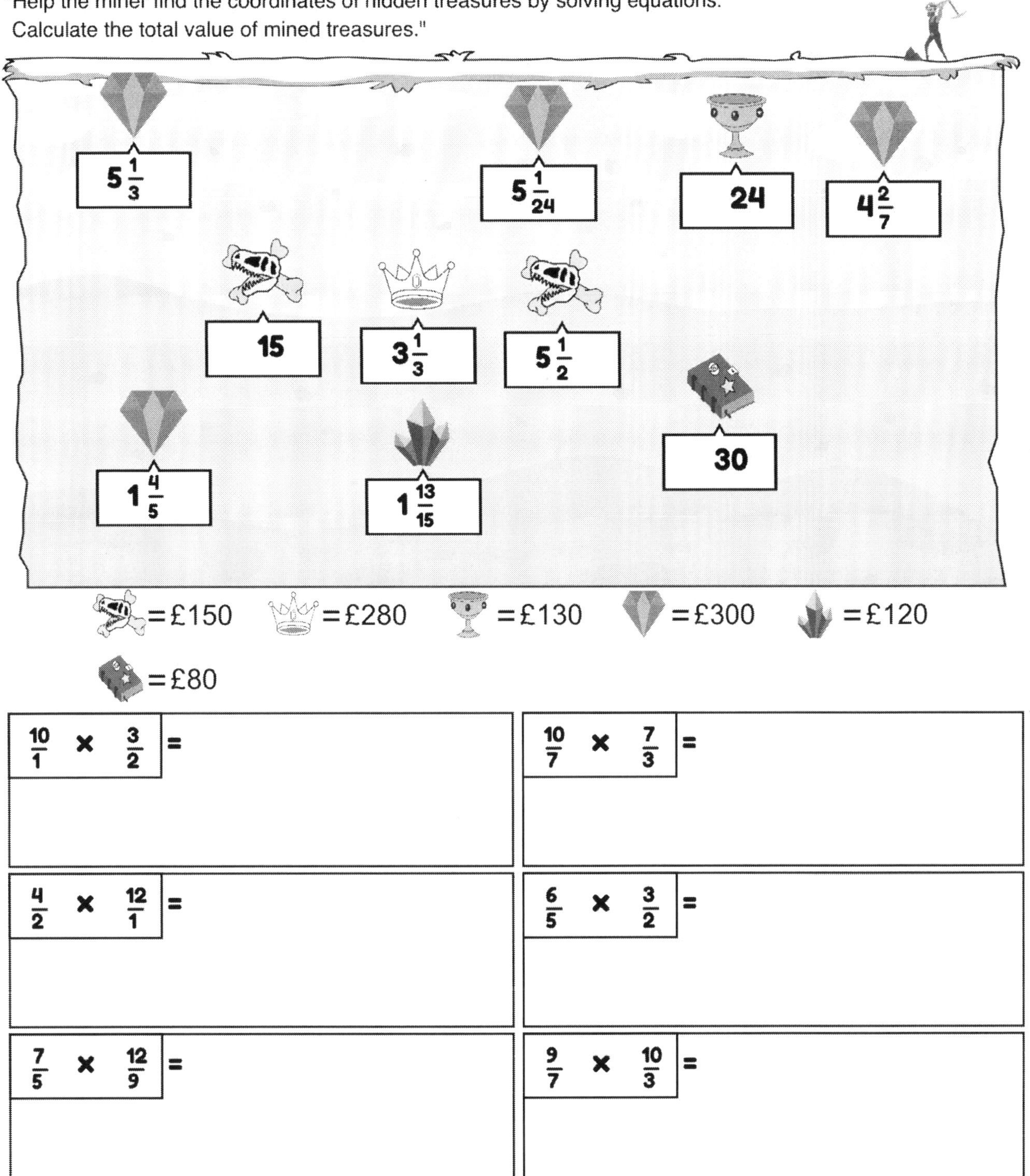

$\frac{10}{1} \times \frac{3}{2} =$	$\frac{10}{7} \times \frac{7}{3} =$
$\frac{4}{2} \times \frac{12}{1} =$	$\frac{6}{5} \times \frac{3}{2} =$
$\frac{7}{5} \times \frac{12}{9} =$	$\frac{9}{7} \times \frac{10}{3} =$

The total value of mined treasures = £

FRACTIONS PUZZLE 42

MULTIPLYING IMPROPER FRACTIONS

"Help the miner find the coordinates of hidden treasures by solving equations.
Calculate the total value of mined treasures."

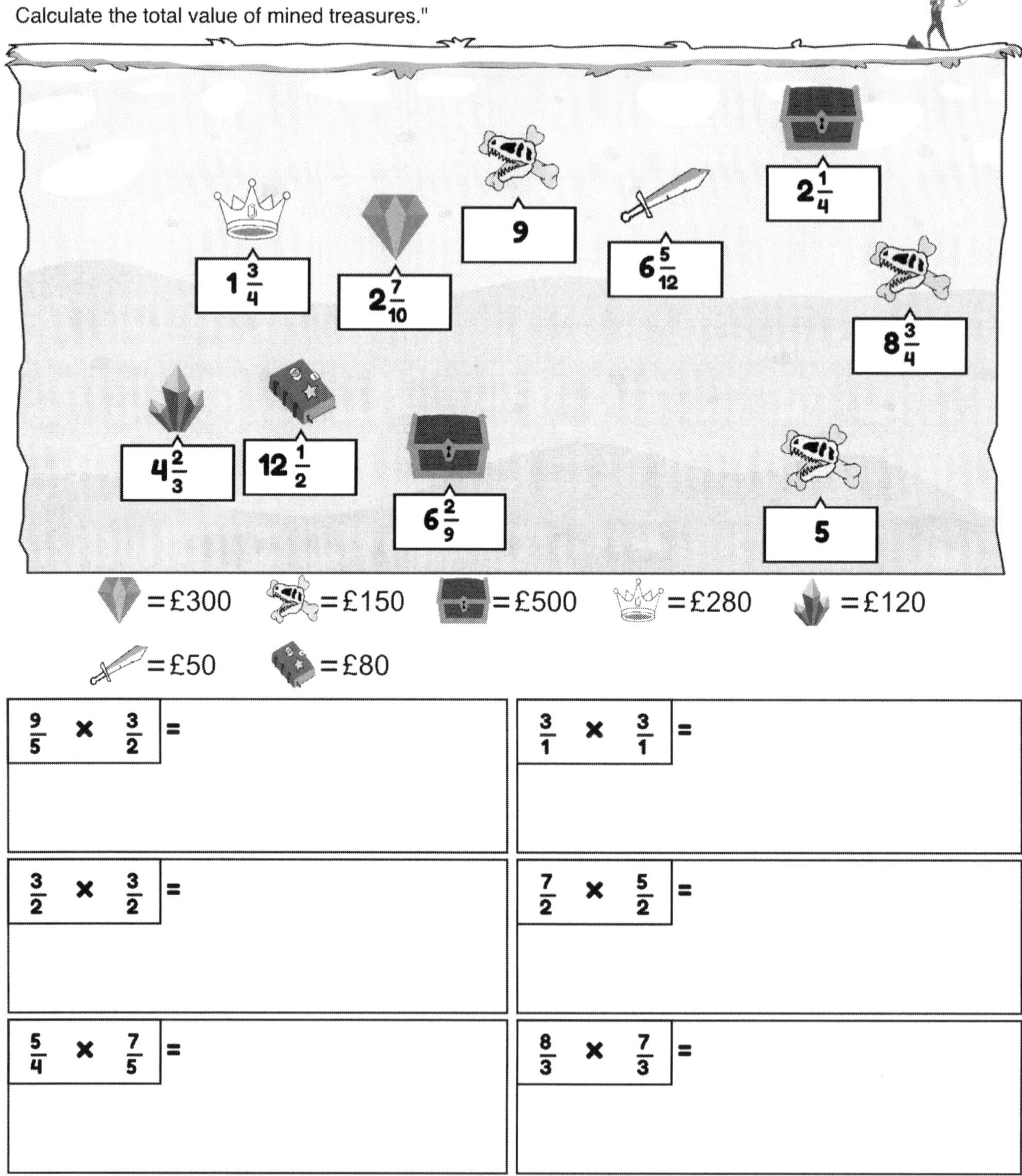

$\frac{9}{5} \times \frac{3}{2} =$	$\frac{3}{1} \times \frac{3}{1} =$
$\frac{3}{2} \times \frac{3}{2} =$	$\frac{7}{2} \times \frac{5}{2} =$
$\frac{5}{4} \times \frac{7}{5} =$	$\frac{8}{3} \times \frac{7}{3} =$

The total value of mined treasures = £

FRACTIONS PUZZLE 43

MULTIPLYING IMPROPER FRACTIONS

Fix the leaking pipes by solving equations.
Find which pipes still have leakages after all possible leaks are fixed

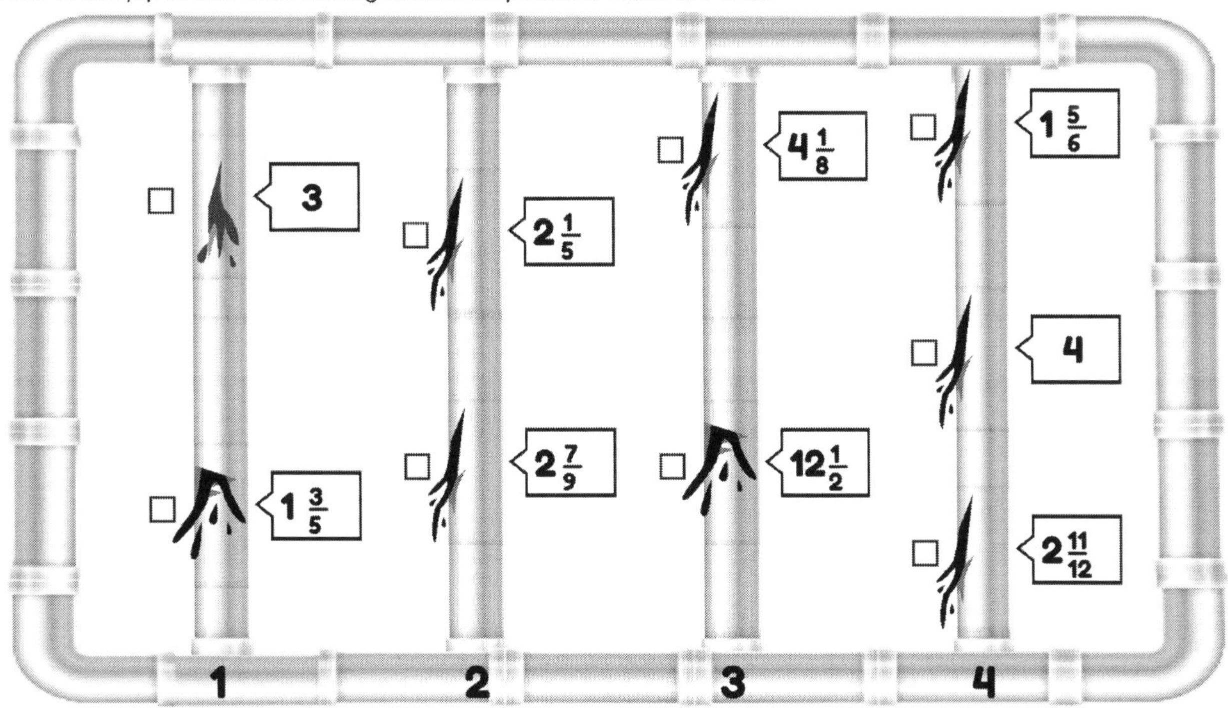

$\frac{5}{2} \times \frac{5}{1} =$	$\frac{11}{7} \times \frac{7}{5} =$
$\frac{3}{2} \times \frac{11}{4} =$	$\frac{4}{3} \times \frac{3}{1} =$
$\frac{4}{2} \times \frac{9}{6} =$	$\frac{5}{3} \times \frac{10}{6} =$

The numbers of the pipes which still have leaks are:

FRACTIONS PUZZLE 44

MULTIPLYING IMPROPER FRACTIONS

Fix the leaking pipes by solving equations.
Find which pipes still have leakages after all possible leaks are fixed

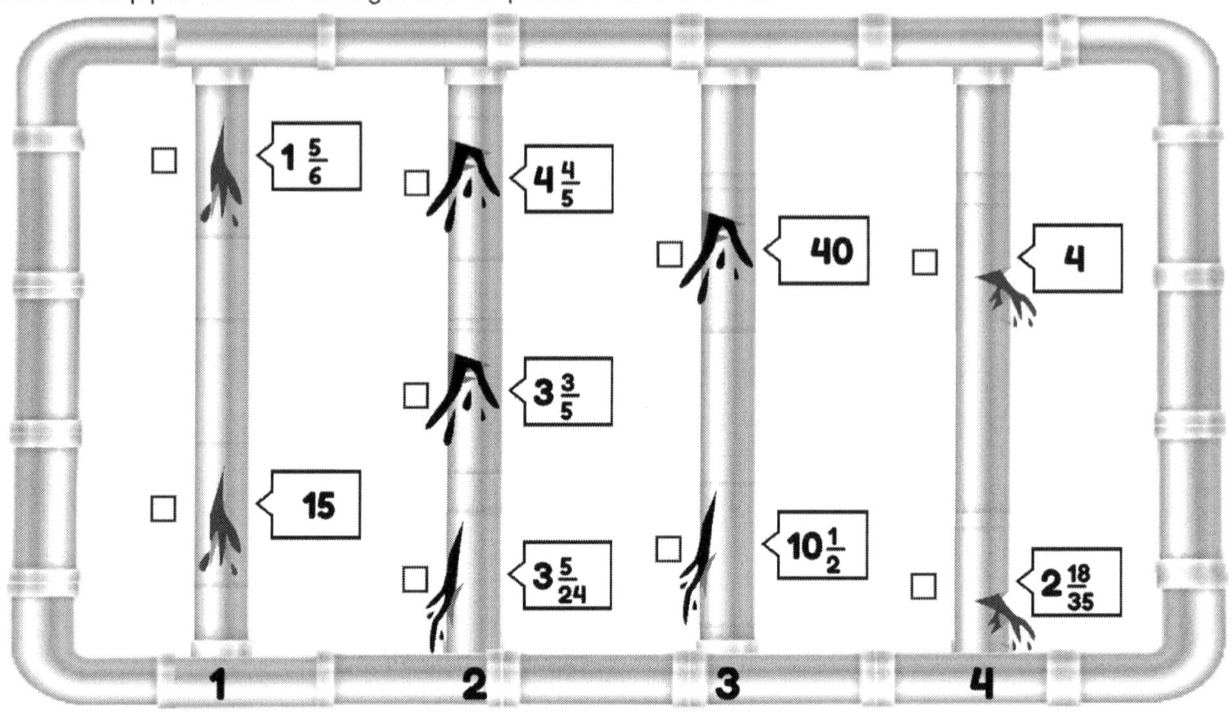

$\frac{8}{5} \times \frac{6}{2} =$	$\frac{9}{5} \times \frac{8}{4} =$
$\frac{10}{4} \times \frac{6}{1} =$	$\frac{11}{7} \times \frac{8}{5} =$
$\frac{10}{1} \times \frac{12}{3} =$	$\frac{4}{2} \times \frac{4}{2} =$

The numbers of the pipes which still have leaks are:

FRACTIONS PUZZLE 45

MULTIPLYING MIXED FRACTIONS

"Help the miner find the coordinates of hidden treasures by solving equations.
Calculate the total value of mined treasures."

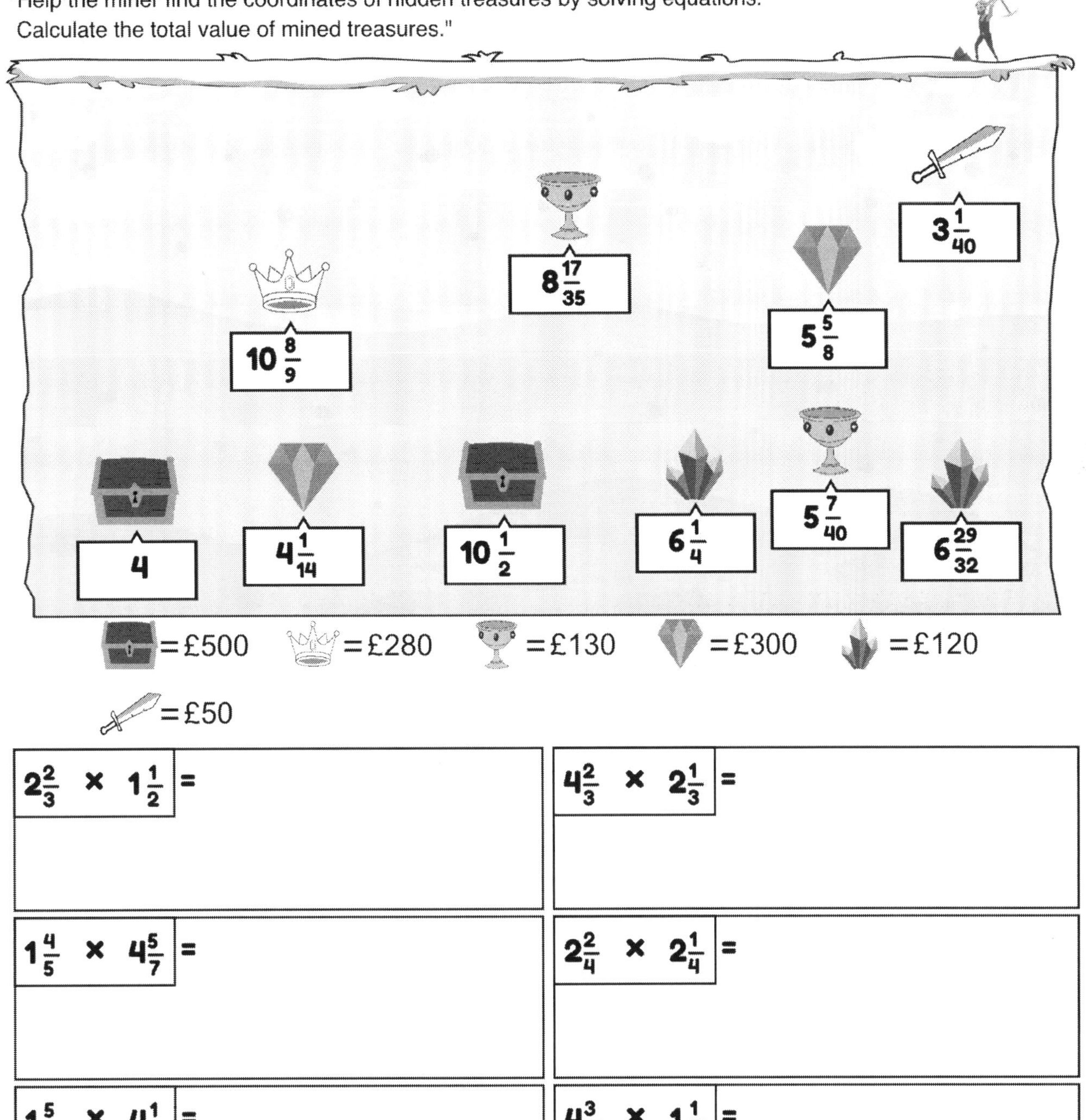

$2\frac{2}{3} \times 1\frac{1}{2} =$	$4\frac{2}{3} \times 2\frac{1}{3} =$
$1\frac{4}{5} \times 4\frac{5}{7} =$	$2\frac{2}{4} \times 2\frac{1}{4} =$
$1\frac{5}{8} \times 4\frac{1}{4} =$	$4\frac{3}{5} \times 1\frac{1}{8} =$

The total value of mined treasures = £

FRACTIONS PUZZLE 46

MULTIPLYING MIXED FRACTIONS

"Help the miner find the coordinates of hidden treasures by solving equations.
Calculate the total value of mined treasures."

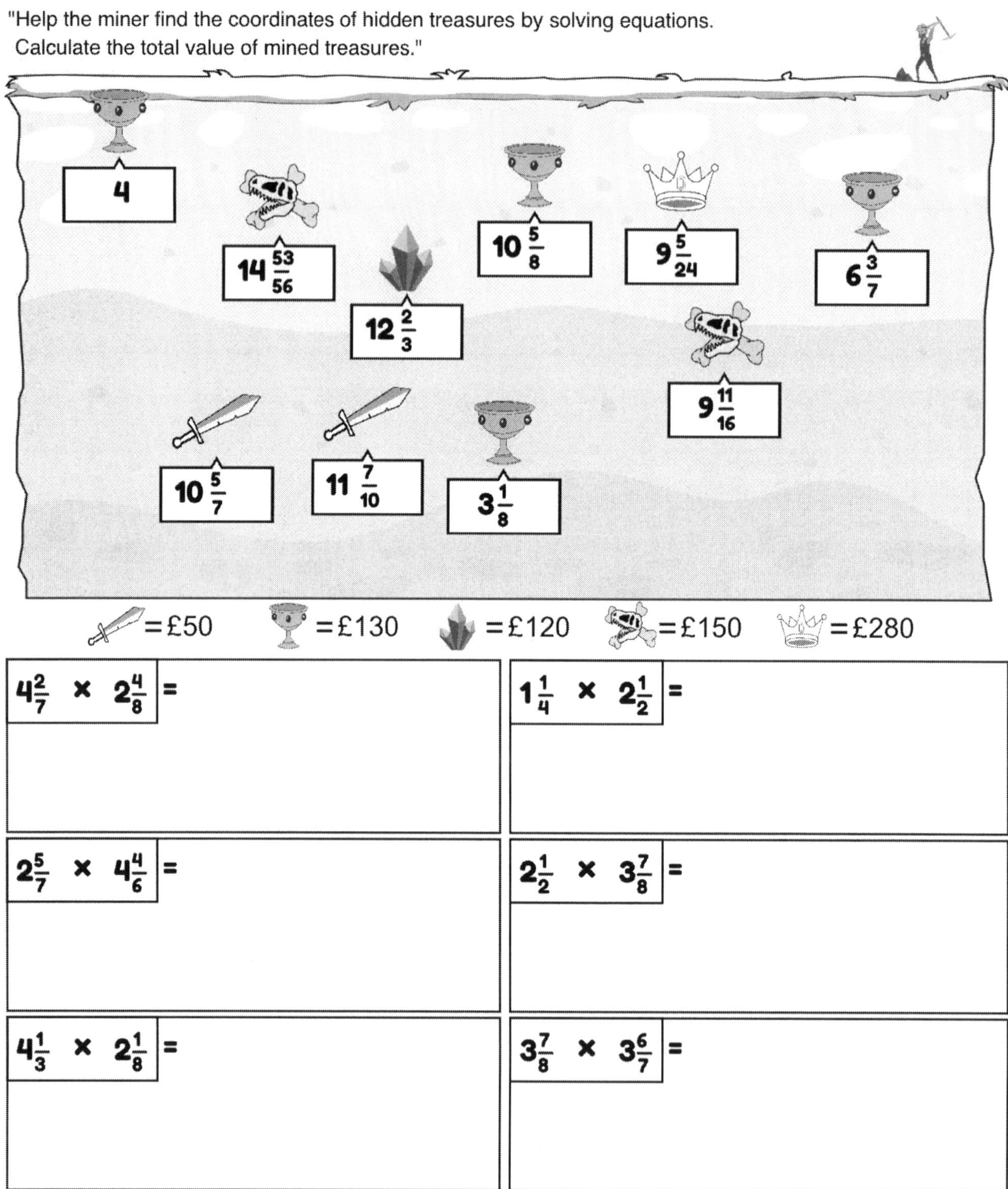

$4\frac{2}{7} \times 2\frac{4}{8} =$

$1\frac{1}{4} \times 2\frac{1}{2} =$

$2\frac{5}{7} \times 4\frac{4}{6} =$

$2\frac{1}{2} \times 3\frac{7}{8} =$

$4\frac{1}{3} \times 2\frac{1}{8} =$

$3\frac{7}{8} \times 3\frac{6}{7} =$

The total value of mined treasures = £

FRACTIONS PUZZLE 47

MULTIPLYING MIXED FRACTIONS

Fix the leaking pipes by solving equations.
Find which pipes still have leakages after all possible leaks are fixed

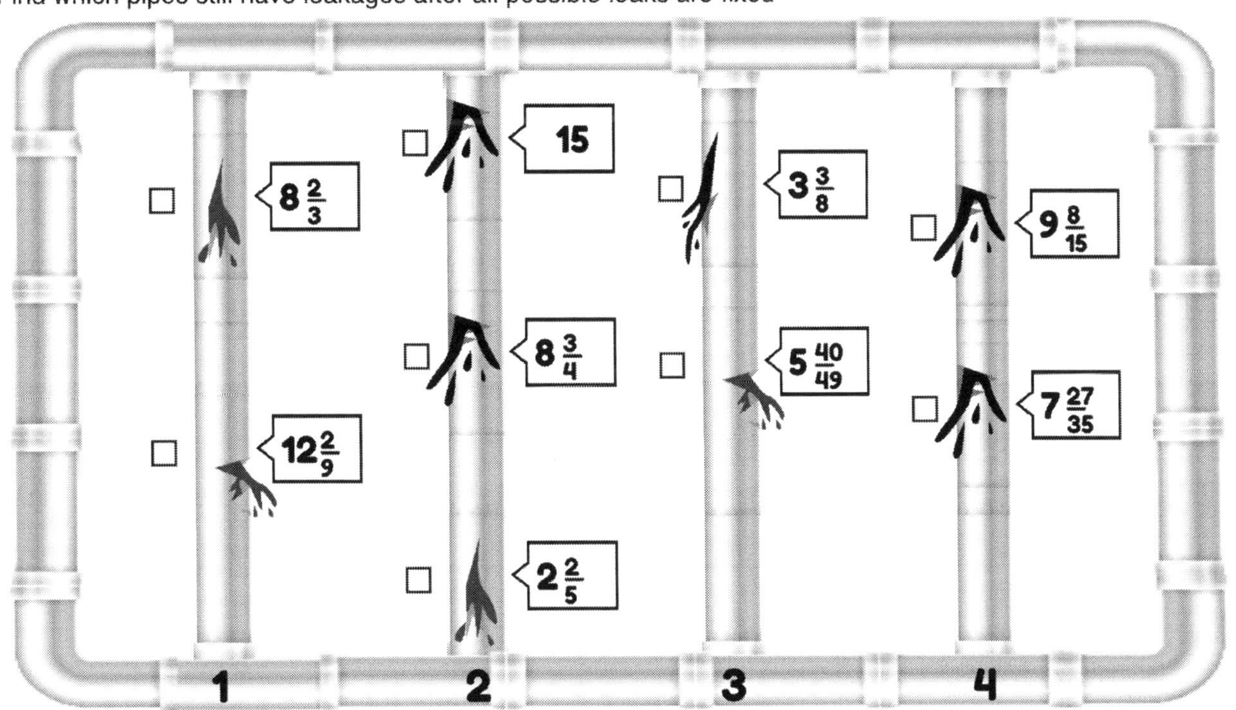

$2\frac{1}{7} \times 2\frac{5}{7} =$	$4\frac{2}{7} \times 3\frac{1}{2} =$
$3\frac{3}{4} \times 2\frac{1}{3} =$	$3\frac{1}{3} \times 2\frac{3}{5} =$
$3\frac{2}{6} \times 3\frac{2}{3} =$	$4\frac{2}{6} \times 2\frac{1}{5} =$

The numbers of the pipes which still have leaks are:

FRACTIONS PUZZLE 48

MULTIPLYING MIXED FRACTIONS

Fix the leaking pipes by solving equations.
Find which pipes still have leakages after all possible leaks are fixed

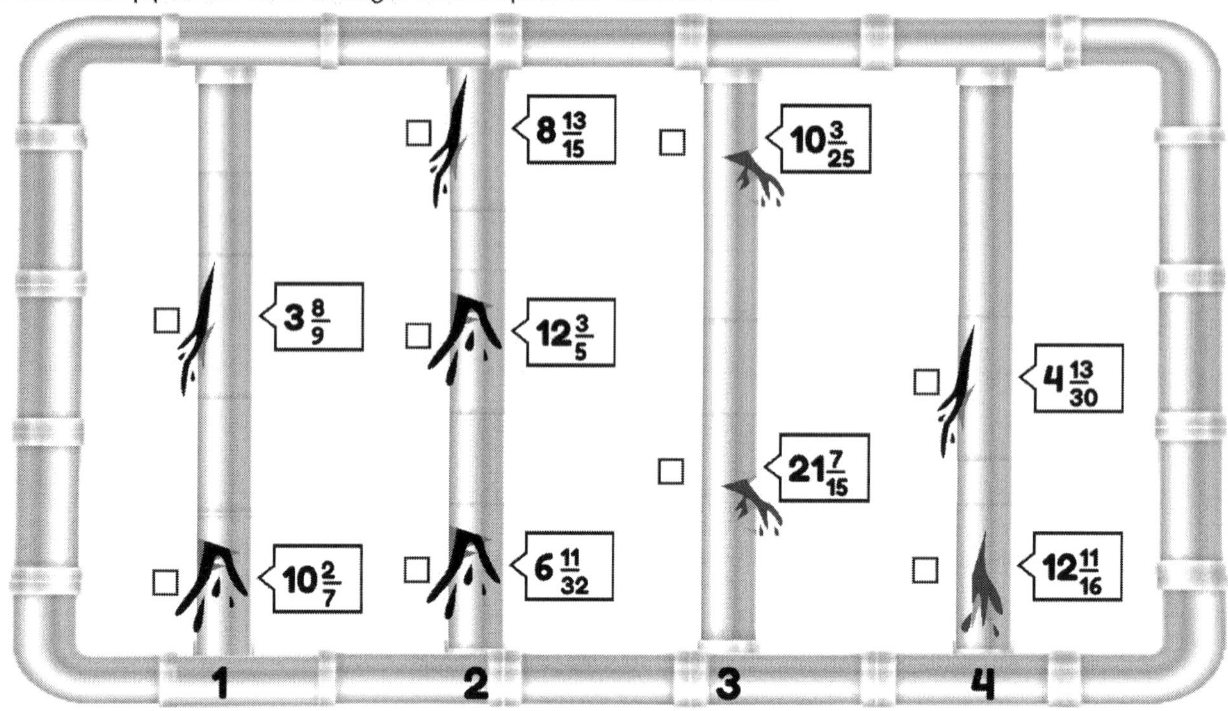

$1\frac{2}{5} \times 3\frac{1}{6} =$	$3\frac{5}{8} \times 1\frac{3}{4} =$
$4\frac{4}{6} \times 4\frac{3}{5} =$	$2\frac{1}{5} \times 4\frac{3}{5} =$
$2\frac{1}{7} \times 4\frac{4}{5} =$	$1\frac{2}{3} \times 2\frac{1}{3} =$

The numbers of the pipes which still have leaks are:

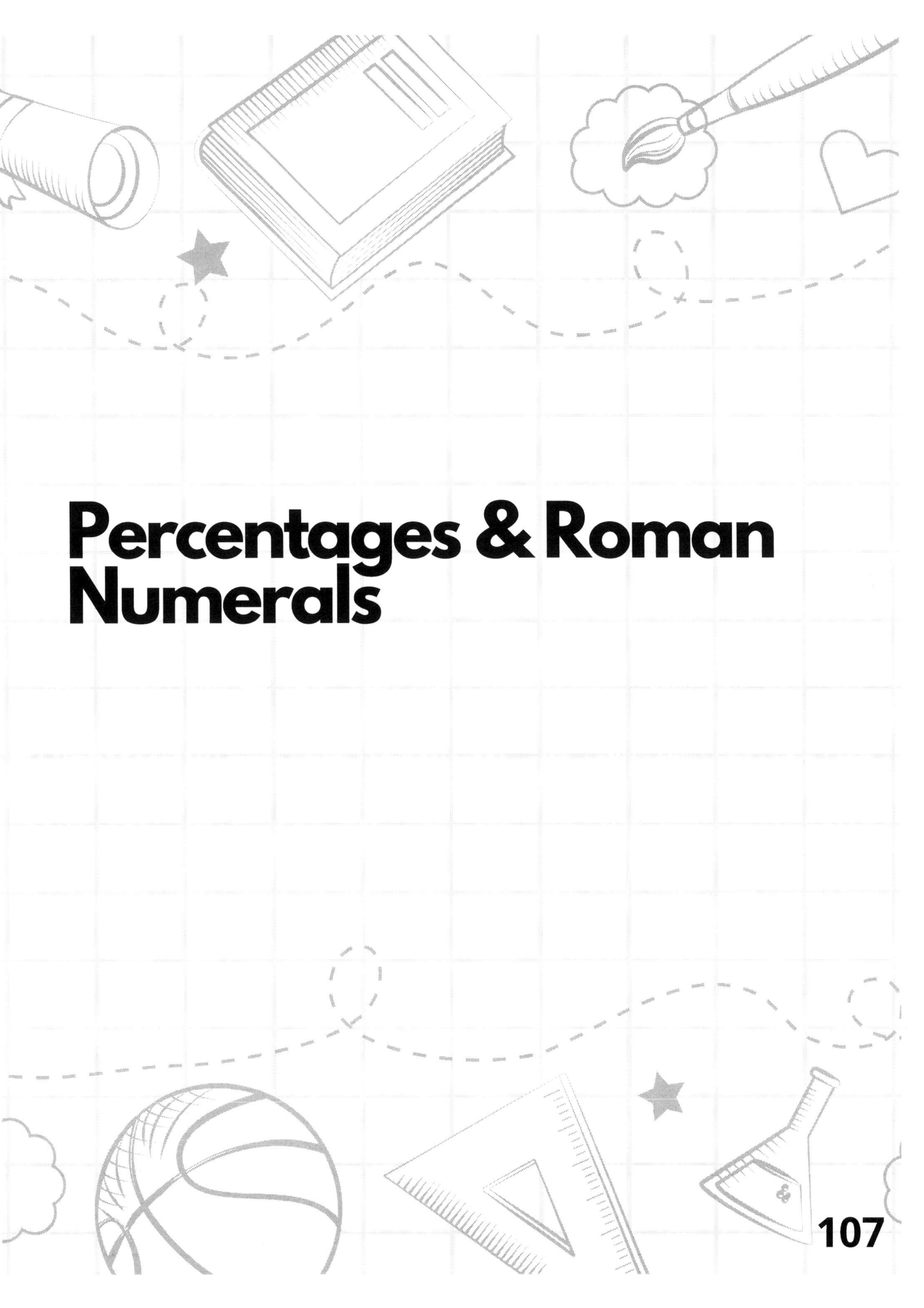

Percentages & Roman Numerals

FINDING PERCENTAGES CHEAT SHEET

Thousands , Hundreds Tens Ones ● DECIMAL POINT Tenths Hundredths Thousandths

Divide By 10 = Move Decimal point to the left

Example: 325 ÷ 10 = 3 2 5 . 0 = 3 2 . 5 0 = 32.5

Divide By 100 = Move Decimal point to the left twice

Example: 85 ÷ 100 = 8 5 . 0 = 0 . 8 5 = 0.85

TIP: BREAK THE QUESTION INTO PARTS

50% of a number = 1/2 the number

25% of a number = 1/2 of 50%

10% of a number = divide by 10

5% of a number = 1/2 of 10%

1% of a number = divide by 100

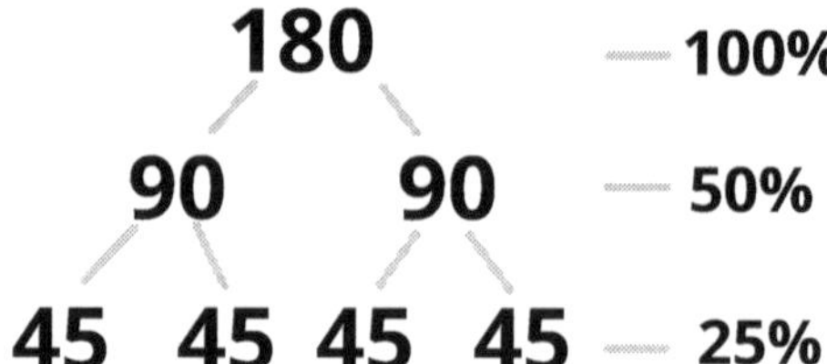

EXAMPLES

15% of 160 = 15% = 10% + 5%
10% = 16 (160 divided by 10)
5% = 8 (half of 10%)

Therefore 16 + 8 = 24

62% of 840 = 62% = 50% + 10% + 1% + 1%
50% = 420
10% = 84
1% = 8.4
2% = 16.8

Therefore 420 + 84 + 8.4 + 16.8 = 529.2

18% of 300 = 10% + 5% + 1% + 1% + 1%
10% = 30
5% = 15
1% = 3
3% = 9 (3 x 1%)

Therefore 18% = 9 + 15 + 30 = 54

SOMETIMES IT'S BETTER TO SUBTRACT PARTS TO FIND AN ANSWER

VIA ADDITION

89% of 95 = 50% + 25% + 10% + 1% +1% + 1% + 1%
50% = 47.5 25% = 23.75
10% = 9.5. 1% = 0.95
4% = 3.8

Therefore 47.5 + 23.75 + 9.5 + 3.8 = 84.55

VIA SUBTRACTION

89% of 95 = 100% - 10% - 1%
10% = 9.5
1% = 0.95

Therefore 95 - 9.5 - 0.95 = 84.55

It is up to you how to break the percentages into parts!

Gumball Puzzle 1

Finding Percentages

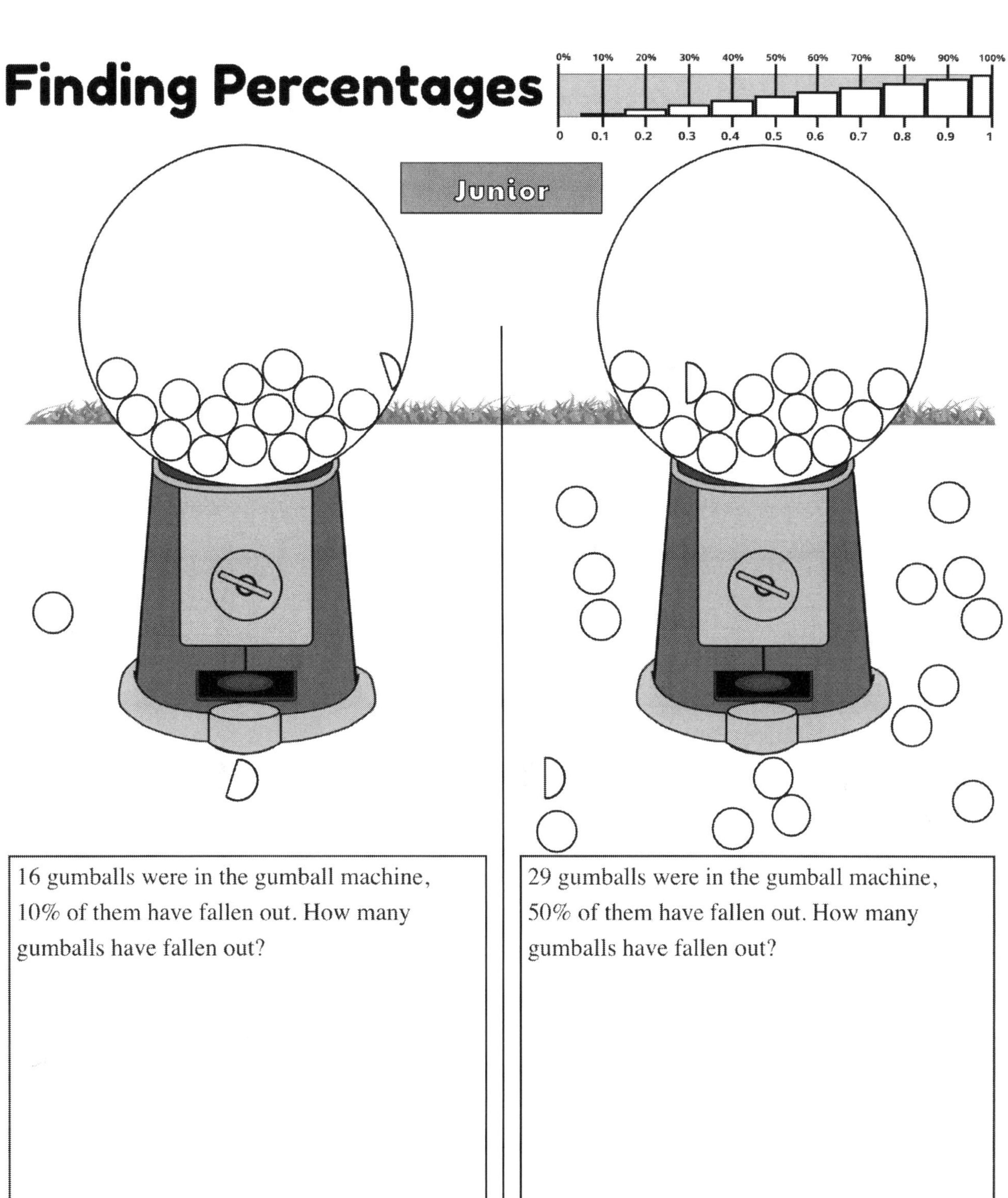

16 gumballs were in the gumball machine, 10% of them have fallen out. How many gumballs have fallen out?

29 gumballs were in the gumball machine, 50% of them have fallen out. How many gumballs have fallen out?

Gumball Puzzle 2

Finding Percentages

Junior

10 gumballs were in the gumball machine, 25% of them have fallen out. How many gumballs have fallen out?	20 gumballs were in the gumball machine, 50% of them have fallen out. How many gumballs have fallen out?

Gumball Puzzle 3

Finding Percentages

Junior

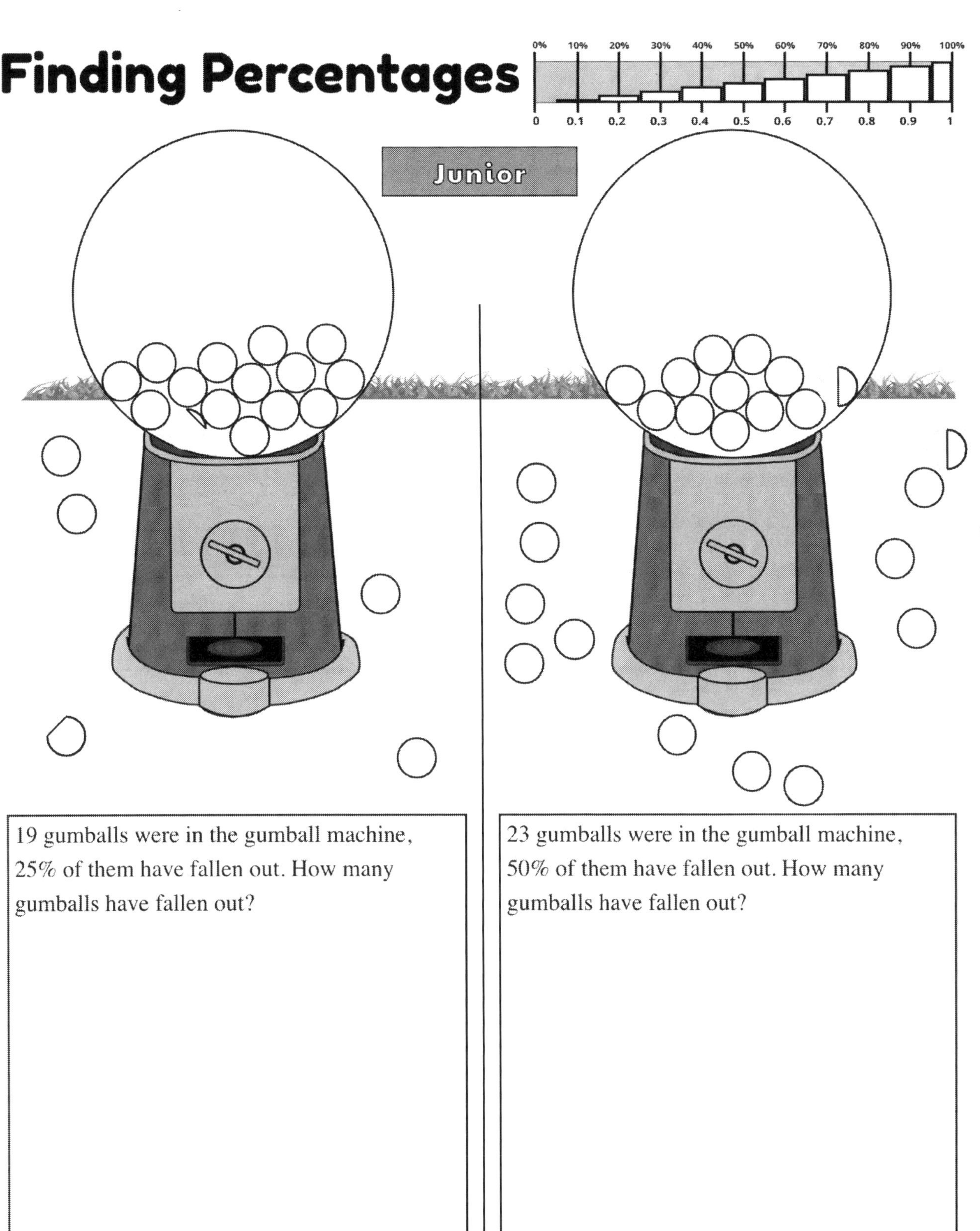

19 gumballs were in the gumball machine, 25% of them have fallen out. How many gumballs have fallen out?

23 gumballs were in the gumball machine, 50% of them have fallen out. How many gumballs have fallen out?

Gumball Puzzle 4

Finding Percentages

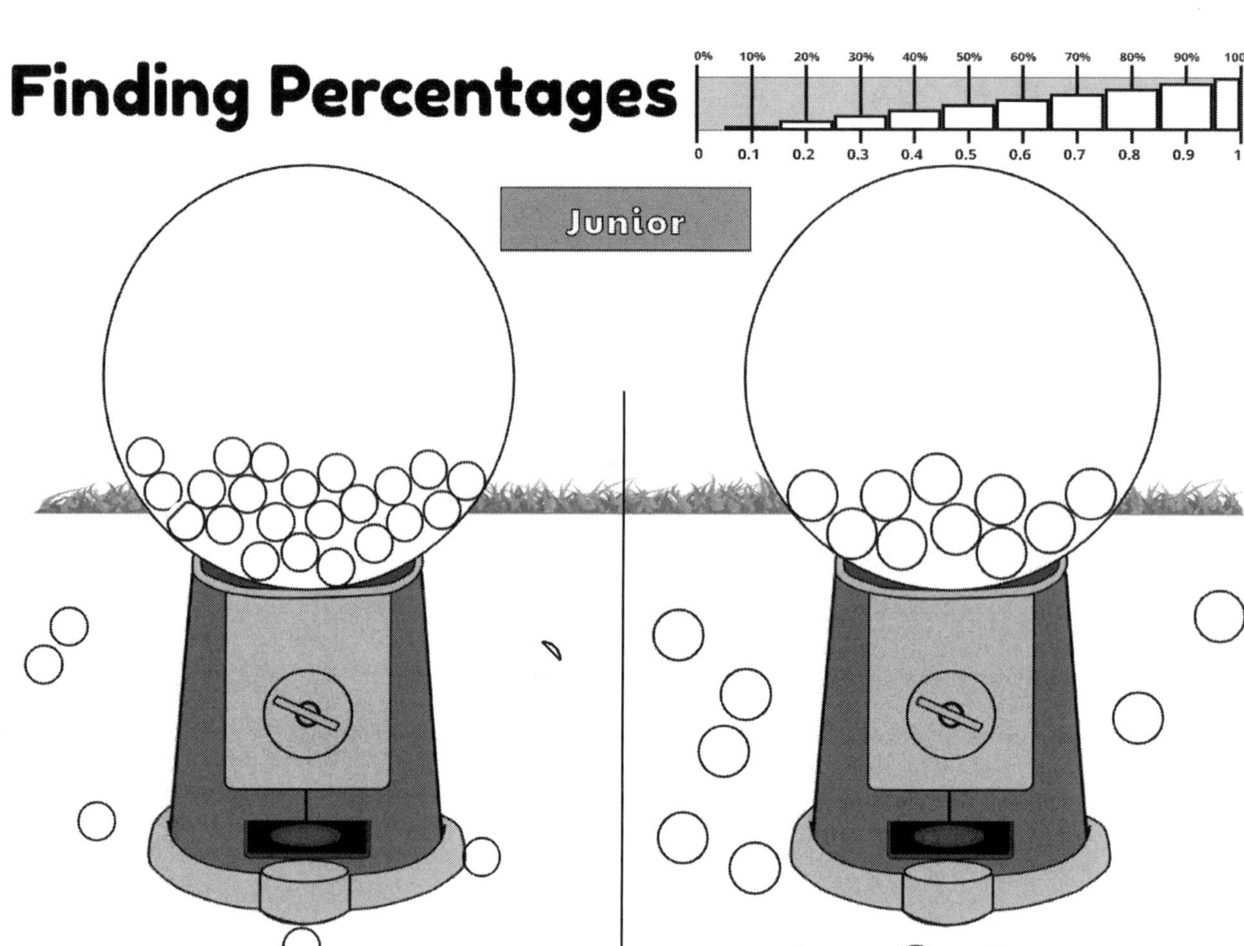

29 gumballs were in the gumball machine, 25% of them have fallen out. How many gumballs have fallen out?

20 gumballs were in the gumball machine, 50% of them have fallen out. How many gumballs have fallen out?

Gumball Puzzle 5

Finding Percentages

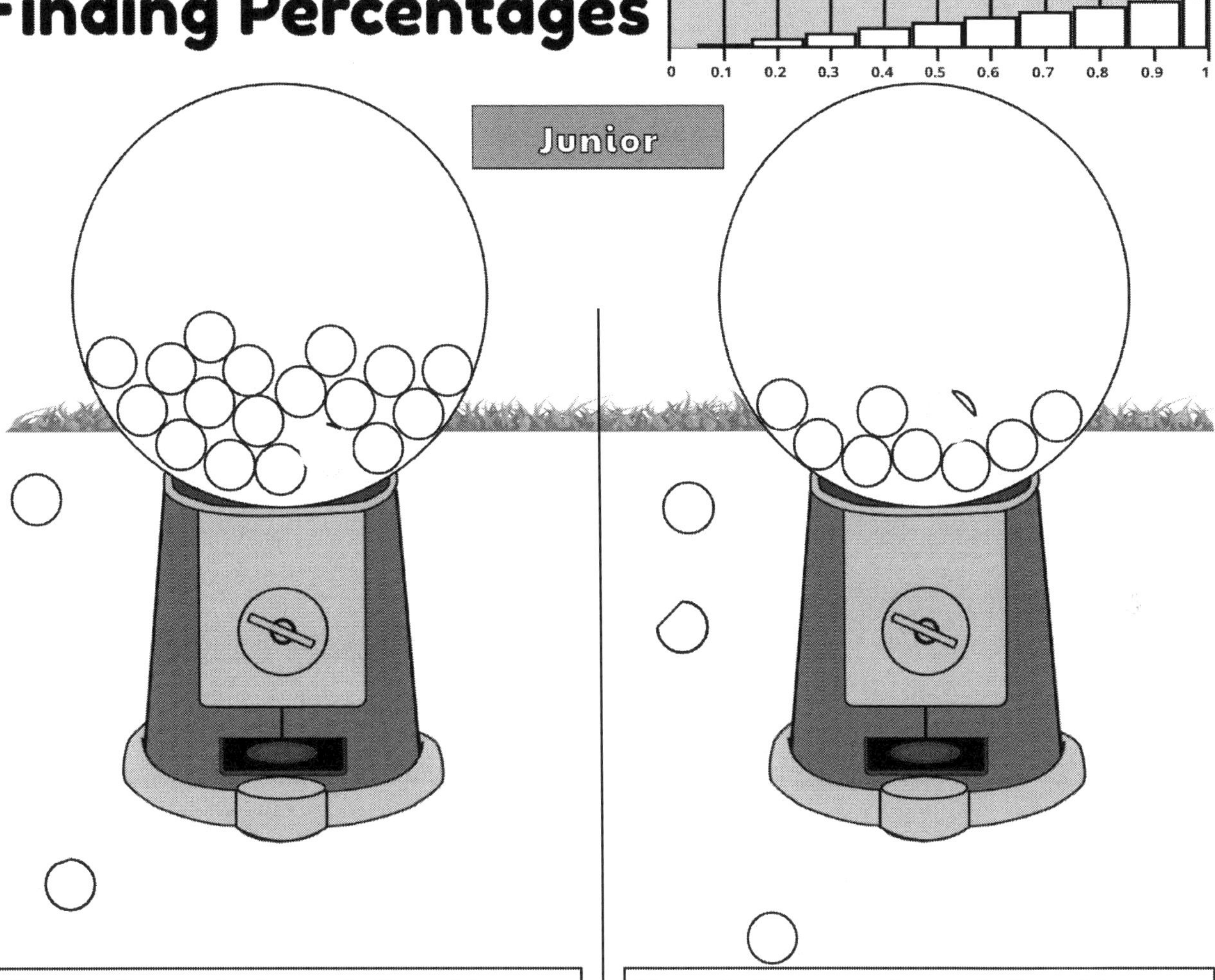

19 gumballs were in the gumball machine, 10% of them have fallen out. How many gumballs have fallen out?

11 gumballs were in the gumball machine, 25% of them have fallen out. How many gumballs have fallen out?

Gumball Puzzle 6

Finding Percentages

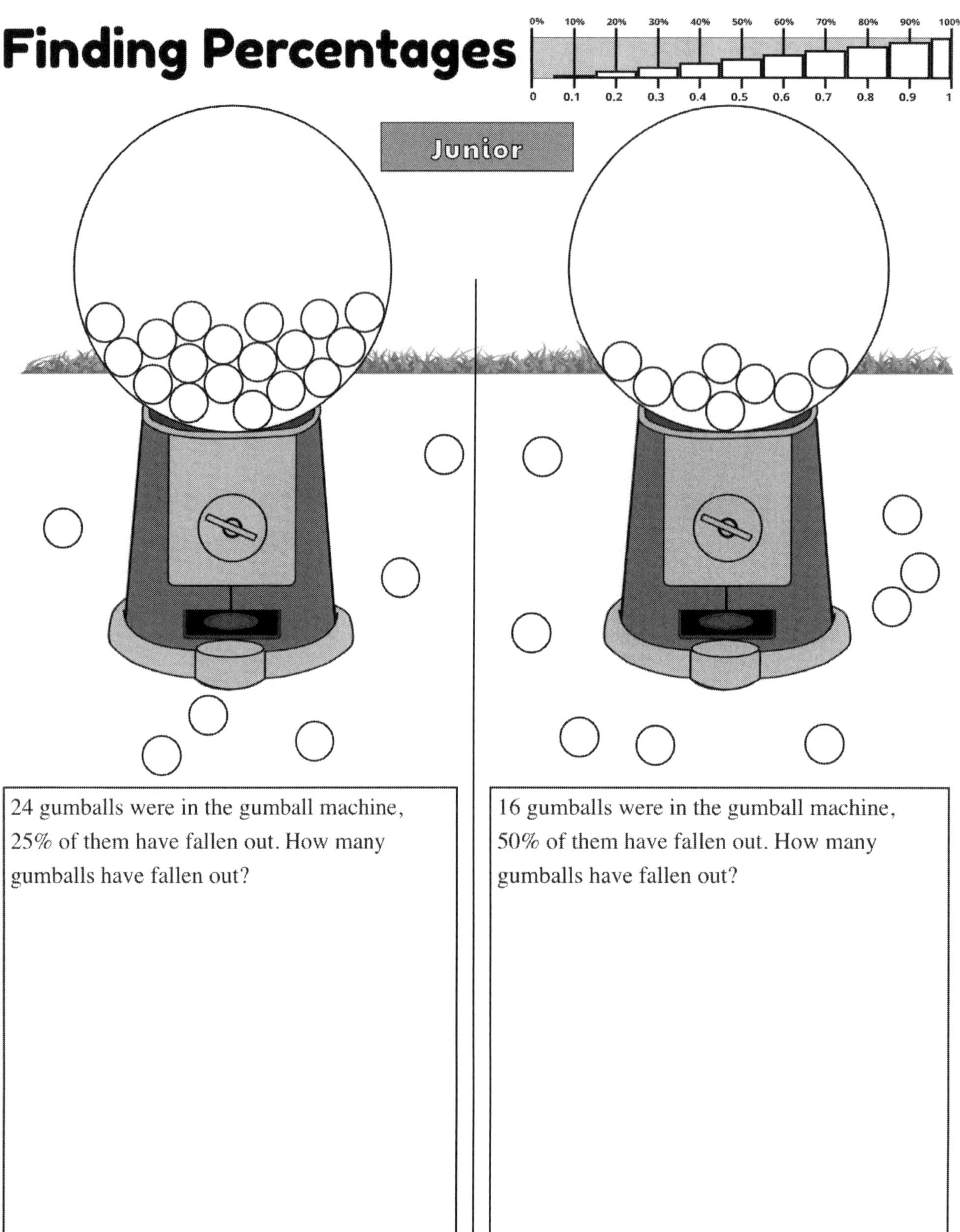

24 gumballs were in the gumball machine, 25% of them have fallen out. How many gumballs have fallen out?

16 gumballs were in the gumball machine, 50% of them have fallen out. How many gumballs have fallen out?

Gumball Puzzle 7

Finding Percentages

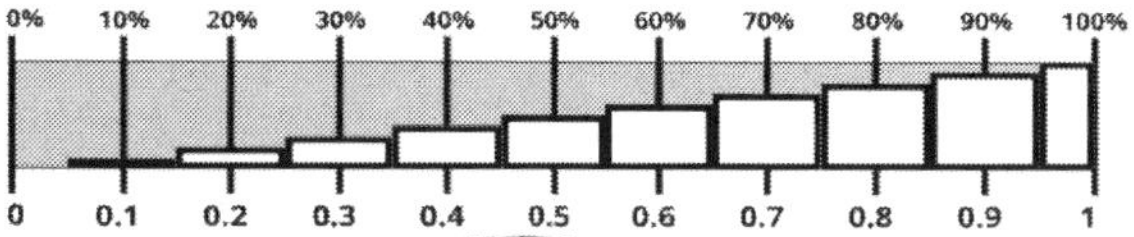

0% 10% 20% 30% 40% 50% 60% 70% 80% 90% 100%
0 0.1 0.2 0.3 0.4 0.5 0.6 0.7 0.8 0.9 1

Junior

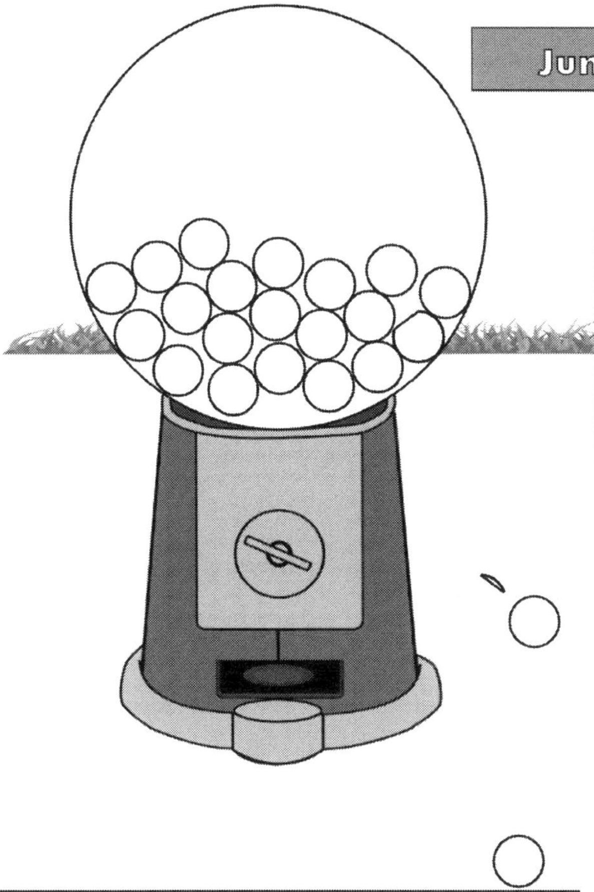

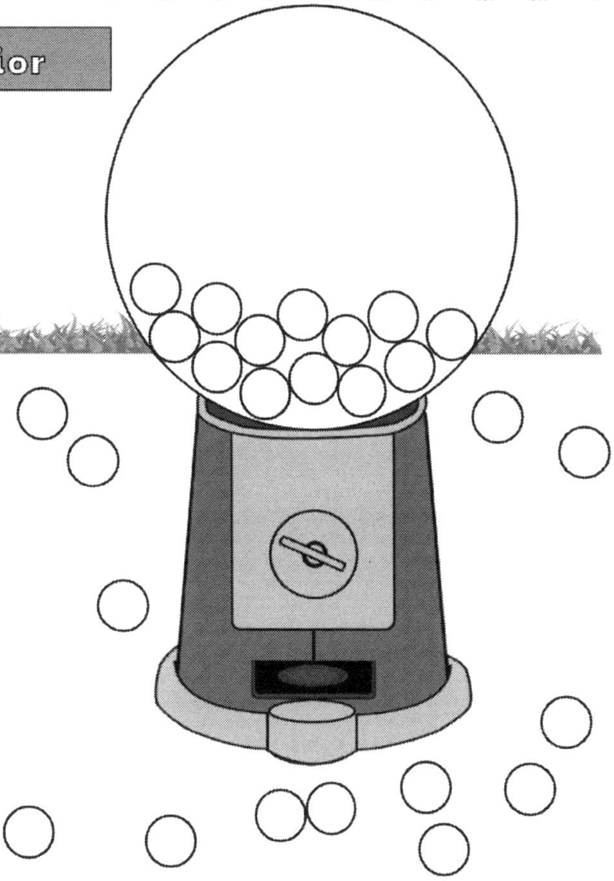

22 gumballs were in the gumball machine, 10% of them have fallen out. How many gumballs have fallen out?

26 gumballs were in the gumball machine, 50% of them have fallen out. How many gumballs have fallen out?

Gumball Puzzle 8

Finding Percentages

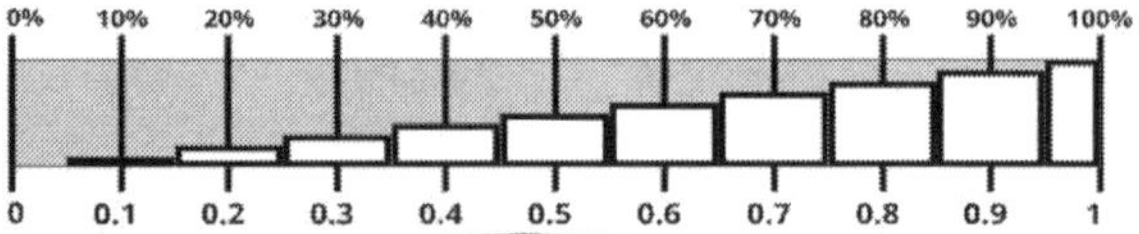

0% 10% 20% 30% 40% 50% 60% 70% 80% 90% 100%

0 0.1 0.2 0.3 0.4 0.5 0.6 0.7 0.8 0.9 1

Junior

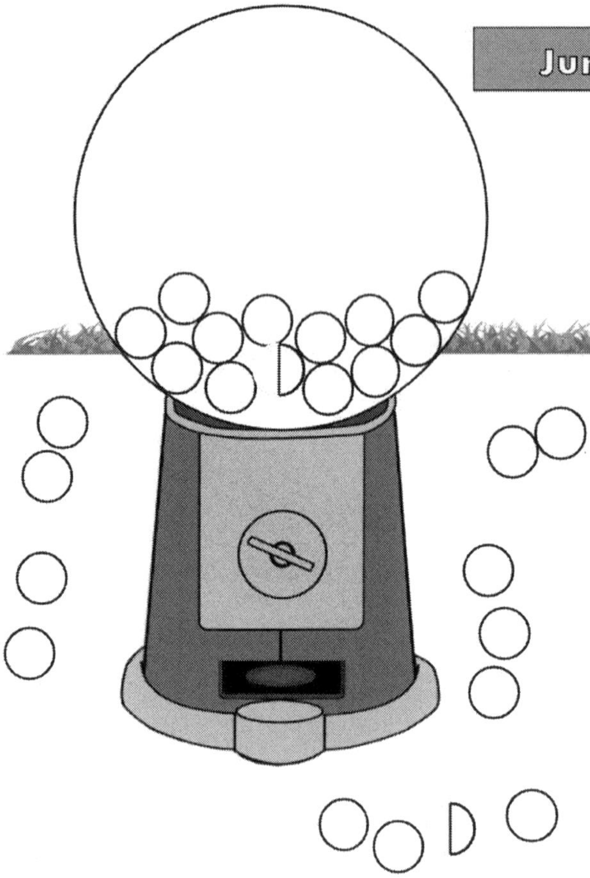

25 gumballs were in the gumball machine, 50% of them have fallen out. How many gumballs have fallen out?

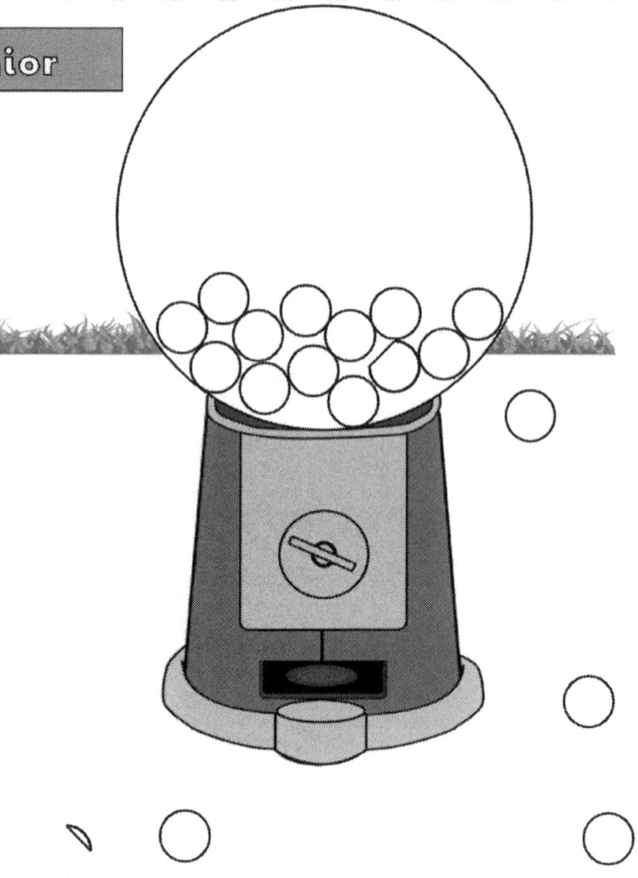

17 gumballs were in the gumball machine, 25% of them have fallen out. How many gumballs have fallen out?

Gumball Puzzle 9

Finding Percentages

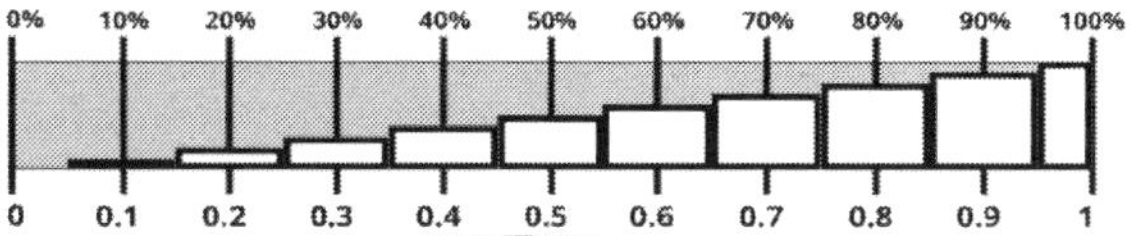

0% 10% 20% 30% 40% 50% 60% 70% 80% 90% 100%

0 0.1 0.2 0.3 0.4 0.5 0.6 0.7 0.8 0.9 1

Medium

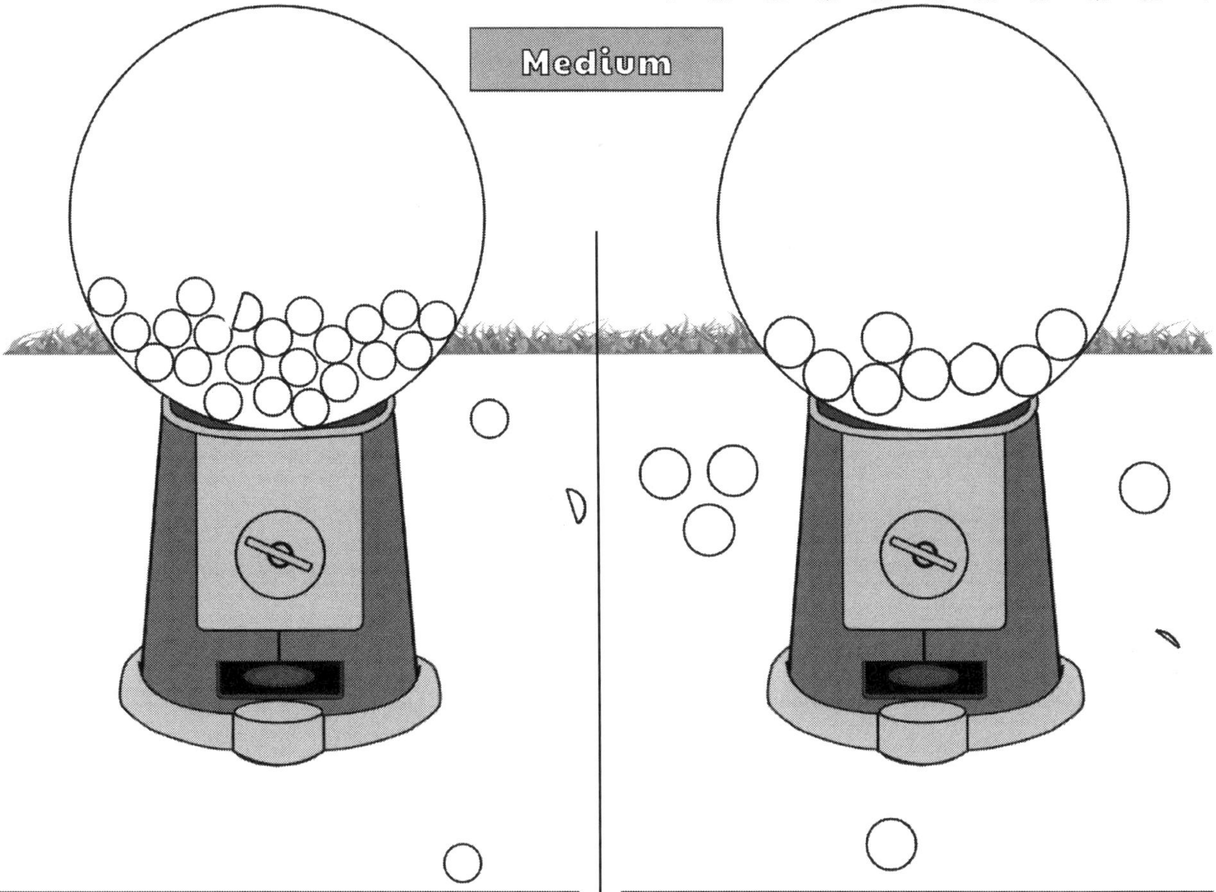

24 gumballs were in the gumball machine, 10% of them have fallen out. How many gumballs have fallen out?

13 gumballs were in the gumball machine, 40% of them have fallen out. How many gumballs have fallen out?

Gumball Puzzle 10

Finding Percentages

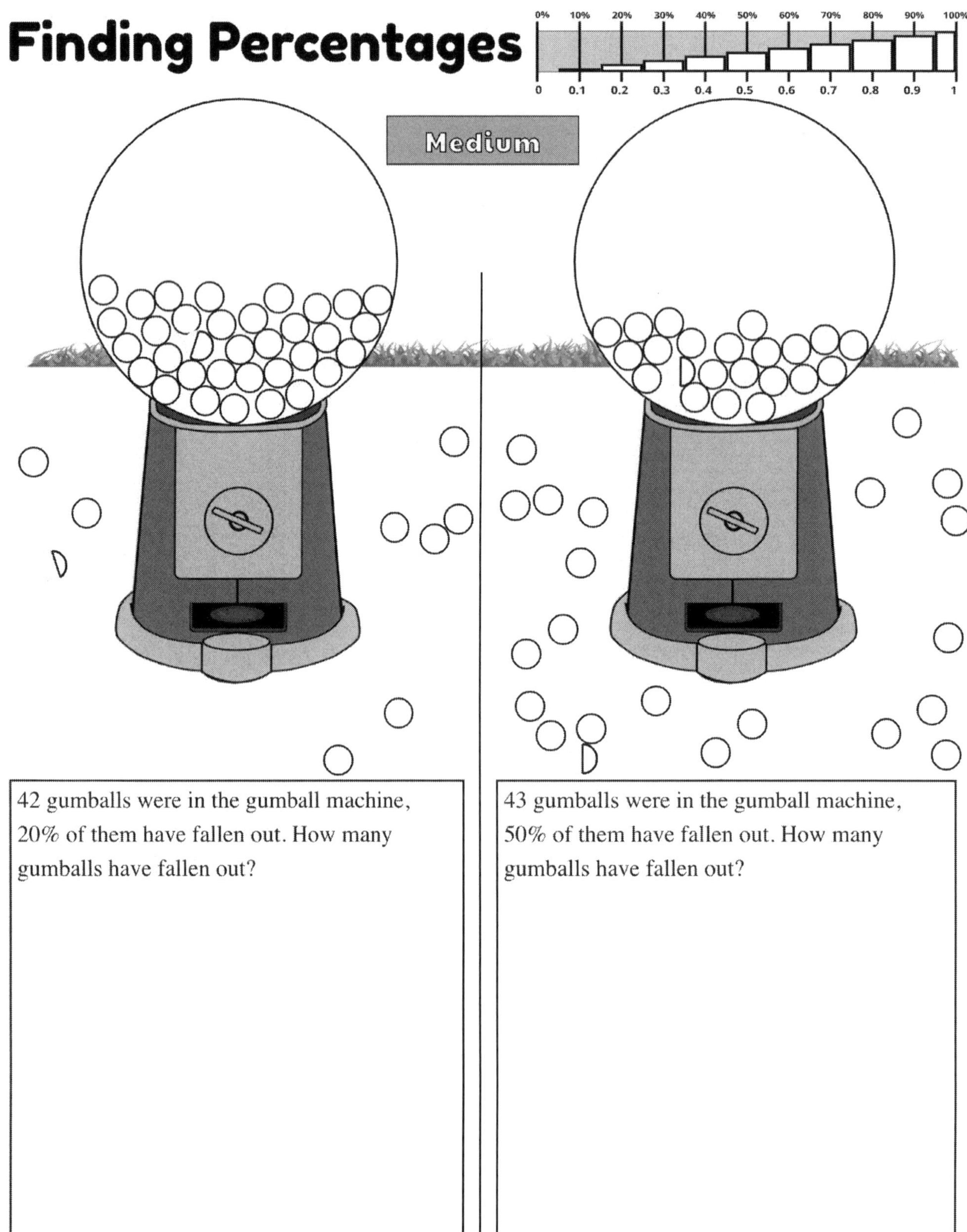

42 gumballs were in the gumball machine, 20% of them have fallen out. How many gumballs have fallen out?

43 gumballs were in the gumball machine, 50% of them have fallen out. How many gumballs have fallen out?

Gumball Puzzle 11

Finding Percentages

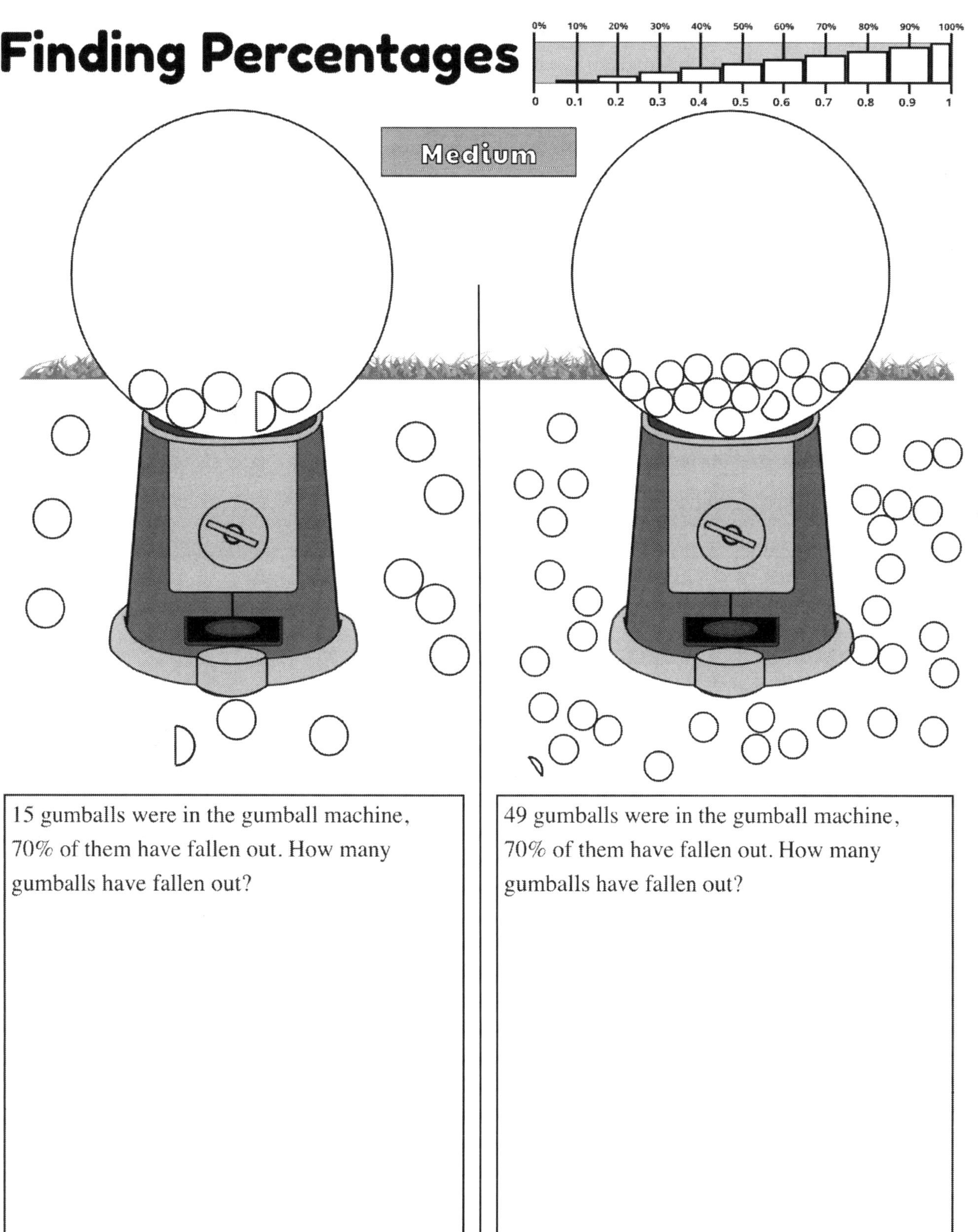

15 gumballs were in the gumball machine, 70% of them have fallen out. How many gumballs have fallen out?

49 gumballs were in the gumball machine, 70% of them have fallen out. How many gumballs have fallen out?

Gumball Puzzle 12

Finding Percentages

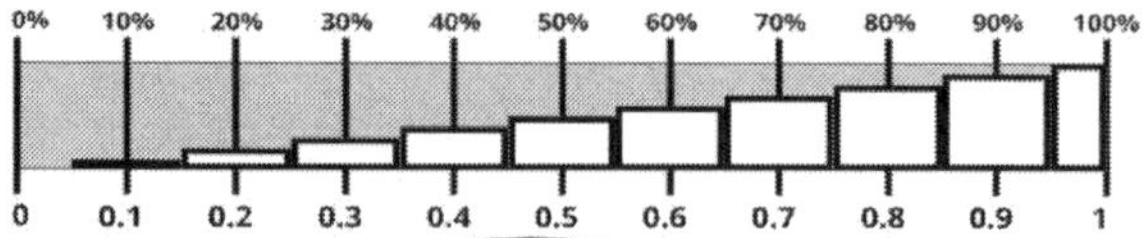

0% 10% 20% 30% 40% 50% 60% 70% 80% 90% 100%

0 0.1 0.2 0.3 0.4 0.5 0.6 0.7 0.8 0.9 1

Medium

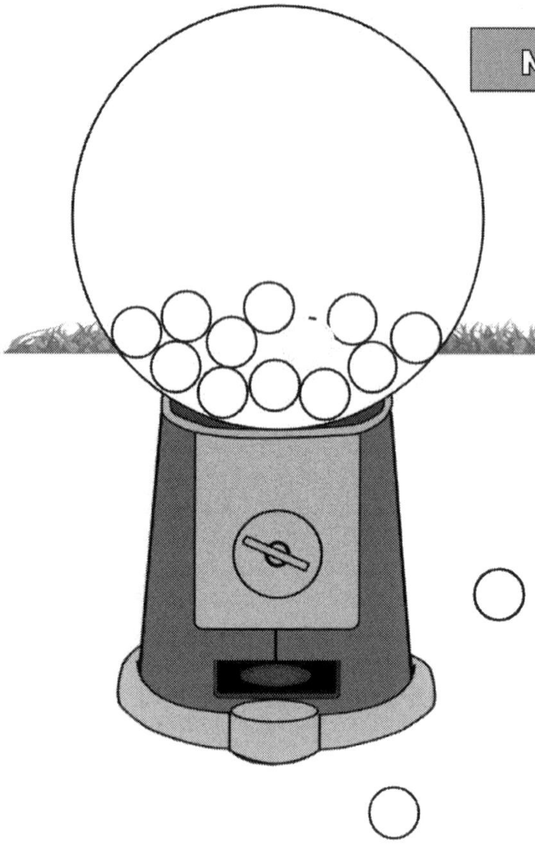

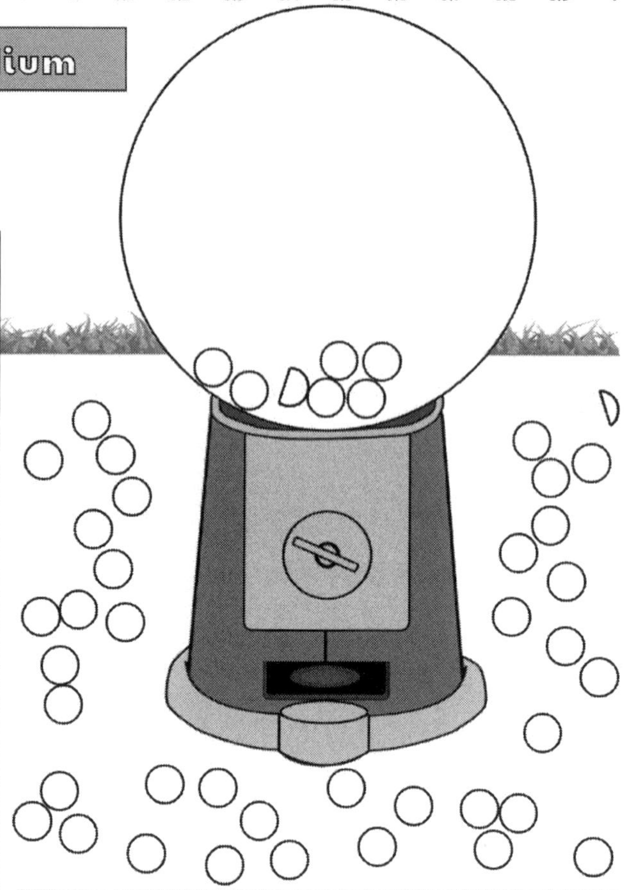

13 gumballs were in the gumball machine, 15% of them have fallen out. How many gumballs have fallen out?

44 gumballs were in the gumball machine, 85% of them have fallen out. How many gumballs have fallen out?

Gumball Puzzle 13

Finding Percentages

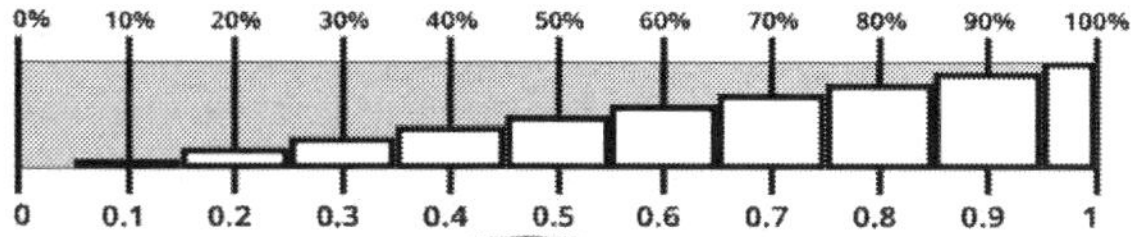

0% 10% 20% 30% 40% 50% 60% 70% 80% 90% 100%

0 0.1 0.2 0.3 0.4 0.5 0.6 0.7 0.8 0.9 1

Medium

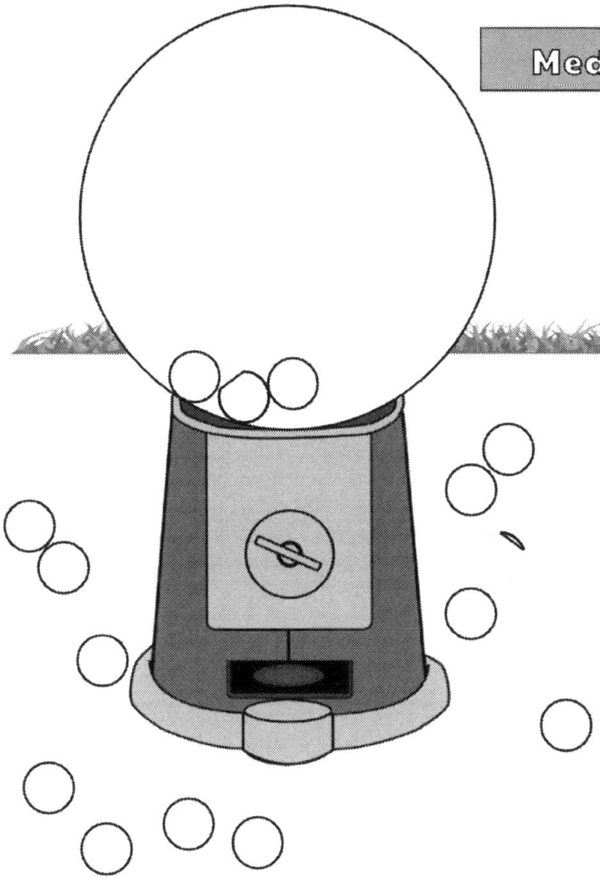

14 gumballs were in the gumball machine, 80% of them have fallen out. How many gumballs have fallen out?

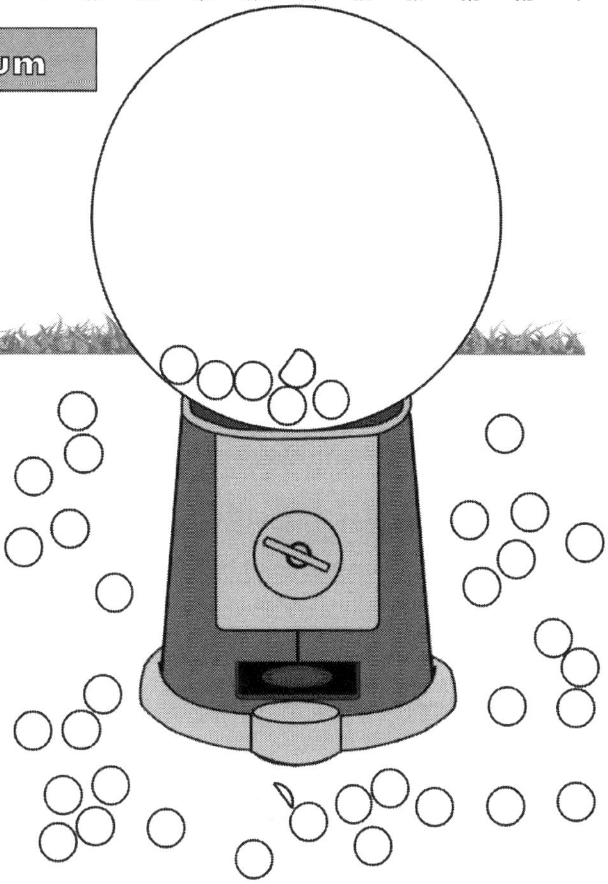

38 gumballs were in the gumball machine, 85% of them have fallen out. How many gumballs have fallen out?

Gumball Puzzle 14

Finding Percentages

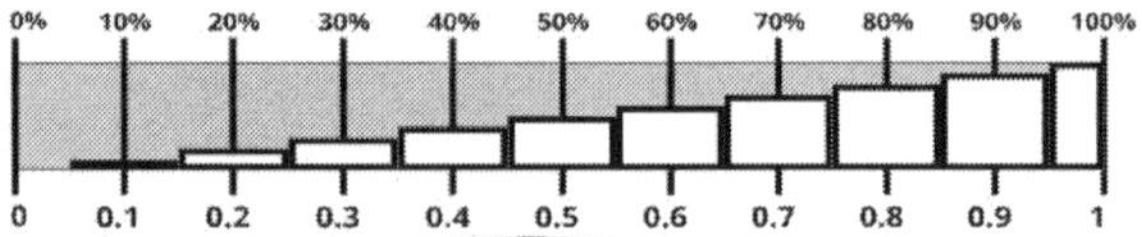

0% 10% 20% 30% 40% 50% 60% 70% 80% 90% 100%

0 0.1 0.2 0.3 0.4 0.5 0.6 0.7 0.8 0.9 1

Medium

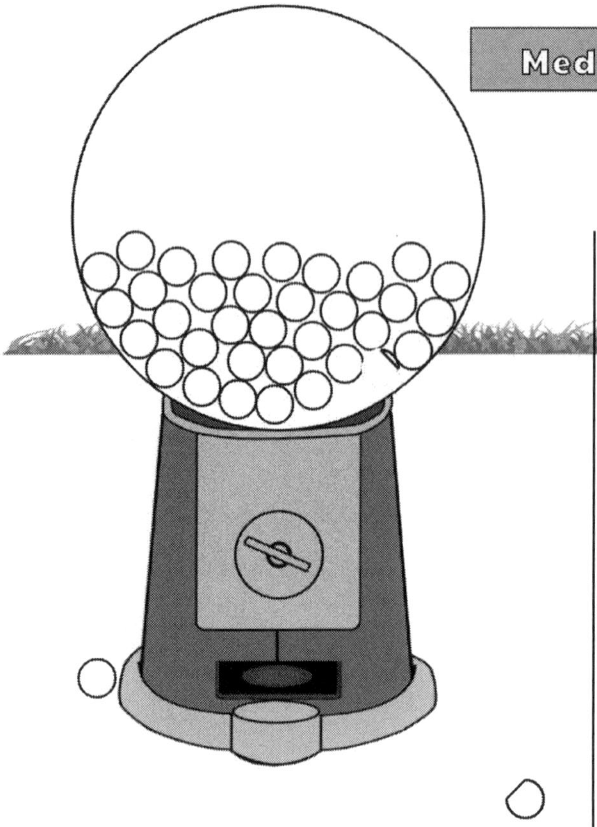

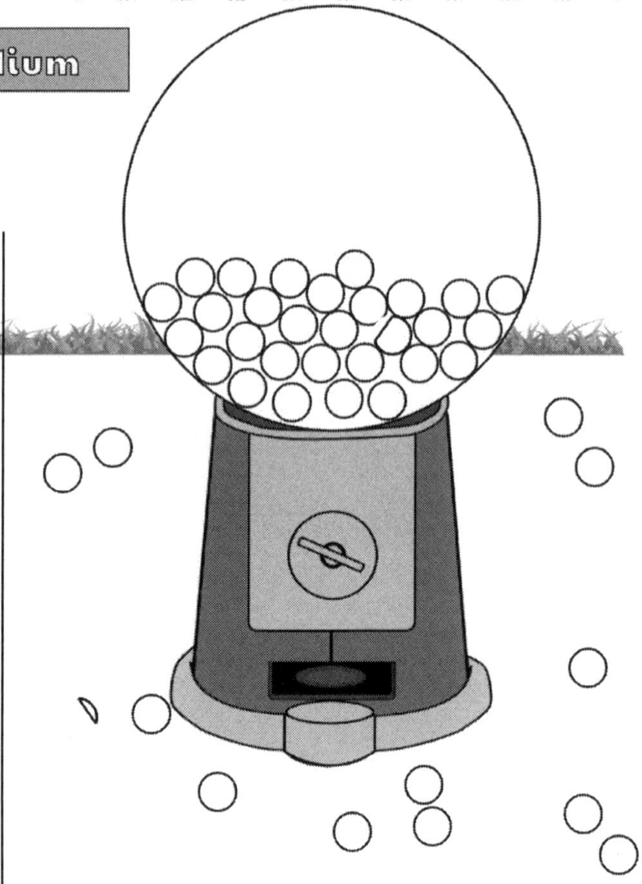

35 gumballs were in the gumball machine, 5% of them have fallen out. How many gumballs have fallen out?

41 gumballs were in the gumball machine, 30% of them have fallen out. How many gumballs have fallen out?

Gumball Puzzle 15

Finding Percentages

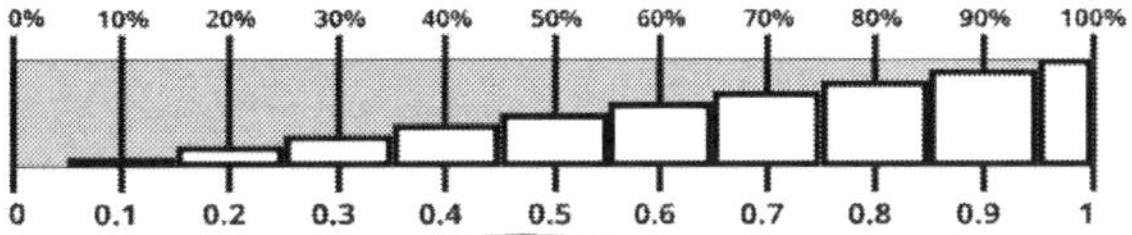

0% 10% 20% 30% 40% 50% 60% 70% 80% 90% 100%

0 0.1 0.2 0.3 0.4 0.5 0.6 0.7 0.8 0.9 1

Medium

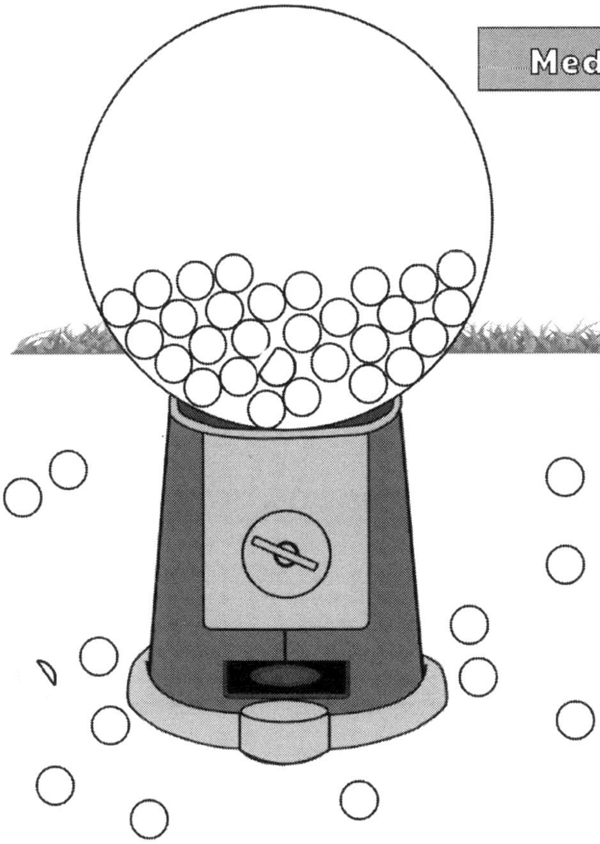

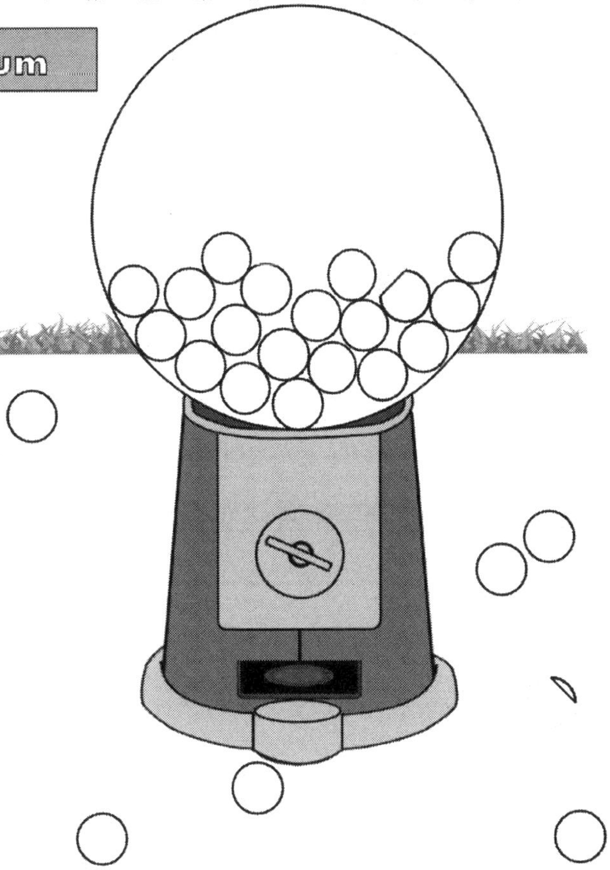

41 gumballs were in the gumball machine, 30% of them have fallen out. How many gumballs have fallen out?

25 gumballs were in the gumball machine, 25% of them have fallen out. How many gumballs have fallen out?

Gumball Puzzle 16

Finding Percentages

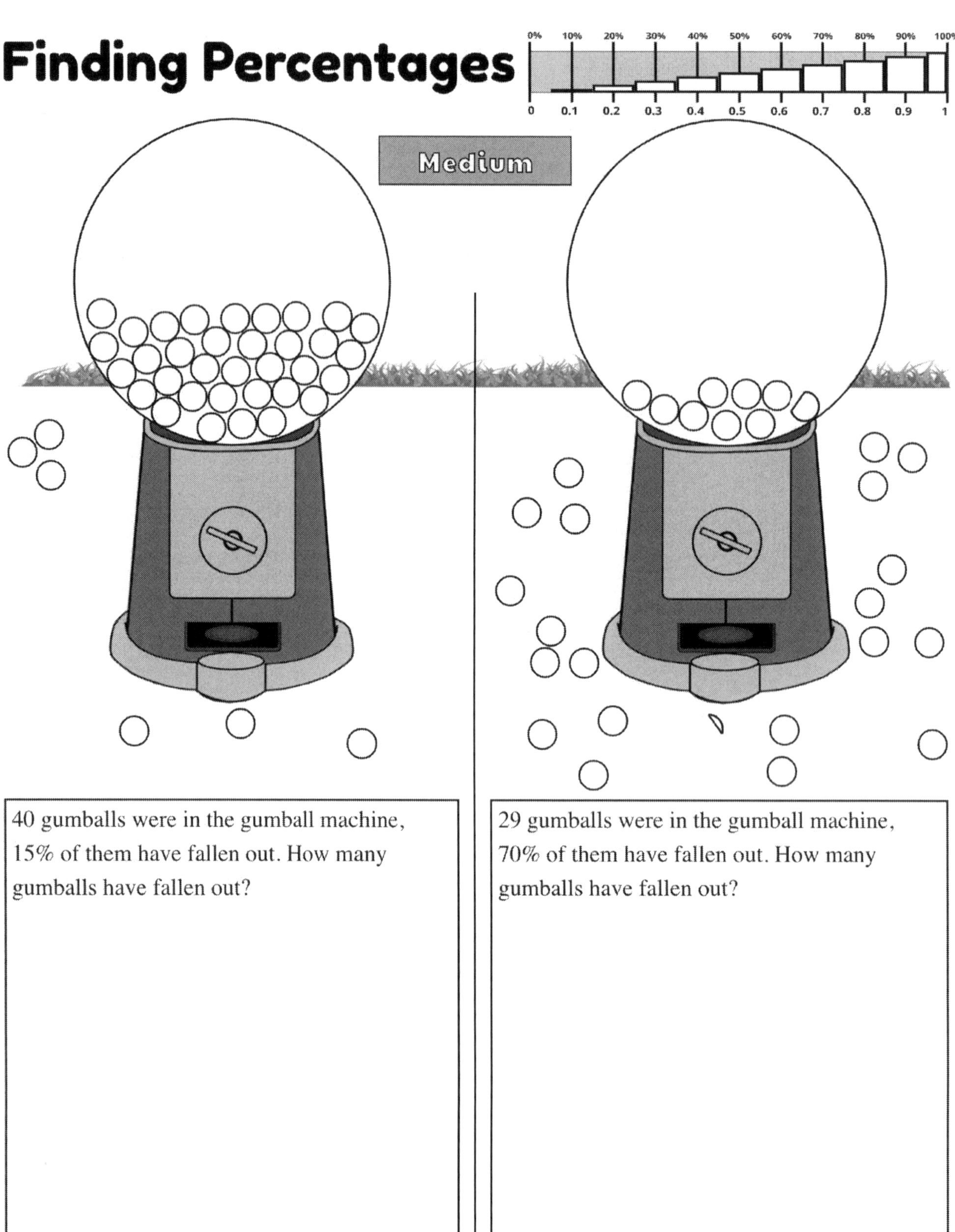

40 gumballs were in the gumball machine, 15% of them have fallen out. How many gumballs have fallen out?

29 gumballs were in the gumball machine, 70% of them have fallen out. How many gumballs have fallen out?

Gumball Puzzle 17

Finding Percentages

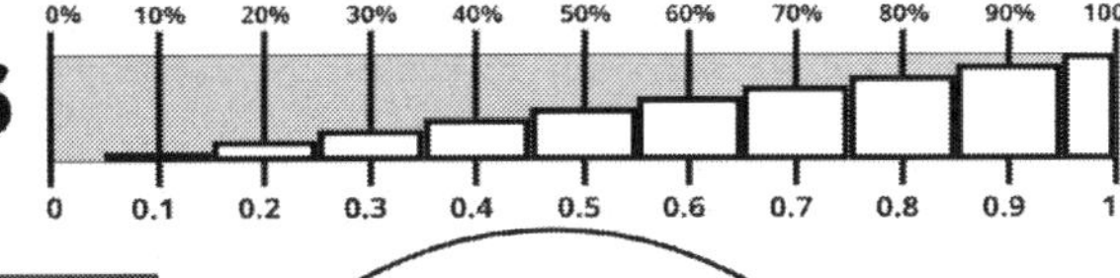

Hard

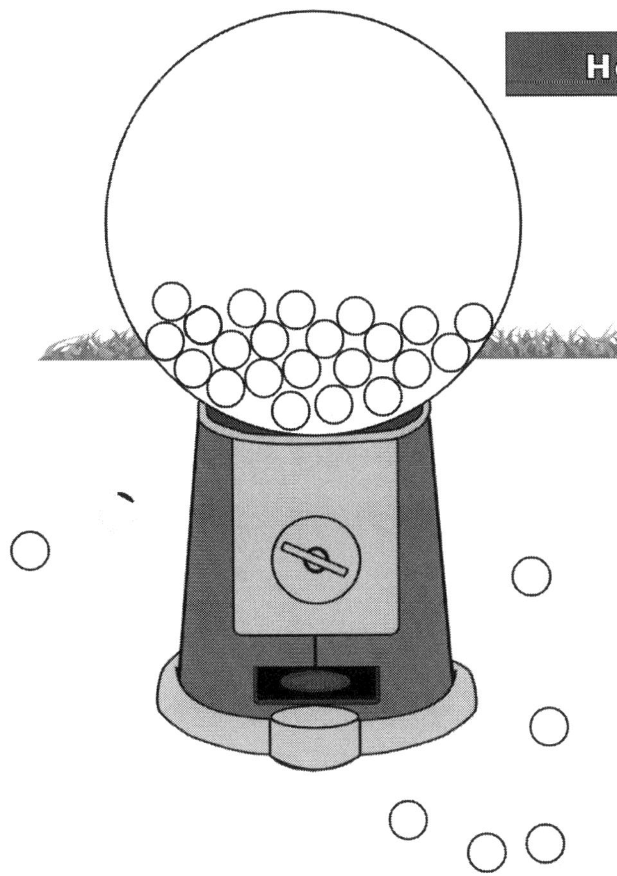

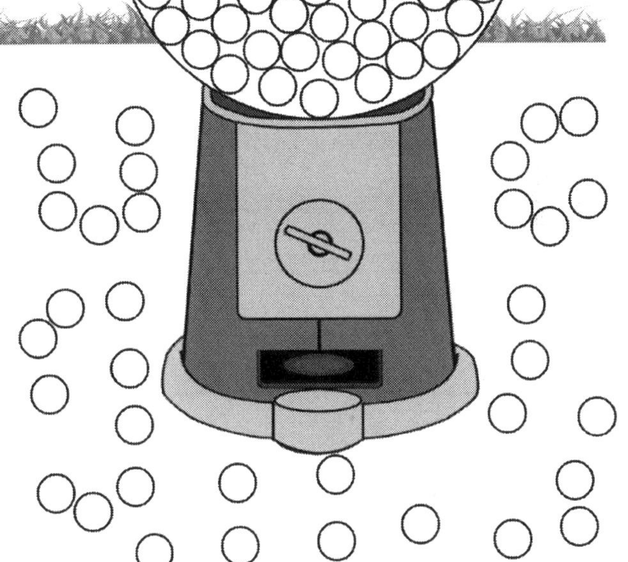

28 gumballs were in the gumball machine, 22% of them have fallen out. How many gumballs have fallen out?

Extra Challenge:
87% of the gumballs on the ground have been eaten by birds. How many were eaten?

70 gumballs were in the gumball machine, 50% of them have fallen out. How many gumballs have fallen out?

Extra Challenge:
96% of the gumballs on the ground have been eaten by birds. How many were eaten?

Gumball Puzzle 18

Finding Percentages

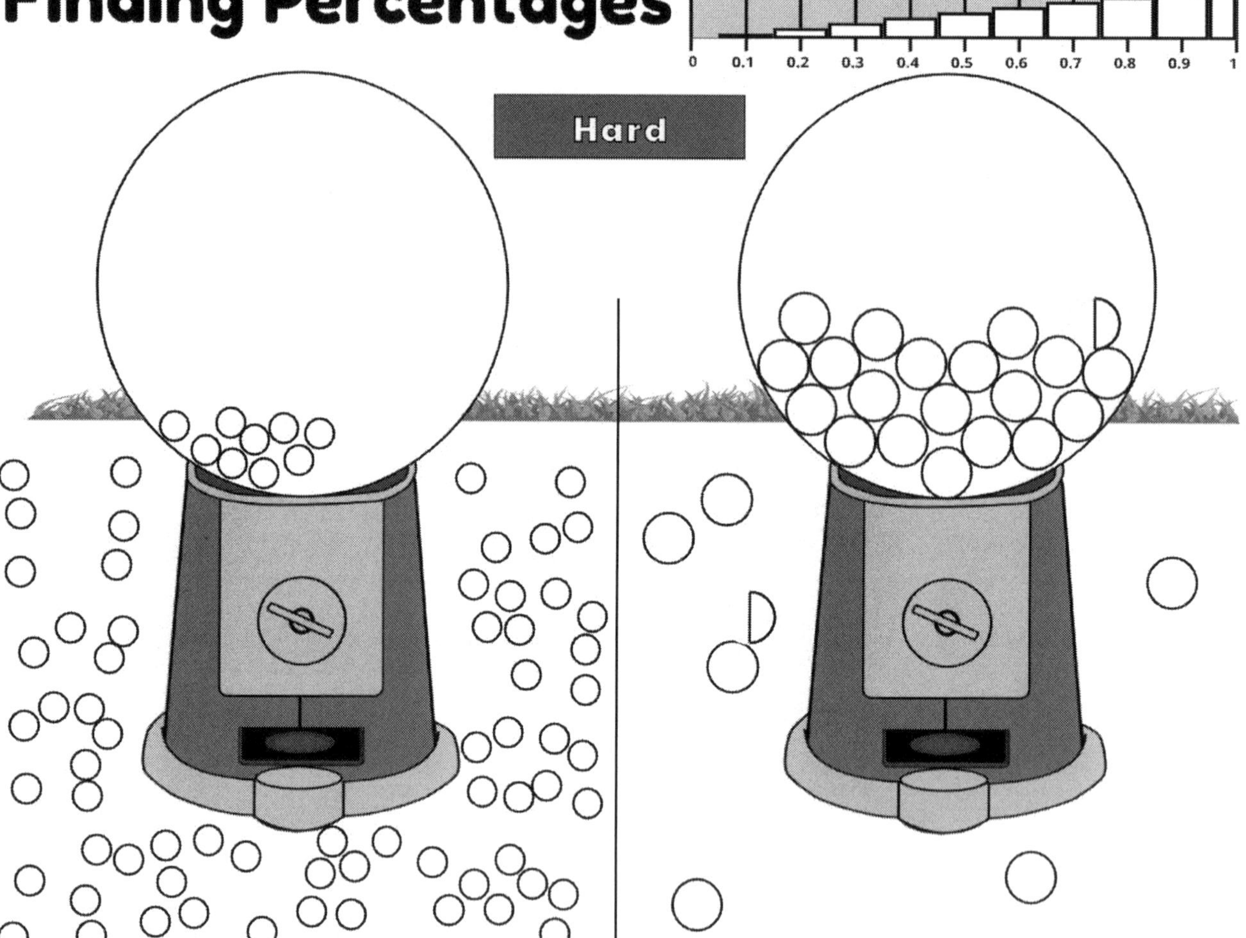

75 gumballs were in the gumball machine, 88% of them have fallen out. How many gumballs have fallen out?

Extra Challenge:
52% of the gumballs on the ground have been eaten by birds. How many were eaten?

26 gumballs were in the gumball machine, 25% of them have fallen out. How many gumballs have fallen out?

Extra Challenge:
93% of the gumballs on the ground have been eaten by birds. How many were eaten?

Gumball Puzzle 19

Finding Percentages

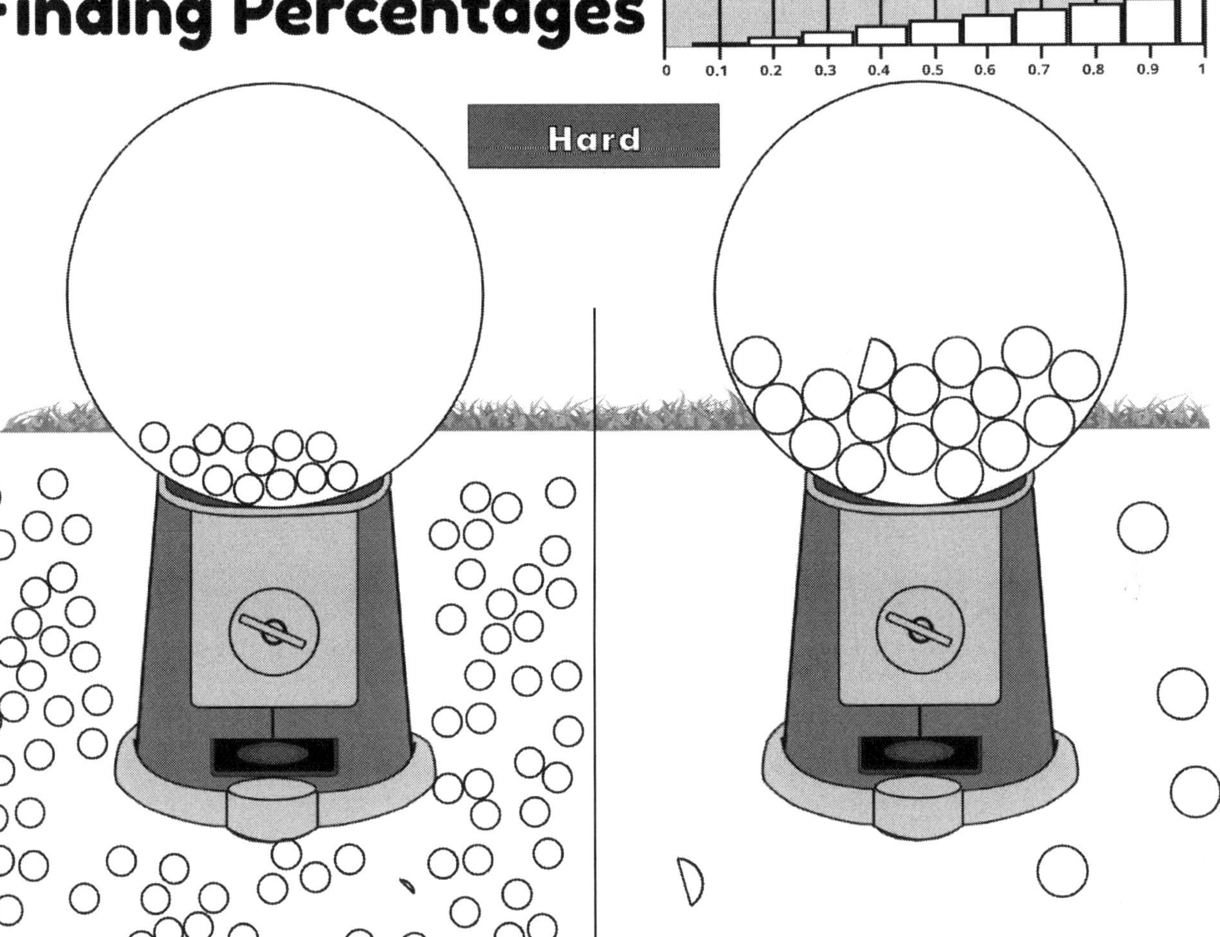

84 gumballs were in the gumball machine, 86% of them have fallen out. How many gumballs have fallen out?

Extra Challenge:
57% of the gumballs on the ground have been eaten by birds. How many were eaten?

21 gumballs were in the gumball machine, 21% of them have fallen out. How many gumballs have fallen out?

Extra Challenge:
85% of the gumballs on the ground have been eaten by birds. How many were eaten?

Gumball Puzzle 20

Finding Percentages

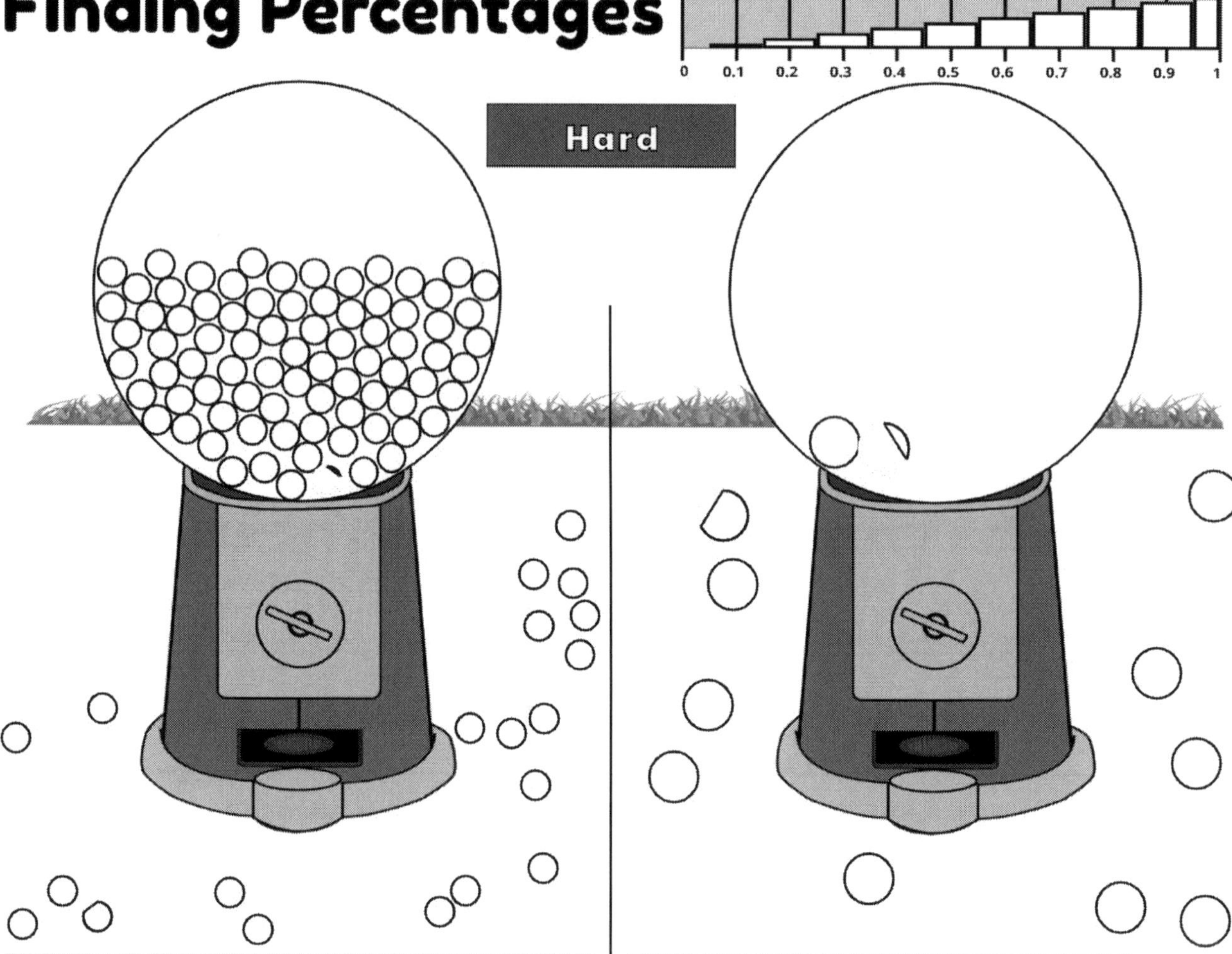

99 gumballs were in the gumball machine, 20% of them have fallen out. How many gumballs have fallen out?

Extra Challenge:
19% of the gumballs on the ground have been eaten by birds. How many were eaten?

11 gumballs were in the gumball machine, 88% of them have fallen out. How many gumballs have fallen out?

Extra Challenge:
61% of the gumballs on the ground have been eaten by birds. How many were eaten?

Gumball Puzzle 21

Finding Percentages

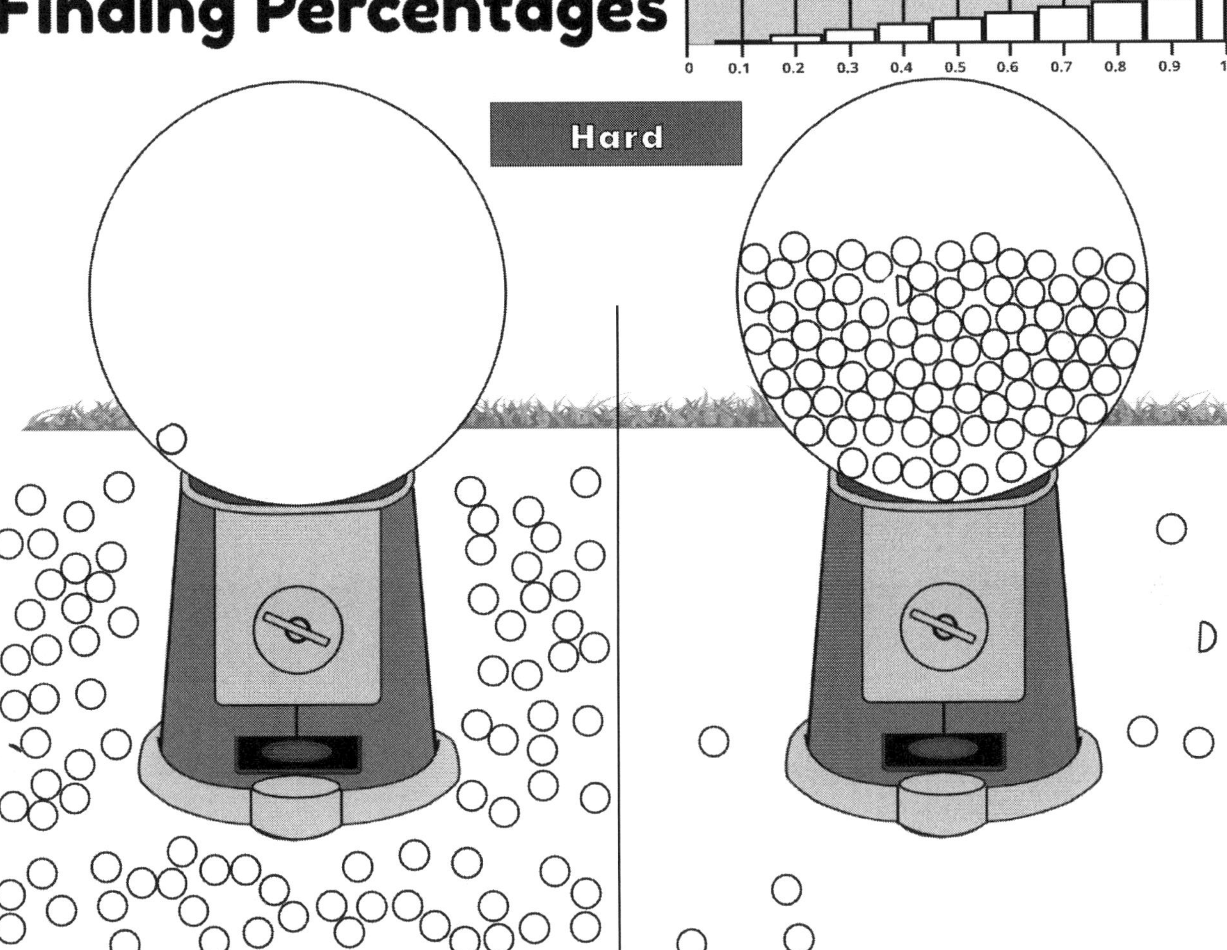

84 gumballs were in the gumball machine, 99% of them have fallen out. How many gumballs have fallen out?

Extra Challenge:
55% of the gumballs on the ground have been eaten by birds. How many were eaten?

94 gumballs were in the gumball machine, 8% of them have fallen out. How many gumballs have fallen out?

Extra Challenge:
74% of the gumballs on the ground have been eaten by birds. How many were eaten?

Gumball Puzzle 22

Finding Percentages

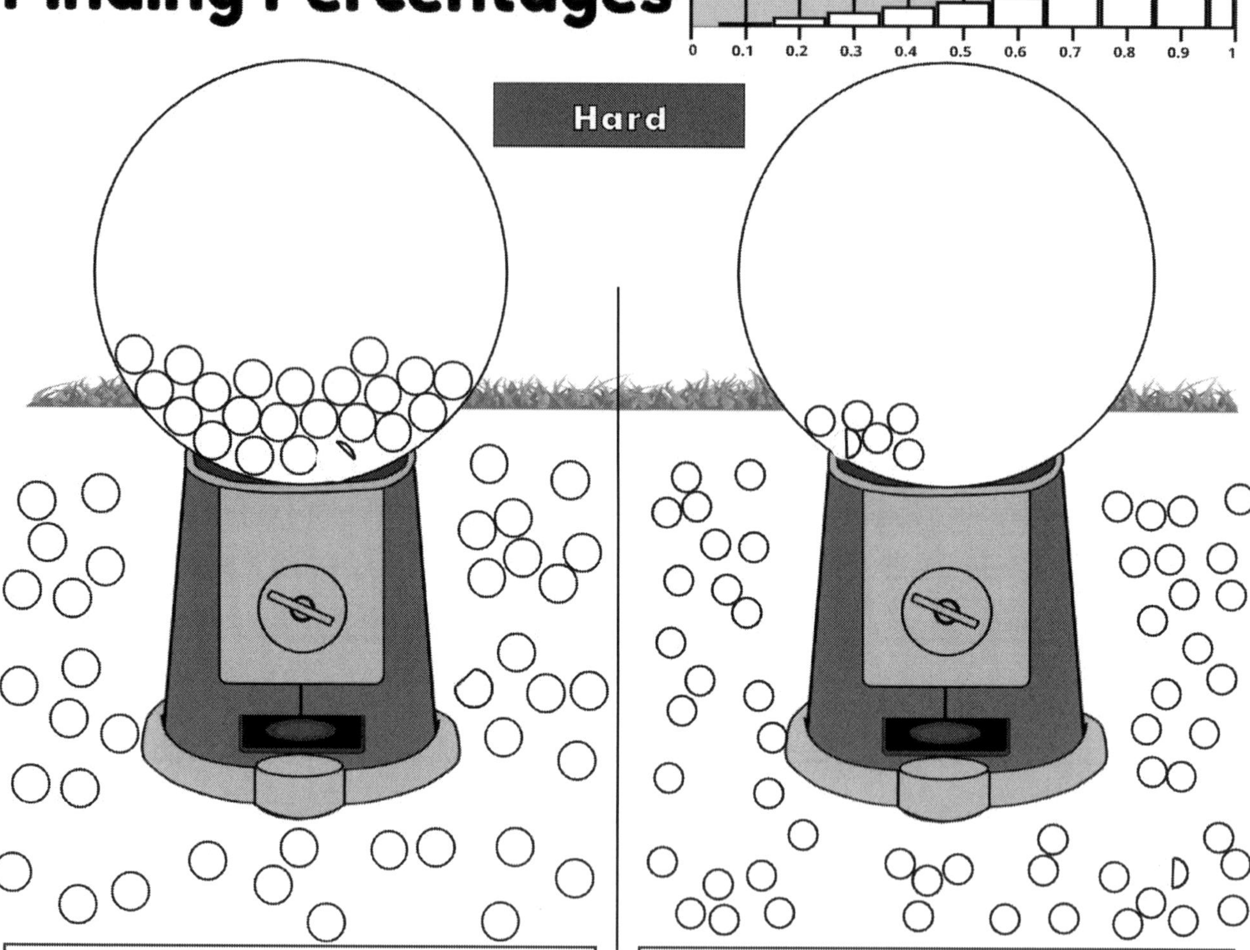

59 gumballs were in the gumball machine, 64% of them have fallen out. How many gumballs have fallen out?

Extra Challenge:
28% of the gumballs on the ground have been eaten by birds. How many were eaten?

61 gumballs were in the gumball machine, 91% of them have fallen out. How many gumballs have fallen out?

Extra Challenge:
82% of the gumballs on the ground have been eaten by birds. How many were eaten?

Gumball Puzzle 23

Finding Percentages

0% 10% 20% 30% 40% 50% 60% 70% 80% 90% 100%

0 0.1 0.2 0.3 0.4 0.5 0.6 0.7 0.8 0.9 1

Hard

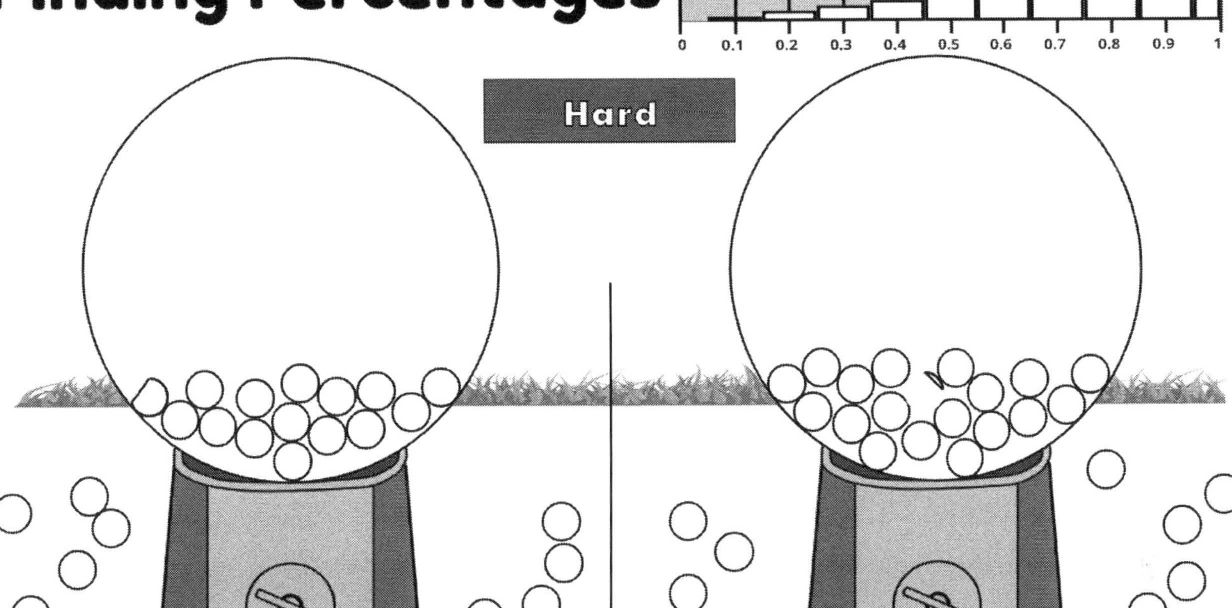

42 gumballs were in the gumball machine, 65% of them have fallen out. How many gumballs have fallen out?

Extra Challenge:
48% of the gumballs on the ground have been eaten by birds. How many were eaten?

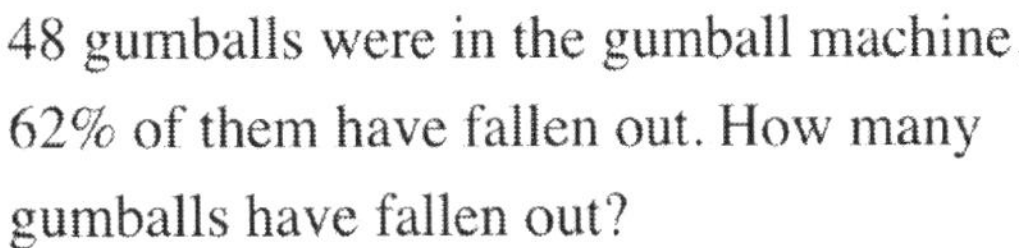

48 gumballs were in the gumball machine, 62% of them have fallen out. How many gumballs have fallen out?

Extra Challenge:
18% of the gumballs on the ground have been eaten by birds. How many were eaten?

Gumball Puzzle 24

Finding Percentages

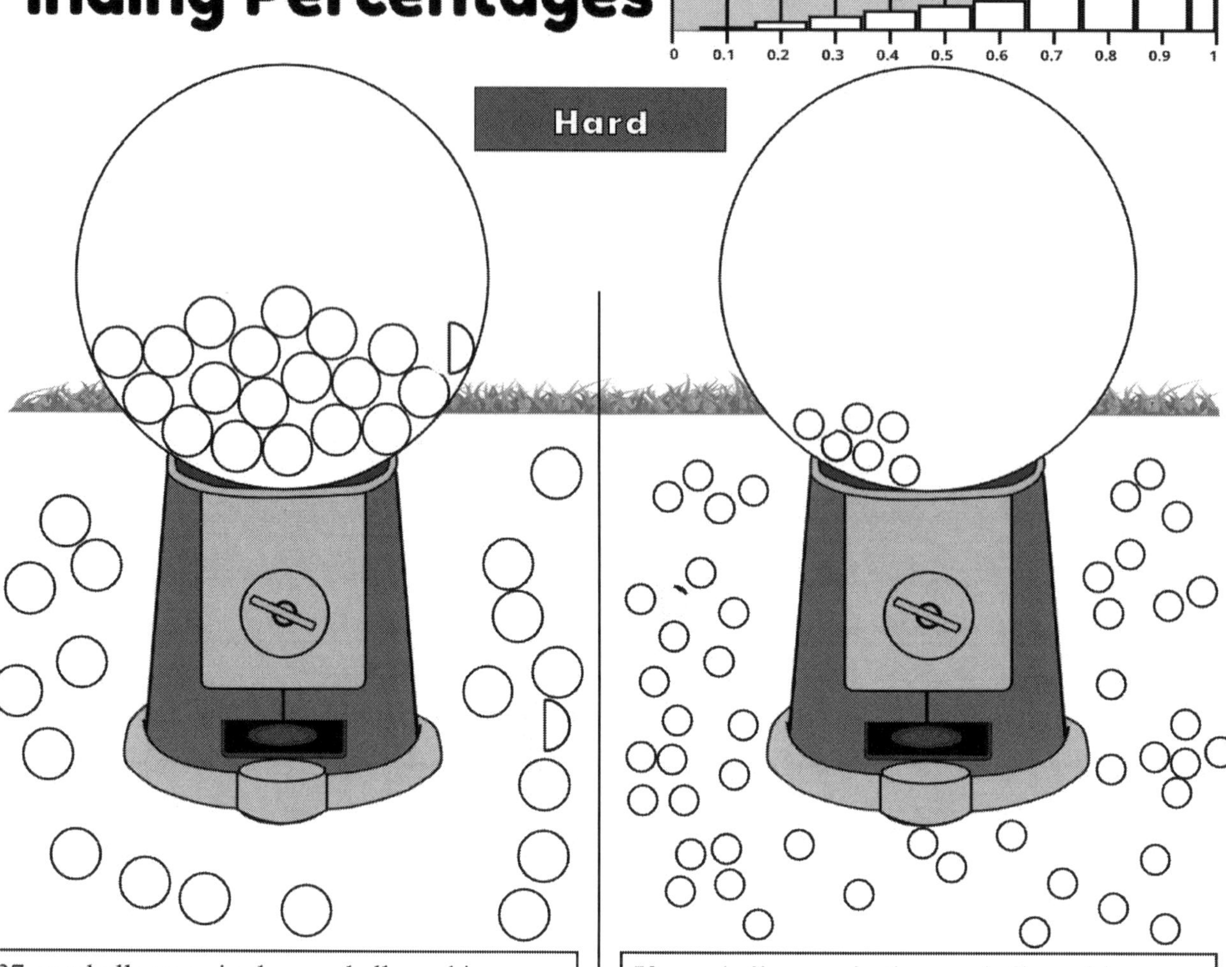

37 gumballs were in the gumball machine, 50% of them have fallen out. How many gumballs have fallen out?

Extra Challenge:
58% of the gumballs on the ground have been eaten by birds. How many were eaten?

53 gumballs were in the gumball machine, 89% of them have fallen out. How many gumballs have fallen out?

Extra Challenge:
66% of the gumballs on the ground have been eaten by birds. How many were eaten?

ROMAN NUMERALS CHEAT SHEET

Roman Numerals

1	2	3	4	5	6	7	8	9	10
I	II	III	IV	V	VI	VII	VIII	IX	X

10	20	30	40	50	60	70	80	90	100
X	XX	XXX	XL	L	LX	LXX	LXXX	XC	C

500	1000
D	M

HOW TO CONVERT ROMAN NUMERALS

Rules:		**Examples:**	
(1):	When a smaller symbol is after a greater symbol, it's added	**XV**	= 10 + 5 = 15
(2):	If a symbol comes after itself, it's added	**VII**	= 5 + 2 = 7
(3):	When a smaller symbol appears before a greater symbol, it's subtracted from the greater symbol	**IV**	= 5 - 1 = 4
(4):	The same symbol cannot be used more than 3x in a row	**III** **IIII**	= 3 ✓ = Invalid ✗

FURTHER EXAMPLES

LXX	= 70	**CDLXXXV**	= 485	**LXXXVI**	= 86
XCVII	= 97	**CMLXX**	= 970	**XC**	= 90
LXVII	= 67	**DXVI**	= 516	**XLIX**	= 49

Roman Numerals Sheet 1

Roman Numerals

1	2	3	4	5	6	7	8	9	10
I	II	III	IV	V	VI	VII	VIII	IX	X

10	20	30	40	50	60	70	80	90	100
X	XX	XXX	XL	L	LX	LXX	LXXX	XC	C

500	1000
D	M

Junior

Write the correct number next to each Roman numeral:

1) XVIII =
2) II =
3) XXX =
4) XIV =
5) X =
6) XVI =
7) XXI =
8) XXIV =
9) II =
10) I =
11) XVIII =
12) XXIII =
13) XIV =
14) XXVII =
15) XXIV =
16) XXVI =
17) XIII =
18) IV =
19) XII =
20) XII =

Write the correct Roman numeral next to each number:

1) 4 =
2) 21 =
3) 23 =
4) 9 =
5) 11 =
6) 23 =
7) 10 =
8) 21 =
9) 9 =
10) 18 =
11) 13 =
12) 1 =
13) 23 =
14) 15 =
15) 10 =
16) 10 =
17) 12 =
18) 13 =
19) 13 =
20) 7 =

Roman Numerals Sheet 2

Roman Numerals

1	2	3	4	5	6	7	8	9	10
I	II	III	IV	V	VI	VII	VIII	IX	X

10	20	30	40	50	60	70	80	90	100
X	XX	XXX	XL	L	LX	LXX	LXXX	XC	C

500	1000
D	M

Junior

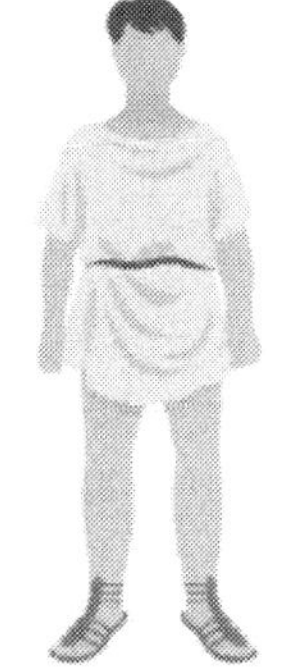

Write the correct number next to each Roman numeral:

1) VIII =
2) XXI =
3) XVIII =
4) XXII =
5) XVII =
6) XIX =
7) XVIII =
8) IX =
9) XVIII =
10) VII =
11) XI =
12) XII =
13) XIII =
14) XIII =
15) XXX =
16) XI =
17) XXVI =
18) IX =
19) XVII =
20) XXIX =

Write the correct Roman numeral next to each number:

1) 13 =
2) 14 =
3) 8 =
4) 10 =
5) 29 =
6) 20 =
7) 9 =
8) 15 =
9) 12 =
10) 20 =
11) 24 =
12) 24 =
13) 24 =
14) 19 =
15) 3 =
16) 28 =
17) 16 =
18) 12 =
19) 13 =
20) 5 =

Roman Numerals Sheet 3

Roman Numerals

1	2	3	4	5	6	7	8	9	10
I	II	III	IV	V	VI	VII	VIII	IX	X

10	20	30	40	50	60	70	80	90	100
X	XX	XXX	XL	L	LX	LXX	LXXX	XC	C

500	1000
D	M

Medium

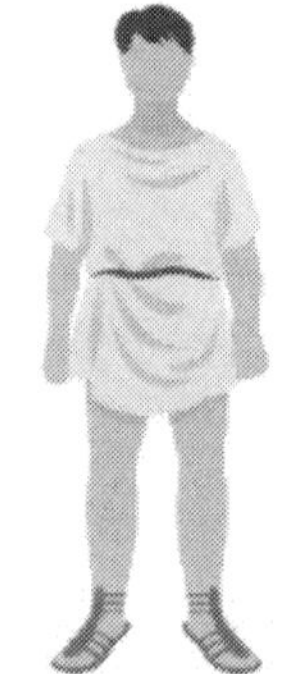

Write the correct number next to each Roman numeral:

1) XCVI =
2) LXXXV =
3) XCI =
4) LXXIV =
5) LXXXVI =
6) LXXXVII =
7) LXXX =
8) LXIII =
9) LVIII =
10) XCIV =
11) LI =
12) LVIII =
13) XCIV =
14) XCII =
15) XXXIX =
16) LXXXIX =
17) LVIII =
18) LXVI =
19) LXXXII =
20) LIX =

Write the correct Roman numeral next to each number:

1) 57 =
2) 63 =
3) 79 =
4) 44 =
5) 79 =
6) 55 =
7) 52 =
8) 54 =
9) 75 =
10) 64 =
11) 55 =
12) 39 =
13) 35 =
14) 99 =
15) 95 =
16) 49 =
17) 96 =
18) 92 =
19) 91 =
20) 54 =

Roman Numerals Sheet 4

Roman Numerals

1	2	3	4	5	6	7	8	9	10
I	II	III	IV	V	VI	VII	VIII	IX	X

10	20	30	40	50	60	70	80	90	100
X	XX	XXX	XL	L	LX	LXX	LXXX	XC	C

500	1000
D	M

Medium

Write the correct number next to each Roman numeral:

1) XL =
2) LXXXI =
3) XLIII =
4) LIV =
5) LII =
6) XL =
7) L =
8) XLVIII =
9) LXXXIII =
10) LXXXI =
11) XC =
12) LXXXVII =
13) XLIV =
14) XCVII =
15) LXII =
16) LXXXVIII =
17) LXXXIX =
18) XXXIX =
19) LXXXVIII =
20) LVI =

Write the correct Roman numeral next to each number:

1) 94 =
2) 90 =
3) 64 =
4) 34 =
5) 96 =
6) 87 =
7) 100 =
8) 55 =
9) 99 =
10) 92 =
11) 50 =
12) 82 =
13) 68 =
14) 66 =
15) 100 =
16) 92 =
17) 91 =
18) 33 =
19) 70 =
20) 97 =

Roman Numerals Sheet 5

Roman Numerals

1	2	3	4	5	6	7	8	9	10
I	II	III	IV	V	VI	VII	VIII	IX	X

10	20	30	40	50	60	70	80	90	100
X	XX	XXX	XL	L	LX	LXX	LXXX	XC	C

500	1000
D	M

Hard

Write the correct number next to each Roman numeral:

1) DCCXI =
2) DCCXV =
3) CMXXXI =
4) DCCLXIV =
5) DXXXII =
6) CDXCVIII =
7) DCCXLIII =
8) DCXCV =
9) DCCLXXV =
10) DCCXCIX =
11) DLXXVI =
12) CMXCI =
13) CMXLVII =
14) CDXCVII =
15) DCCCXCI =
16) MIII =
17) DCCLXXXVII =
18) DCCCIV =
19) DCXXXIV =
20) DCCXLIX =

Write the correct Roman numeral next to each number:

1) 789 =
2) 519 =
3) 488 =
4) 628 =
5) 719 =
6) 584 =
7) 968 =
8) 580 =
9) 884 =
10) 812 =
11) 1000 =
12) 877 =
13) 906 =
14) 623 =
15) 826 =
16) 982 =
17) 824 =
18) 526 =
19) 956 =
20) 713 =

Roman Numerals Sheet 6

Roman Numerals

1	2	3	4	5	6	7	8	9	10
I	II	III	IV	V	VI	VII	VIII	IX	X

10	20	30	40	50	60	70	80	90	100
X	XX	XXX	XL	L	LX	LXX	LXXX	XC	C

500	1000
D	M

Hard

Write the correct number next to each Roman numeral:

1) DCXCVII =
2) DCCXXVIII =
3) CDXCVIII =
4) DCCLXXVII =
5) DCCCLXXVI =
6) DXXVI =
7) DCCLIX =
8) DLVII =
9) CMXLVII =
10) DCCLVII =
11) DLXXXIII =
12) MX =
13) DLXXXVIII =
14) DCCCLXXVII =
15) DCCCLXXVIII =
16) CMXXIV =
17) DCLXXXVI =
18) DCCXXXVI =
19) CDXCIII =
20) DXCV =

Write the correct Roman numeral next to each number:

1) 877 =
2) 631 =
3) 548 =
4) 524 =
5) 720 =
6) 677 =
7) 704 =
8) 530 =
9) 765 =
10) 879 =
11) 839 =
12) 923 =
13) 691 =
14) 972 =
15) 754 =
16) 882 =
17) 712 =
18) 514 =
19) 538 =
20) 828 =

Roman Numerals Sheet 7

Roman Numerals Market

1	2	3	4	5	6	7	8	9	10
I	II	III	IV	V	VI	VII	VIII	IX	X

10	20	30	40	50	60	70	80	90	100
X	XX	XXX	XL	L	LX	LXX	LXXX	XC	C

500	1000
D	M

Junior

There is a sale on at the Roman markets! Convert the Roman numeral price tags to Arabic numerals and calculate the final sale price of each item (after reductions). Round answer to 2 decimal places

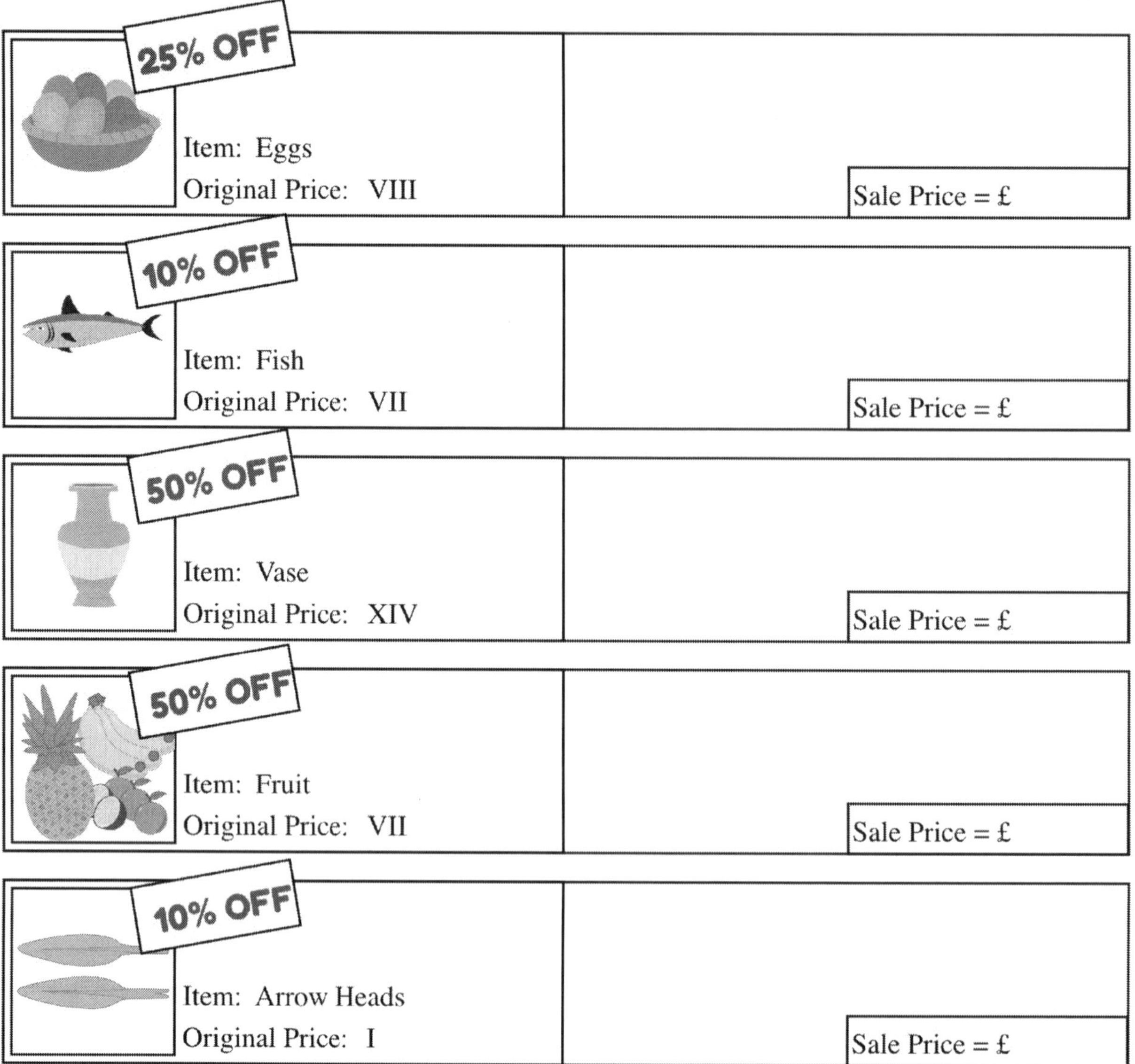

Roman Numerals Sheet 8

Roman Numerals Market

1	2	3	4	5	6	7	8	9	10
I	II	III	IV	V	VI	VII	VIII	IX	X

10	20	30	40	50	60	70	80	90	100
X	XX	XXX	XL	L	LX	LXX	LXXX	XC	C

500	1000
D	M

Junior

There is a sale on at the Roman markets! Convert the Roman numeral price tags to Arabic numerals and calculate the final sale price of each item (after reductions). Round answer to 2 decimal places

10% OFF
Item: Vase
Original Price: XIV
Sale Price = £

25% OFF
Item: Eggs
Original Price: II
Sale Price = £

50% OFF
Item: Chicken
Original Price: IX
Sale Price = £

25% OFF
Item: Books
Original Price: X
Sale Price = £

10% OFF
Item: Fruit
Original Price: II
Sale Price = £

Roman Numerals Sheet 9

Roman Numerals Market

1	2	3	4	5	6	7	8	9	10
I	II	III	IV	V	VI	VII	VIII	IX	X

10	20	30	40	50	60	70	80	90	100
X	XX	XXX	XL	L	LX	LXX	LXXX	XC	C

500	1000
D	M

Junior

There is a sale on at the Roman markets! Convert the Roman numeral price tags to Arabic numerals and calculate the final sale price of each item (after reductions). Round answer to 2 decimal places

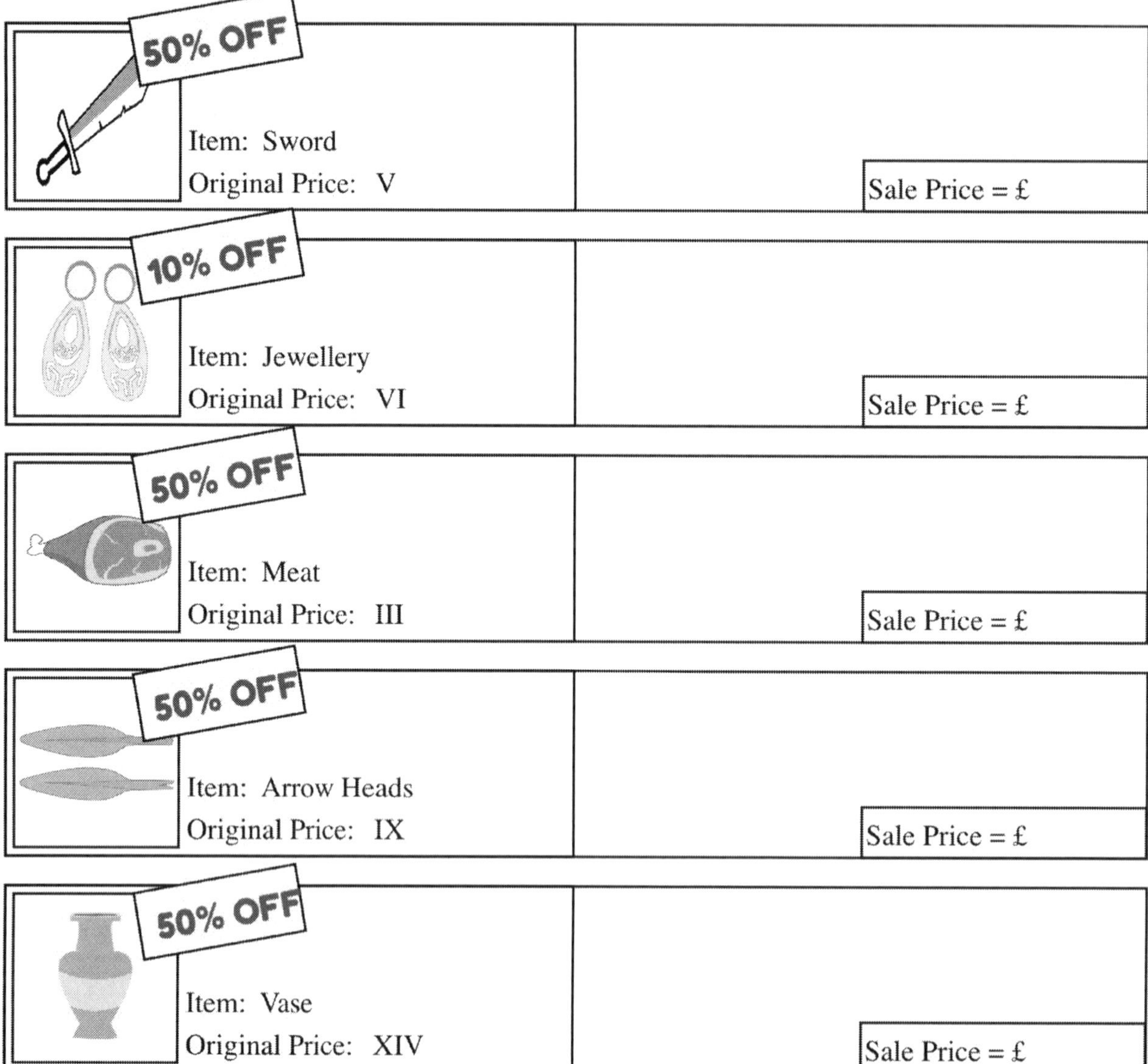

Roman Numerals Sheet 10

Roman Numerals Market

1	2	3	4	5	6	7	8	9	10
I	II	III	IV	V	VI	VII	VIII	IX	X

10	20	30	40	50	60	70	80	90	100
X	XX	XXX	XL	L	LX	LXX	LXXX	XC	C

500	1000
D	M

Junior

There is a sale on at the Roman markets! Convert the Roman numeral price tags to Arabic numerals and calculate the final sale price of each item (after reductions). Round answer to 2 decimal places

50% OFF

Item: Beans

Original Price: XI

Sale Price = £

10% OFF

Item: Chicken

Original Price: X

Sale Price = £

25% OFF

Item: Eggs

Original Price: XI

Sale Price = £

25% OFF

Item: Books

Original Price: IX

Sale Price = £

10% OFF

Item: Bread

Original Price: V

Sale Price = £

Roman Numerals Sheet 11

Roman Numerals Market

1	2	3	4	5	6	7	8	9	10
I	II	III	IV	V	VI	VII	VIII	IX	X

10	20	30	40	50	60	70	80	90	100
X	XX	XXX	XL	L	LX	LXX	LXXX	XC	C

500	1000
D	M

Junior

There is a sale on at the Roman markets! Convert the Roman numeral price tags to Arabic numerals and calculate the final sale price of each item (after reductions). Round answer to 2 decimal places

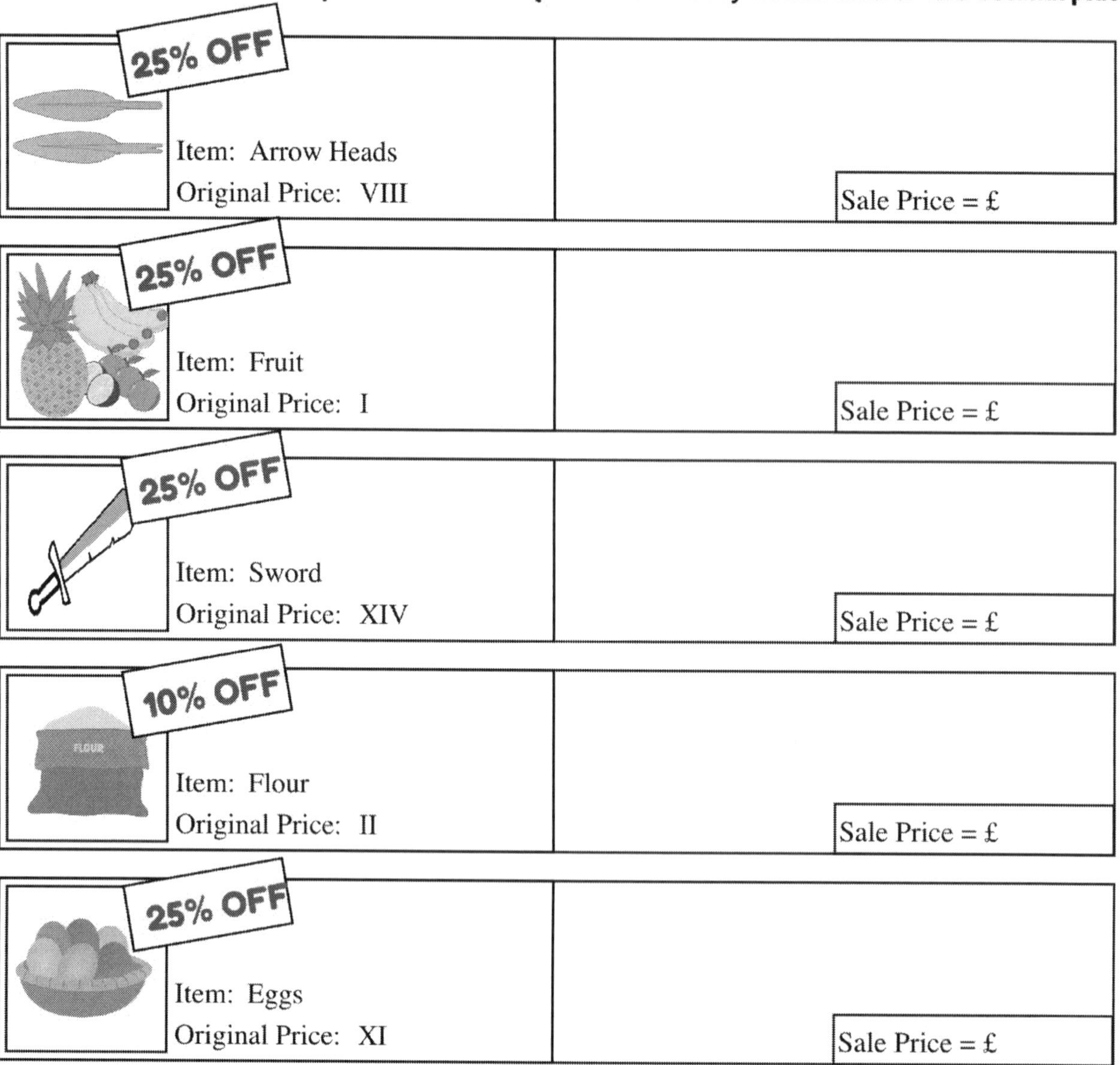

Roman Numerals Sheet 12

Roman Numerals Market

1	2	3	4	5	6	7	8	9	10
I	II	III	IV	V	VI	VII	VIII	IX	X

10	20	30	40	50	60	70	80	90	100
X	XX	XXX	XL	L	LX	LXX	LXXX	XC	C

500	1000
D	M

Junior

There is a sale on at the Roman markets! Convert the Roman numeral price tags to Arabic numerals and calculate the final sale price of each item (after reductions). Round answer to 2 decimal places

10% OFF
Item: Beans
Original Price: VI
Sale Price = £

25% OFF
Item: Arrow Heads
Original Price: XII
Sale Price = £

50% OFF
Item: Goblet
Original Price: IV
Sale Price = £

50% OFF
Item: Vase
Original Price: XIV
Sale Price = £

10% OFF
Item: Sword
Original Price: XI
Sale Price = £

Roman Numerals Sheet 13

Roman Numerals Market

1	2	3	4	5	6	7	8	9	10
I	II	III	IV	V	VI	VII	VIII	IX	X

10	20	30	40	50	60	70	80	90	100
X	XX	XXX	XL	L	LX	LXX	LXXX	XC	C

500	1000
D	M

Junior

There is a sale on at the Roman markets! Convert the Roman numeral price tags to Arabic numerals and calculate the final sale price of each item (after reductions). Round answer to 2 decimal places

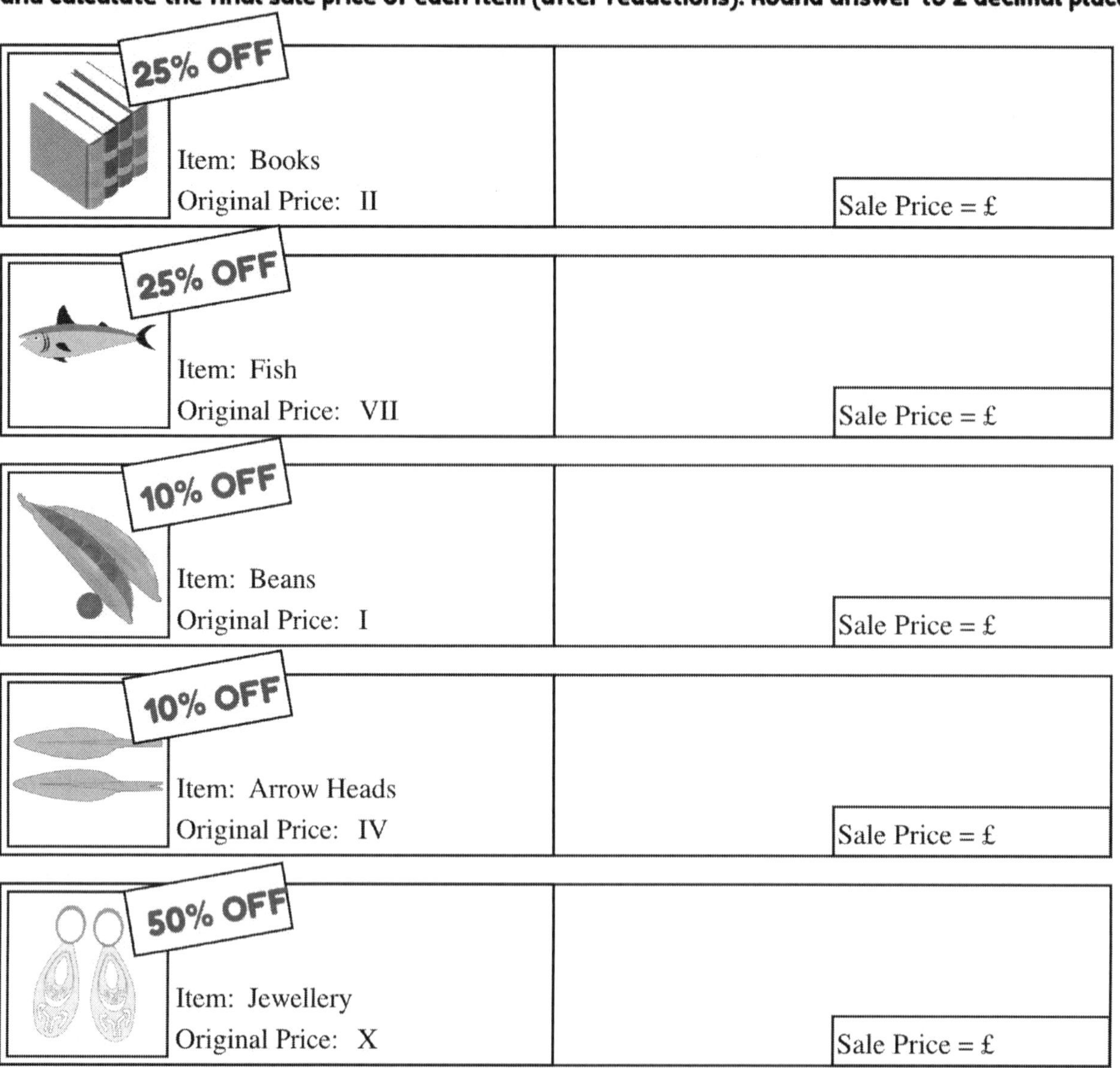

Roman Numerals Sheet 14

Roman Numerals Market

1	2	3	4	5	6	7	8	9	10
I	II	III	IV	V	VI	VII	VIII	IX	X

10	20	30	40	50	60	70	80	90	100
X	XX	XXX	XL	L	LX	LXX	LXXX	XC	C

500	1000
D	M

Junior

There is a sale on at the Roman markets! Convert the Roman numeral price tags to Arabic numerals and calculate the final sale price of each item (after reductions). Round answer to 2 decimal places

50% OFF

Item: Vase
Original Price: XI

Sale Price = £

25% OFF

Item: Meat
Original Price: XII

Sale Price = £

50% OFF

Item: Beans
Original Price: VIII

Sale Price = £

50% OFF

Item: Vase
Original Price: VII

Sale Price = £

10% OFF

Item: Eggs
Original Price: I

Sale Price = £

Roman Numerals Sheet 15

Roman Numerals Market

1	2	3	4	5	6	7	8	9	10
I	II	III	IV	V	VI	VII	VIII	IX	X

10	20	30	40	50	60	70	80	90	100
X	XX	XXX	XL	L	LX	LXX	LXXX	XC	C

500	1000
D	M

Medium

There is a sale on at the Roman markets! Convert the Roman numeral price tags to Arabic numerals and calculate the final sale price of each item (after reductions). Round answer to 2 decimal places

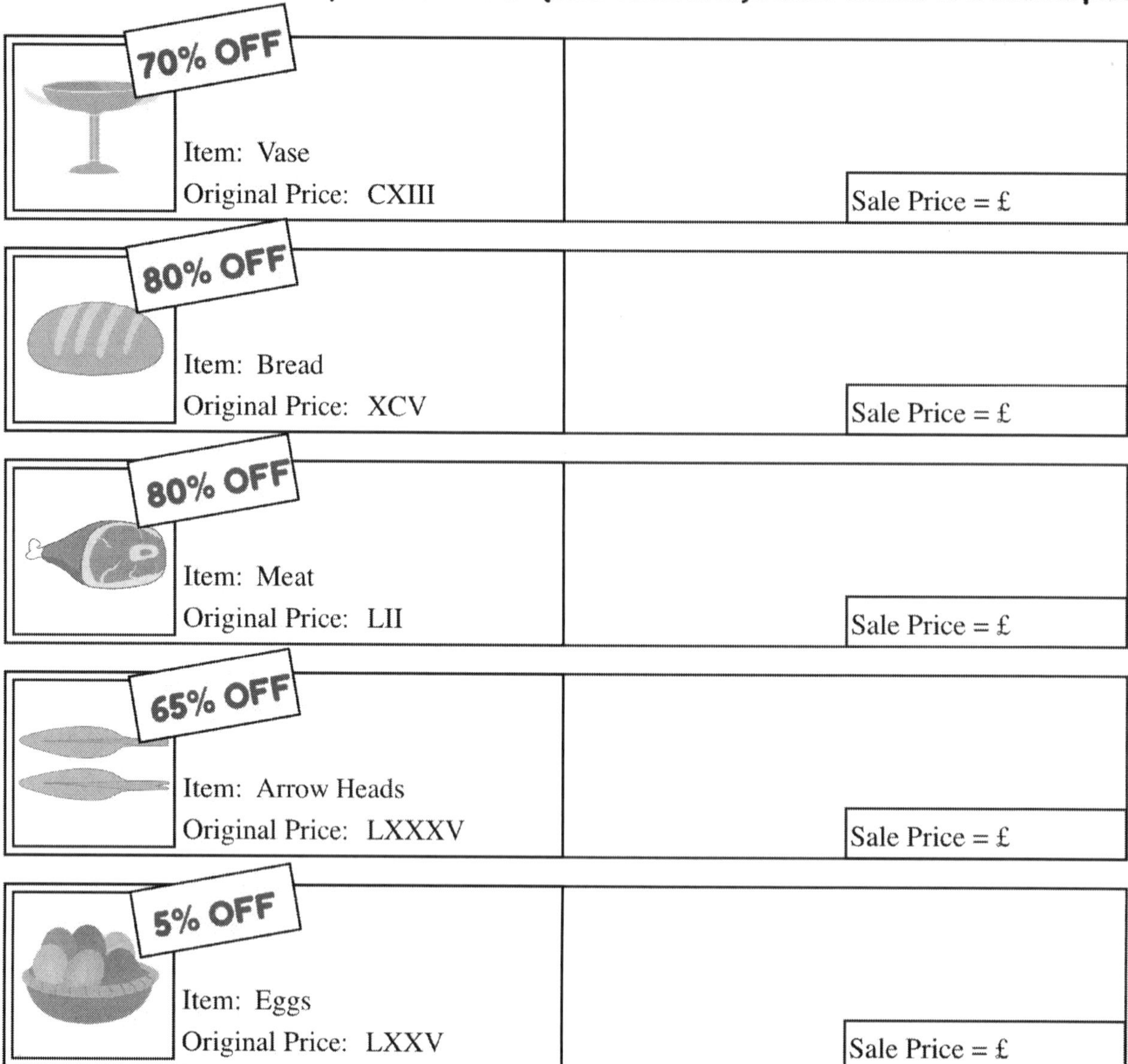

Roman Numerals Sheet 16

Roman Numerals Market

1	2	3	4	5	6	7	8	9	10
I	II	III	IV	V	VI	VII	VIII	IX	X

10	20	30	40	50	60	70	80	90	100
X	XX	XXX	XL	L	LX	LXX	LXXX	XC	C

500	1000
D	M

Medium

There is a sale on at the Roman markets! Convert the Roman numeral price tags to Arabic numerals and calculate the final sale price of each item (after reductions). Round answer to 2 decimal places

15% OFF

Item: Fish
Original Price: LXII

Sale Price = £

10% OFF

Item: Chicken
Original Price: XCVIII

Sale Price = £

90% OFF

Item: Goblet
Original Price: CXI

Sale Price = £

85% OFF

Item: Vase
Original Price: CXXVI

Sale Price = £

75% OFF

Item: Jewellery
Original Price: CXLV

Sale Price = £

Roman Numerals Sheet 17

Roman Numerals Market

1	2	3	4	5	6	7	8	9	10
I	II	III	IV	V	VI	VII	VIII	IX	X

10	20	30	40	50	60	70	80	90	100
X	XX	XXX	XL	L	LX	LXX	LXXX	XC	C

500	1000
D	M

Medium

There is a sale on at the Roman markets! Convert the Roman numeral price tags to Arabic numerals and calculate the final sale price of each item (after reductions). Round answer to 2 decimal places

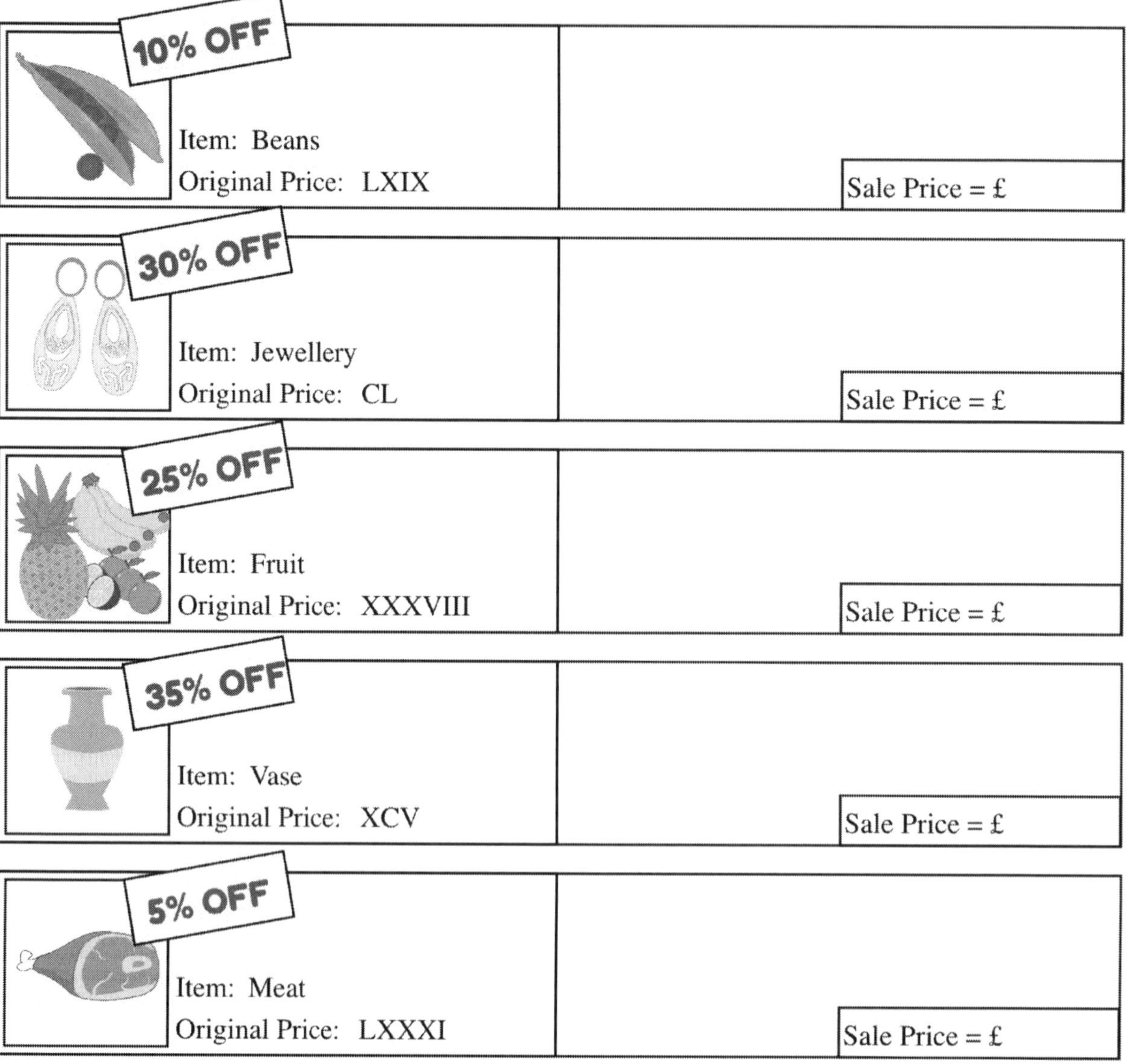

Roman Numerals Sheet 18

Roman Numerals Market

1	2	3	4	5	6	7	8	9	10
I	II	III	IV	V	VI	VII	VIII	IX	X

10	20	30	40	50	60	70	80	90	100
X	XX	XXX	XL	L	LX	LXX	LXXX	XC	C

500	1000
D	M

Medium

There is a sale on at the Roman markets! Convert the Roman numeral price tags to Arabic numerals and calculate the final sale price of each item (after reductions). Round answer to 2 decimal places

35% OFF

Item: Goblet
Original Price: CXXXV

Sale Price = £

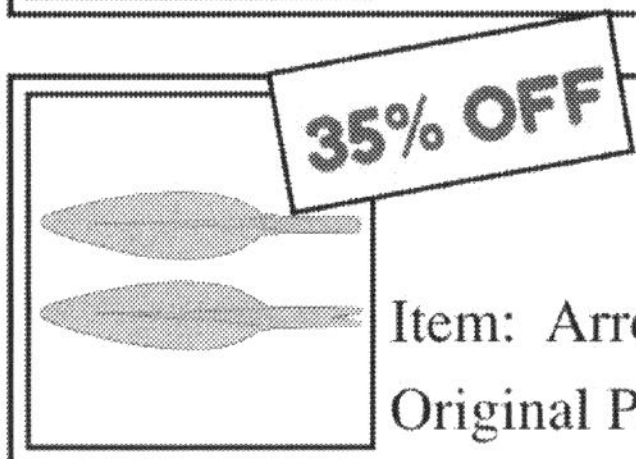

35% OFF

Item: Arrow Heads
Original Price: XLIX

Sale Price = £

10% OFF

Item: Chicken
Original Price: CXVII

Sale Price = £

20% OFF

Item: Sword
Original Price: LXX

Sale Price = £

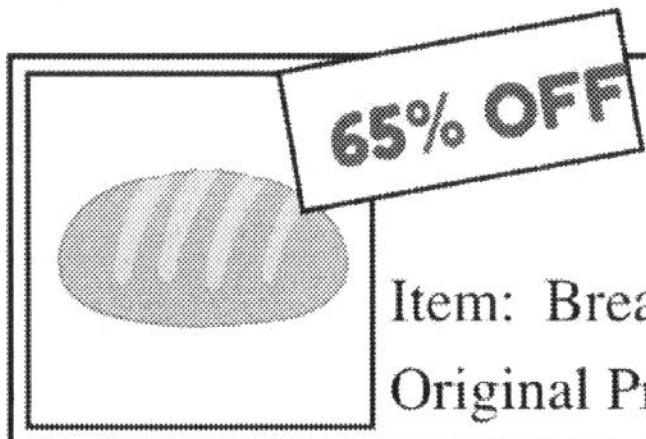

65% OFF

Item: Bread
Original Price: XXXIX

Sale Price = £

Roman Numerals Sheet 19

Roman Numerals Market

1	2	3	4	5	6	7	8	9	10
I	II	III	IV	V	VI	VII	VIII	IX	X

10	20	30	40	50	60	70	80	90	100
X	XX	XXX	XL	L	LX	LXX	LXXX	XC	C

500	1000
D	M

Medium

There is a sale on at the Roman markets! Convert the Roman numeral price tags to Arabic numerals and calculate the final sale price of each item (after reductions). Round answer to 2 decimal places

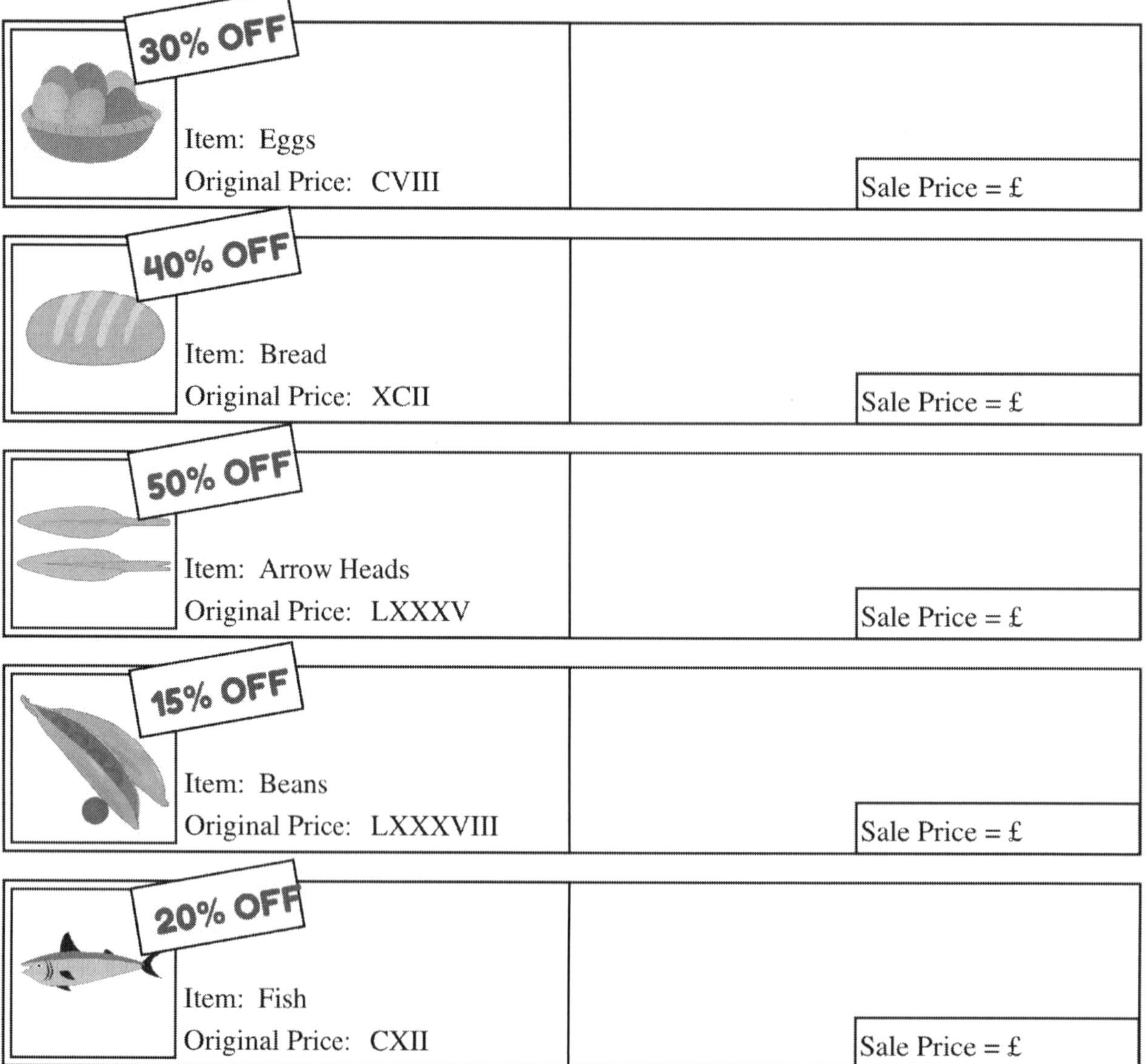

30% OFF
Item: Eggs
Original Price: CVIII
Sale Price = £

40% OFF
Item: Bread
Original Price: XCII
Sale Price = £

50% OFF
Item: Arrow Heads
Original Price: LXXXV
Sale Price = £

15% OFF
Item: Beans
Original Price: LXXXVIII
Sale Price = £

20% OFF
Item: Fish
Original Price: CXII
Sale Price = £

Roman Numerals Sheet 20

Roman Numerals Market

1	2	3	4	5	6	7	8	9	10
I	II	III	IV	V	VI	VII	VIII	IX	X

10	20	30	40	50	60	70	80	90	100
X	XX	XXX	XL	L	LX	LXX	LXXX	XC	C

500	1000
D	M

Medium

There is a sale on at the Roman markets! Convert the Roman numeral price tags to Arabic numerals and calculate the final sale price of each item (after reductions). Round answer to 2 decimal places

55% OFF

Item: Beans
Original Price: CVIII

Sale Price = £

5% OFF

Item: Sword
Original Price: CX

Sale Price = £

25% OFF

Item: Fruit
Original Price: CV

Sale Price = £

45% OFF

Item: Bread
Original Price: XXXVIII

Sale Price = £

10% OFF

Item: Arrow Heads
Original Price: LX

Sale Price = £

Roman Numerals Sheet 21

Roman Numerals Market

1	2	3	4	5	6	7	8	9	10
I	II	III	IV	V	VI	VII	VIII	IX	X

10	20	30	40	50	60	70	80	90	100
X	XX	XXX	XL	L	LX	LXX	LXXX	XC	C

500	1000
D	M

Medium

There is a sale on at the Roman markets! Convert the Roman numeral price tags to Arabic numerals and calculate the final sale price of each item (after reductions). Round answer to 2 decimal places

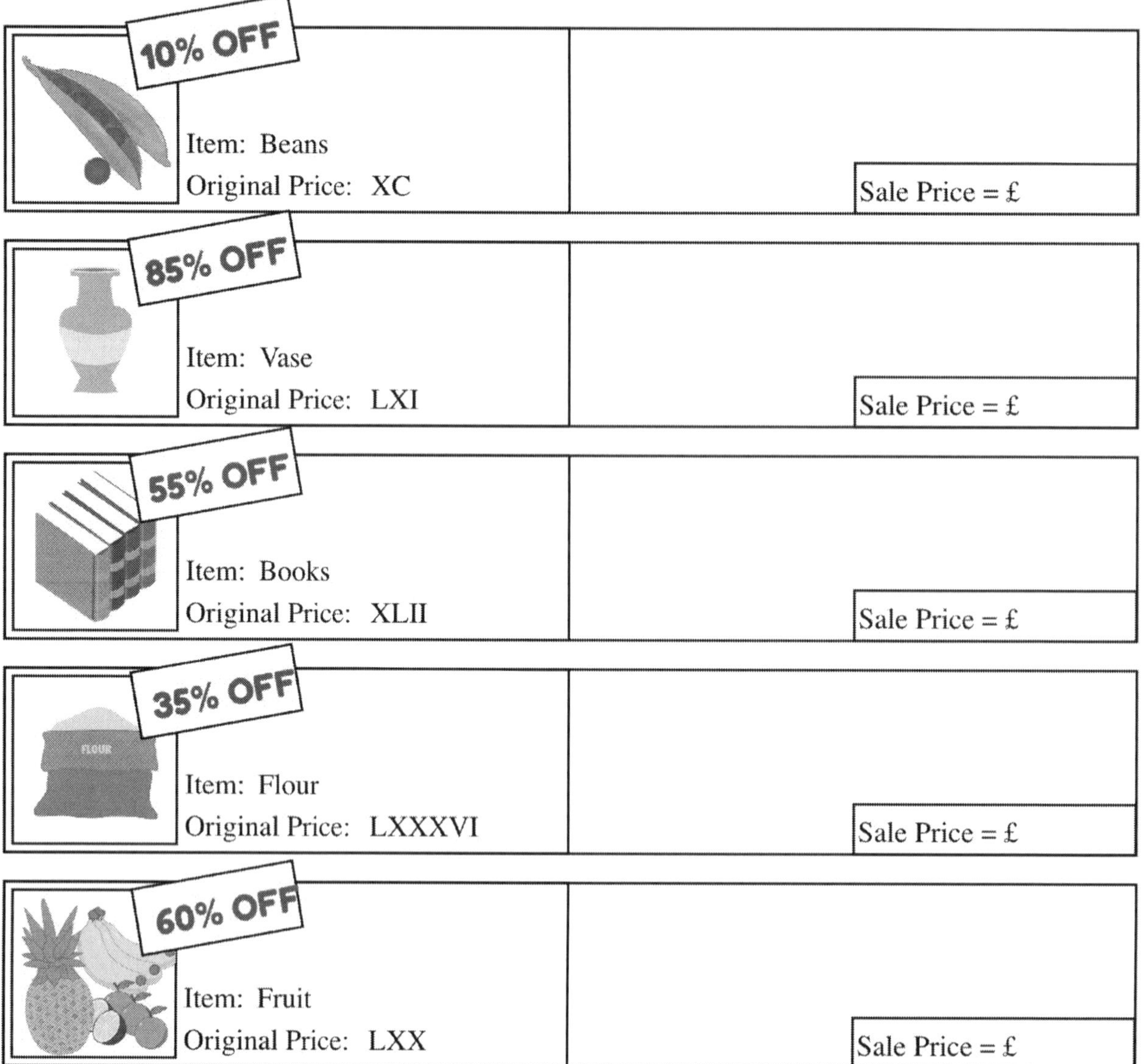

Roman Numerals Sheet 22

Roman Numerals Market

1	2	3	4	5	6	7	8	9	10
I	II	III	IV	V	VI	VII	VIII	IX	X

10	20	30	40	50	60	70	80	90	100
X	XX	XXX	XL	L	LX	LXX	LXXX	XC	C

500	1000
D	M

Medium

There is a sale on at the Roman markets! Convert the Roman numeral price tags to Arabic numerals and calculate the final sale price of each item (after reductions). Round answer to 2 decimal places

50% OFF

Item: Fruit
Original Price: XC

Sale Price = £

85% OFF

Item: Flour
Original Price: LXXX

Sale Price = £

55% OFF

Item: Bread
Original Price: CI

Sale Price = £

25% OFF

Item: Arrow Heads
Original Price: CXII

Sale Price = £

85% OFF

Item: Goblet
Original Price: XLVIII

Sale Price = £

Roman Numerals Sheet 23

Roman Numerals Market

1	2	3	4	5	6	7	8	9	10
I	II	III	IV	V	VI	VII	VIII	IX	X

10	20	30	40	50	60	70	80	90	100
X	XX	XXX	XL	L	LX	LXX	LXXX	XC	C

500	1000
D	M

Hard

There is a sale on at the Roman markets! Convert the Roman numeral price tags to Arabic numerals and calculate the final sale price of each item (after reductions). Round answer to 2 decimal places

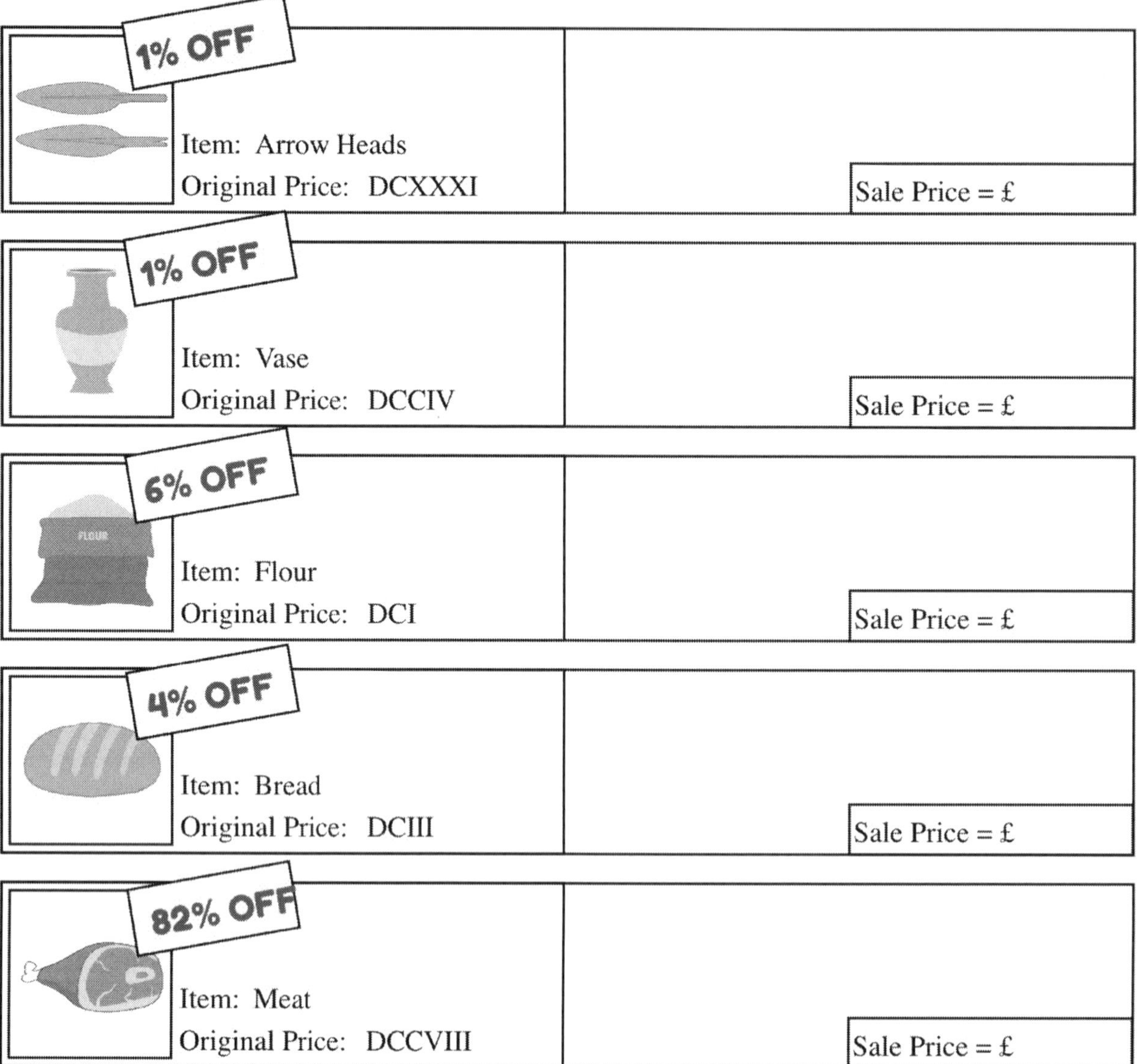

1% OFF
Item: Arrow Heads
Original Price: DCXXXI
Sale Price = £

1% OFF
Item: Vase
Original Price: DCCIV
Sale Price = £

6% OFF
Item: Flour
Original Price: DCI
Sale Price = £

4% OFF
Item: Bread
Original Price: DCIII
Sale Price = £

82% OFF
Item: Meat
Original Price: DCCVIII
Sale Price = £

Roman Numerals Sheet 24

Roman Numerals Market

1	2	3	4	5	6	7	8	9	10
I	II	III	IV	V	VI	VII	VIII	IX	X

10	20	30	40	50	60	70	80	90	100
X	XX	XXX	XL	L	LX	LXX	LXXX	XC	C

500	1000
D	M

Hard

There is a sale on at the Roman markets! Convert the Roman numeral price tags to Arabic numerals and calculate the final sale price of each item (after reductions). Round answer to 2 decimal places

76% OFF

Item: Arrow Heads
Original Price: DCXVIII

Sale Price = £

76% OFF

Item: Chicken
Original Price: DCLXX

Sale Price = £

64% OFF

Item: Eggs
Original Price: DXXXVII

Sale Price = £

93% OFF

Item: Vase
Original Price: DCCLVI

Sale Price = £

58% OFF

Item: Jewellery
Original Price: DCCLXXX

Sale Price = £

Roman Numerals Sheet 25

Roman Numerals Market

1	2	3	4	5	6	7	8	9	10
I	II	III	IV	V	VI	VII	VIII	IX	X

10	20	30	40	50	60	70	80	90	100
X	XX	XXX	XL	L	LX	LXX	LXXX	XC	C

500	1000
D	M

Hard

There is a sale on at the Roman markets! Convert the Roman numeral price tags to Arabic numerals and calculate the final sale price of each item (after reductions). Round answer to 2 decimal places

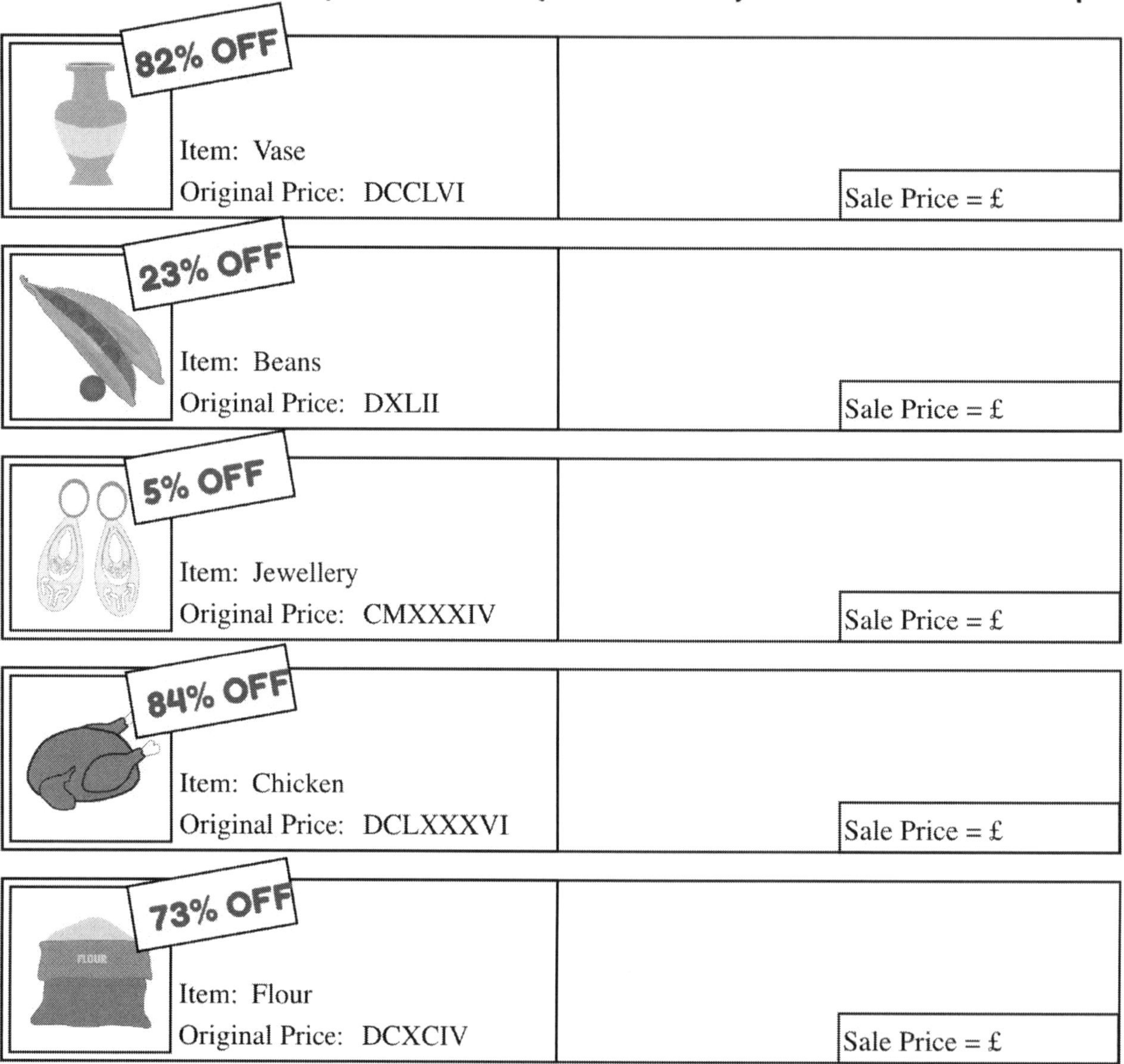

Roman Numerals Sheet 26

Roman Numerals Market

1	2	3	4	5	6	7	8	9	10
I	II	III	IV	V	VI	VII	VIII	IX	X

10	20	30	40	50	60	70	80	90	100
X	XX	XXX	XL	L	LX	LXX	LXXX	XC	C

500	1000
D	M

Hard

There is a sale on at the Roman markets! Convert the Roman numeral price tags to Arabic numerals and calculate the final sale price of each item (after reductions). Round answer to 2 decimal places

92% OFF

Item: Jewellery
Original Price: DCCCLXIV

Sale Price = £

83% OFF

Item: Books
Original Price: DCXXXVIII

Sale Price = £

83% OFF

Item: Goblet
Original Price: DCCLIX

Sale Price = £

77% OFF

Item: Fruit
Original Price: DCXXVI

Sale Price = £

43% OFF

Item: Eggs
Original Price: DCXLIV

Sale Price = £

Roman Numerals Sheet 27

Roman Numerals Market

1	2	3	4	5	6	7	8	9	10
I	II	III	IV	V	VI	VII	VIII	IX	X

10	20	30	40	50	60	70	80	90	100
X	XX	XXX	XL	L	LX	LXX	LXXX	XC	C

500	1000
D	M

Hard

There is a sale on at the Roman markets! Convert the Roman numeral price tags to Arabic numerals and calculate the final sale price of each item (after reductions). Round answer to 2 decimal places

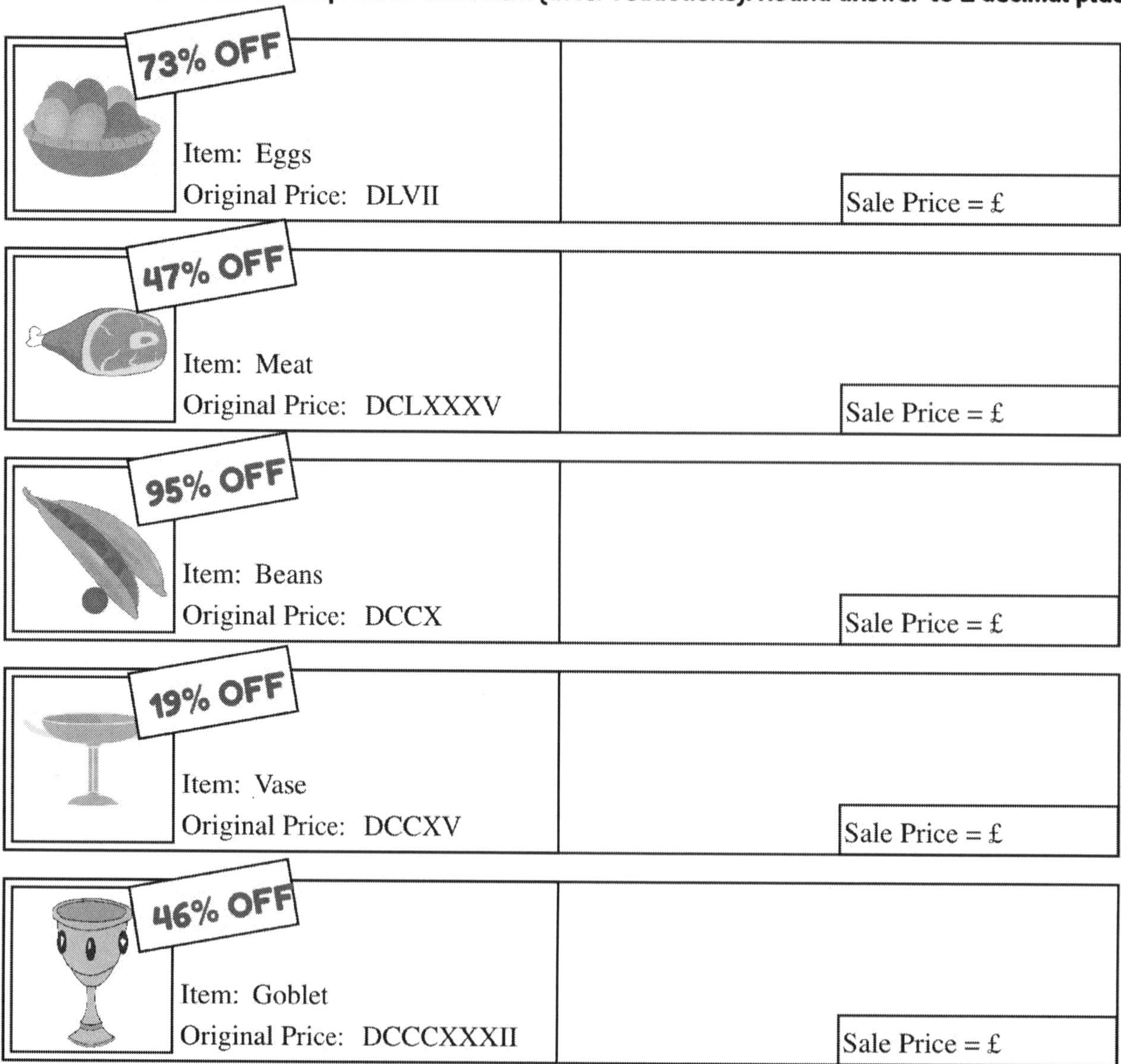

73% OFF
Item: Eggs
Original Price: DLVII
Sale Price = £

47% OFF
Item: Meat
Original Price: DCLXXXV
Sale Price = £

95% OFF
Item: Beans
Original Price: DCCX
Sale Price = £

19% OFF
Item: Vase
Original Price: DCCXV
Sale Price = £

46% OFF
Item: Goblet
Original Price: DCCCXXXII
Sale Price = £

Roman Numerals Sheet 28

Roman Numerals Market

1	2	3	4	5	6	7	8	9	10
I	II	III	IV	V	VI	VII	VIII	IX	X

10	20	30	40	50	60	70	80	90	100
X	XX	XXX	XL	L	LX	LXX	LXXX	XC	C

500	1000
D	M

Hard

There is a sale on at the Roman markets! Convert the Roman numeral price tags to Arabic numerals and calculate the final sale price of each item (after reductions). Round answer to 2 decimal places

86% OFF

Item: Meat
Original Price: DCI

Sale Price = £

3% OFF

Item: Sword
Original Price: DCXCIV

Sale Price = £

10% OFF

Item: Beans
Original Price: DLXXIV

Sale Price = £

14% OFF

Item: Bread
Original Price: DLXXXI

Sale Price = £

83% OFF

Item: Chicken
Original Price: DCCLXXI

Sale Price = £

Roman Numerals Sheet 29

Roman Numerals Market

1	2	3	4	5	6	7	8	9	10
I	II	III	IV	V	VI	VII	VIII	IX	X

10	20	30	40	50	60	70	80	90	100
X	XX	XXX	XL	L	LX	LXX	LXXX	XC	C

500	1000
D	M

Hard

There is a sale on at the Roman markets! Convert the Roman numeral price tags to Arabic numerals and calculate the final sale price of each item (after reductions). Round answer to 2 decimal places

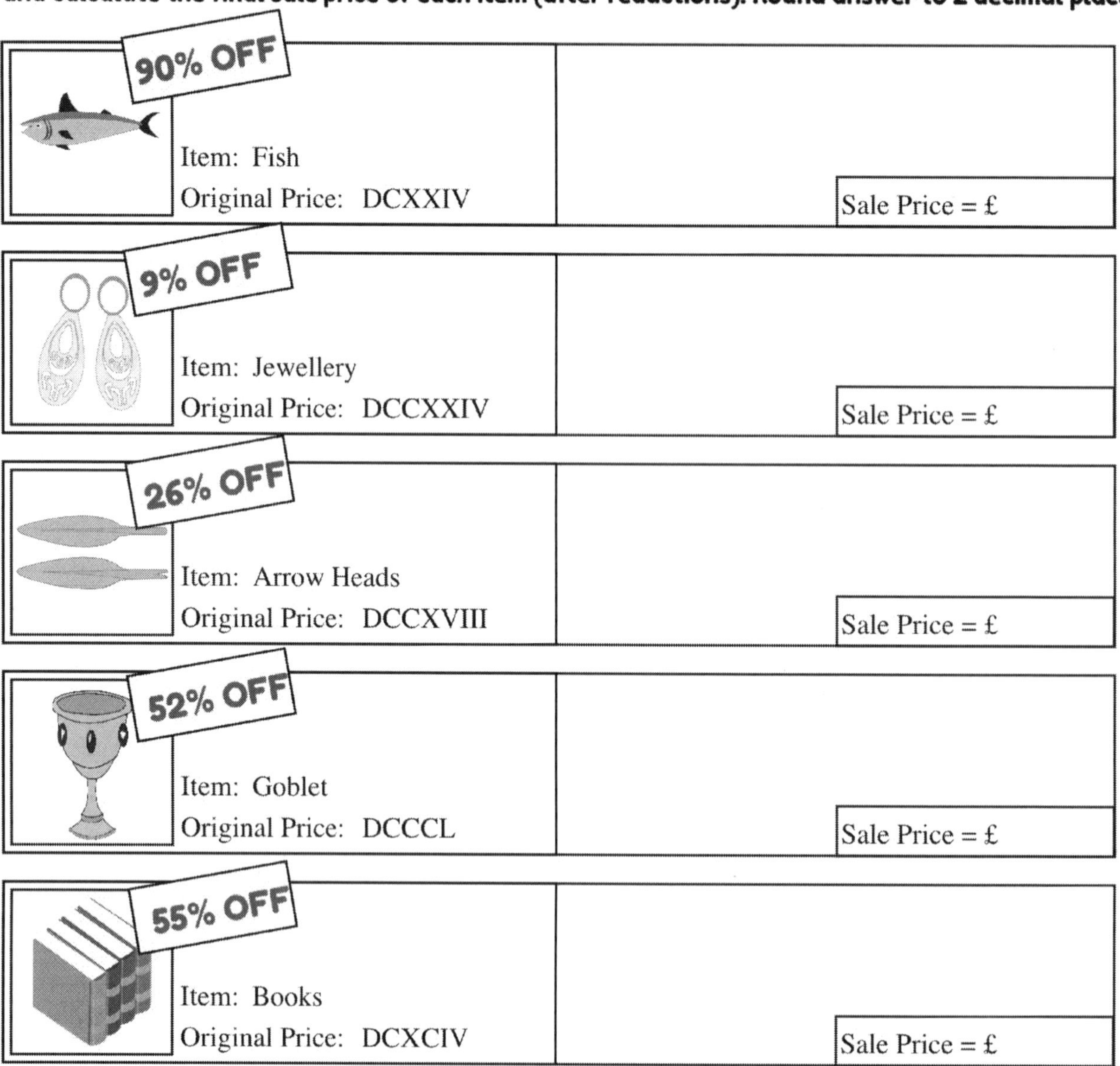
90% OFF
Item: Fish
Original Price: DCXXIV
Sale Price = £

9% OFF
Item: Jewellery
Original Price: DCCXXIV
Sale Price = £

26% OFF
Item: Arrow Heads
Original Price: DCCXVIII
Sale Price = £

52% OFF
Item: Goblet
Original Price: DCCCL
Sale Price = £

55% OFF
Item: Books
Original Price: DCXCIV
Sale Price = £

Roman Numerals Sheet 30

Roman Numerals Market

1	2	3	4	5	6	7	8	9	10
I	II	III	IV	V	VI	VII	VIII	IX	X

10	20	30	40	50	60	70	80	90	100
X	XX	XXX	XL	L	LX	LXX	LXXX	XC	C

500	1000
D	M

Hard

There is a sale on at the Roman markets! Convert the Roman numeral price tags to Arabic numerals and calculate the final sale price of each item (after reductions). Round answer to 2 decimal places

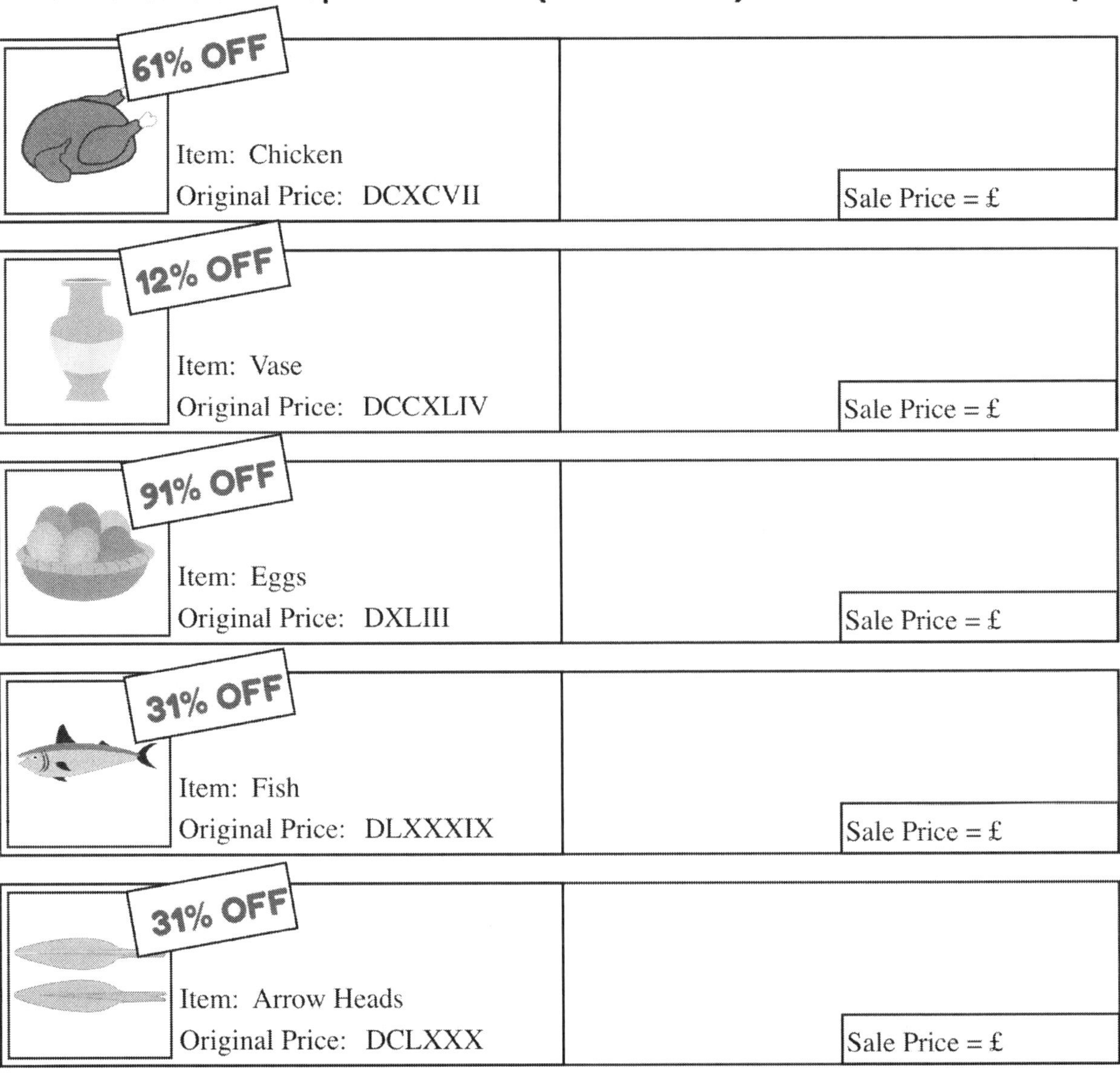

Logic Puzzles

LOGIC PUZZLES

8 x Sudoku Puzzles

6 x Two Dimensional Mazes

14 x Three Dimensional Mazes

Sudoku

The goal of a sudoku is to fill in the missing numbers. Via logical deduction, the player must place the numbers 1-9 in every row, column and in each of the nine square grids.

	4			6	8			7
9			7	5			2	1
7		5		2		6		4
5		1	3			7		
					1	9	3	5
3	9	7	8			2		
		8	4					
	7	9	6	1		5	8	3
2	1	3		8	7	4		

Mazes

Either climb ladders, or navigate through walls to solve each maze.

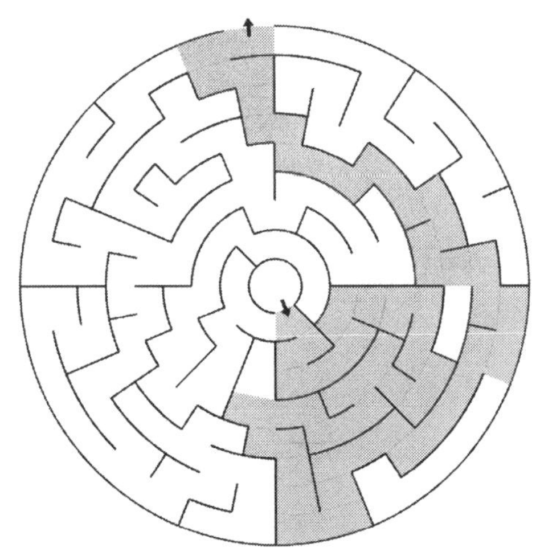

(Climb up/down the ladders)

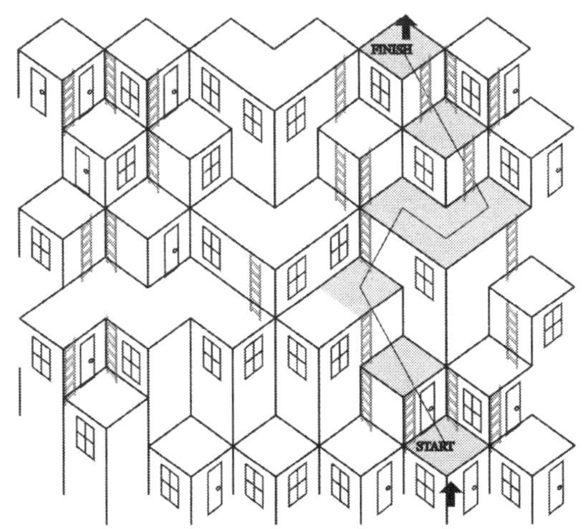

Sudoku Sheet 1
(Single)

	7	9			3	6		1
	3						5	
		2	6	4				8
		3	2		6	5		
9				8				3
6	2	5	9		4	1		7
		7		9		8		
	9	4	1		8	7		6
1		8			7	4	2	

Sudoku Sheet 2
(Single)

8		3		5	4		1	
	2		7	1			4	
9			2	3		5		7
		4	1	9	7	6	5	2
		5		4	2	8		
2				8	6	4	7	
4				2	1			6
6				7				
		2		6	3		8	

Sudoku Sheet 3
(Double)

9			5			7	3	1						
	8	3	6		7			4						
		1		2				6						
8		6			5		4	7						
7	3	5			1		6	2						
1		9				3								
	5			7		8			1			7		
	9	7	8		6	4			6	7			5	9
3						6		5	2	9		1		3
							3	7	8		9	6		4
								1			7	8		5
							8				6			7
							5	2		3		4	6	
									4		5		7	
							4	6						1

Sudoku Sheet 4
(Double)

						9		4	5			3		6
						7			9	6				
							8	3		4		9		2
									2		9	4		
						5	3	9			6		8	
						2		6				1	9	5
	9	8	1		2	3			8			6		9
	3				5	8	9			3		7	2	4
7			3				6		1	9	7		3	
5		9		3			1	6						
	2	3				9	4	8						
	4	7	8	9			3							
	6			4	3	5		9						
3		2		5				4						
		4		2	8	1	7							

Sudoku Sheet 5
(Triple)

									4		2	9								
						9				1			6							
						8	4	3				5								
							7	9	1	8	5	6		2						
						6	8		3				1	9						
								2	9	6		7	8							
8	7	1		3		2		6			3			7	9		8	6		5
	4			1			5				1		9		5	1			7	3
6	5					7	1		2	9	6				7	2		1		9
		5	8			4	6	2				5	7	1					9	
					3		8	9						2	3	9				1
	8	2	6				7					3					1		5	
1				4		9	2						2	5	4					
9	2		1			8		7				6		8			9	4	3	7
		7	9	8		6	4					9	3	4		8	7			

Sudoku Sheet 6
(Triple)

									4			9	5	6						
											5		3	7						
						5	8	7		6	3	2	4	1						
						8	4			2		3	7							
							2		3	4	9	5	1							
									5	7	8			4						
		8	6	5	4	1	3	2					8		3	2		9		1
		3	8	1		9					2	1	6		4			2	8	
		1	9	3		6				3		4			5	8		6	3	7
		4	7		1	3	2	6				2	5		1		9		7	
		9		6	5	4	8	7				6		4	7			1		
6	7												7			4	3	5	6	8
	4				8	2		9				3		9		7			5	4
	8					7	6	3					4			1		3		
		7		2	6			5						6					1	

Sudoku Sheet 7
(Hard)

6		3	7			9		1				3	6	9	7		2	8	1	
		1	9			7	4	2					2	5	6		1		7	
	9	4			1	3	6								9	8		3		2
4			6				7	8				5	8	2	3		4		9	
				7		5	9	3						1	8	5		2		
8	7				2	6	1	4						3	1					
1	6	8	5	2			3			6		2	1			9				
9			8		3	1			4			9		6		7	8	1		4
3	5			9		8				9			5		2	1		9	8	3
						3	9				2	6	7	1						
							4			1			2							
						2	7	1	6	5	9									
	7	9	2	6		5	1	3	2	8		7			3		1	5		
	6		9	4	1	7	8	2	9			1			8	2	7	4	3	9
	2		3		7	9	6				1	3	8	2	9		5			
7		6	1	9	3		4	8				2			6		3		5	
	9	8	7			3		6						3		9	2	6		
2	3											6				8			9	3
	8						2	1				5	2	6	1					4
5			6	1	2		7	9				4		1	2	7				
		2												8	4		6	3	1	2

Sudoku Sheet 8
(Hard)

	5	1			4		3					5			8			1		7
	4	9	2			5		6					8	2	6			9		4
		6		1			7	2					7	4	9	1	2		6	8
8				5		6	4	1									4	8		5
4	3			8								7	9		1		8			6
	1	7	9		2	3						8	4	3					1	
		4	8	9					4	8		6	2	1	3		5			9
9		3	1	2	5					2			3						5	
	6					1		9	3						2					
													4							
						4	3	1	2		8	7	6	9						
						6	8	2					1	5						
9			8			5			8	6		2	9	4	3	5	6			7
	2		4			3	9		5					6	8					
		8			3	2	4				7				2	1				9
3		5			8		6	2					4	9			5		3	
	6		3			1		4						7		3	9		1	
	4			2	6									5			2			
1	8						3					4						9	7	
4	9		2	3	1	8	7	5						8		7	1			6
5	7					4						7	6	2	9		3	8	5	1

Maze Puzzle 1
(Square)

Maze Puzzle 2
(Square)

Maze Puzzle 3
(Spiral)

Maze Puzzle 4
(Spiral)

Maze Puzzle 5
(Diamond)

Maze Puzzle 6
(Diamond)

Maze Puzzle 7
(Medium)

Maze Puzzle 8
(Medium)

Maze Puzzle 9
(Medium)

Maze Puzzle 10
(Medium)

Maze Puzzle 11
(Medium)

Maze Puzzle 12
(Medium)

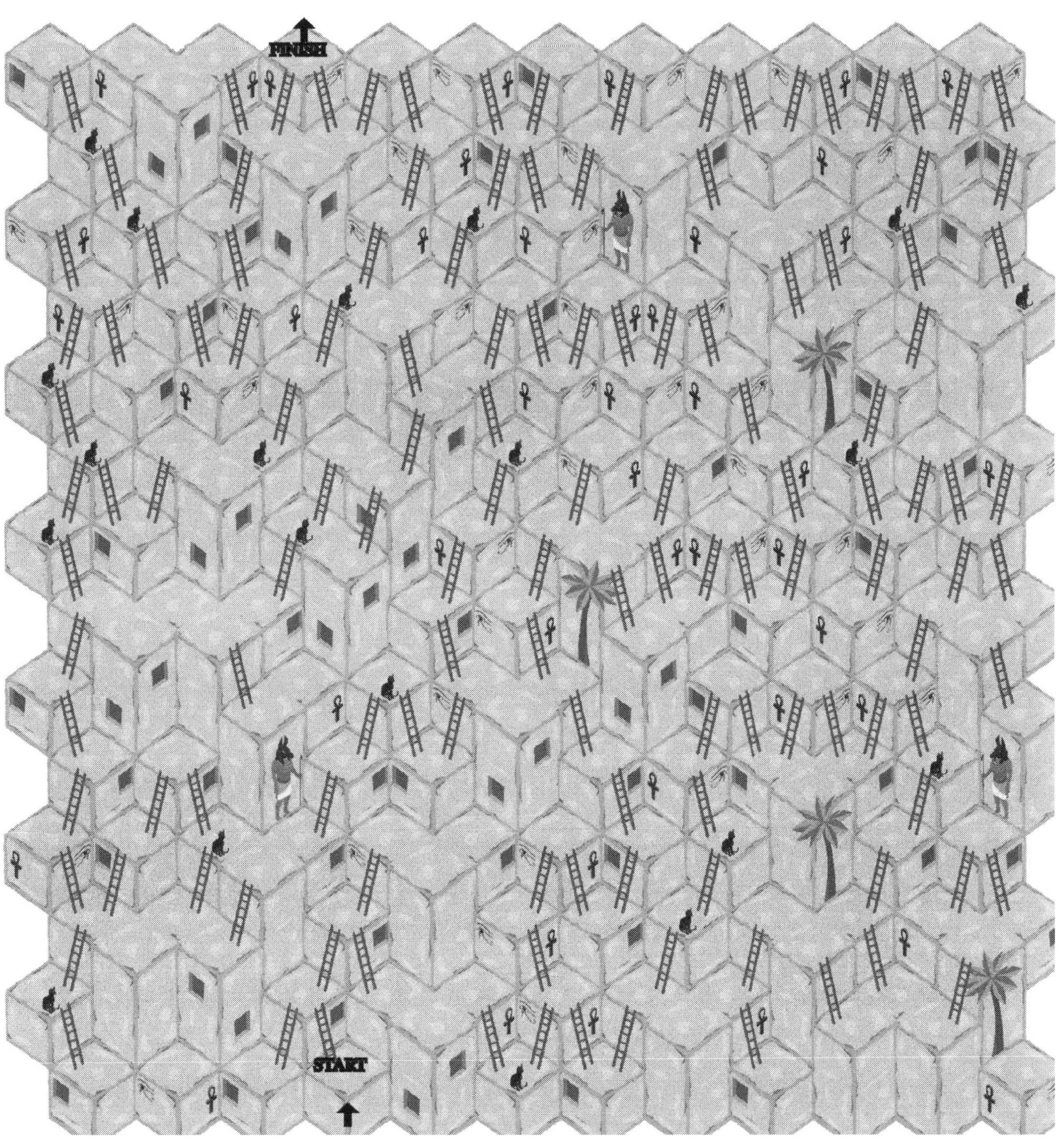

Maze Puzzle 13 (Medium)

Maze Puzzle 14
(Medium)

Maze Puzzle 15
(Medium)

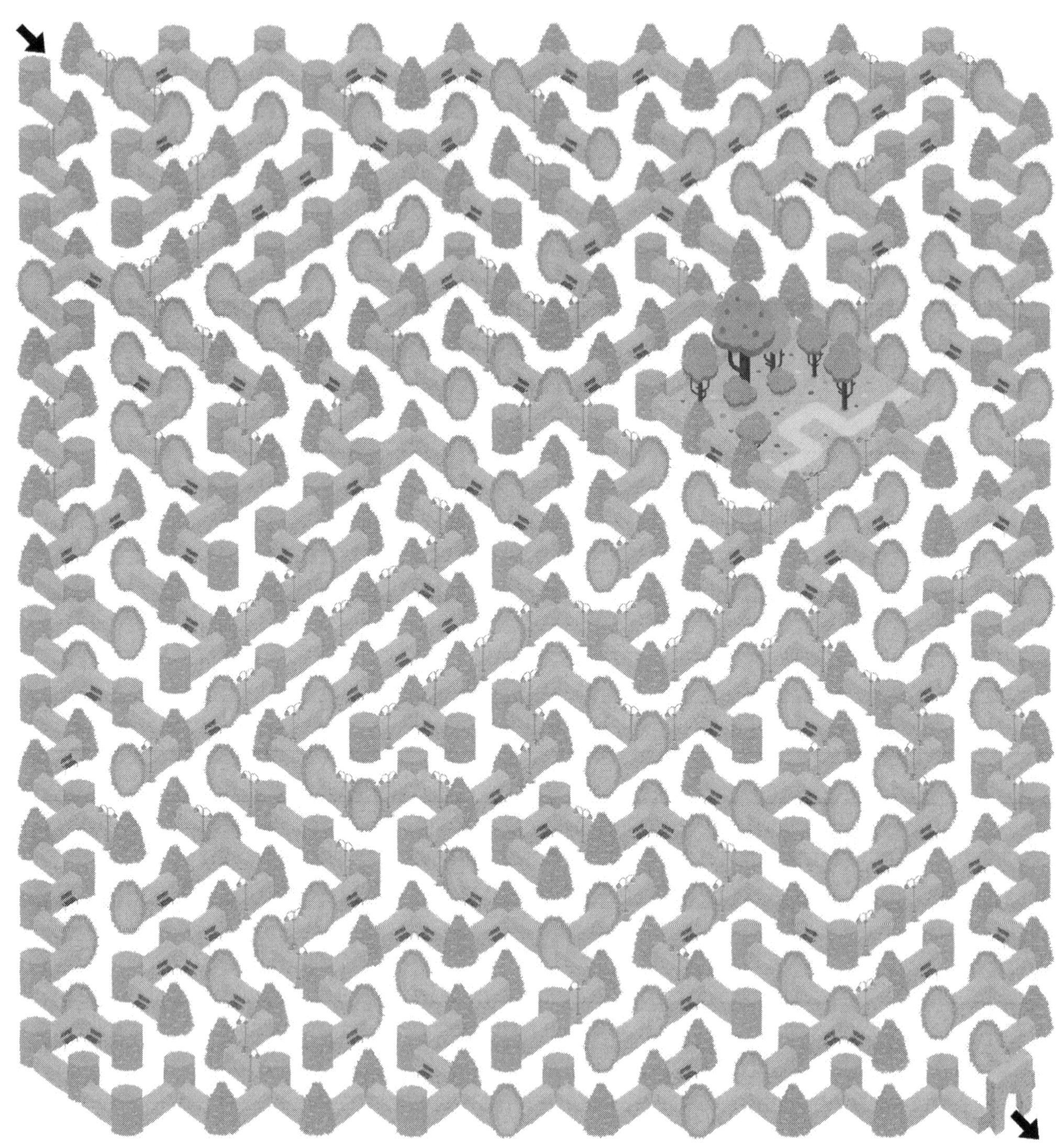

Maze Puzzle 16
(Hard)

Maze Puzzle 17
(Hard)

Maze Puzzle 18
(Hard)

Maze Puzzle 19
(Hard)

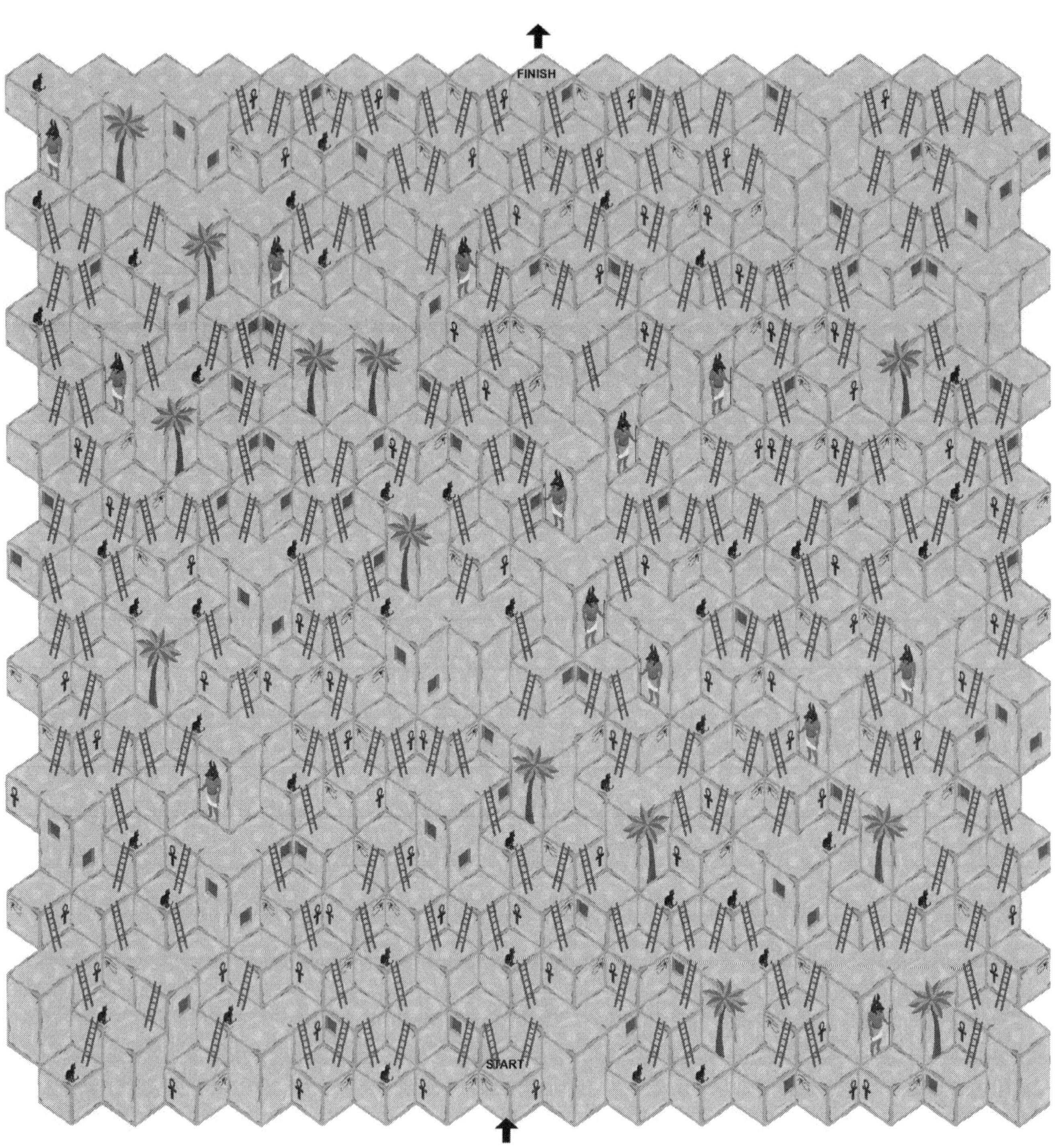

Maze Puzzle 20
(Hard)

All Puzzles Solutions

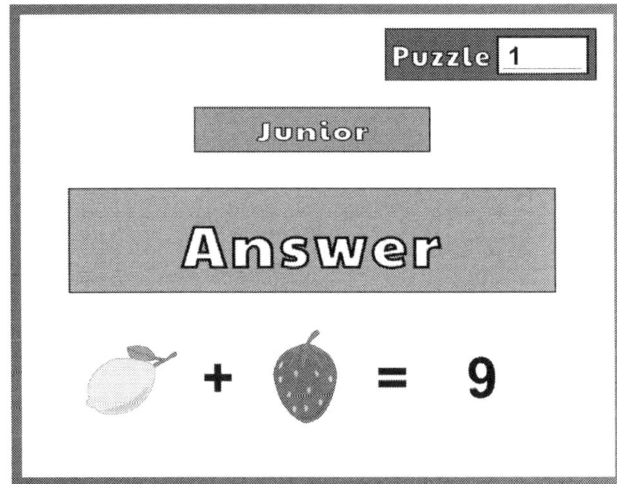
Puzzle 1
Junior
Answer
+ = 9

Puzzle 2
Junior
Answer
- = 1

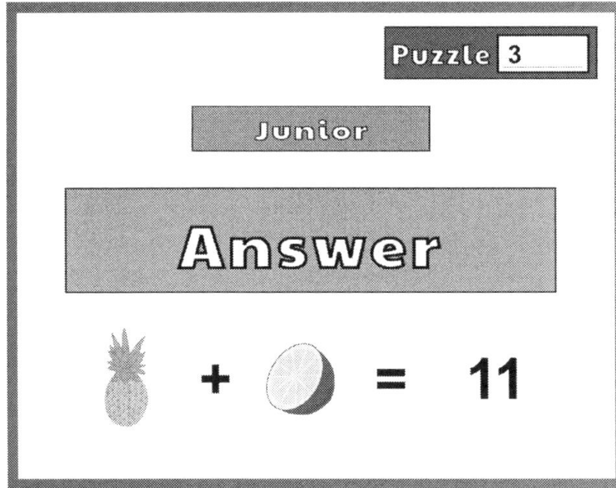
Puzzle 3
Junior
Answer
+ = 11

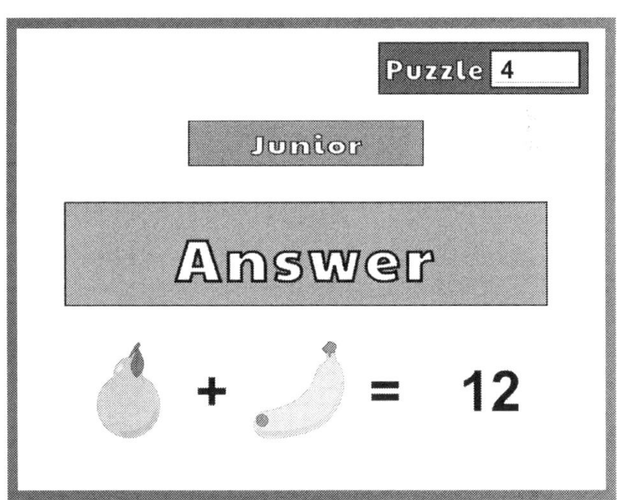
Puzzle 4
Junior
Answer
+ = 12

Puzzle 5
Junior
Answer
+ = 16

Puzzle 6
Junior
Answer
- = 3

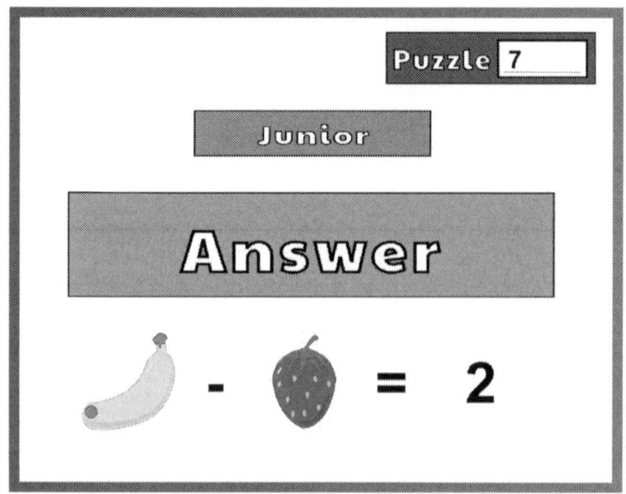
Puzzle 7
Junior
Answer
- = 2

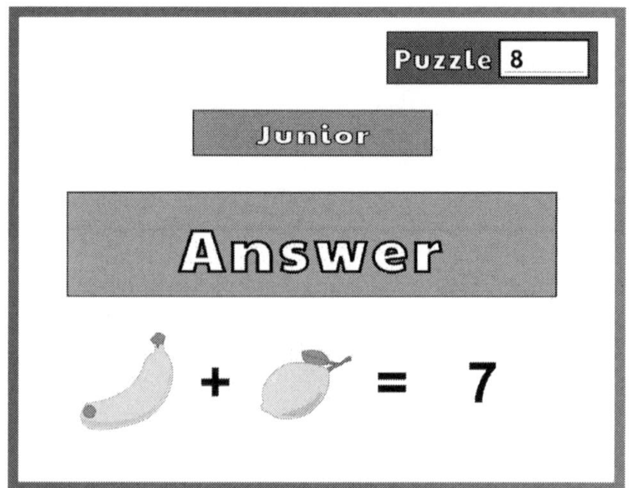
Puzzle 8
Junior
Answer
+ = 7

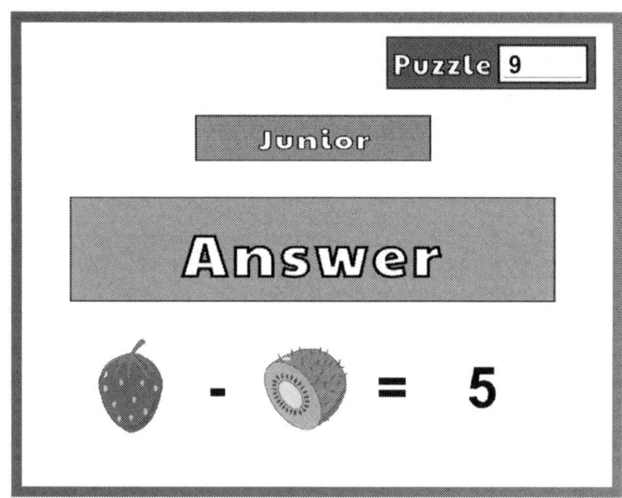
Puzzle 9
Junior
Answer
- = 5

Puzzle 10
Junior
Answer
+ = 13

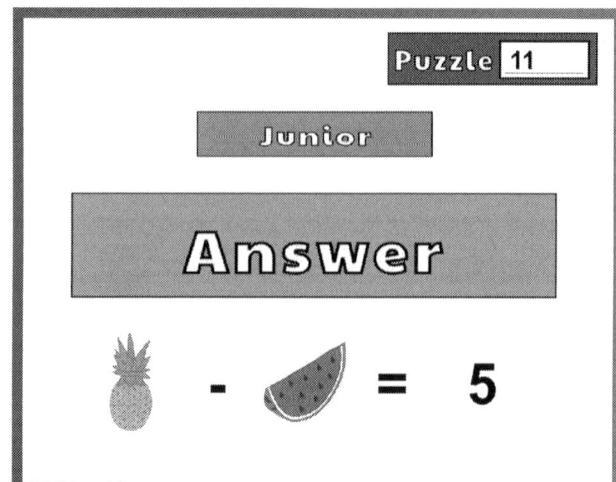
Puzzle 11
Junior
Answer
- = 5

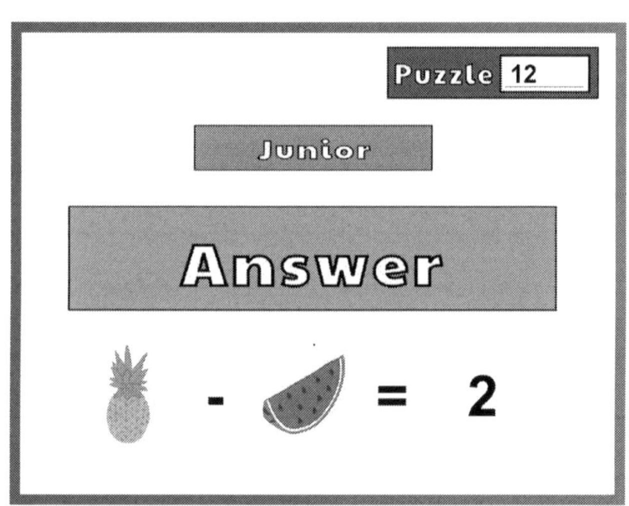
Puzzle 12
Junior
Answer
- = 2

Puzzle 13
Junior
Answer
+ = 5

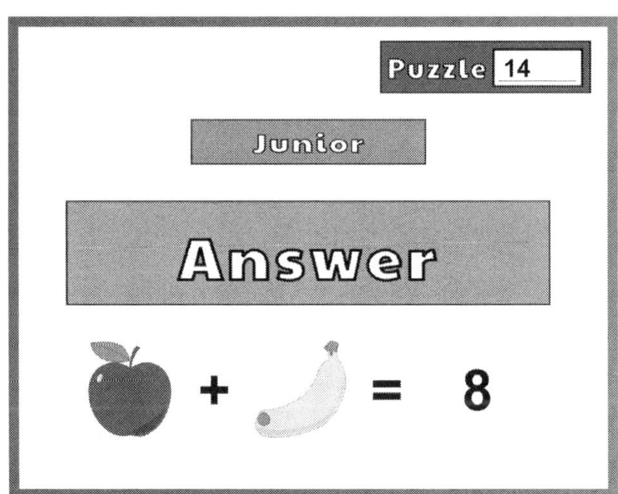
Puzzle 14
Junior
Answer
+ = 8

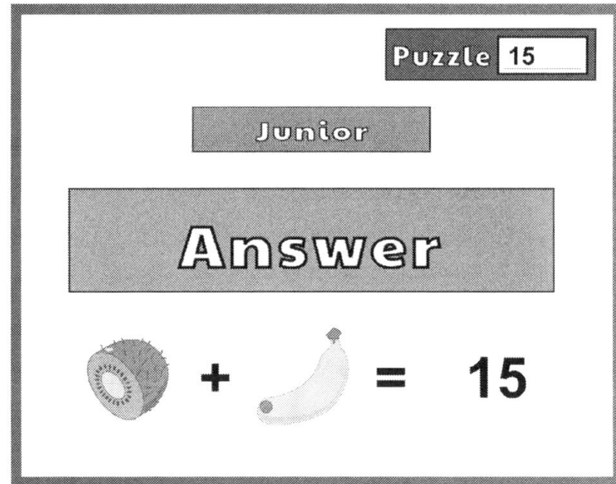
Puzzle 15
Junior
Answer
+ = 15

Puzzle 16
Junior
Answer
+ = 10

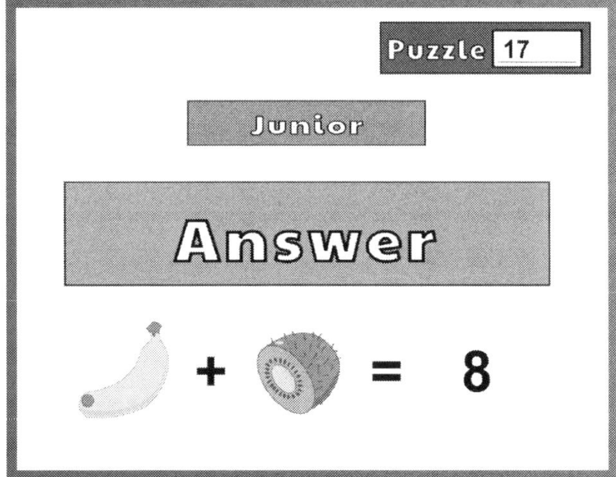
Puzzle 17
Junior
Answer
+ = 8

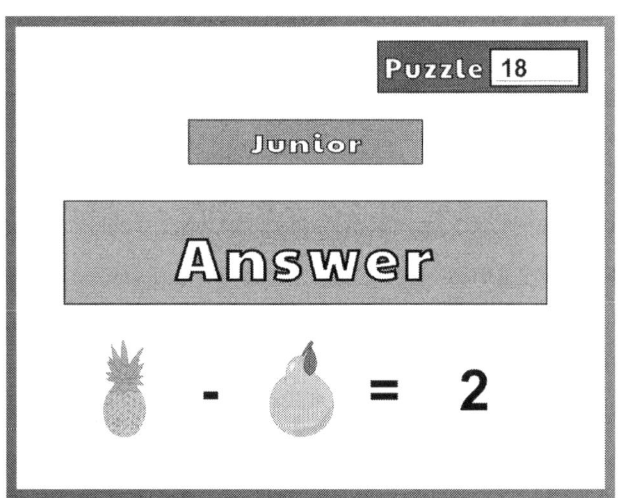
Puzzle 18
Junior
Answer
- = 2

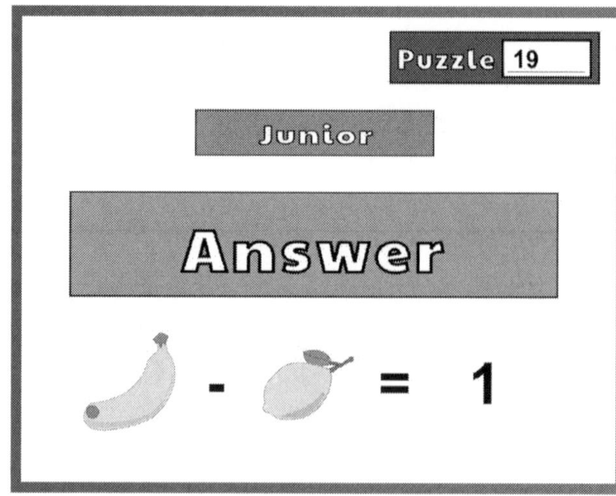
Puzzle 19
Junior
Answer
- = 1

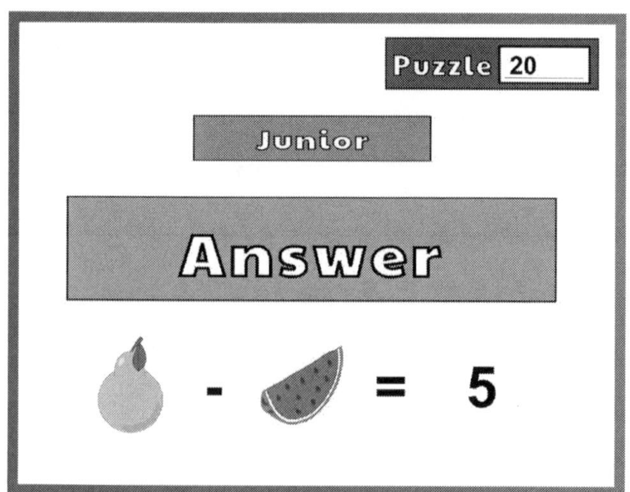
Puzzle 20
Junior
Answer
- = 5

Puzzle 21
Junior
Answer
- = 3

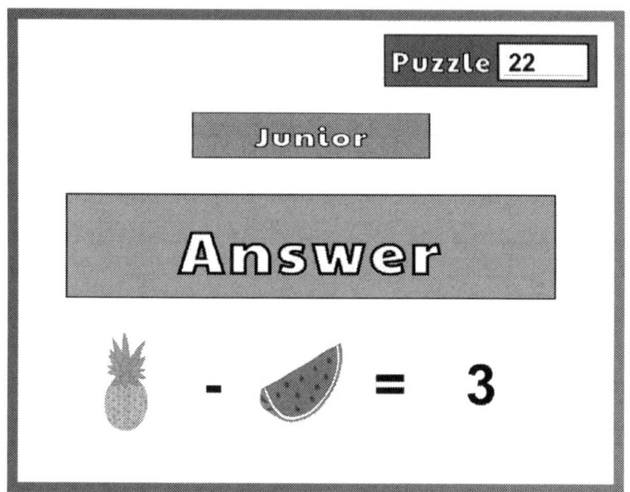
Puzzle 22
Junior
Answer
- = 3

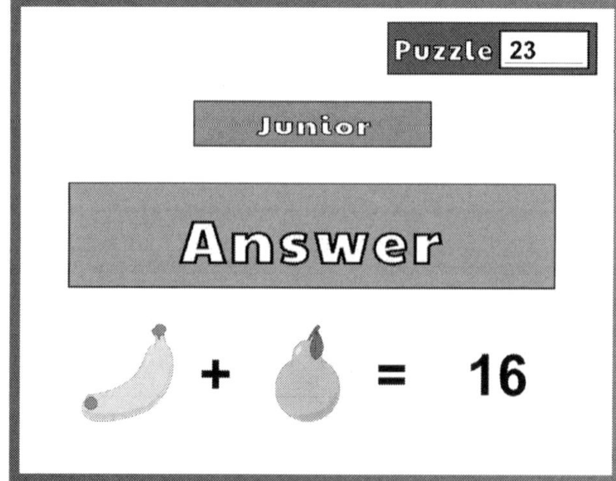
Puzzle 23
Junior
Answer
+ = 16

Puzzle 24
Junior
Answer
+ = 17

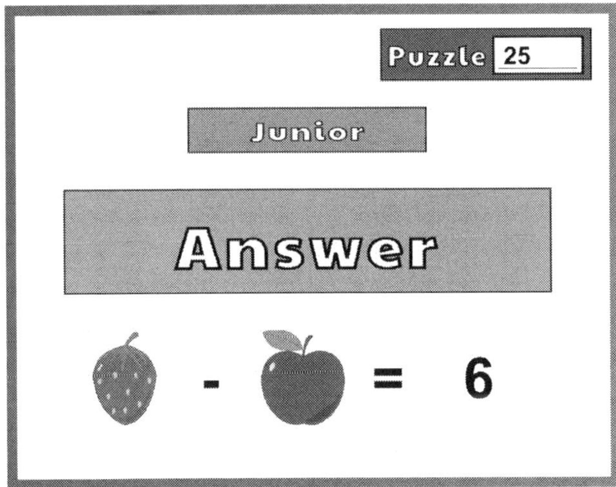
Puzzle 25
Junior
Answer
- = 6

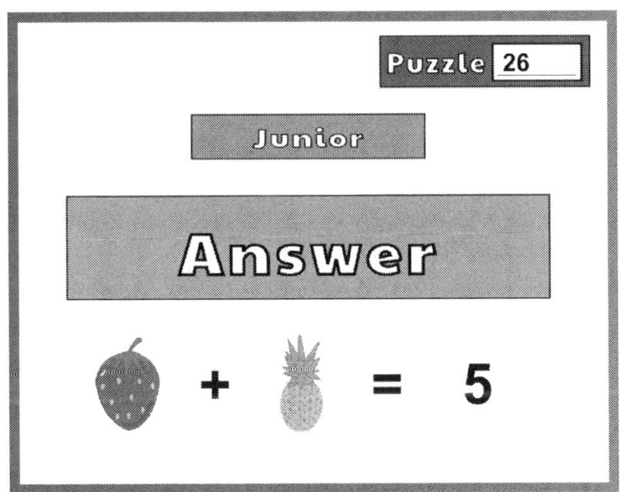
Puzzle 26
Junior
Answer
+ = 5

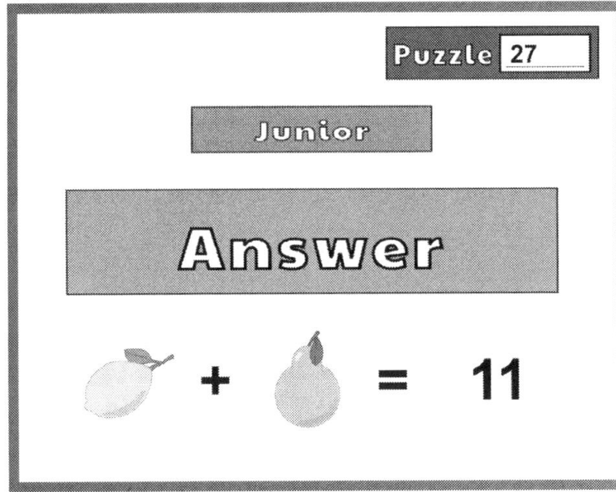
Puzzle 27
Junior
Answer
+ = 11

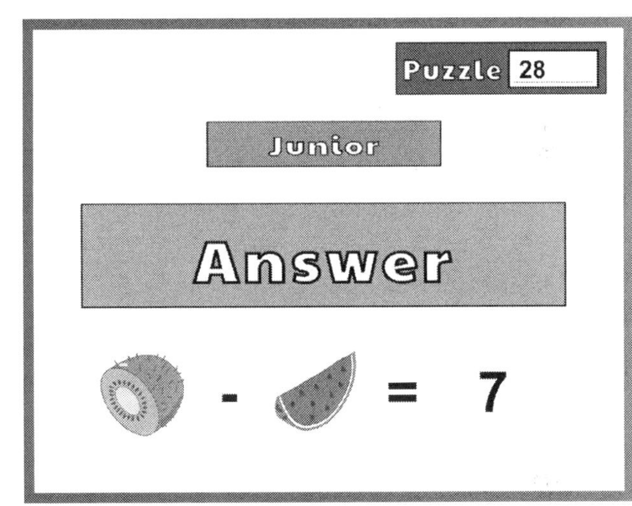
Puzzle 28
Junior
Answer
- = 7

Puzzle 29
Junior
Answer
- = 4

Puzzle 30
Junior
Answer
+ = 13

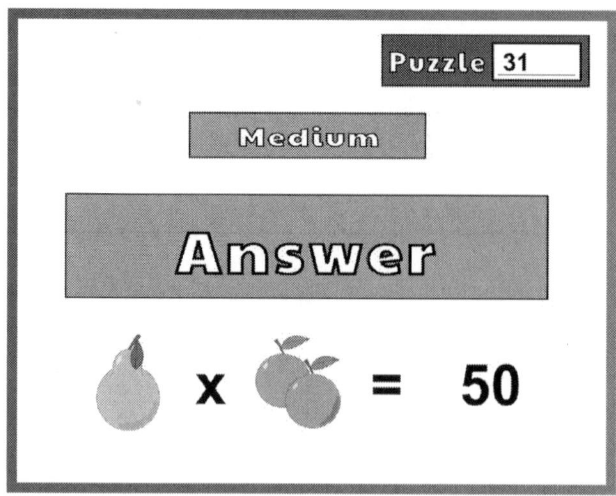
Puzzle 31
Medium
Answer
x
=
50

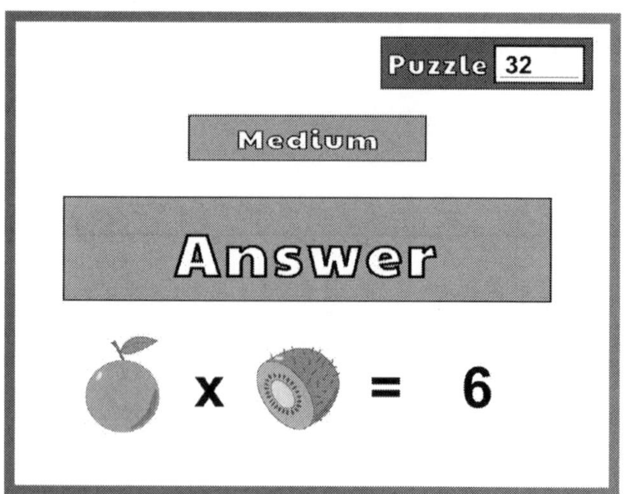
Puzzle 32
Medium
Answer
x
=
6

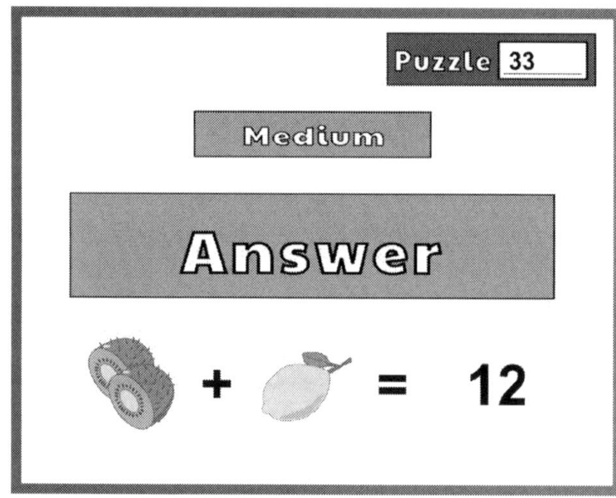
Puzzle 33
Medium
Answer
+
=
12

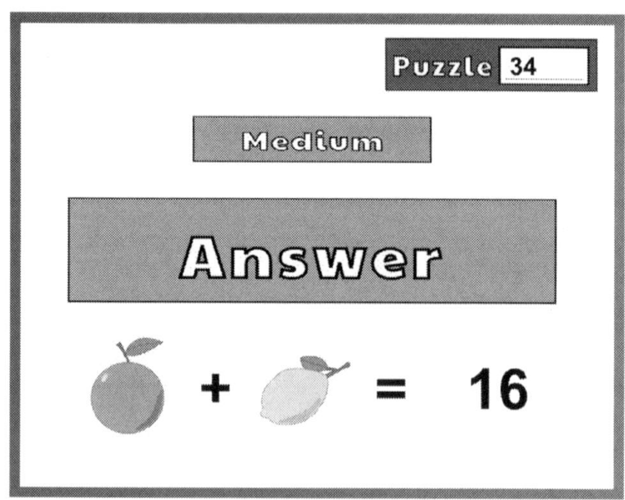
Puzzle 34
Medium
Answer
+
=
16

Puzzle 35
Medium
Answer
-
=
5

Puzzle 36
Medium
Answer
+
=
32

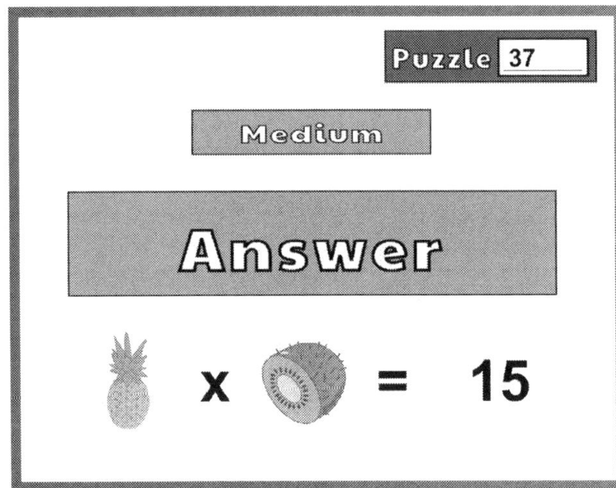

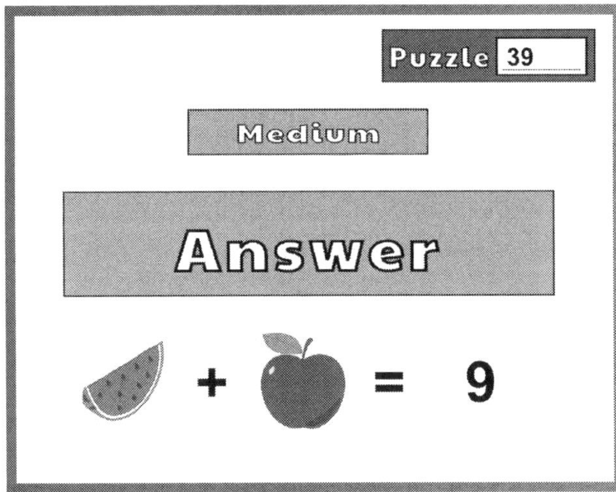

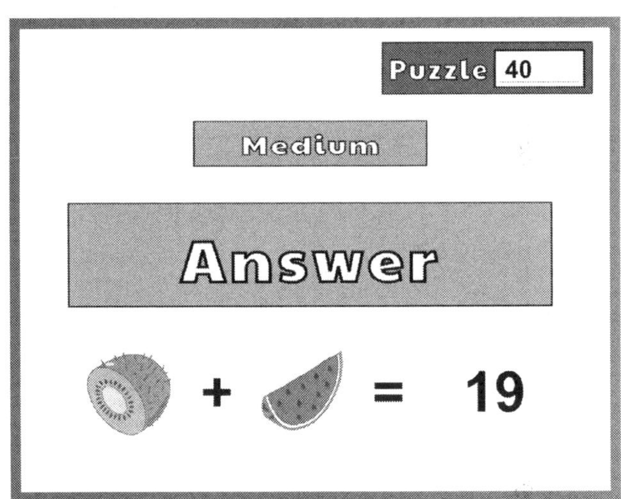

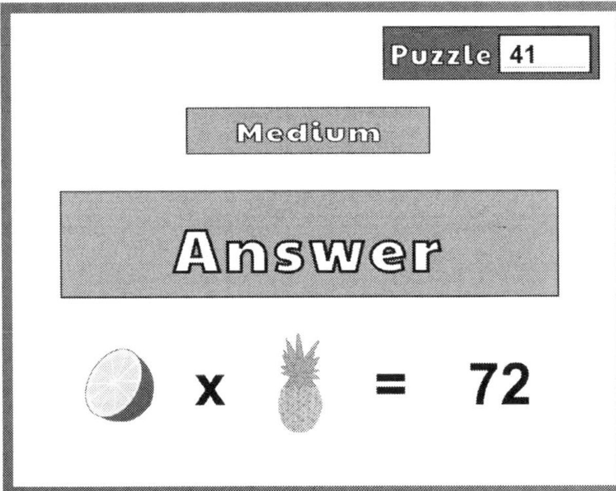

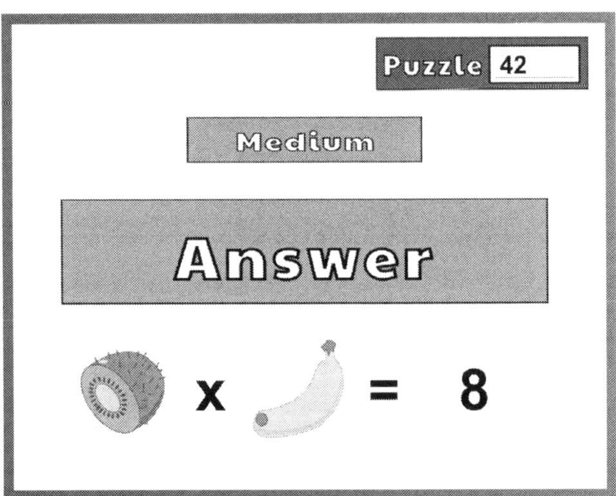

MEDIUM FRUIT PUZZLES

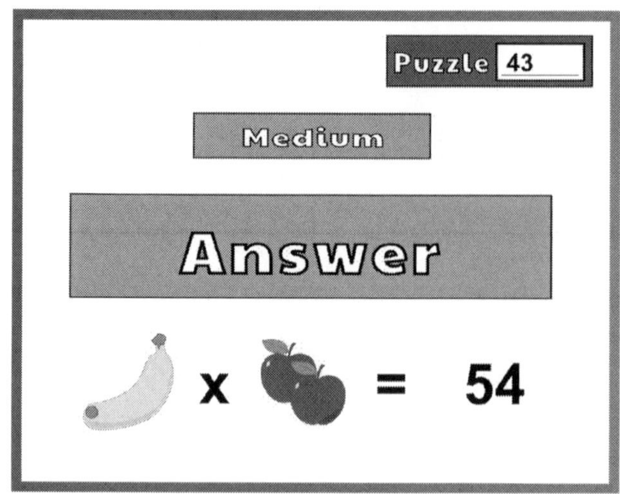
Puzzle 43
Medium
Answer
x = 54

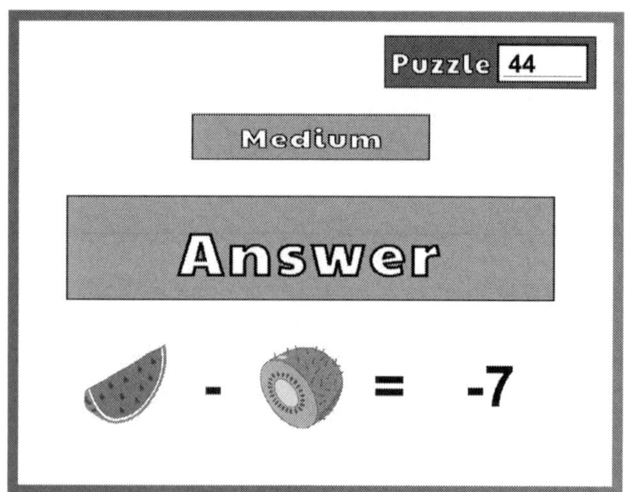
Puzzle 44
Medium
Answer
- = -7

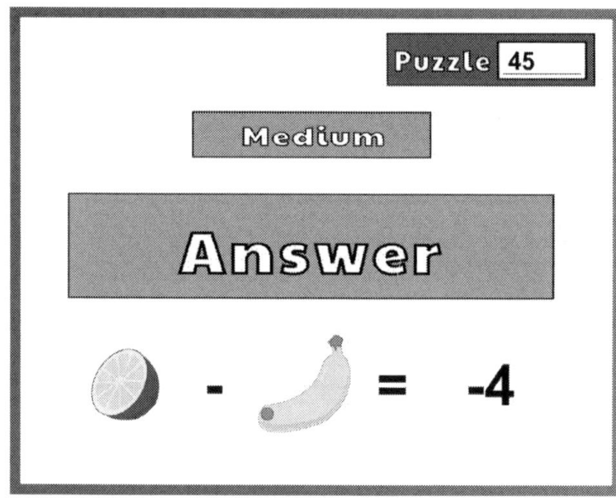
Puzzle 45
Medium
Answer
- = -4

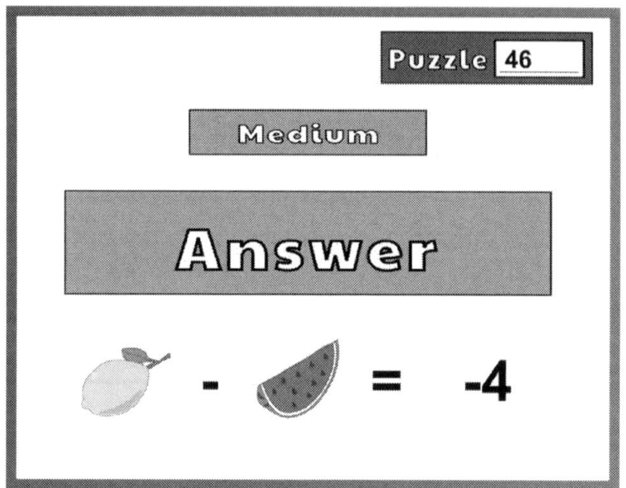
Puzzle 46
Medium
Answer
- = -4

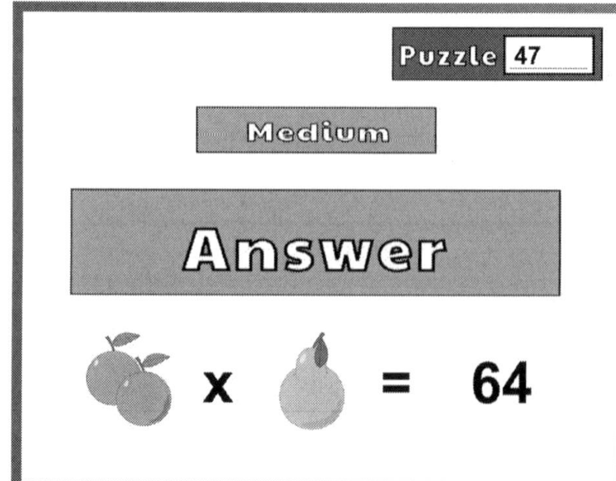
Puzzle 47
Medium
Answer
x = 64

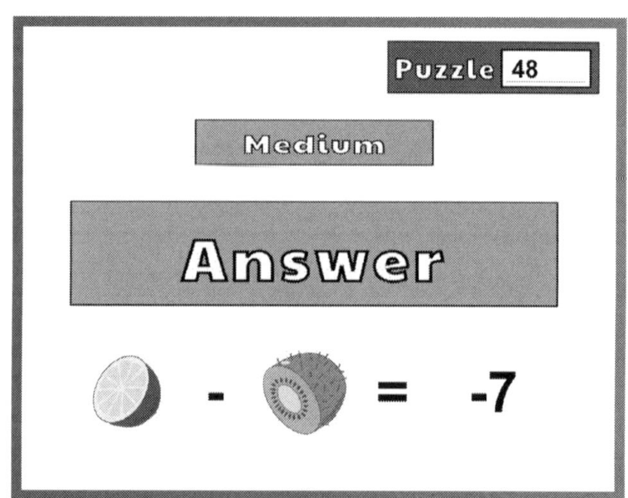
Puzzle 48
Medium
Answer
- = -7

Puzzle 49
Medium
Answer
- = 0

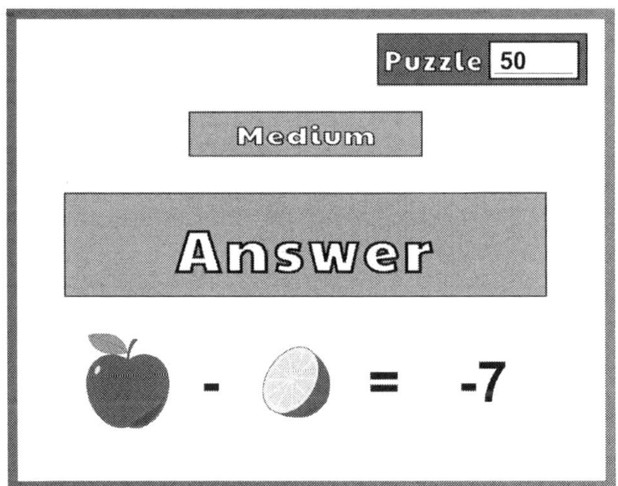

Puzzle 50
Medium
Answer
- = -7

Puzzle 51
Medium
Answer
- = 10

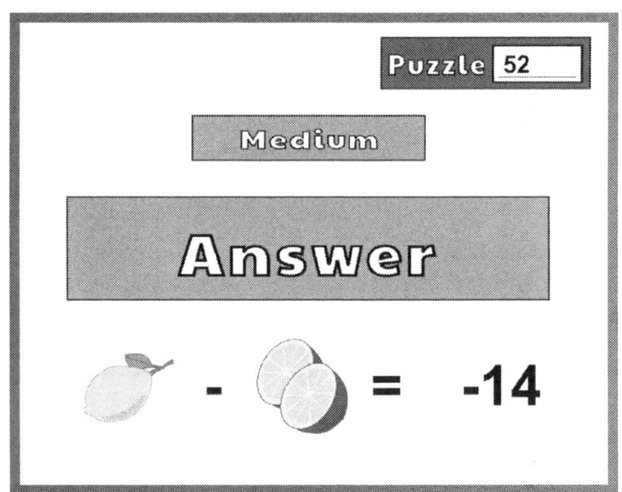

Puzzle 52
Medium
Answer
- = -14

Puzzle 53
Medium
Answer
+ = 5

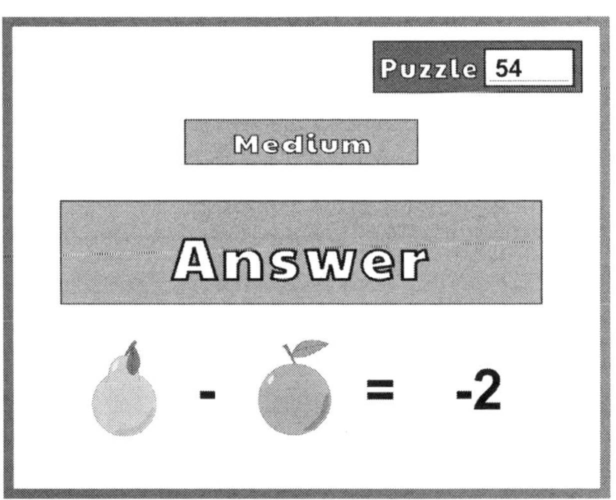

Puzzle 54
Medium
Answer
- = -2

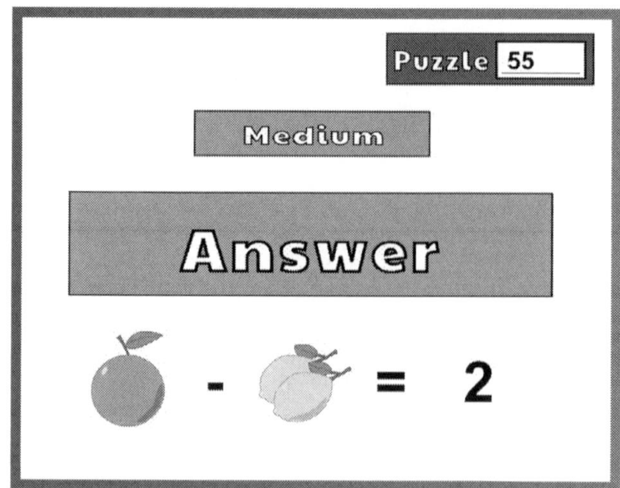
Puzzle 55
Medium
Answer
- = 2

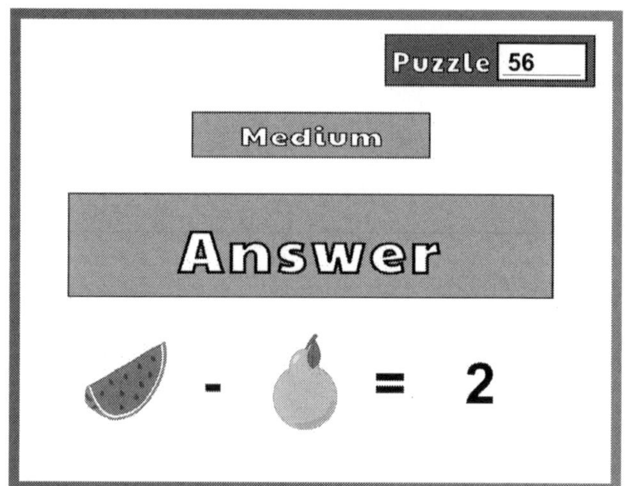
Puzzle 56
Medium
Answer
- = 2

Puzzle 57
Medium
Answer
- = -1

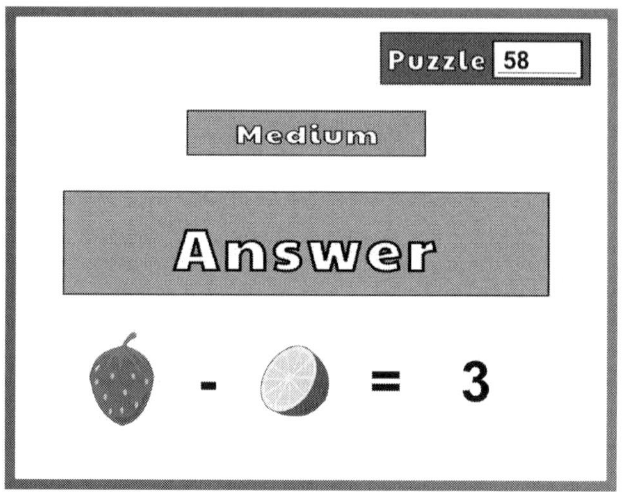
Puzzle 58
Medium
Answer
- = 3

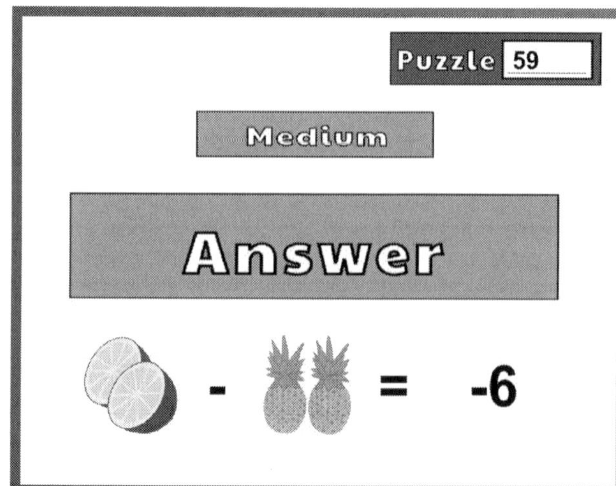
Puzzle 59
Medium
Answer
- = -6

Puzzle 60
Medium
Answer
+ = 10

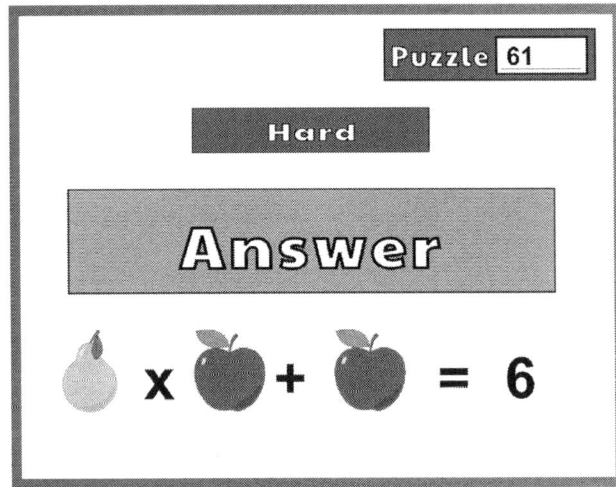
Puzzle 61
Hard
Answer
x + = 6

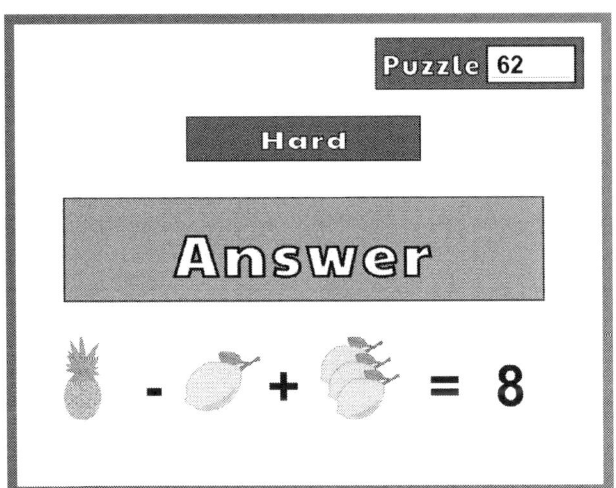
Puzzle 62
Hard
Answer
- + = 8

Puzzle 63
Hard
Answer
x - = 2

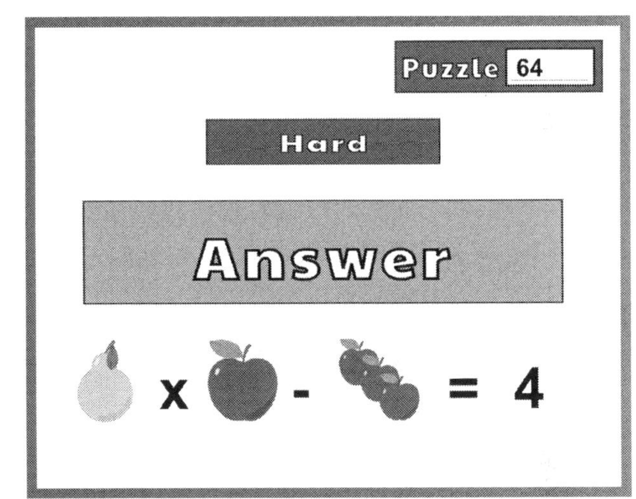
Puzzle 64
Hard
Answer
x - = 4

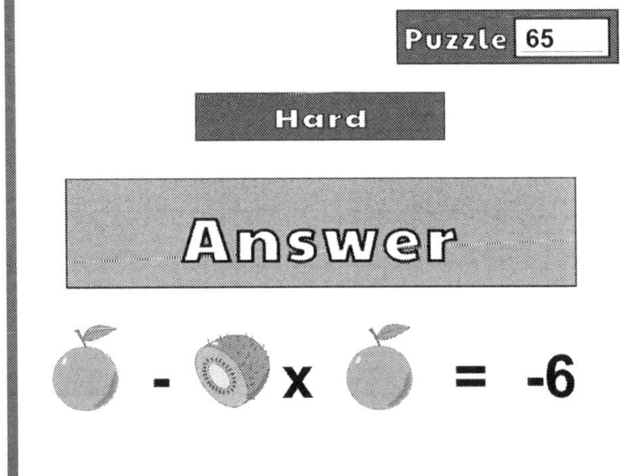
Puzzle 65
Hard
Answer
- x = -6

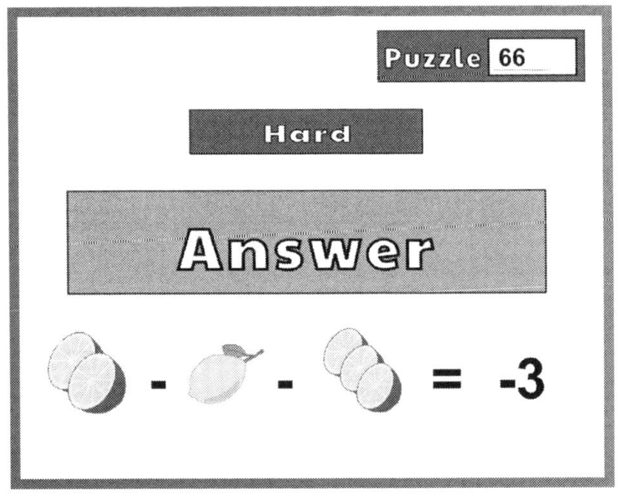
Puzzle 66
Hard
Answer
- - = -3

Puzzle 67
Hard
Answer
x + = 30

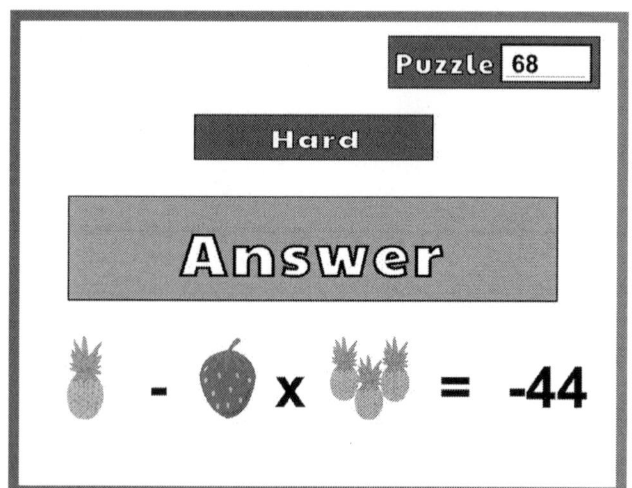
Puzzle 68
Hard
Answer
- x = -44

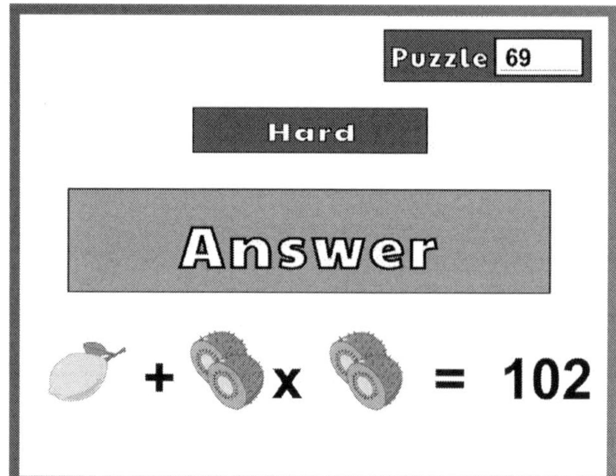
Puzzle 69
Hard
Answer
+ x = 102

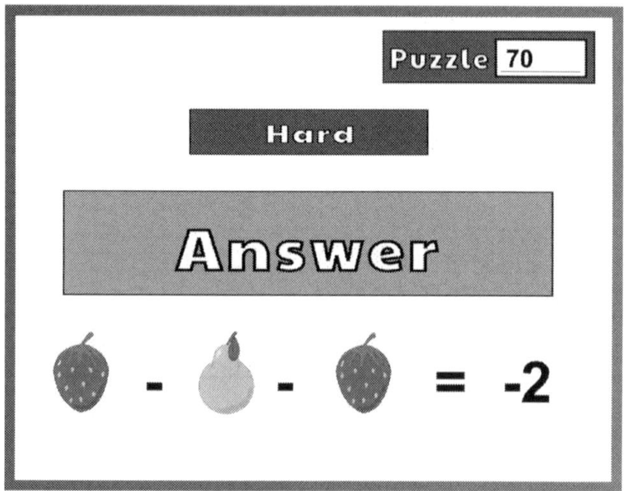
Puzzle 70
Hard
Answer
- - = -2

Puzzle 71
Hard
Answer
+ + = 11

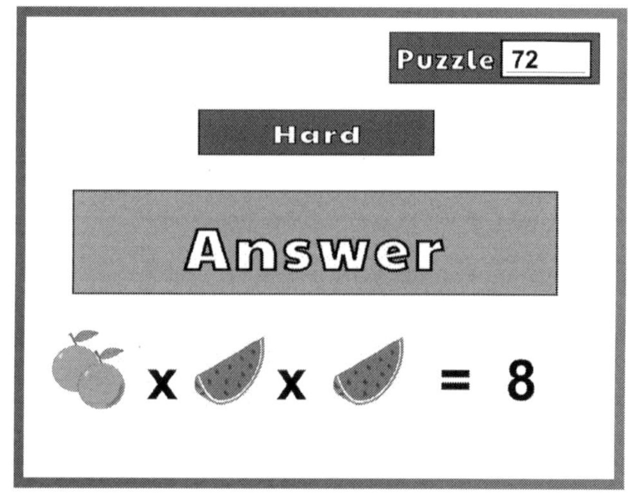
Puzzle 72
Hard
Answer
x x = 8

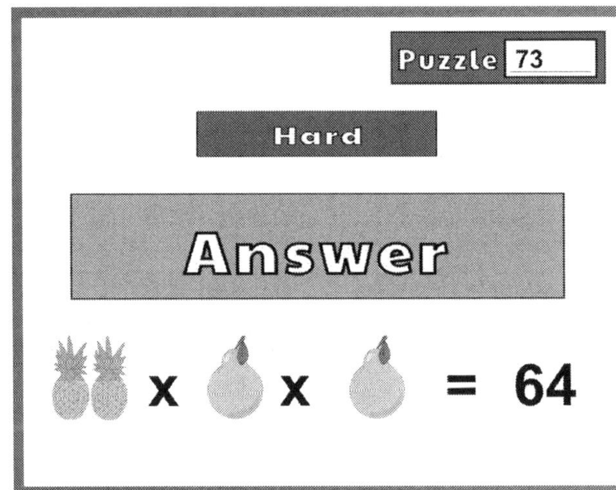

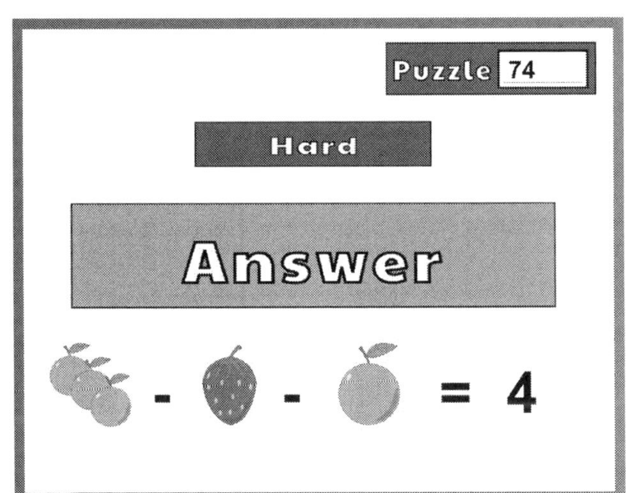

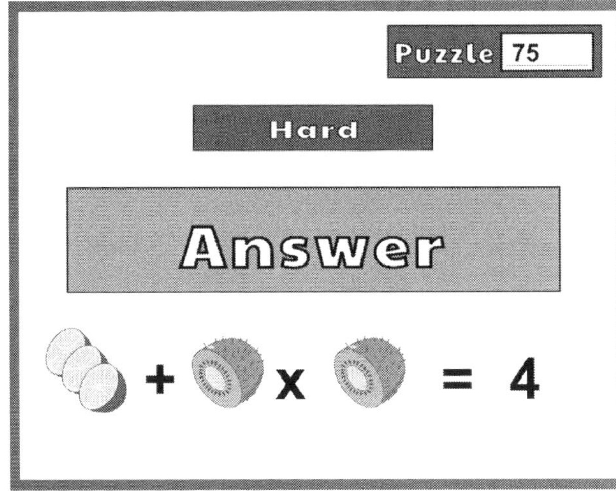

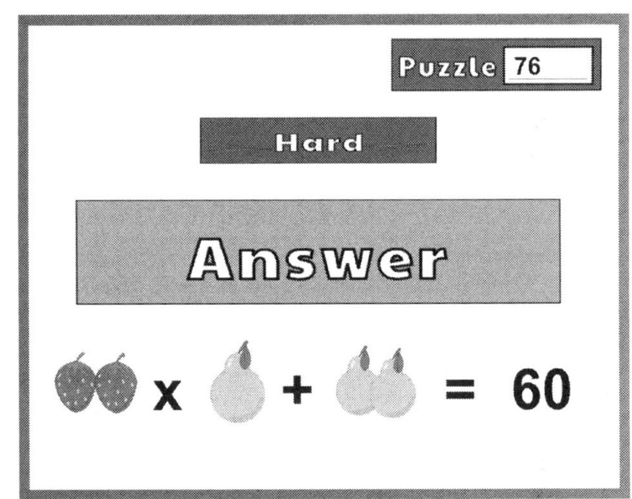

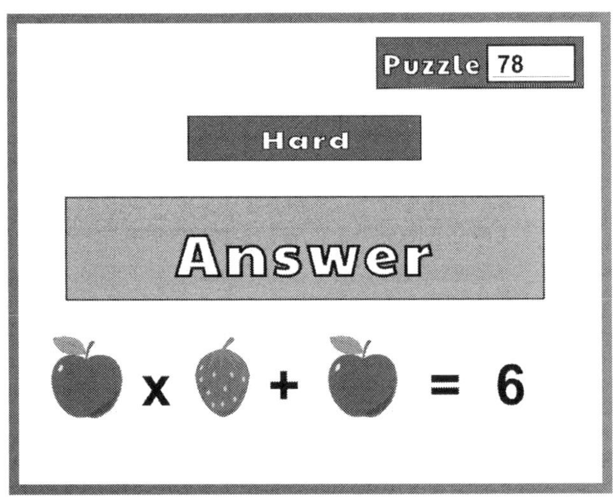

HARD FRUIT PUZZLES

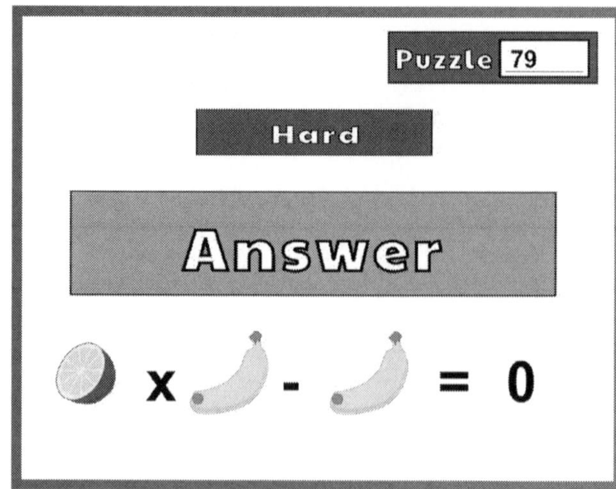
Puzzle 79
Hard
Answer
x - = 0

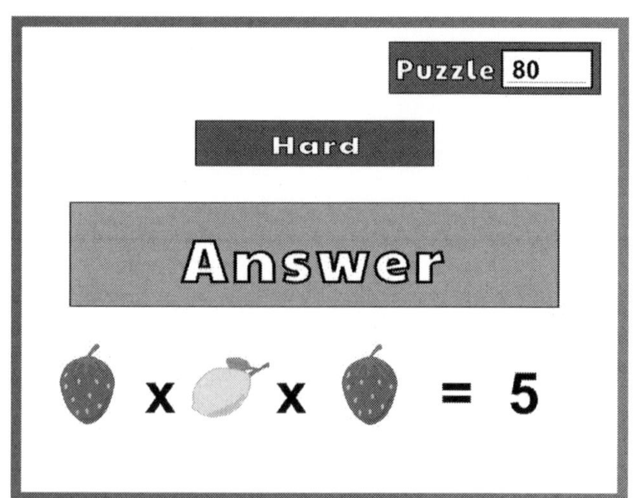
Puzzle 80
Hard
Answer
x x = 5

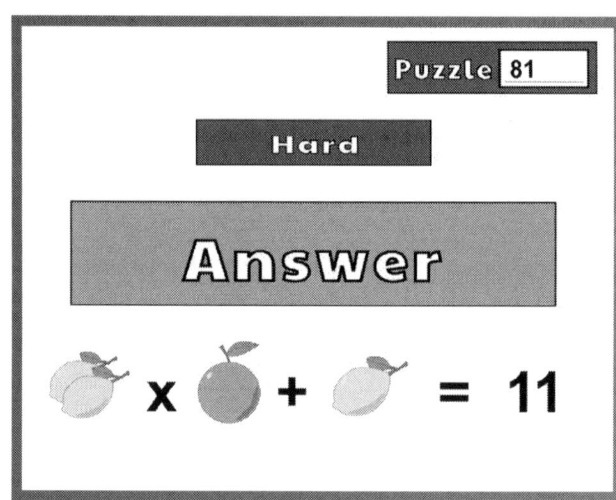
Puzzle 81
Hard
Answer
x + = 11

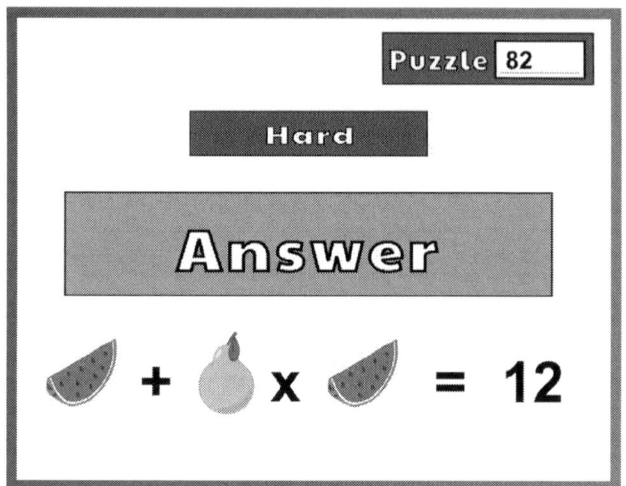
Puzzle 82
Hard
Answer
+ x = 12

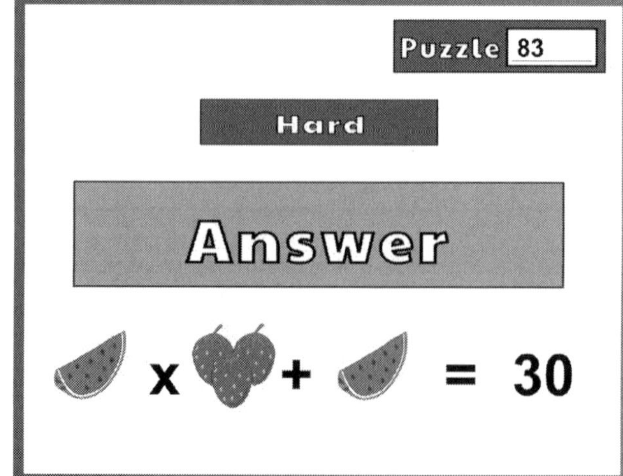
Puzzle 83
Hard
Answer
x + = 30

Puzzle 84
Hard
Answer
+ - = 2

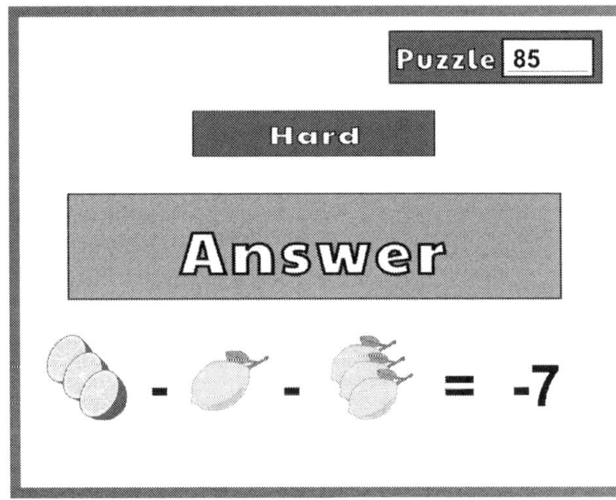
Puzzle 85
Hard
Answer
- - = -7

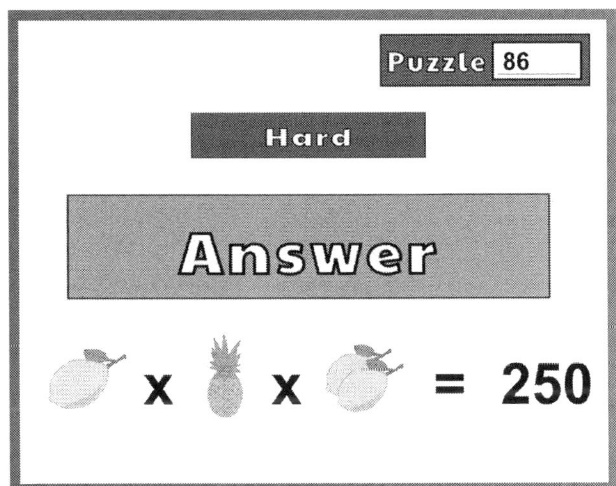
Puzzle 86
Hard
Answer
x x = 250

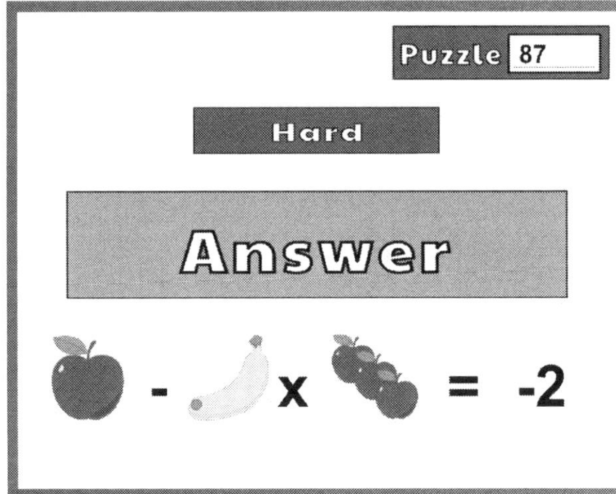
Puzzle 87
Hard
Answer
- x = -2

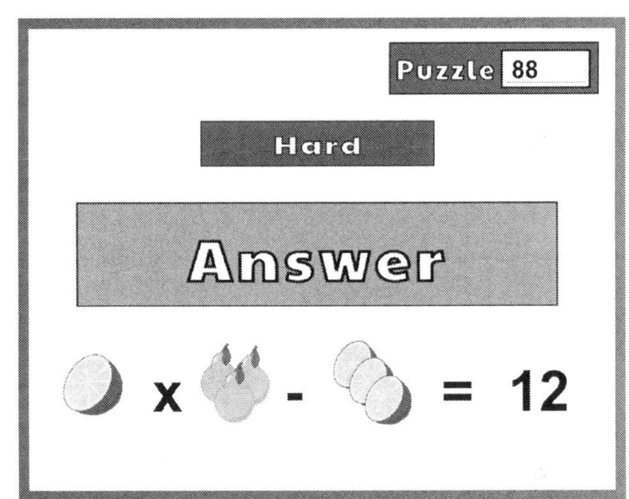
Puzzle 88
Hard
Answer
x - = 12

Puzzle 89
Hard
Answer
+ - = 8

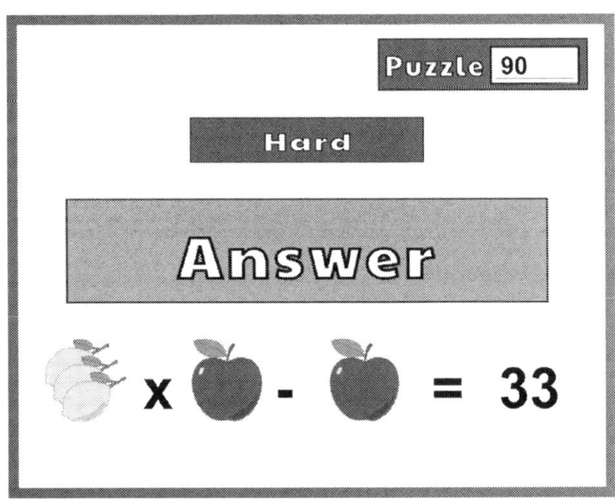
Puzzle 90
Hard
Answer
x - = 33

SINGLE ADDITION SHEET 1

2 + 1 = 3 | 3 + 8 = 11 | 2 + 2 = 4 | 8 + 2 = 10 | 8 + 7 = 15 | 6 + 5 = 11

0 + 4 = 4 | 2 + 6 = 8 | 5 + 0 = 5 | 8 + 3 = 11 | 1 + 4 = 5 | 8 + 7 = 15

7 + 8 = 15 | 0 + 2 = 2 | 1 + 2 = 3 | 4 + 8 = 12 | 0 + 7 = 7 | 8 + 7 = 15

2 + 8 = 10 | 0 + 2 = 2 | 2 + 7 = 9 | 6 + 7 = 13 | 1 + 5 = 6 | 7 + 8 = 15

6 + 3 = 9 | 5 + 0 = 5 | 5 + 2 = 7 | 6 + 4 = 10 | 8 + 5 = 13 | 8 + 5 = 13

1 + 6 = 7 | 1 + 8 = 9 | 8 + 3 = 11 | 6 + 8 = 14 | 7 + 4 = 11 | 6 + 7 = 13

3 + 6 = 9 | 8 + 2 = 10 | 2 + 2 = 4 | 7 + 1 = 8 | 0 + 0 = 0 | 5 + 8 = 13

SINGLE ADDITION SHEET 2

6 + 0 = 6 | 4 + 5 = 9 | 1 + 6 = 7 | 1 + 6 = 7 | 0 + 4 = 4 | 8 + 1 = 9

4 + 5 = 9 | 2 + 3 = 5 | 8 + 6 = 14 | 0 + 2 = 2 | 7 + 7 = 14 | 0 + 6 = 6

8 + 4 = 12 | 0 + 3 = 3 | 0 + 2 = 2 | 7 + 0 = 7 | 8 + 8 = 16 | 6 + 7 = 13

3 + 0 = 3 | 8 + 3 = 11 | 2 + 1 = 3 | 0 + 0 = 0 | 0 + 6 = 6 | 8 + 8 = 16

1 + 4 = 5 | 1 + 2 = 3 | 4 + 6 = 10 | 5 + 1 = 6 | 5 + 0 = 5 | 5 + 4 = 9

4 + 4 = 8 | 6 + 6 = 12 | 4 + 6 = 10 | 1 + 4 = 5 | 0 + 5 = 5 | 6 + 4 = 10

1 + 1 = 2 | 6 + 6 = 12 | 7 + 5 = 12 | 1 + 4 = 5 | 5 + 2 = 7 | 3 + 8 = 11

SINGLE ADDITION SHEET 3

2 + 0 = 2 | 0 + 6 = 6 | 5 + 0 = 5 | 1 + 5 = 6 | 3 + 4 = 7 | 8 + 4 = 12

0 + 5 = 5 | 4 + 3 = 7 | 6 + 5 = 11 | 8 + 1 = 9 | 6 + 4 = 10 | 0 + 5 = 5

2 + 7 = 9 | 1 + 6 = 7 | 5 + 3 = 8 | 8 + 7 = 15 | 6 + 3 = 9 | 1 + 6 = 7

6 + 3 = 9 | 0 + 5 = 5 | 8 + 4 = 12 | 1 + 1 = 2 | 2 + 7 = 9 | 5 + 0 = 5

5 + 7 = 12 | 7 + 7 = 14 | 8 + 3 = 11 | 1 + 6 = 7 | 2 + 8 = 10 | 4 + 1 = 5

2 + 2 = 4 | 8 + 6 = 14 | 5 + 8 = 13 | 6 + 5 = 11 | 5 + 6 = 11 | 7 + 3 = 10

5 + 6 = 11 | 3 + 8 = 11 | 2 + 2 = 4 | 0 + 2 = 2 | 6 + 1 = 7 | 1 + 1 = 2

SINGLE ADDITION SHEET 4

3 + 0 = 3 | 3 + 3 = 6 | 4 + 3 = 7 | 5 + 8 = 13 | 8 + 0 = 8 | 5 + 6 = 11

2 + 1 = 3 | 1 + 7 = 8 | 3 + 3 = 6 | 3 + 1 = 4 | 2 + 5 = 7 | 6 + 0 = 6

8 + 7 = 15 | 0 + 6 = 6 | 3 + 4 = 7 | 8 + 0 = 8 | 2 + 1 = 3 | 1 + 2 = 3

8 + 7 = 15 | 2 + 0 = 2 | 6 + 6 = 12 | 7 + 3 = 10 | 7 + 6 = 13 | 1 + 3 = 4

8 + 5 = 13 | 4 + 8 = 12 | 1 + 5 = 6 | 7 + 4 = 11 | 1 + 8 = 9 | 6 + 1 = 7

0 + 0 = 0 | 6 + 2 = 8 | 3 + 8 = 11 | 3 + 8 = 11 | 5 + 5 = 10 | 5 + 3 = 8

5 + 4 = 9 | 4 + 8 = 12 | 7 + 6 = 13 | 8 + 1 = 9 | 8 + 5 = 13 | 7 + 4 = 11

DOUBLE ADDITION SHEET 1

30 + 22 = 52 | 57 + 50 = 107 | 46 + 52 = 98 | 23 + 58 = 81 | 48 + 25 = 73 | 61 + 38 = 99

19 + 21 = 40 | 25 + 66 = 91 | 73 + 61 = 134 | 92 + 72 = 164 | 93 + 94 = 187 | 50 + 92 = 142

92 + 98 = 190 | 67 + 80 = 147 | 77 + 82 = 159 | 20 + 69 = 89 | 49 + 36 = 85 | 15 + 42 = 57

95 + 51 = 146 | 14 + 67 = 81 | 16 + 46 = 62 | 51 + 15 = 66 | 83 + 35 = 118 | 31 + 79 = 110

15 + 51 = 66 | 10 + 52 = 62 | 61 + 15 = 76 | 65 + 60 = 125 | 27 + 23 = 50 | 93 + 61 = 154

32 + 87 = 119 | 40 + 96 = 136 | 15 + 50 = 65 | 69 + 98 = 167 | 43 + 28 = 71 | 92 + 14 = 106

30 + 94 = 124 | 86 + 22 = 108 | 85 + 33 = 118 | 42 + 61 = 103 | 51 + 86 = 137 | 27 + 43 = 70

DOUBLE ADDITION SHEET 2

75 + 92 = 167 | 59 + 15 = 74 | 99 + 13 = 112 | 46 + 12 = 58 | 49 + 17 = 66 | 10 + 60 = 70

96 + 22 = 118 | 69 + 60 = 129 | 37 + 28 = 65 | 35 + 23 = 58 | 52 + 59 = 111 | 62 + 63 = 125

19 + 68 = 87 | 82 + 81 = 163 | 76 + 74 = 150 | 88 + 27 = 115 | 19 + 20 = 39 | 36 + 48 = 84

37 + 35 = 72 | 70 + 20 = 90 | 69 + 33 = 102 | 97 + 89 = 186 | 49 + 89 = 138 | 90 + 39 = 129

58 + 77 = 135 | 34 + 97 = 131 | 61 + 67 = 128 | 17 + 46 = 63 | 89 + 86 = 175 | 95 + 29 = 124

49 + 99 = 148 | 42 + 92 = 134 | 22 + 18 = 40 | 88 + 67 = 155 | 47 + 10 = 57 | 40 + 23 = 63

86 + 53 = 139 | 27 + 50 = 77 | 22 + 28 = 50 | 39 + 42 = 81 | 83 + 32 = 115 | 98 + 33 = 131

DOUBLE ADDITION SHEET 3

80 + 16 = 96 | 37 + 32 = 69 | 32 + 19 = 51 | 30 + 26 = 56 | 32 + 94 = 126 | 21 + 99 = 120

55 + 72 = 127 | 27 + 61 = 88 | 14 + 26 = 40 | 76 + 76 = 152 | 53 + 66 = 119 | 43 + 92 = 135

23 + 19 = 42 | 70 + 66 = 136 | 31 + 87 = 118 | 30 + 63 = 93 | 32 + 92 = 124 | 10 + 55 = 65

84 + 54 = 138 | 71 + 57 = 128 | 47 + 86 = 133 | 12 + 36 = 48 | 99 + 43 = 142 | 46 + 52 = 98

75 + 56 = 131 | 98 + 58 = 156 | 41 + 62 = 103 | 78 + 87 = 165 | 35 + 25 = 60 | 20 + 62 = 82

40 + 63 = 103 | 77 + 79 = 156 | 11 + 72 = 83 | 43 + 51 = 94 | 47 + 60 = 107 | 96 + 12 = 108

59 + 55 = 114 | 64 + 58 = 122 | 63 + 40 = 103 | 45 + 45 = 90 | 57 + 52 = 109 | 60 + 23 = 83

DOUBLE ADDITION SHEET 4

77 + 24 = 101 | 40 + 14 = 54 | 11 + 82 = 93 | 40 + 15 = 55 | 10 + 61 = 71 | 98 + 47 = 145

34 + 72 = 106 | 19 + 52 = 71 | 48 + 54 = 102 | 46 + 98 = 144 | 33 + 42 = 75 | 80 + 13 = 93

74 + 48 = 122 | 38 + 23 = 61 | 64 + 82 = 146 | 99 + 98 = 197 | 18 + 11 = 29 | 49 + 99 = 148

71 + 16 = 87 | 37 + 31 = 68 | 93 + 87 = 180 | 61 + 50 = 111 | 69 + 37 = 106 | 69 + 67 = 136

32 + 66 = 98 | 94 + 90 = 184 | 33 + 57 = 90 | 73 + 82 = 155 | 19 + 83 = 102 | 88 + 64 = 152

38 + 60 = 98 | 15 + 85 = 100 | 61 + 83 = 144 | 73 + 17 = 90 | 36 + 92 = 128 | 83 + 52 = 135

80 + 33 = 113 | 51 + 11 = 62 | 51 + 47 = 98 | 67 + 29 = 96 | 98 + 28 = 126 | 13 + 70 = 83

TRIPLE ADDITION SHEET 1

277 + 860 = 1137	435 + 793 = 1228	229 + 662 = 891	606 + 892 = 1498	121 + 929 = 1050	773 + 238 = 1011
317 + 501 = 818	664 + 802 = 1466	337 + 331 = 668	401 + 447 = 848	933 + 469 = 1402	406 + 179 = 585
907 + 255 = 1162	148 + 171 = 319	662 + 935 = 1597	362 + 990 = 1352	583 + 950 = 1533	823 + 650 = 1473
445 + 209 = 654	822 + 364 = 1186	928 + 874 = 1802	188 + 922 = 1110	539 + 692 = 1231	333 + 117 = 450
380 + 507 = 887	514 + 532 = 1046	148 + 972 = 1120	979 + 877 = 1856	154 + 480 = 634	534 + 896 = 1430
937 + 614 = 1551	485 + 485 = 970	265 + 138 = 403	216 + 690 = 906	654 + 439 = 1093	945 + 734 = 1679
658 + 263 = 921	764 + 428 = 1192	353 + 639 = 992	502 + 734 = 1236	655 + 605 = 1260	937 + 451 = 1388

TRIPLE ADDITION SHEET 2

680 + 894 = 1574	975 + 431 = 1406	229 + 913 = 1142	182 + 660 = 842	800 + 365 = 1165	208 + 570 = 778
816 + 269 = 1085	169 + 851 = 1020	183 + 454 = 637	448 + 722 = 1170	227 + 834 = 1061	957 + 770 = 1727
150 + 813 = 963	453 + 717 = 1170	224 + 426 = 650	675 + 990 = 1665	797 + 938 = 1735	936 + 235 = 1171
850 + 881 = 1731	554 + 194 = 748	402 + 605 = 1007	342 + 431 = 773	633 + 606 = 1239	460 + 420 = 880
936 + 681 = 1617	316 + 717 = 1033	775 + 726 = 1501	975 + 832 = 1807	422 + 849 = 1271	366 + 852 = 1218
488 + 599 = 1087	747 + 233 = 980	628 + 751 = 1379	208 + 273 = 481	978 + 356 = 1334	774 + 750 = 1524
651 + 339 = 990	209 + 219 = 428	246 + 901 = 1147	518 + 832 = 1350	670 + 488 = 1158	600 + 179 = 779

TRIPLE ADDITION SHEET 3

254 + 389 = 643	366 + 944 = 1310	189 + 588 = 777	933 + 400 = 1333	793 + 889 = 1682	790 + 284 = 1074
977 + 531 = 1508	595 + 290 = 885	338 + 775 = 1113	598 + 252 = 850	449 + 682 = 1131	436 + 671 = 1107
110 + 226 = 336	525 + 794 = 1319	883 + 852 = 1735	322 + 125 = 447	302 + 544 = 846	991 + 123 = 1114
867 + 881 = 1748	935 + 831 = 1766	393 + 555 = 948	688 + 305 = 993	469 + 124 = 593	822 + 270 = 1092
738 + 342 = 1080	390 + 678 = 1068	983 + 367 = 1350	178 + 538 = 716	629 + 464 = 1093	571 + 388 = 959
770 + 204 = 974	683 + 675 = 1358	273 + 538 = 811	180 + 358 = 538	147 + 438 = 585	577 + 130 = 707
226 + 116 = 342	722 + 720 = 1442	250 + 166 = 416	854 + 560 = 1414	461 + 444 = 905	906 + 408 = 1314

TRIPLE ADDITION SHEET 4

578 + 433 = 1011	415 + 619 = 1034	224 + 934 = 1158	655 + 610 = 1265	256 + 962 = 1218	268 + 525 = 793
760 + 701 = 1461	659 + 412 = 1071	217 + 720 = 937	313 + 637 = 950	797 + 565 = 1362	109 + 453 = 562
615 + 709 = 1324	841 + 234 = 1075	620 + 883 = 1503	776 + 433 = 1209	500 + 137 = 637	705 + 793 = 1498
707 + 543 = 1250	790 + 354 = 1144	500 + 503 = 1003	542 + 588 = 1130	411 + 824 = 1235	956 + 967 = 1923
547 + 458 = 1005	790 + 748 = 1538	352 + 822 = 1174	566 + 558 = 1124	951 + 988 = 1939	231 + 248 = 479
213 + 716 = 929	200 + 887 = 1087	899 + 243 = 1142	154 + 948 = 1102	128 + 288 = 416	737 + 954 = 1691
763 + 748 = 1511	736 + 335 = 1071	166 + 659 = 825	996 + 989 = 1985	587 + 755 = 1342	988 + 735 = 1723

SINGLE SUBTRACTION SHEET 1

8 - 6 = 2 | 5 - 4 = 1 | 8 - 6 = 2 | 7 - 4 = 3 | 5 - 2 = 3 | 4 - 3 = 1

7 - 6 = 1 | 4 - 0 = 4 | 2 - 1 = 1 | 5 - 0 = 5 | 5 - 3 = 2 | 3 - 1 = 2

8 - 5 = 3 | 8 - 1 = 7 | 6 - 1 = 5 | 7 - 1 = 6 | 6 - 1 = 5 | 3 - 1 = 2

7 - 4 = 3 | 1 - 1 = 0 | 5 - 0 = 5 | 7 - 0 = 7 | 8 - 0 = 8 | 5 - 1 = 4

8 - 7 = 1 | 8 - 2 = 6 | 8 - 7 = 1 | 3 - 2 = 1 | 6 - 1 = 5 | 8 - 2 = 6

8 - 5 = 3 | 8 - 1 = 7 | 2 - 1 = 1 | 8 - 0 = 8 | 8 - 4 = 4 | 5 - 5 = 0

6 - 0 = 6 | 6 - 0 = 6 | 4 - 3 = 1 | 7 - 7 = 0 | 1 - 1 = 0 | 7 - 1 = 6

SINGLE SUBTRACTION SHEET 2

6 - 3 = 3 | 6 - 3 = 3 | 7 - 2 = 5 | 8 - 1 = 7 | 3 - 2 = 1 | 7 - 0 = 7

6 - 0 = 6 | 6 - 1 = 5 | 6 - 3 = 3 | 6 - 1 = 5 | 8 - 1 = 7 | 7 - 6 = 1

7 - 1 = 6 | 7 - 0 = 7 | 8 - 6 = 2 | 1 - 0 = 1 | 5 - 0 = 5 | 8 - 1 = 7

6 - 0 = 6 | 3 - 0 = 3 | 5 - 4 = 1 | 3 - 0 = 3 | 4 - 2 = 2 | 5 - 5 = 0

4 - 2 = 2 | 2 - 0 = 2 | 8 - 7 = 1 | 3 - 2 = 1 | 8 - 4 = 4 | 6 - 1 = 5

2 - 2 = 0 | 0 - 0 = 0 | 8 - 7 = 1 | 4 - 2 = 2 | 2 - 1 = 1 | 6 - 0 = 6

6 - 0 = 6 | 4 - 0 = 4 | 4 - 4 = 0 | 6 - 0 = 6 | 7 - 6 = 1 | 4 - 1 = 3

SINGLE SUBTRACTION SHEET 3

8 - 2 = 6 | 7 - 0 = 7 | 8 - 0 = 8 | 8 - 5 = 3 | 5 - 0 = 5 | 2 - 0 = 2

0 - 0 = 0 | 6 - 1 = 5 | 8 - 4 = 4 | 8 - 5 = 3 | 7 - 1 = 6 | 3 - 2 = 1

6 - 4 = 2 | 5 - 2 = 3 | 8 - 0 = 8 | 5 - 0 = 5 | 2 - 1 = 1 | 7 - 1 = 6

8 - 5 = 3 | 3 - 1 = 2 | 5 - 2 = 3 | 7 - 4 = 3 | 5 - 0 = 5 | 3 - 2 = 1

6 - 0 = 6 | 7 - 5 = 2 | 5 - 3 = 2 | 4 - 3 = 1 | 6 - 2 = 4 | 2 - 2 = 0

7 - 5 = 2 | 6 - 5 = 1 | 7 - 7 = 0 | 5 - 4 = 1 | 4 - 3 = 1 | 4 - 0 = 4

8 - 4 = 4 | 4 - 4 = 0 | 8 - 7 = 1 | 1 - 1 = 0 | 4 - 4 = 0 | 7 - 6 = 1

SINGLE SUBTRACTION SHEET 4

8 - 6 = 2 | 6 - 6 = 0 | 8 - 7 = 1 | 7 - 4 = 3 | 5 - 2 = 3 | 8 - 8 = 0

8 - 3 = 5 | 8 - 5 = 3 | 8 - 3 = 5 | 8 - 4 = 4 | 4 - 3 = 1 | 6 - 6 = 0

4 - 2 = 2 | 8 - 0 = 8 | 3 - 3 = 0 | 5 - 2 = 3 | 5 - 2 = 3 | 7 - 6 = 1

8 - 1 = 7 | 8 - 0 = 8 | 1 - 1 = 0 | 8 - 5 = 3 | 7 - 5 = 2 | 4 - 2 = 2

7 - 7 = 0 | 3 - 2 = 1 | 8 - 5 = 3 | 2 - 2 = 0 | 8 - 7 = 1 | 7 - 3 = 4

7 - 2 = 5 | 8 - 6 = 2 | 7 - 6 = 1 | 8 - 4 = 4 | 3 - 1 = 2 | 8 - 5 = 3

6 - 3 = 3 | 5 - 4 = 1 | 7 - 3 = 4 | 3 - 3 = 0 | 6 - 3 = 3 | 8 - 7 = 1

DOUBLE SUBTRACTION SHEET 1

98 - 79 = 19   90 - 15 = 75   99 - 95 = 4   65 - 60 = 5   65 - 62 = 3   88 - 45 = 43

94 - 59 = 35   85 - 79 = 6   74 - 55 = 19   94 - 59 = 35   68 - 32 = 36   87 - 83 = 4

81 - 63 = 18   93 - 56 = 37   52 - 34 = 18   95 - 86 = 9   85 - 80 = 5   48 - 34 = 14

69 - 60 = 9   53 - 11 = 42   58 - 22 = 36   69 - 21 = 48   78 - 59 = 19   66 - 58 = 8

79 - 25 = 54   92 - 79 = 13   65 - 11 = 54   84 - 30 = 54   68 - 67 = 1   78 - 78 = 0

53 - 23 = 30   88 - 25 = 63   98 - 77 = 21   85 - 84 = 1   34 - 26 = 8   60 - 38 = 22

88 - 48 = 40   87 - 64 = 23   44 - 42 = 2   48 - 14 = 34   65 - 18 = 47   72 - 18 = 54

DOUBLE SUBTRACTION SHEET 2

93 - 24 = 69   92 - 87 = 5   92 - 89 = 3   84 - 43 = 41   88 - 59 = 29   44 - 25 = 19

63 - 57 = 6   84 - 29 = 55   84 - 29 = 55   70 - 17 = 53   98 - 15 = 83   99 - 93 = 6

62 - 37 = 25   66 - 37 = 29   68 - 24 = 44   66 - 65 = 1   81 - 46 = 35   51 - 31 = 20

57 - 11 = 46   96 - 54 = 42   18 - 13 = 5   89 - 79 = 10   30 - 25 = 5   45 - 44 = 1

89 - 23 = 66   88 - 73 = 15   84 - 67 = 17   97 - 32 = 65   99 - 53 = 46   67 - 22 = 45

60 - 55 = 5   31 - 11 = 20   75 - 10 = 65   63 - 45 = 18   94 - 89 = 5   85 - 35 = 50

72 - 71 = 1   92 - 21 = 71   69 - 54 = 15   49 - 38 = 11   66 - 38 = 28   84 - 26 = 58

DOUBLE SUBTRACTION SHEET 3

83 - 56 = 27   91 - 34 = 57   95 - 44 = 51   90 - 39 = 51   88 - 42 = 46   69 - 17 = 52

84 - 53 = 31   85 - 54 = 31   85 - 52 = 33   72 - 63 = 9   88 - 85 = 3   84 - 28 = 56

72 - 16 = 56   83 - 24 = 59   53 - 32 = 21   69 - 68 = 1   82 - 52 = 30   36 - 12 = 24

94 - 89 = 5   52 - 39 = 13   69 - 47 = 22   28 - 13 = 15   93 - 40 = 53   51 - 31 = 20

85 - 17 = 68   85 - 13 = 72   23 - 21 = 2   39 - 18 = 21   53 - 33 = 20   95 - 38 = 57

97 - 86 = 11   87 - 76 = 11   19 - 19 = 0   65 - 33 = 32   34 - 20 = 14   73 - 65 = 8

43 - 12 = 31   74 - 73 = 1   80 - 39 = 41   95 - 70 = 25   44 - 25 = 19   97 - 84 = 13

DOUBLE SUBTRACTION SHEET 4

61 - 53 = 8   89 - 75 = 14   92 - 32 = 60   33 - 30 = 3   78 - 65 = 13   40 - 38 = 2

90 - 73 = 17   77 - 49 = 28   91 - 87 = 4   70 - 44 = 26   24 - 22 = 2   50 - 33 = 17

86 - 37 = 49   90 - 30 = 60   99 - 48 = 51   74 - 66 = 8   91 - 42 = 49   97 - 43 = 54

71 - 57 = 14   77 - 41 = 36   58 - 34 = 24   93 - 65 = 28   65 - 14 = 51   84 - 82 = 2

65 - 13 = 52   92 - 23 = 69   33 - 19 = 14   43 - 29 = 14   98 - 92 = 6   79 - 14 = 65

65 - 62 = 3   45 - 40 = 5   83 - 38 = 45   65 - 60 = 5   76 - 72 = 4   28 - 22 = 6

95 - 43 = 52   87 - 45 = 42   79 - 49 = 30   89 - 31 = 58   63 - 57 = 6   51 - 30 = 21

TRIPLE SUBTRACTION SHEET 1

569 - 229 340	757 - 369 388	815 - 326 489	243 - 194 49	809 - 271 538	596 - 487 109
247 - 131 116	713 - 175 538	658 - 623 35	578 - 135 443	891 - 111 780	477 - 372 105
313 - 190 123	525 - 297 228	451 - 341 110	395 - 143 252	782 - 477 305	630 - 590 40
379 - 220 159	979 - 422 557	513 - 205 308	998 - 736 262	855 - 656 199	874 - 506 368
571 - 305 266	853 - 479 374	696 - 543 153	921 - 183 738	831 - 690 141	703 - 329 374
891 - 418 473	491 - 387 104	459 - 356 103	860 - 320 540	891 - 184 707	248 - 112 136
986 - 971 15	333 - 169 164	715 - 416 299	824 - 499 325	720 - 139 581	835 - 154 681

TRIPLE SUBTRACTION SHEET 2

316 - 229 87	459 - 285 174	761 - 423 338	739 - 214 525	835 - 626 209	450 - 449 1
847 - 303 544	724 - 351 373	725 - 521 204	423 - 256 167	958 - 340 618	261 - 200 61
754 - 709 45	154 - 103 51	793 - 152 641	604 - 459 145	671 - 612 59	804 - 281 523
966 - 552 414	955 - 686 269	622 - 225 397	382 - 330 52	677 - 385 292	952 - 144 808
980 - 248 732	754 - 450 304	768 - 312 456	614 - 243 371	460 - 201 259	784 - 266 518
671 - 496 175	272 - 253 19	284 - 138 146	643 - 172 471	362 - 204 158	570 - 560 10
482 - 260 222	499 - 297 202	648 - 337 311	742 - 728 14	620 - 483 137	743 - 358 385

TRIPLE SUBTRACTION SHEET 3

756 - 682 74	387 - 292 95	284 - 244 40	809 - 370 439	535 - 330 205	514 - 176 338
988 - 883 105	719 - 304 415	923 - 253 670	332 - 310 22	718 - 615 103	699 - 258 441
321 - 191 130	797 - 459 338	768 - 537 231	598 - 392 206	717 - 485 232	745 - 438 307
728 - 461 267	360 - 117 243	810 - 217 593	333 - 103 230	243 - 220 23	874 - 578 296
510 - 303 207	919 - 824 95	634 - 403 231	881 - 298 583	870 - 732 138	843 - 552 291
762 - 239 523	623 - 360 263	254 - 162 92	891 - 680 211	657 - 428 229	916 - 896 20
668 - 120 548	835 - 793 42	684 - 562 122	399 - 257 142	578 - 280 298	674 - 423 251

TRIPLE SUBTRACTION SHEET 4

782 - 128 654	873 - 815 58	840 - 692 148	566 - 125 441	638 - 465 173	849 - 745 104
634 - 351 283	988 - 487 501	907 - 496 411	792 - 347 445	580 - 185 395	976 - 828 148
615 - 265 350	520 - 214 306	515 - 132 383	440 - 244 196	950 - 743 207	715 - 641 74
992 - 950 42	888 - 841 47	682 - 266 416	901 - 529 372	859 - 809 50	521 - 162 359
881 - 250 631	562 - 559 3	933 - 383 550	841 - 419 422	980 - 463 517	703 - 378 325
894 - 726 168	633 - 236 397	780 - 448 332	911 - 263 648	777 - 706 71	871 - 596 275
587 - 314 273	466 - 142 324	536 - 445 91	710 - 479 231	739 - 423 316	889 - 800 89

SINGLE MULTIPLICATION SHEET 1

20 x 7 = 140	88 x 1 = 88	980 x 4 = 3920	10 x 0 = 0	1 x 6 = 6
1 x 5 = 5	24 x 3 = 72	879 x 4 = 3516	542 x 2 = 1084	424 x 5 = 2120
205 x 7 = 1435	74 x 5 = 370	1 x 7 = 7	81 x 0 = 0	72 x 2 = 144
98 x 4 = 392	3 x 6 = 18	1 x 4 = 4	368 x 6 = 2208	7 x 0 = 0
77 x 7 = 539	4 x 1 = 4	54 x 0 = 0	943 x 3 = 2829	642 x 7 = 4494
882 x 2 = 1764	6 x 1 = 6	4 x 0 = 0	7 x 8 = 56	59 x 8 = 472
6 x 3 = 18	3 x 4 = 12	971 x 2 = 1942	3 x 1 = 3	257 x 5 = 1285

SINGLE MULTIPLICATION SHEET 2

884 x 0 = 0	848 x 4 = 3392	78 x 2 = 156	8 x 3 = 24	7 x 4 = 28
443 x 0 = 0	290 x 6 = 1740	7 x 8 = 56	41 x 7 = 287	54 x 7 = 378
62 x 3 = 186	199 x 0 = 0	77 x 7 = 539	7 x 8 = 56	729 x 4 = 2916
0 x 7 = 0	3 x 8 = 24	396 x 5 = 1980	39 x 6 = 234	389 x 2 = 778
900 x 4 = 3600	48 x 1 = 48	947 x 0 = 0	669 x 7 = 4683	815 x 2 = 1630
44 x 5 = 220	2 x 0 = 0	88 x 8 = 704	773 x 7 = 5411	4 x 8 = 32
4 x 1 = 4	6 x 0 = 0	78 x 7 = 546	51 x 1 = 51	2 x 4 = 8

SINGLE MULTIPLICATION SHEET 3

13 x 7 = 91	64 x 0 = 0	105 x 3 = 315	7 x 5 = 35	69 x 5 = 345
809 x 3 = 2427	517 x 7 = 3619	41 x 5 = 205	8 x 0 = 0	8 x 8 = 64
96 x 0 = 0	4 x 0 = 0	38 x 0 = 0	0 x 2 = 0	61 x 4 = 244
67 x 2 = 134	61 x 2 = 122	10 x 6 = 60	109 x 1 = 109	107 x 4 = 428
6 x 3 = 18	747 x 8 = 5976	4 x 4 = 16	783 x 8 = 6264	31 x 3 = 93
0 x 7 = 0	43 x 5 = 215	4 x 6 = 24	245 x 5 = 1225	668 x 2 = 1336
14 x 8 = 112	5 x 6 = 30	5 x 4 = 20	48 x 3 = 144	96 x 5 = 480

SINGLE MULTIPLICATION SHEET 4

19 x 2 = 38	66 x 2 = 132	8 x 4 = 32	7 x 2 = 14	248 x 8 = 1984
610 x 6 = 3660	701 x 7 = 4907	7 x 5 = 35	8 x 0 = 0	92 x 3 = 276
6 x 7 = 42	580 x 1 = 580	566 x 4 = 2264	8 x 7 = 56	823 x 6 = 4938
51 x 1 = 51	4 x 8 = 32	396 x 6 = 2376	79 x 8 = 632	266 x 3 = 798
76 x 7 = 532	684 x 3 = 2052	257 x 1 = 257	578 x 0 = 0	12 x 6 = 72
8 x 7 = 56	28 x 4 = 112	543 x 1 = 543	524 x 4 = 2096	1 x 8 = 8
99 x 3 = 297	562 x 1 = 562	686 x 5 = 3430	7 x 2 = 14	115 x 3 = 345

DOUBLE MULTIPLICATION SHEET 1

51 × 49 = 2499	84 × 91 = 7644	51 × 89 = 4539	35 × 12 = 420	86 × 19 = 1634
40 × 41 = 1640	85 × 29 = 2465	67 × 14 = 938	42 × 14 = 588	22 × 82 = 1804
54 × 40 = 2160	51 × 11 = 561	78 × 53 = 4134	98 × 47 = 4606	41 × 66 = 2706
61 × 52 = 3172	90 × 16 = 1440	26 × 46 = 1196	71 × 89 = 6319	36 × 60 = 2160
39 × 14 = 546	68 × 96 = 6528	47 × 16 = 752	67 × 67 = 4489	75 × 29 = 2175
58 × 67 = 3886	39 × 52 = 2028	30 × 41 = 1230	40 × 23 = 920	31 × 83 = 2573

DOUBLE MULTIPLICATION SHEET 2

76 × 55 = 4180	61 × 48 = 2928	49 × 50 = 2450	86 × 90 = 7740	95 × 45 = 4275
56 × 83 = 4648	71 × 10 = 710	17 × 60 = 1020	72 × 55 = 3960	98 × 56 = 5488
57 × 51 = 2907	69 × 68 = 4692	79 × 44 = 3476	95 × 32 = 3040	99 × 53 = 5247
12 × 66 = 792	65 × 62 = 4030	71 × 20 = 1420	26 × 54 = 1404	58 × 67 = 3886
82 × 81 = 6642	17 × 56 = 952	16 × 24 = 384	56 × 42 = 2352	81 × 80 = 6480
41 × 40 = 1640	62 × 80 = 4960	56 × 53 = 2968	57 × 71 = 4047	10 × 55 = 550

DOUBLE MULTIPLICATION SHEET 3

95 × 87 = 8265	41 × 77 = 3157	77 × 71 = 5467	76 × 54 = 4104	16 × 71 = 1136
93 × 44 = 4092	36 × 61 = 2196	35 × 90 = 3150	75 × 41 = 3075	74 × 95 = 7030
37 × 99 = 3663	18 × 72 = 1296	78 × 88 = 6864	46 × 99 = 4554	56 × 67 = 3752
68 × 73 = 4964	26 × 49 = 1274	29 × 92 = 2668	29 × 77 = 2233	88 × 94 = 8272
69 × 78 = 5382	30 × 81 = 2430	48 × 78 = 3744	58 × 80 = 4640	17 × 67 = 1139
56 × 21 = 1176	55 × 58 = 3190	24 × 13 = 312	60 × 34 = 2040	89 × 44 = 3916

DOUBLE MULTIPLICATION SHEET 4

44 × 69 = 3036	48 × 34 = 1632	26 × 95 = 2470	44 × 30 = 1320	86 × 10 = 860
34 × 46 = 1564	85 × 96 = 8160	76 × 82 = 6232	93 × 13 = 1209	58 × 96 = 5568
75 × 82 = 6150	42 × 79 = 3318	15 × 81 = 1215	44 × 64 = 2816	30 × 94 = 2820
78 × 84 = 6552	96 × 37 = 3552	33 × 25 = 825	70 × 31 = 2170	66 × 31 = 2046
85 × 22 = 1870	43 × 50 = 2150	70 × 64 = 4480	81 × 22 = 1782	39 × 95 = 3705
23 × 74 = 1702	90 × 90 = 8100	39 × 31 = 1209	89 × 20 = 1780	47 × 65 = 3055

TRIPLE MULTIPLICATION SHEET 1

674 x 84 56616	127 x 60 7620	775 x 82 63550	853 x 67 57151
191 x 84 16044	579 x 61 35319	284 x 49 13916	893 x 61 54473
605 x 91 55055	331 x 40 13240	625 x 12 7500	971 x 86 83506
722 x 95 68590	802 x 89 71378	126 x 74 9324	127 x 24 3048
627 x 56 35112	776 x 88 68288	579 x 84 48636	969 x 13 12597
149 x 65 9685	617 x 75 46275	358 x 78 27924	769 x 79 60751

TRIPLE MULTIPLICATION SHEET 2

265 x 83 21995	998 x 19 18962	864 x 67 57888	934 x 48 44832
695 x 15 10425	141 x 99 13959	607 x 80 48560	372 x 38 14136
820 x 34 27880	906 x 54 48924	128 x 19 2432	142 x 70 9940
372 x 37 13764	715 x 27 19305	117 x 92 10764	654 x 78 51012
237 x 58 13746	742 x 37 27454	296 x 25 7400	557 x 82 45674
892 x 17 15164	259 x 73 18907	280 x 11 3080	241 x 95 22895

TRIPLE MULTIPLICATION SHEET 3

334 x 82 27388	781 x 20 15620	975 x 83 80925	487 x 51 24837
944 x 21 19824	716 x 24 17184	612 x 50 30600	876 x 37 32412
147 x 89 13083	371 x 27 10017	746 x 78 58188	837 x 27 22599
206 x 32 6592	701 x 25 17525	794 x 89 70666	706 x 28 19768
508 x 86 43688	268 x 56 15008	911 x 38 34618	380 x 33 12540
289 x 27 7803	384 x 50 19200	520 x 74 38480	461 x 51 23511

TRIPLE MULTIPLICATION SHEET 4

727 x 86 62522	791 x 77 60907	811 x 70 56770	881 x 12 10572
409 x 66 26994	940 x 35 32900	557 x 50 27850	750 x 17 12750
322 x 39 12558	815 x 32 26080	414 x 19 7866	921 x 31 28551
179 x 74 13246	121 x 78 9438	447 x 91 40677	643 x 90 57870
250 x 52 13000	733 x 20 14660	523 x 38 19874	458 x 51 23358
523 x 54 28242	295 x 71 20945	523 x 70 36610	818 x 15 12270

FRACTIONS PUZZLE 1

ADDING PROPER FRACTIONS

"Help the miner find the coordinates of hidden treasures by solving equations. Calculate the total value of mined treasures."

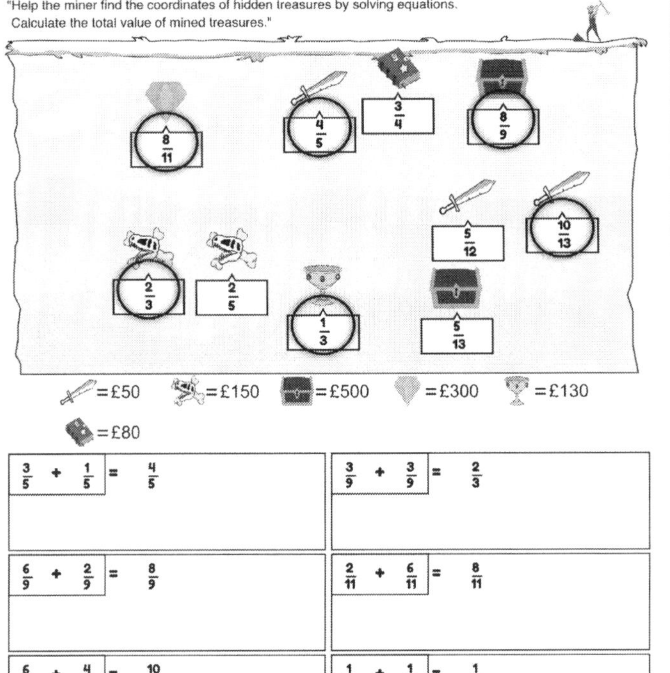

$\frac{3}{5} + \frac{1}{5} = \frac{4}{5}$	$\frac{3}{9} + \frac{3}{9} = \frac{2}{3}$
$\frac{6}{9} + \frac{2}{9} = \frac{8}{9}$	$\frac{2}{11} + \frac{6}{11} = \frac{8}{11}$
$\frac{6}{13} + \frac{4}{13} = \frac{10}{13}$	$\frac{1}{6} + \frac{1}{6} = \frac{1}{3}$

The total value of mined treasures = £ 1180

FRACTIONS PUZZLE 2

ADDING PROPER FRACTIONS

"Help the miner find the coordinates of hidden treasures by solving equations. Calculate the total value of mined treasures."

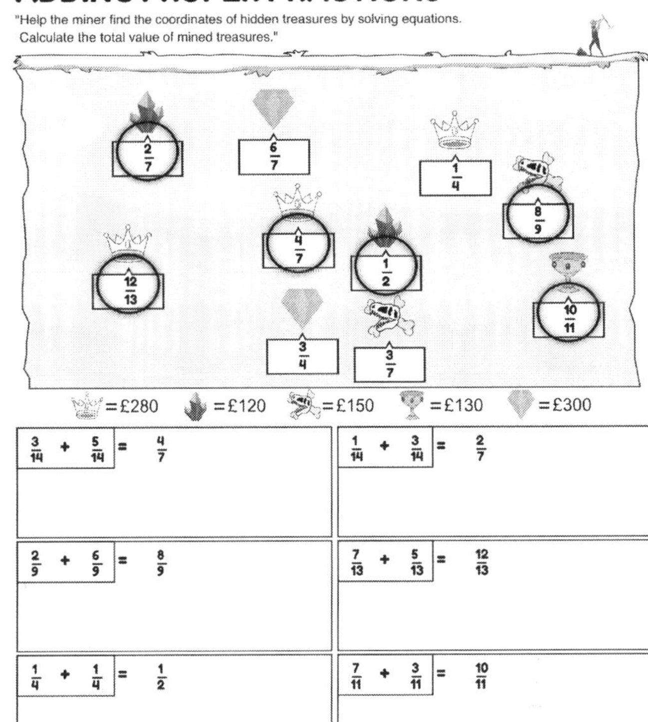

$\frac{3}{14} + \frac{5}{14} = \frac{4}{7}$	$\frac{1}{14} + \frac{3}{14} = \frac{2}{7}$
$\frac{2}{9} + \frac{6}{9} = \frac{8}{9}$	$\frac{7}{13} + \frac{5}{13} = \frac{12}{13}$
$\frac{1}{4} + \frac{1}{4} = \frac{1}{2}$	$\frac{7}{11} + \frac{3}{11} = \frac{10}{11}$

The total value of mined treasures = £ 1080

FRACTIONS PUZZLE 3

ADDING PROPER FRACTIONS

Fix the leaking pipes by solving equations.
Find which pipes still have leakages after all possible leaks are fixed

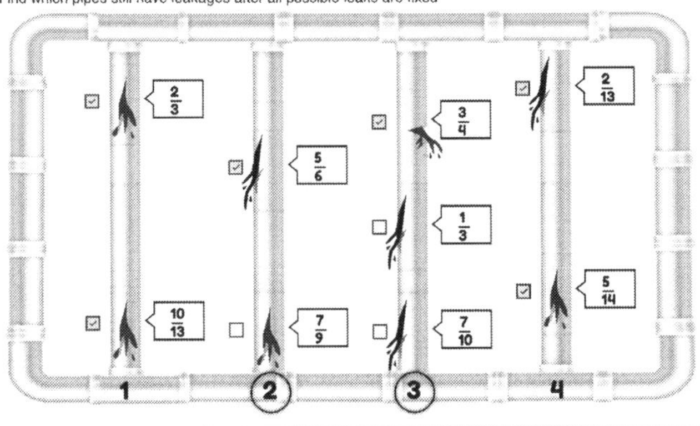

$\frac{4}{6} + \frac{1}{6} = \frac{5}{6}$	$\frac{1}{14} + \frac{4}{14} = \frac{5}{14}$
$\frac{1}{3} + \frac{1}{3} = \frac{2}{3}$	$\frac{1}{13} + \frac{1}{13} = \frac{2}{13}$
$\frac{6}{13} + \frac{4}{13} = \frac{10}{13}$	$\frac{2}{4} + \frac{1}{4} = \frac{3}{4}$

The numbers of the pipes which still have leaks are: 2, 3

FRACTIONS PUZZLE 4

ADDING PROPER FRACTIONS

Fix the leaking pipes by solving equations.
Find which pipes still have leakages after all possible leaks are fixed

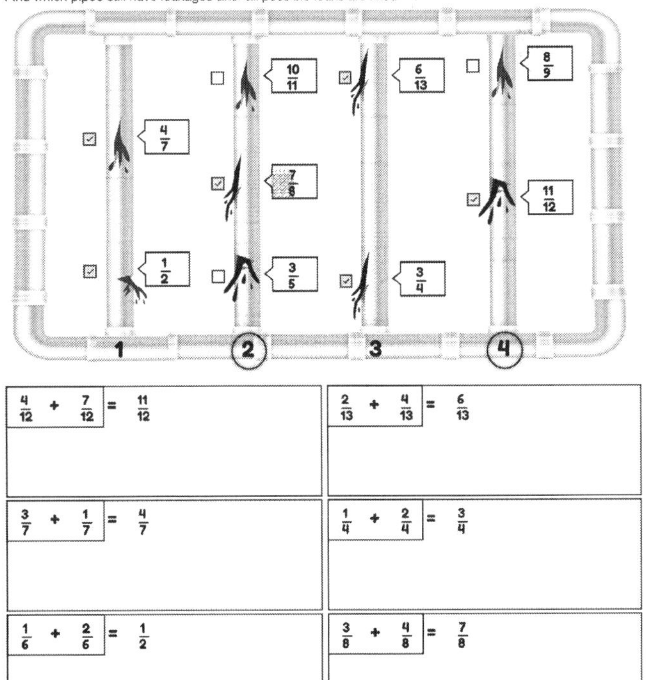

$\frac{4}{12} + \frac{7}{12} = \frac{11}{12}$	$\frac{2}{13} + \frac{4}{13} = \frac{6}{13}$
$\frac{3}{7} + \frac{1}{7} = \frac{4}{7}$	$\frac{1}{4} + \frac{2}{4} = \frac{3}{4}$
$\frac{1}{6} + \frac{2}{6} = \frac{1}{2}$	$\frac{3}{8} + \frac{4}{8} = \frac{7}{8}$

The numbers of the pipes which still have leaks are: 2, 4

FRACTIONS PUZZLE 5

ADDING IMPROPER FRACTIONS

"Help the miner find the coordinates of hidden treasures by solving equations.
Calculate the total value of mined treasures."

=£500 =£150 =£80 =£130 =£300 =£120

$\frac{12}{7} + \frac{3}{2} = 3\frac{3}{14}$	$\frac{12}{8} + \frac{10}{6} = 3\frac{1}{6}$
$\frac{11}{2} + \frac{12}{1} = 17\frac{1}{2}$	$\frac{5}{4} + \frac{4}{2} = 3\frac{1}{4}$
$\frac{4}{3} + \frac{3}{1} = 4\frac{1}{3}$	$\frac{10}{7} + \frac{4}{1} = 5\frac{3}{7}$

The total value of mined treasures = £ 1310

FRACTIONS PUZZLE 6

ADDING IMPROPER FRACTIONS

"Help the miner find the coordinates of hidden treasures by solving equations.
Calculate the total value of mined treasures."

=£150 =£120 =£80 =£280 =£300

$\frac{5}{4} + \frac{3}{1} = 4\frac{1}{4}$	$\frac{4}{3} + \frac{7}{5} = 2\frac{11}{15}$
$\frac{8}{5} + \frac{7}{6} = 2\frac{23}{30}$	$\frac{4}{2} + \frac{5}{1} = 7$
$\frac{7}{4} + \frac{6}{2} = 4\frac{3}{4}$	$\frac{5}{1} + \frac{6}{2} = 8$

The total value of mined treasures = £ 900

FRACTIONS PUZZLE 7

ADDING IMPROPER FRACTIONS

Fix the leaking pipes by solving equations.
Find which pipes still have leakages after all possible leaks are fixed

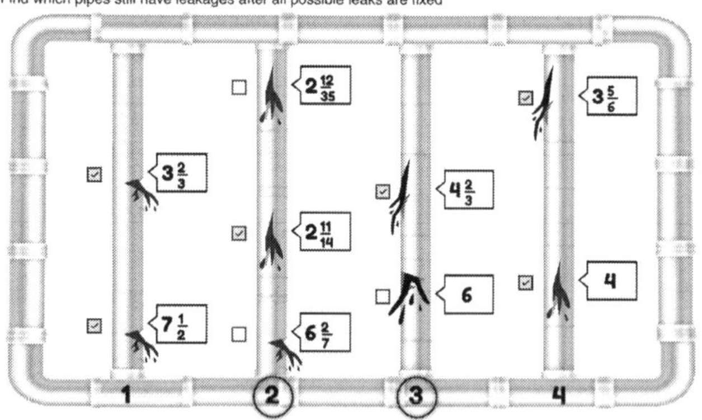

$\frac{12}{9} + \frac{10}{3} = 4\frac{2}{3}$	$\frac{6}{4} + \frac{9}{7} = 2\frac{11}{14}$
$\frac{3}{2} + \frac{10}{4} = 4$	$\frac{8}{6} + \frac{7}{3} = 3\frac{2}{3}$
$\frac{8}{4} + \frac{11}{2} = 7\frac{1}{2}$	$\frac{7}{3} + \frac{9}{6} = 3\frac{5}{6}$

The numbers of the pipes which still have leaks are: 2, 3

FRACTIONS PUZZLE 8

ADDING IMPROPER FRACTIONS

Fix the leaking pipes by solving equations.
Find which pipes still have leakages after all possible leaks are fixed

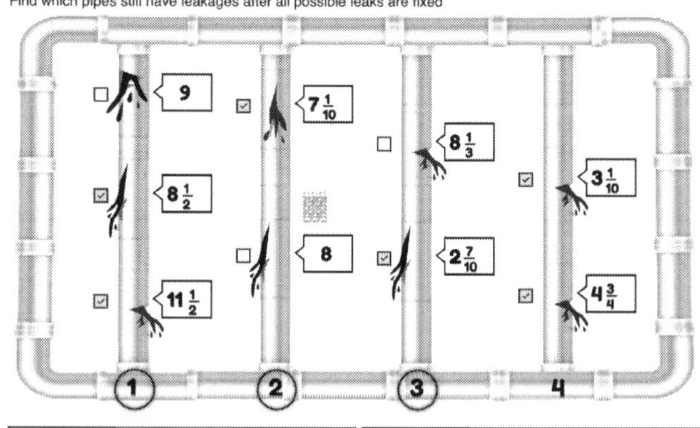

$\frac{3}{1} + \frac{7}{4} = 4\frac{3}{4}$	$\frac{3}{2} + \frac{7}{1} = 8\frac{1}{2}$
$\frac{8}{5} + \frac{3}{2} = 3\frac{1}{10}$	$\frac{11}{2} + \frac{8}{5} = 7\frac{1}{10}$
$\frac{6}{5} + \frac{6}{4} = 2\frac{7}{10}$	$\frac{7}{2} + \frac{8}{1} = 11\frac{1}{2}$

The numbers of the pipes which still have leaks are: 1, 2, 3

FRACTIONS PUZZLE 9

ADDING MIXED FRACTIONS

"Help the miner find the coordinates of hidden treasures by solving equations.
Calculate the total value of mined treasures."

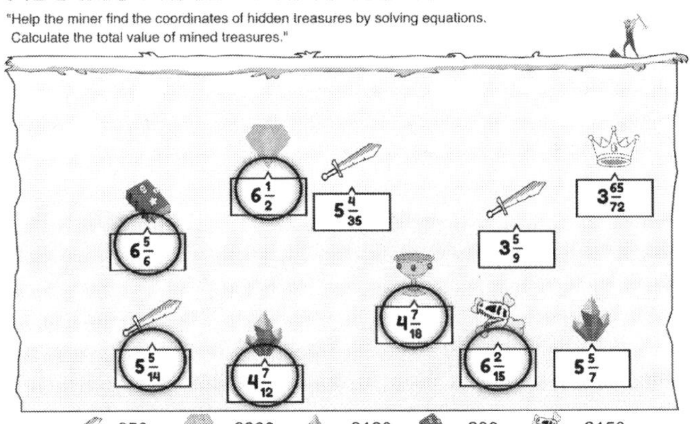

=£50 =£300 =£120 =£80 =£150

=£130 =£280

$1\frac{6}{7} + 3\frac{3}{6} = 5\frac{5}{14}$	$3\frac{2}{3} + 2\frac{5}{6} = 6\frac{1}{2}$
$3\frac{1}{3} + 1\frac{1}{4} = 4\frac{7}{12}$	$3\frac{2}{4} + 3\frac{1}{3} = 6\frac{5}{6}$
$3\frac{4}{5} + 2\frac{1}{3} = 6\frac{2}{15}$	$2\frac{3}{6} + 1\frac{8}{9} = 4\frac{7}{18}$

The total value of mined treasures = £ 830

FRACTIONS PUZZLE 10

ADDING MIXED FRACTIONS

"Help the miner find the coordinates of hidden treasures by solving equations.
Calculate the total value of mined treasures."

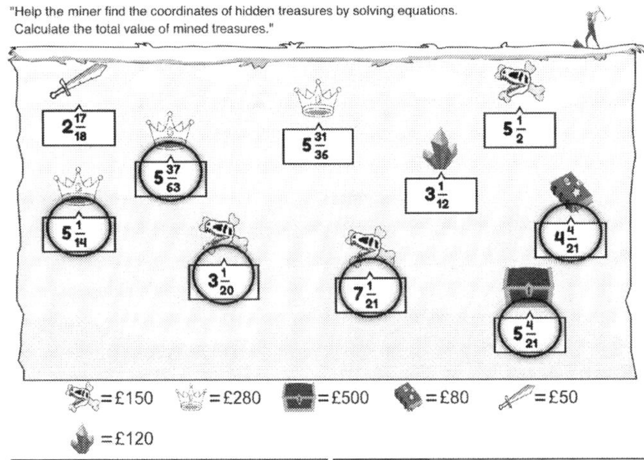

=£150 =£280 =£500 =£80 =£50

=£120

$1\frac{2}{8} + 1\frac{4}{5} = 3\frac{1}{20}$	$3\frac{5}{7} + 3\frac{3}{9} = 7\frac{1}{21}$
$3\frac{1}{7} + 2\frac{4}{9} = 5\frac{37}{63}$	$3\frac{2}{6} + 1\frac{6}{7} = 5\frac{4}{21}$
$3\frac{4}{8} + 1\frac{4}{7} = 5\frac{1}{14}$	$1\frac{6}{7} + 2\frac{1}{3} = 4\frac{4}{21}$

The total value of mined treasures = £ 1440

FRACTIONS PUZZLE 11

ADDING MIXED FRACTIONS

Fix the leaking pipes by solving equations.
Find which pipes still have leakages after all possible leaks are fixed

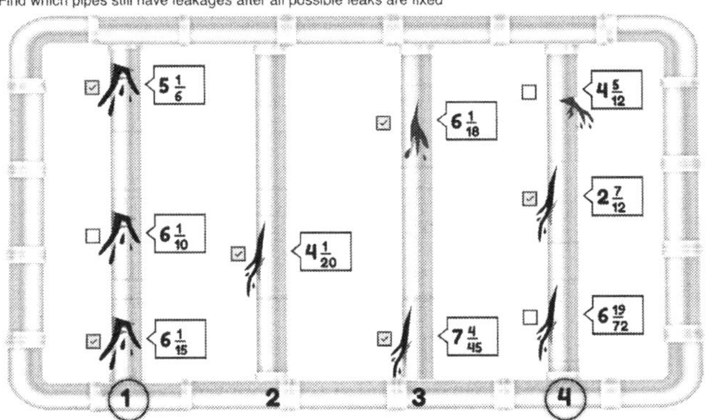

$3\frac{4}{8} + 1\frac{4}{6} = 5\frac{1}{6}$	$3\frac{8}{9} + 3\frac{1}{5} = 7\frac{4}{45}$
$1\frac{1}{4} + 1\frac{1}{3} = 2\frac{7}{12}$	$3\frac{4}{6} + 2\frac{2}{5} = 6\frac{1}{15}$
$3\frac{2}{4} + 2\frac{5}{9} = 6\frac{1}{18}$	$1\frac{4}{5} + 2\frac{1}{4} = 4\frac{1}{20}$

The numbers of the pipes which still have leaks are: 1, 4

FRACTIONS PUZZLE 12

ADDING MIXED FRACTIONS

Fix the leaking pipes by solving equations.
Find which pipes still have leakages after all possible leaks are fixed

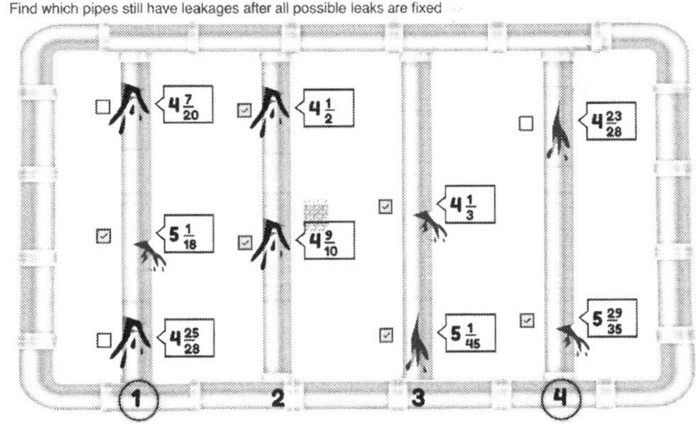

$1\frac{2}{9} + 3\frac{5}{6} = 5\frac{1}{18}$	$3\frac{2}{4} + 1\frac{2}{5} = 4\frac{9}{10}$
$2\frac{3}{7} + 3\frac{2}{5} = 5\frac{29}{35}$	$3\frac{2}{9} + 1\frac{4}{5} = 5\frac{1}{45}$
$3\frac{2}{8} + 1\frac{1}{4} = 4\frac{1}{2}$	$2\frac{3}{6} + 1\frac{5}{6} = 4\frac{1}{3}$

The numbers of the pipes which still have leaks are: 1, 4

FRACTIONS PUZZLE 13

SUBTRACTING PROPER FRACTIONS

"Help the miner find the coordinates of hidden treasures by solving equations. Calculate the total value of mined treasures."

=£120 =£280 =£50 =£80

$\frac{5}{5} - \frac{3}{5} = \frac{2}{5}$	$\frac{9}{10} - \frac{1}{10} = \frac{4}{5}$
$\frac{11}{11} - \frac{7}{11} = \frac{4}{11}$	$\frac{4}{6} - \frac{2}{6} = \frac{1}{3}$
$\frac{7}{7} - \frac{3}{7} = \frac{4}{7}$	$\frac{3}{3} - \frac{1}{3} = \frac{2}{3}$

The total value of mined treasures = £ 630

FRACTIONS PUZZLE 14

SUBTRACTING PROPER FRACTIONS

"Help the miner find the coordinates of hidden treasures by solving equations. Calculate the total value of mined treasures."

=£280 =£120 =£500 =£130 =£50 =£150

$\frac{11}{13} - \frac{3}{13} = \frac{8}{13}$	$\frac{10}{12} - \frac{6}{12} = \frac{1}{3}$
$\frac{3}{5} - \frac{1}{5} = \frac{2}{5}$	$\frac{4}{4} - \frac{2}{4} = \frac{1}{2}$
$\frac{3}{3} - \frac{1}{3} = \frac{2}{3}$	$\frac{11}{13} - \frac{2}{13} = \frac{9}{13}$

The total value of mined treasures = £ 1580

FRACTIONS PUZZLE 15

SUBTRACTING PROPER FRACTIONS

Fix the leaking pipes by solving equations.
Find which pipes still have leakages after all possible leaks are fixed

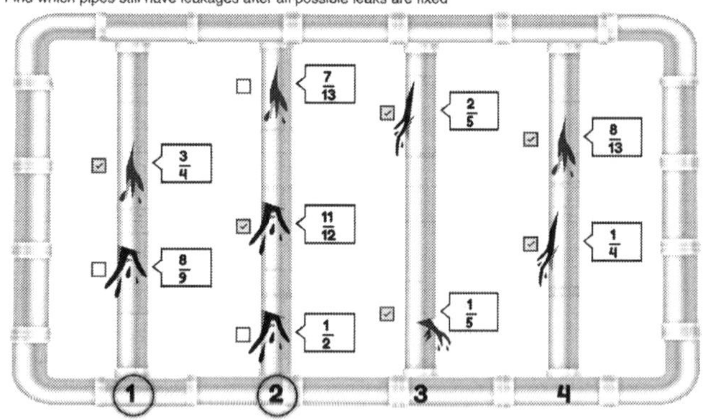

$\frac{12}{12} - \frac{1}{12} = \frac{11}{12}$	$\frac{5}{10} - \frac{3}{10} = \frac{1}{5}$
$\frac{10}{12} - \frac{1}{12} = \frac{3}{4}$	$\frac{13}{13} - \frac{5}{13} = \frac{8}{13}$
$\frac{7}{12} - \frac{4}{12} = \frac{1}{4}$	$\frac{3}{5} - \frac{1}{5} = \frac{2}{5}$

The numbers of the pipes which still have leaks are: 1, 2

FRACTIONS PUZZLE 16

SUBTRACTING PROPER FRACTIONS

Fix the leaking pipes by solving equations.
Find which pipes still have leakages after all possible leaks are fixed

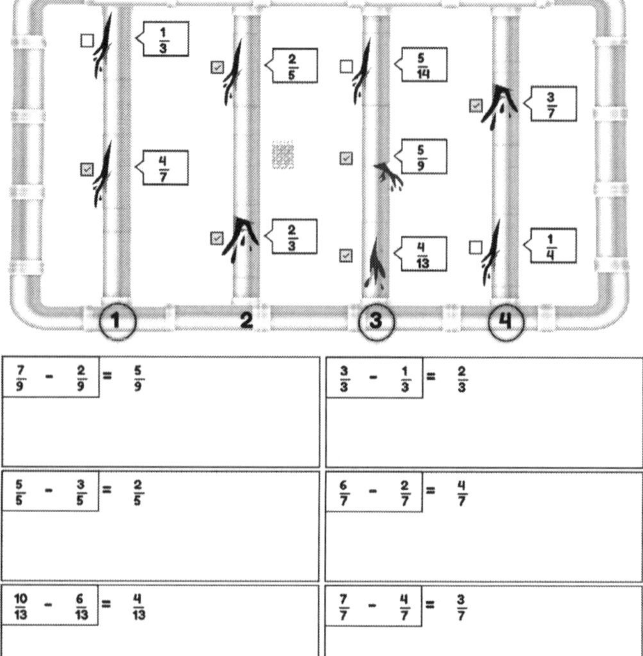

$\frac{7}{9} - \frac{2}{9} = \frac{5}{9}$	$\frac{3}{3} - \frac{1}{3} = \frac{2}{3}$
$\frac{5}{5} - \frac{3}{5} = \frac{2}{5}$	$\frac{6}{7} - \frac{2}{7} = \frac{4}{7}$
$\frac{10}{13} - \frac{6}{13} = \frac{4}{13}$	$\frac{7}{7} - \frac{4}{7} = \frac{3}{7}$

The numbers of the pipes which still have leaks are: 1, 3, 4

FRACTIONS PUZZLE 17

SUBTRACTING IMPROPER FRACTIONS

"Help the miner find the coordinates of hidden treasures by solving equations.
Calculate the total value of mined treasures."

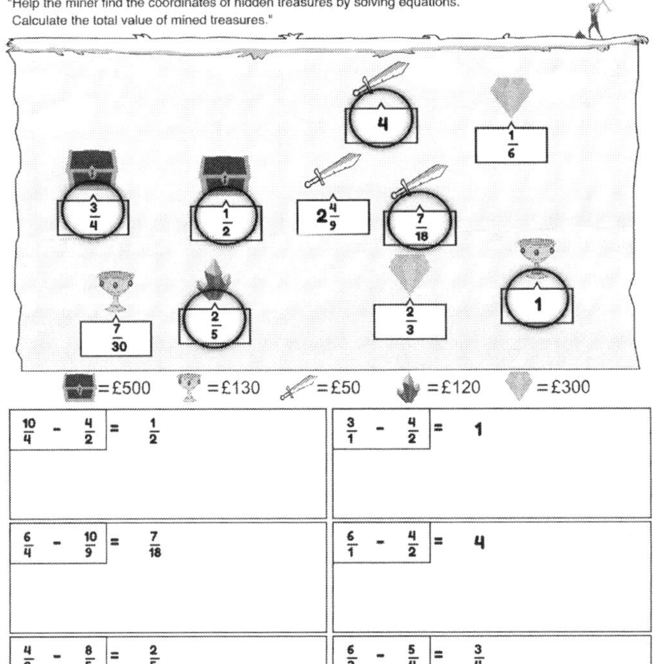

$\frac{10}{4} - \frac{4}{2} = \frac{1}{2}$	$\frac{3}{1} - \frac{4}{2} = 1$
$\frac{6}{4} - \frac{10}{9} = \frac{7}{18}$	$\frac{6}{1} - \frac{4}{2} = 4$
$\frac{4}{2} - \frac{8}{5} = \frac{2}{5}$	$\frac{6}{3} - \frac{5}{4} = \frac{3}{4}$

The total value of mined treasures = £ 1350

FRACTIONS PUZZLE 18

SUBTRACTING IMPROPER FRACTIONS

"Help the miner find the coordinates of hidden treasures by solving equations.
Calculate the total value of mined treasures."

=£120 =£280 =£50 =£80 =£130

$\frac{9}{7} - \frac{5}{4} = \frac{1}{28}$	$\frac{5}{3} - \frac{9}{8} = \frac{13}{24}$
$\frac{7}{1} - \frac{12}{6} = 5$	$\frac{3}{2} - \frac{5}{4} = \frac{1}{4}$
$\frac{9}{3} - \frac{10}{4} = \frac{1}{2}$	$\frac{9}{3} - \frac{5}{4} = 1\frac{3}{4}$

The total value of mined treasures = £ 1130

FRACTIONS PUZZLE 19

SUBTRACTING IMPROPER FRACTIONS

Fix the leaking pipes by solving equations.
Find which pipes still have leakages after all possible leaks are fixed

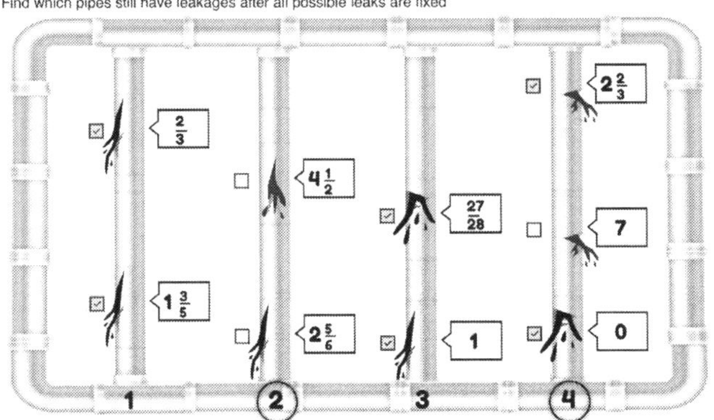

$\frac{3}{1} - \frac{7}{5} = 1\frac{3}{5}$	$\frac{8}{6} - \frac{12}{9} = 0$
$\frac{4}{1} - \frac{4}{3} = 2\frac{2}{3}$	$\frac{3}{1} - \frac{4}{2} = 1$
$\frac{8}{3} - \frac{4}{2} = \frac{2}{3}$	$\frac{9}{4} - \frac{9}{7} = \frac{27}{28}$

The numbers of the pipes which still have leaks are: 2, 4

FRACTIONS PUZZLE 20

SUBTRACTING IMPROPER FRACTIONS

Fix the leaking pipes by solving equations.
Find which pipes still have leakages after all possible leaks are fixed

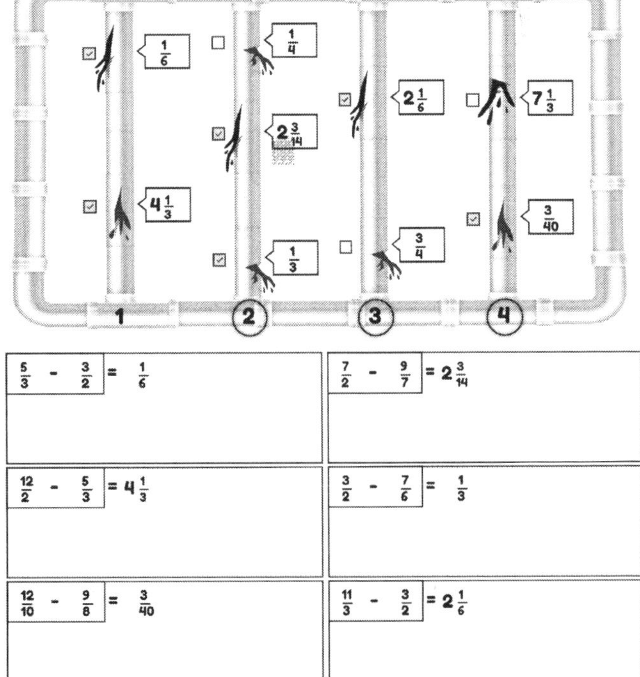

$\frac{5}{3} - \frac{3}{2} = \frac{1}{6}$	$\frac{7}{2} - \frac{9}{7} = 2\frac{3}{14}$
$\frac{12}{2} - \frac{5}{3} = 4\frac{1}{3}$	$\frac{3}{2} - \frac{7}{6} = \frac{1}{3}$
$\frac{12}{10} - \frac{9}{8} = \frac{3}{40}$	$\frac{11}{3} - \frac{3}{2} = 2\frac{1}{6}$

The numbers of the pipes which still have leaks are: 2, 3, 4

FRACTIONS PUZZLE 21

SUBTRACTING MIXED FRACTIONS

"Help the miner find the coordinates of hidden treasures by solving equations.
Calculate the total value of mined treasures."

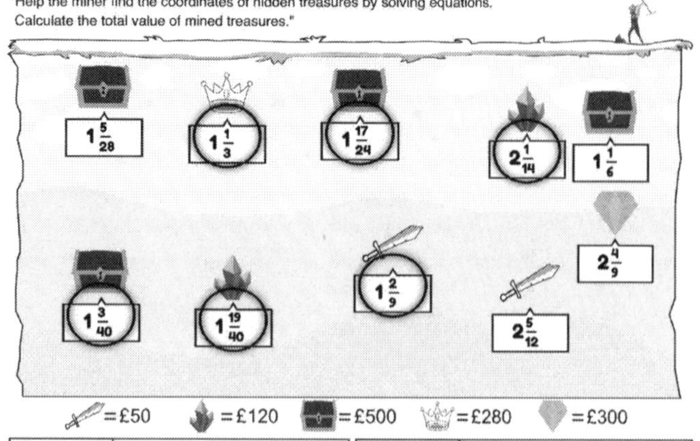

$3\frac{8}{9} - 2\frac{2}{3} = 1\frac{2}{9}$	$2\frac{3}{5} - 1\frac{1}{8} = 1\frac{19}{40}$
$3\frac{7}{8} - 2\frac{4}{5} = 1\frac{3}{40}$	$3\frac{4}{7} - 1\frac{3}{6} = 2\frac{1}{14}$
$2\frac{4}{8} - 1\frac{1}{6} = 1\frac{1}{3}$	$3\frac{3}{8} - 1\frac{2}{3} = 1\frac{17}{24}$

The total value of mined treasures = £ 1570

FRACTIONS PUZZLE 22

SUBTRACTING MIXED FRACTIONS

"Help the miner find the coordinates of hidden treasures by solving equations.
Calculate the total value of mined treasures."

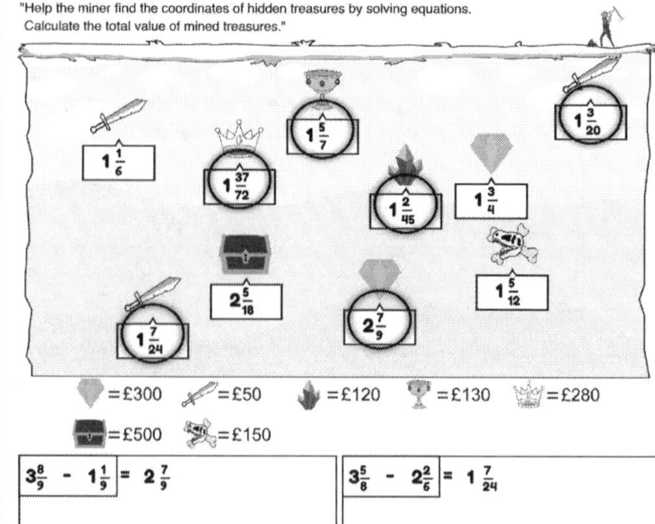

$3\frac{8}{9} - 1\frac{1}{9} = 2\frac{7}{9}$	$3\frac{5}{8} - 2\frac{2}{6} = 1\frac{7}{24}$
$3\frac{4}{9} - 2\frac{2}{5} = 1\frac{2}{45}$	$3\frac{2}{7} - 1\frac{4}{7} = 1\frac{5}{7}$
$3\frac{2}{5} - 2\frac{2}{8} = 1\frac{3}{20}$	$3\frac{8}{9} - 2\frac{3}{8} = 1\frac{37}{72}$

The total value of mined treasures = £ 930

FRACTIONS PUZZLE 23

SUBTRACTING MIXED FRACTIONS

Fix the leaking pipes by solving equations.
Find which pipes still have leakages after all possible leaks are fixed

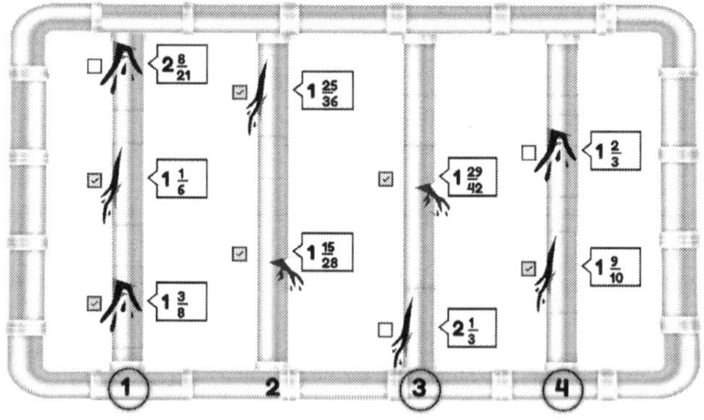

$3\frac{2}{7} - 1\frac{6}{8} = 1\frac{15}{28}$	$3\frac{2}{5} - 1\frac{2}{4} = 1\frac{9}{10}$
$2\frac{2}{3} - 1\frac{2}{4} = 1\frac{1}{6}$	$2\frac{5}{6} - 1\frac{1}{7} = 1\frac{29}{42}$
$3\frac{4}{9} - 1\frac{3}{4} = 1\frac{25}{36}$	$3\frac{5}{8} - 2\frac{1}{4} = 1\frac{3}{8}$

The numbers of the pipes which still have leaks are: 1, 3, 4

FRACTIONS PUZZLE 24

SUBTRACTING MIXED FRACTIONS

Fix the leaking pipes by solving equations.
Find which pipes still have leakages after all possible leaks are fixed

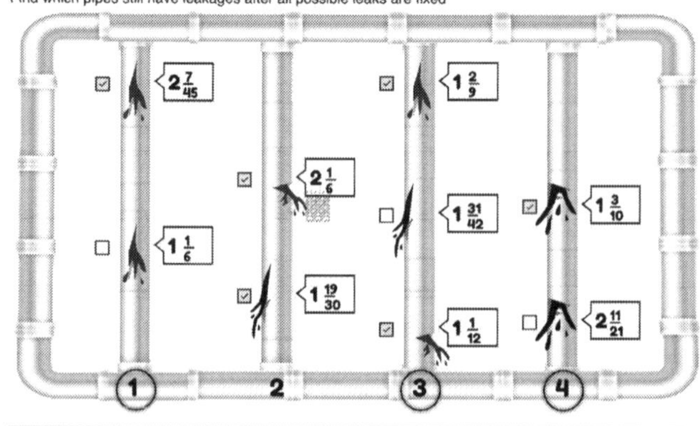

$3\frac{3}{5} - 1\frac{4}{9} = 2\frac{7}{45}$	$2\frac{2}{4} - 1\frac{1}{5} = 1\frac{3}{10}$
$2\frac{4}{5} - 1\frac{1}{6} = 1\frac{19}{30}$	$3\frac{6}{9} - 1\frac{4}{8} = 2\frac{1}{6}$
$3\frac{1}{3} - 2\frac{1}{4} = 1\frac{1}{12}$	$3\frac{5}{9} - 2\frac{3}{9} = 1\frac{2}{9}$

The numbers of the pipes which still have leaks are: 1, 3, 4

FRACTIONS PUZZLE 25

DIVIDING PROPER FRACTIONS

"Help the miner find the coordinates of hidden treasures by solving equations.
Calculate the total value of mined treasures."

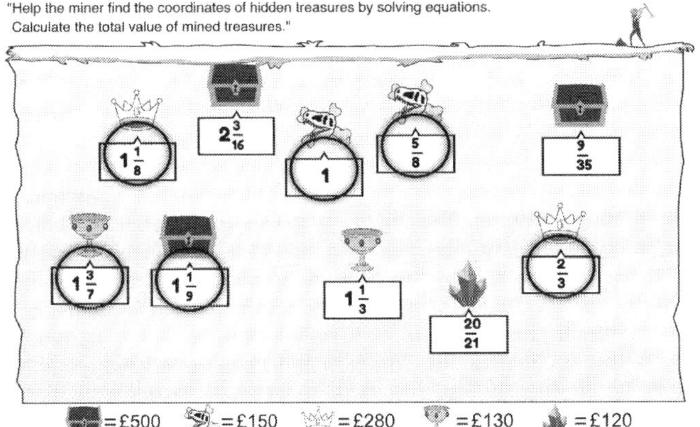

=£500 =£150 =£280 =£130 =£120

$\frac{4}{9} \div \frac{2}{5} = 1\frac{1}{9}$	$\frac{3}{6} \div \frac{4}{5} = \frac{5}{8}$
$\frac{2}{3} \div \frac{6}{9} = 1$	$\frac{4}{9} \div \frac{2}{3} = \frac{2}{3}$
$\frac{6}{7} \div \frac{3}{5} = 1\frac{3}{7}$	$\frac{1}{4} \div \frac{2}{9} = 1\frac{1}{8}$

The total value of mined treasures = £ 1490

FRACTIONS PUZZLE 26

DIVIDING PROPER FRACTIONS

"Help the miner find the coordinates of hidden treasures by solving equations.
Calculate the total value of mined treasures."

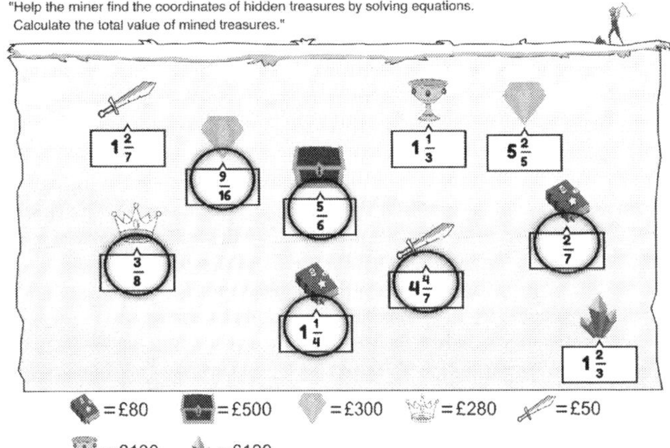

=£80 =£500 =£300 =£280 =£50

=£130 =£120

$\frac{2}{4} \div \frac{2}{5} = 1\frac{1}{4}$	$\frac{5}{8} \div \frac{3}{4} = \frac{5}{6}$
$\frac{2}{4} \div \frac{8}{9} = \frac{9}{16}$	$\frac{2}{8} \div \frac{6}{9} = \frac{3}{8}$
$\frac{1}{4} \div \frac{7}{8} = \frac{2}{7}$	$\frac{4}{7} \div \frac{1}{8} = 4\frac{4}{7}$

The total value of mined treasures = £ 1290

FRACTIONS PUZZLE 27

DIVIDING PROPER FRACTIONS

Fix the leaking pipes by solving equations.
Find which pipes still have leakages after all possible leaks are fixed

$\frac{7}{18}$
$1\frac{11}{24}$
3
$\frac{3}{4}$
$1\frac{5}{9}$
$\frac{9}{20}$
$4\frac{1}{2}$
$3\frac{1}{5}$
$\frac{2}{5}$
1 2 3 4

$\frac{3}{4} \div \frac{1}{6} = 4\frac{1}{2}$	$\frac{5}{8} \div \frac{3}{7} = 1\frac{11}{24}$
$\frac{4}{5} \div \frac{1}{4} = 3\frac{1}{5}$	$\frac{3}{9} \div \frac{6}{7} = \frac{7}{18}$
$\frac{1}{4} \div \frac{5}{9} = \frac{9}{20}$	$\frac{3}{9} \div \frac{5}{6} = \frac{2}{5}$

The numbers of the pipes which still have leaks are: 1, 2

FRACTIONS PUZZLE 28

DIVIDING PROPER FRACTIONS

Fix the leaking pipes by solving equations.
Find which pipes still have leakages after all possible leaks are fixed

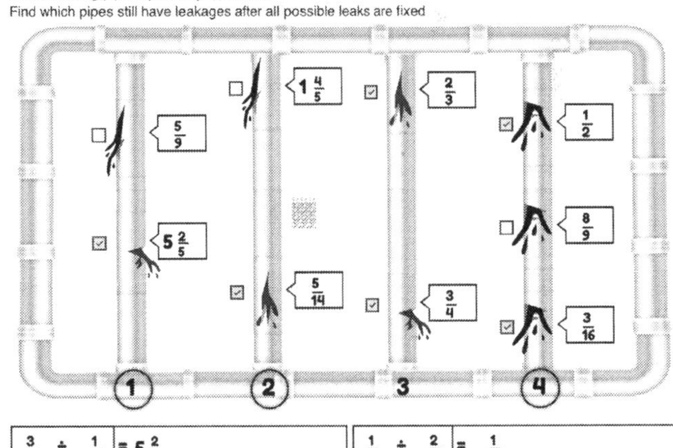

$\frac{3}{5} \div \frac{1}{9} = 5\frac{2}{5}$	$\frac{1}{3} \div \frac{2}{3} = \frac{1}{2}$
$\frac{4}{6} \div \frac{8}{9} = \frac{3}{4}$	$\frac{1}{8} \div \frac{4}{6} = \frac{3}{16}$
$\frac{2}{8} \div \frac{3}{8} = \frac{2}{3}$	$\frac{2}{7} \div \frac{4}{5} = \frac{5}{14}$

The numbers of the pipes which still have leaks are: 1, 2, 4

FRACTIONS PUZZLE 29

DIVIDING IMPROPER FRACTIONS

"Help the miner find the coordinates of hidden treasures by solving equations. Calculate the total value of mined treasures."

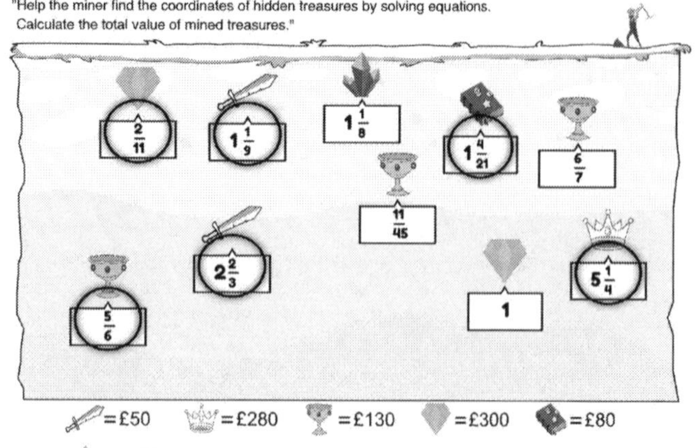

=£50 =£280 =£130 =£300 =£80 =£120

$\frac{4}{1} \div \frac{12}{8} = 2\frac{2}{3}$	$\frac{7}{1} \div \frac{8}{6} = 5\frac{1}{4}$
$\frac{7}{6} \div \frac{7}{5} = \frac{5}{6}$	$\frac{4}{2} \div \frac{11}{1} = \frac{2}{11}$
$\frac{5}{3} \div \frac{7}{5} = 1\frac{4}{21}$	$\frac{10}{1} \div \frac{9}{1} = 1\frac{1}{9}$

The total value of mined treasures = £ 890

FRACTIONS PUZZLE 30

DIVIDING IMPROPER FRACTIONS

"Help the miner find the coordinates of hidden treasures by solving equations. Calculate the total value of mined treasures."

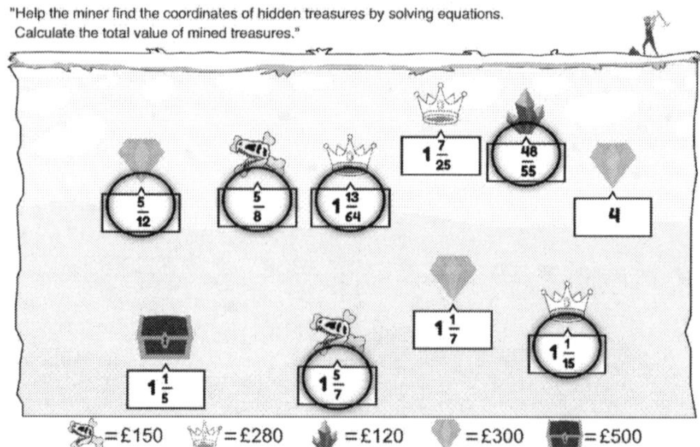

=£150 =£280 =£120 =£300 =£500

$\frac{10}{8} \div \frac{4}{2} = \frac{5}{8}$	$\frac{11}{8} \div \frac{8}{7} = 1\frac{13}{64}$
$\frac{12}{11} \div \frac{5}{4} = \frac{48}{55}$	$\frac{6}{1} \div \frac{7}{2} = 1\frac{5}{7}$
$\frac{5}{4} \div \frac{3}{1} = \frac{5}{12}$	$\frac{8}{5} \div \frac{12}{8} = 1\frac{1}{15}$

The total value of mined treasures = £ 1280

FRACTIONS PUZZLE 31

DIVIDING IMPROPER FRACTIONS

Fix the leaking pipes by solving equations.
Find which pipes still have leakages after all possible leaks are fixed

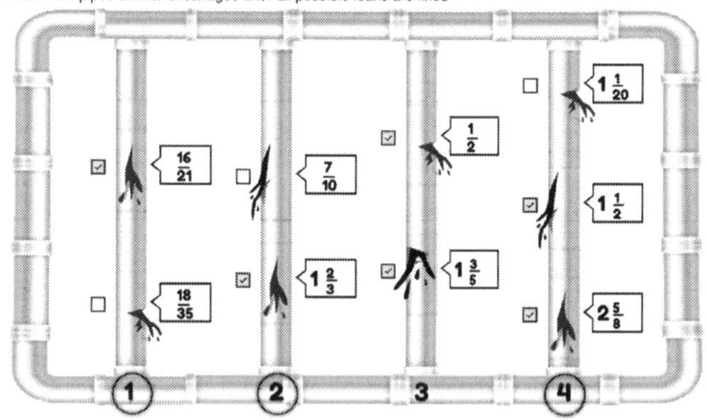

$\frac{4}{2} \div \frac{4}{3} = 1\frac{1}{2}$	$\frac{4}{2} \div \frac{4}{1} = \frac{1}{2}$
$\frac{5}{2} \div \frac{9}{6} = 1\frac{2}{3}$	$\frac{8}{7} \div \frac{3}{2} = \frac{16}{21}$
$\frac{7}{2} \div \frac{8}{6} = 2\frac{5}{8}$	$\frac{4}{2} \div \frac{5}{4} = 1\frac{3}{5}$

The numbers of the pipes which still have leaks are: 1, 2, 4

FRACTIONS PUZZLE 32

DIVIDING IMPROPER FRACTIONS

Fix the leaking pipes by solving equations.
Find which pipes still have leakages after all possible leaks are fixed

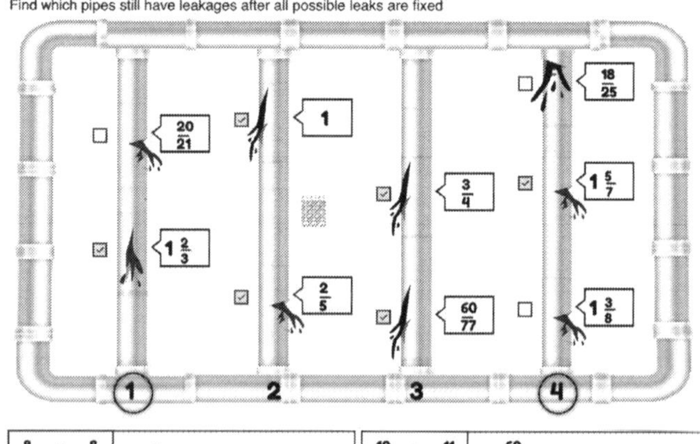

$\frac{8}{1} \div \frac{8}{1} = 1$	$\frac{10}{7} \div \frac{11}{6} = \frac{60}{77}$
$\frac{3}{1} \div \frac{7}{4} = 1\frac{5}{7}$	$\frac{4}{2} \div \frac{5}{1} = \frac{2}{5}$
$\frac{10}{8} \div \frac{5}{3} = \frac{3}{4}$	$\frac{3}{1} \div \frac{9}{5} = 1\frac{2}{3}$

The numbers of the pipes which still have leaks are: 1, 4

FRACTIONS PUZZLE 33

DIVIDING MIXED FRACTIONS

"Help the miner find the coordinates of hidden treasures by solving equations.
Calculate the total value of mined treasures."

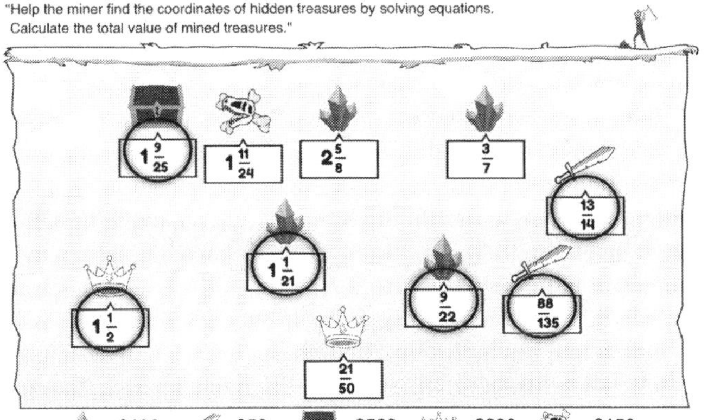

=£120 =£50 =£500 =£280 =£150

$1\frac{2}{4} \div 3\frac{4}{6} = \frac{9}{22}$	$2\frac{1}{5} \div 3\frac{3}{8} = \frac{88}{135}$
$3\frac{2}{5} \div 2\frac{2}{4} = 1\frac{9}{25}$	$3\frac{2}{3} \div 3\frac{3}{6} = 1\frac{1}{21}$
$3\frac{6}{8} \div 2\frac{1}{2} = 1\frac{1}{2}$	$3\frac{2}{8} \div 3\frac{1}{2} = \frac{13}{14}$

The total value of mined treasures = £ 1120

FRACTIONS PUZZLE 34

DIVIDING MIXED FRACTIONS

"Help the miner find the coordinates of hidden treasures by solving equations.
Calculate the total value of mined treasures."

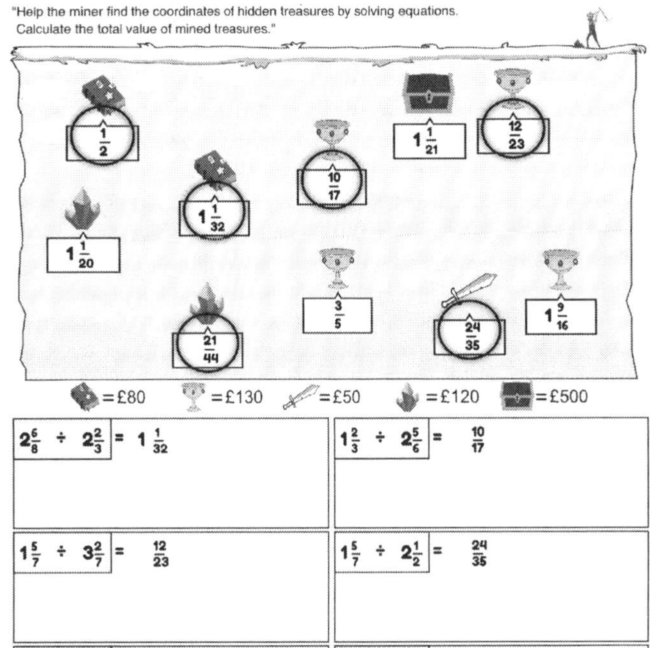

=£80 =£130 =£50 =£120 =£500

$2\frac{6}{8} \div 2\frac{2}{3} = 1\frac{1}{32}$	$1\frac{2}{3} \div 2\frac{5}{6} = \frac{10}{17}$
$1\frac{5}{7} \div 3\frac{2}{7} = \frac{12}{23}$	$1\frac{5}{7} \div 2\frac{1}{2} = \frac{24}{35}$
$1\frac{1}{2} \div 3\frac{1}{7} = \frac{21}{44}$	$1\frac{1}{3} \div 2\frac{2}{3} = \frac{1}{2}$

The total value of mined treasures = £ 590

FRACTIONS PUZZLE 35

DIVIDING MIXED FRACTIONS

Fix the leaking pipes by solving equations.
Find which pipes still have leakages after all possible leaks are fixed

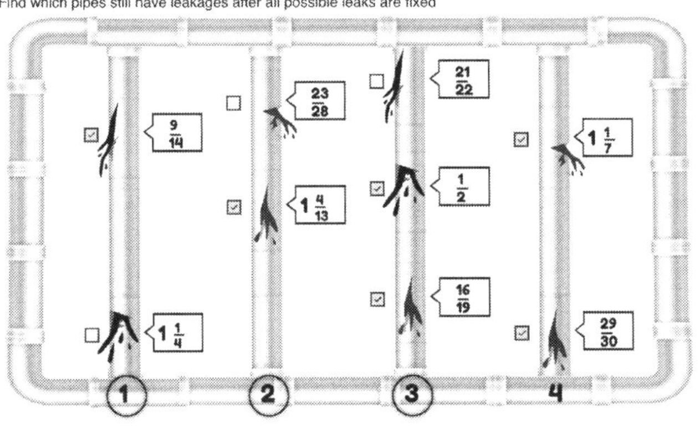

$1\frac{6}{8} \div 3\frac{1}{2} = \frac{1}{2}$	$3\frac{5}{8} \div 3\frac{6}{8} = \frac{29}{30}$
$3\frac{2}{5} \div 2\frac{3}{5} = 1\frac{4}{13}$	$1\frac{5}{7} \div 1\frac{2}{4} = 1\frac{1}{7}$
$2\frac{2}{3} \div 3\frac{1}{6} = \frac{16}{19}$	$1\frac{3}{6} \div 2\frac{1}{3} = \frac{9}{14}$

The numbers of the pipes which still have leaks are: 1, 2, 3

FRACTIONS PUZZLE 36

DIVIDING MIXED FRACTIONS

Fix the leaking pipes by solving equations.
Find which pipes still have leakages after all possible leaks are fixed

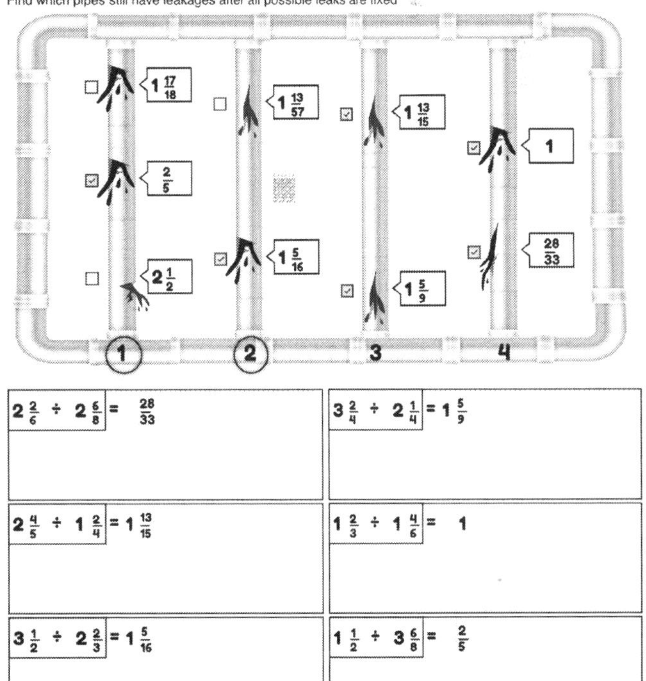

$2\frac{2}{6} \div 2\frac{6}{8} = \frac{28}{33}$	$3\frac{2}{4} \div 2\frac{1}{4} = 1\frac{5}{9}$
$2\frac{4}{5} \div 1\frac{2}{4} = 1\frac{13}{15}$	$1\frac{2}{3} \div 1\frac{4}{6} = 1$
$3\frac{1}{2} \div 2\frac{2}{3} = 1\frac{5}{16}$	$1\frac{1}{2} \div 3\frac{6}{8} = \frac{2}{5}$

The numbers of the pipes which still have leaks are: 1, 2

FRACTIONS PUZZLE 37

MULTIPLYING PROPER FRACTIONS

"Help the miner find the coordinates of hidden treasures by solving equations.
Calculate the total value of mined treasures."

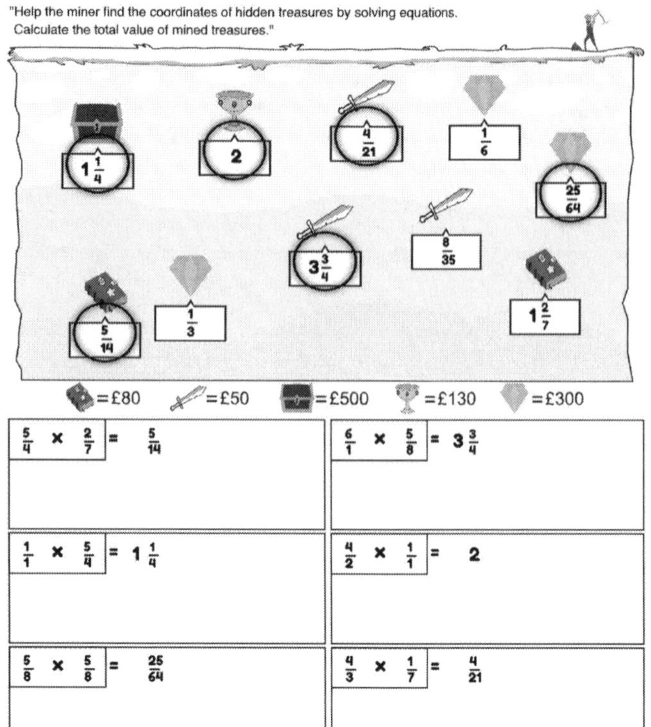

$\frac{5}{4} \times \frac{2}{7} = \frac{5}{14}$	$\frac{6}{1} \times \frac{5}{8} = 3\frac{3}{4}$
$\frac{1}{1} \times \frac{5}{4} = 1\frac{1}{4}$	$\frac{4}{2} \times \frac{1}{1} = 2$
$\frac{5}{8} \times \frac{5}{8} = \frac{25}{64}$	$\frac{4}{3} \times \frac{1}{7} = \frac{4}{21}$

The total value of mined treasures = £ 1110

FRACTIONS PUZZLE 38

MULTIPLYING PROPER FRACTIONS

"Help the miner find the coordinates of hidden treasures by solving equations.
Calculate the total value of mined treasures."

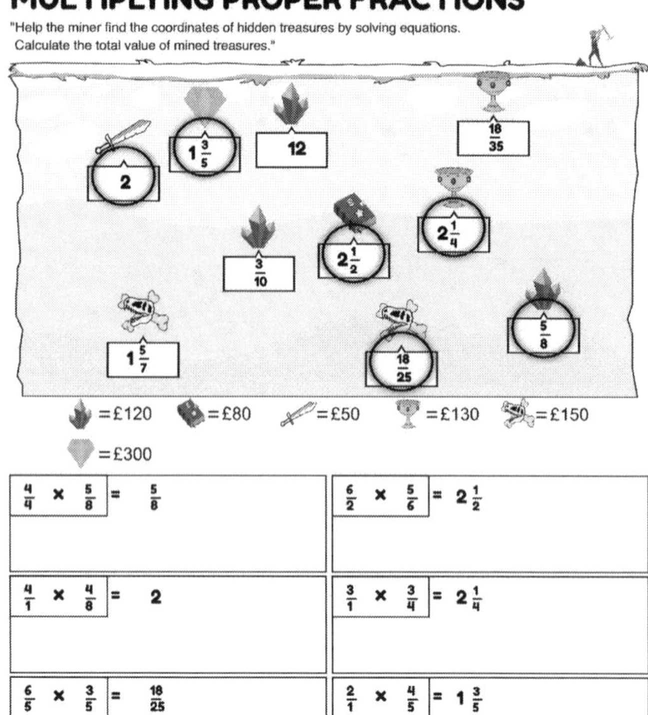

$\frac{4}{4} \times \frac{5}{8} = \frac{5}{8}$	$\frac{6}{2} \times \frac{5}{6} = 2\frac{1}{2}$
$\frac{4}{1} \times \frac{4}{8} = 2$	$\frac{3}{1} \times \frac{3}{4} = 2\frac{1}{4}$
$\frac{6}{5} \times \frac{3}{5} = \frac{18}{25}$	$\frac{2}{1} \times \frac{4}{5} = 1\frac{3}{5}$

The total value of mined treasures = £ 830

FRACTIONS PUZZLE 39

MULTIPLYING PROPER FRACTIONS

Fix the leaking pipes by solving equations.
Find which pipes still have leakages after all possible leaks are fixed

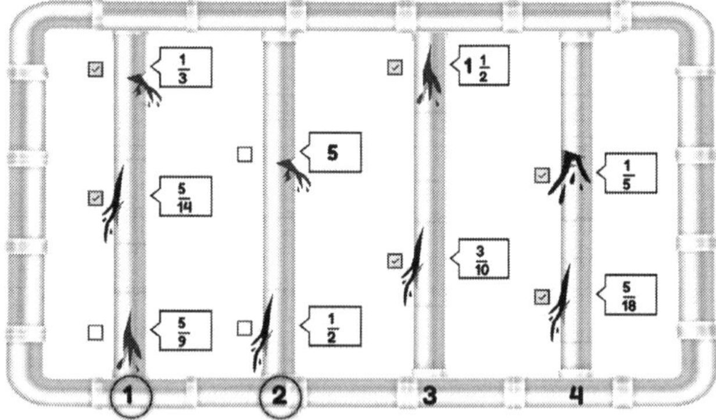

$\frac{1}{5} \times \frac{5}{5} = \frac{1}{5}$	$\frac{5}{3} \times \frac{1}{5} = \frac{1}{3}$
$\frac{5}{2} \times \frac{1}{7} = \frac{5}{14}$	$\frac{3}{5} \times \frac{3}{6} = \frac{3}{10}$
$\frac{5}{3} \times \frac{1}{6} = \frac{5}{18}$	$\frac{3}{1} \times \frac{4}{8} = 1\frac{1}{2}$

The numbers of the pipes which still have leaks are: 1, 2

FRACTIONS PUZZLE 40

MULTIPLYING PROPER FRACTIONS

Fix the leaking pipes by solving equations.
Find which pipes still have leakages after all possible leaks are fixed

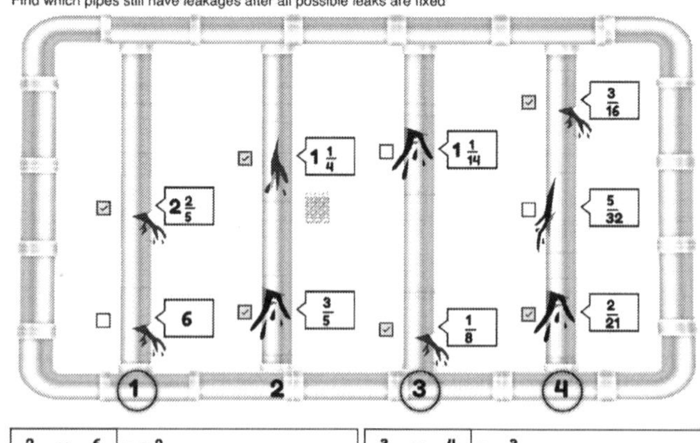

$\frac{2}{5} \times \frac{6}{1} = 2\frac{2}{5}$	$\frac{3}{4} \times \frac{4}{5} = \frac{3}{5}$
$\frac{6}{3} \times \frac{5}{8} = 1\frac{1}{4}$	$\frac{2}{7} \times \frac{2}{6} = \frac{2}{21}$
$\frac{2}{8} \times \frac{3}{4} = \frac{3}{16}$	$\frac{1}{8} \times \frac{3}{3} = \frac{1}{8}$

The numbers of the pipes which still have leaks are: 1, 3, 4

FRACTIONS PUZZLE 41

MULTIPLYING IMPROPER FRACTIONS

"Help the miner find the coordinates of hidden treasures by solving equations.
Calculate the total value of mined treasures."

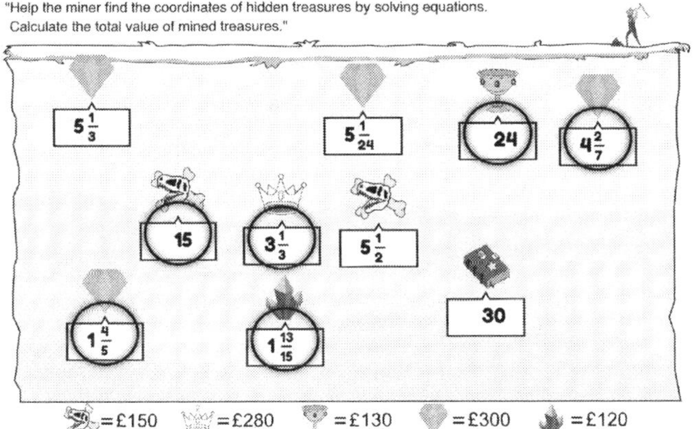

=£150 =£280 =£130 =£300 =£120 =£80

$\frac{10}{1} \times \frac{3}{2} = 15$	$\frac{10}{7} \times \frac{7}{3} = 3\frac{1}{3}$
$\frac{4}{2} \times \frac{12}{1} = 24$	$\frac{6}{5} \times \frac{3}{2} = 1\frac{4}{5}$
$\frac{7}{5} \times \frac{12}{9} = 1\frac{13}{15}$	$\frac{9}{7} \times \frac{10}{3} = 4\frac{2}{7}$

The total value of mined treasures = £ 1280

FRACTIONS PUZZLE 42

MULTIPLYING IMPROPER FRACTIONS

"Help the miner find the coordinates of hidden treasures by solving equations.
Calculate the total value of mined treasures."

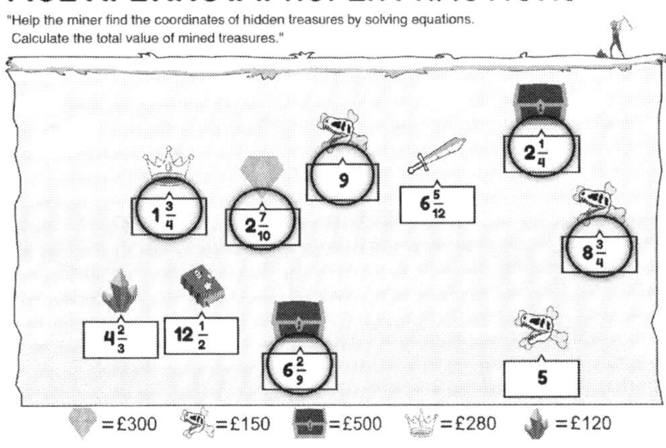

=£300 =£150 =£500 =£280 =£120 =£50 =£80

$\frac{9}{5} \times \frac{3}{2} = 2\frac{7}{10}$	$\frac{3}{1} \times \frac{3}{1} = 9$
$\frac{3}{2} \times \frac{3}{2} = 2\frac{1}{4}$	$\frac{7}{2} \times \frac{5}{2} = 8\frac{3}{4}$
$\frac{5}{4} \times \frac{7}{5} = 1\frac{3}{4}$	$\frac{8}{3} \times \frac{7}{3} = 6\frac{2}{9}$

The total value of mined treasures = £ 1880

FRACTIONS PUZZLE 43

MULTIPLYING IMPROPER FRACTIONS

Fix the leaking pipes by solving equations.
Find which pipes still have leakages after all possible leaks are fixed

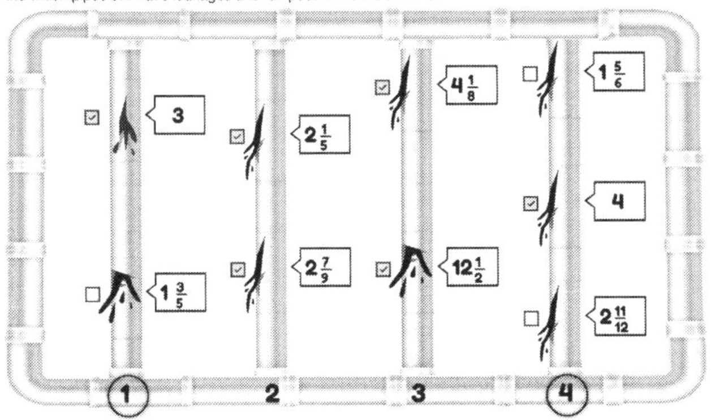

$\frac{5}{2} \times \frac{5}{1} = 12\frac{1}{2}$	$\frac{11}{7} \times \frac{7}{5} = 2\frac{1}{5}$
$\frac{3}{2} \times \frac{11}{4} = 4\frac{1}{8}$	$\frac{4}{3} \times \frac{3}{1} = 4$
$\frac{4}{2} \times \frac{9}{6} = 3$	$\frac{5}{3} \times \frac{10}{6} = 2\frac{7}{9}$

The numbers of the pipes which still have leaks are: 1, 4

FRACTIONS PUZZLE 44

MULTIPLYING IMPROPER FRACTIONS

Fix the leaking pipes by solving equations.
Find which pipes still have leakages after all possible leaks are fixed

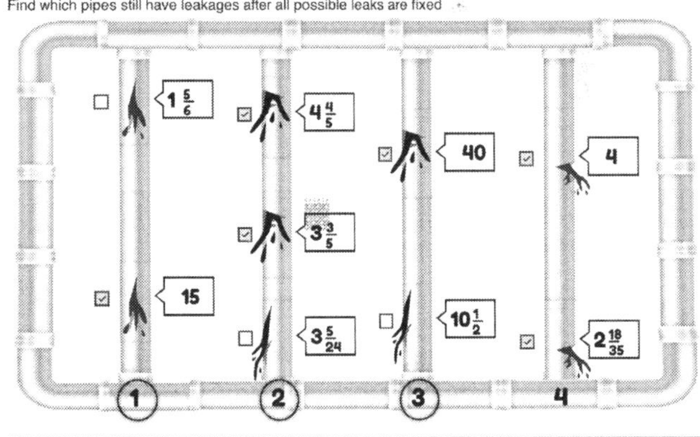

$\frac{8}{5} \times \frac{6}{2} = 4\frac{4}{5}$	$\frac{9}{5} \times \frac{8}{4} = 3\frac{3}{5}$
$\frac{10}{4} \times \frac{6}{1} = 15$	$\frac{11}{7} \times \frac{8}{5} = 2\frac{18}{35}$
$\frac{10}{1} \times \frac{12}{3} = 40$	$\frac{4}{2} \times \frac{4}{2} = 4$

The numbers of the pipes which still have leaks are: 1, 2, 3

FRACTIONS PUZZLE 45

MULTIPLYING MIXED FRACTIONS

"Help the miner find the coordinates of hidden treasures by solving equations.
Calculate the total value of mined treasures."

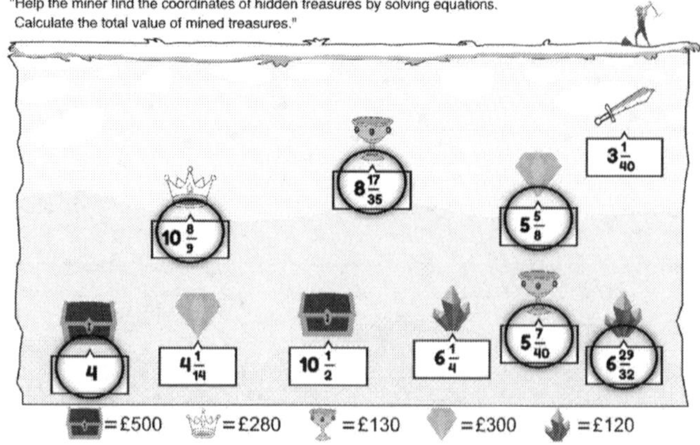

=£50

$2\frac{2}{3} \times 1\frac{1}{2} = 4$	$4\frac{2}{3} \times 2\frac{1}{3} = 10\frac{8}{9}$
$1\frac{4}{5} \times 4\frac{5}{7} = 8\frac{17}{35}$	$2\frac{2}{4} \times 2\frac{1}{4} = 5\frac{5}{8}$
$1\frac{5}{8} \times 4\frac{1}{4} = 6\frac{29}{32}$	$4\frac{3}{5} \times 1\frac{1}{8} = 5\frac{7}{40}$

The total value of mined treasures = £ 1460

FRACTIONS PUZZLE 46

MULTIPLYING MIXED FRACTIONS

"Help the miner find the coordinates of hidden treasures by solving equations.
Calculate the total value of mined treasures."

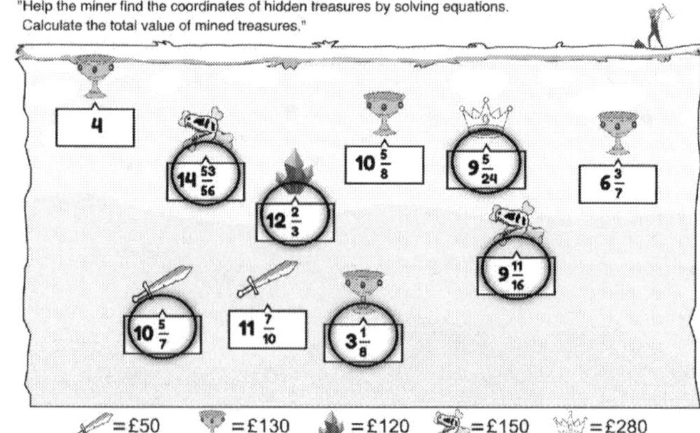

$4\frac{2}{7} \times 2\frac{4}{8} = 10\frac{5}{7}$	$1\frac{1}{4} \times 2\frac{1}{2} = 3\frac{1}{8}$
$2\frac{5}{7} \times 4\frac{4}{6} = 12\frac{2}{3}$	$2\frac{1}{2} \times 3\frac{7}{8} = 9\frac{11}{16}$
$4\frac{1}{3} \times 2\frac{1}{8} = 9\frac{5}{24}$	$3\frac{7}{8} \times 3\frac{6}{7} = 14\frac{53}{56}$

The total value of mined treasures = £ 880

FRACTIONS PUZZLE 47

MULTIPLYING MIXED FRACTIONS

Fix the leaking pipes by solving equations.
Find which pipes still have leakages after all possible leaks are fixed

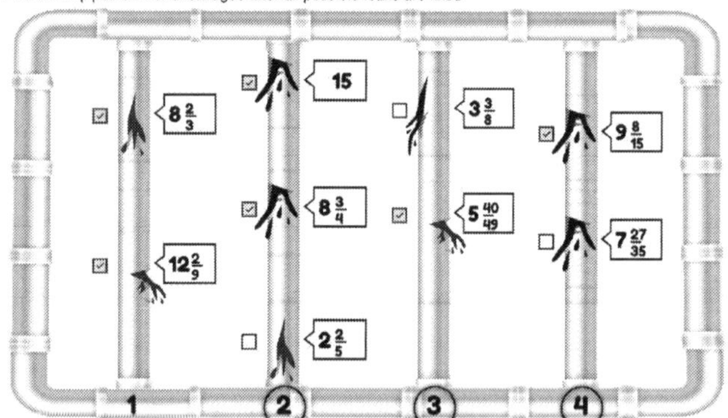

$2\frac{1}{7} \times 2\frac{5}{7} = 5\frac{40}{49}$	$4\frac{2}{7} \times 3\frac{1}{2} = 15$
$3\frac{3}{4} \times 2\frac{1}{3} = 8\frac{3}{4}$	$3\frac{1}{3} \times 2\frac{3}{5} = 8\frac{2}{3}$
$3\frac{2}{6} \times 3\frac{2}{3} = 12\frac{2}{9}$	$4\frac{2}{6} \times 2\frac{1}{5} = 9\frac{8}{15}$

The numbers of the pipes which still have leaks are: 2, 3, 4

FRACTIONS PUZZLE 48

MULTIPLYING MIXED FRACTIONS

Fix the leaking pipes by solving equations.
Find which pipes still have leakages after all possible leaks are fixed

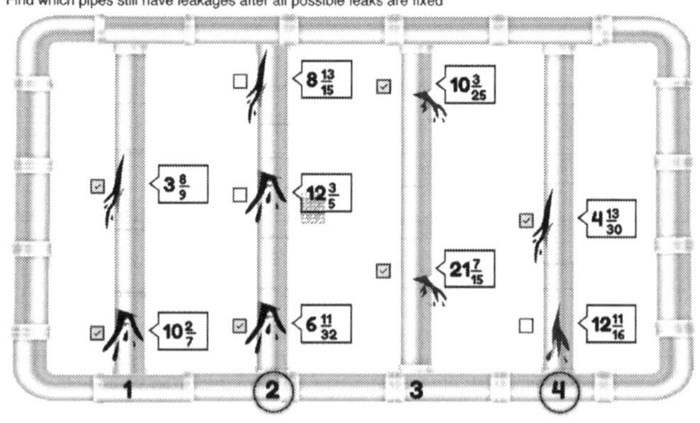

$1\frac{2}{5} \times 3\frac{1}{6} = 4\frac{13}{30}$	$3\frac{5}{8} \times 1\frac{3}{4} = 6\frac{11}{32}$
$4\frac{4}{6} \times 4\frac{3}{5} = 21\frac{7}{15}$	$2\frac{1}{5} \times 4\frac{3}{5} = 10\frac{3}{25}$
$2\frac{1}{7} \times 4\frac{4}{5} = 10\frac{2}{7}$	$1\frac{2}{3} \times 2\frac{1}{3} = 3\frac{8}{9}$

The numbers of the pipes which still have leaks are: 2, 4

Gumball Puzzle 1

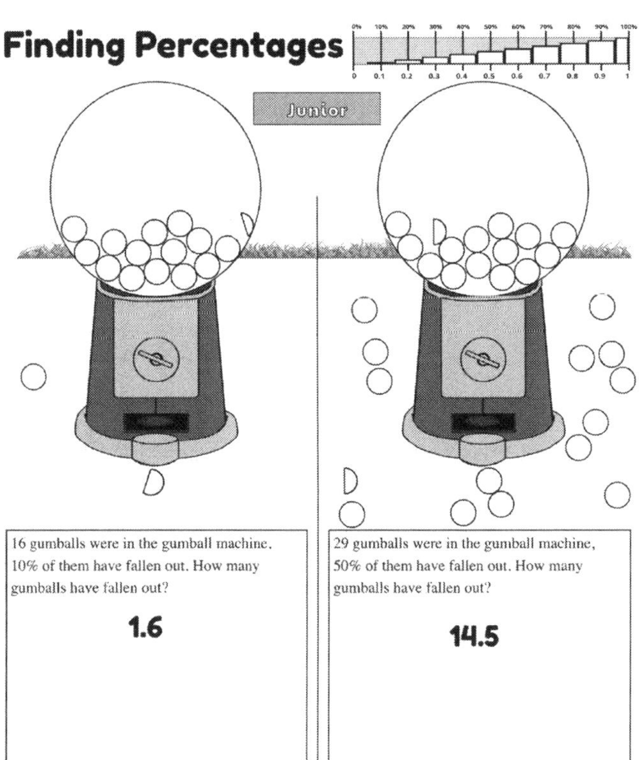

16 gumballs were in the gumball machine, 10% of them have fallen out. How many gumballs have fallen out?

1.6

29 gumballs were in the gumball machine, 50% of them have fallen out. How many gumballs have fallen out?

14.5

Gumball Puzzle 2

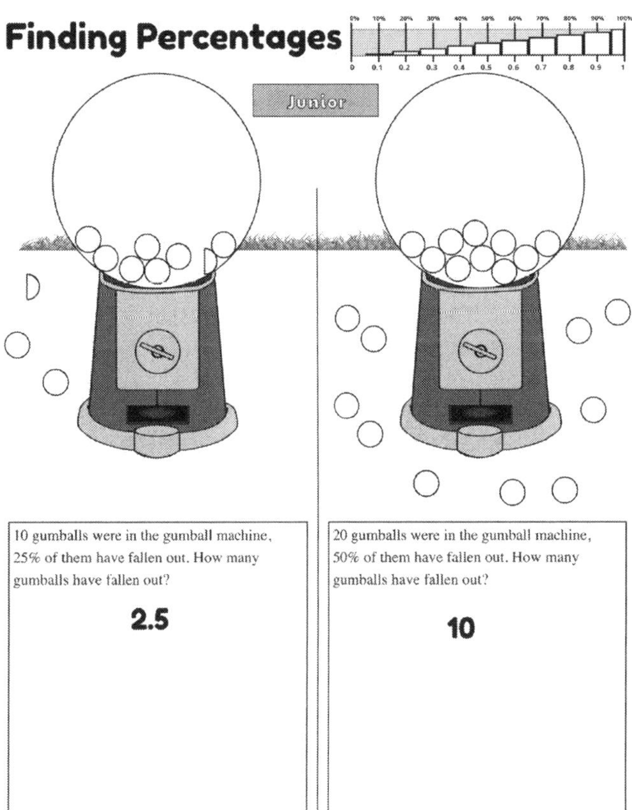

10 gumballs were in the gumball machine, 25% of them have fallen out. How many gumballs have fallen out?

2.5

20 gumballs were in the gumball machine, 50% of them have fallen out. How many gumballs have fallen out?

10

Gumball Puzzle 3

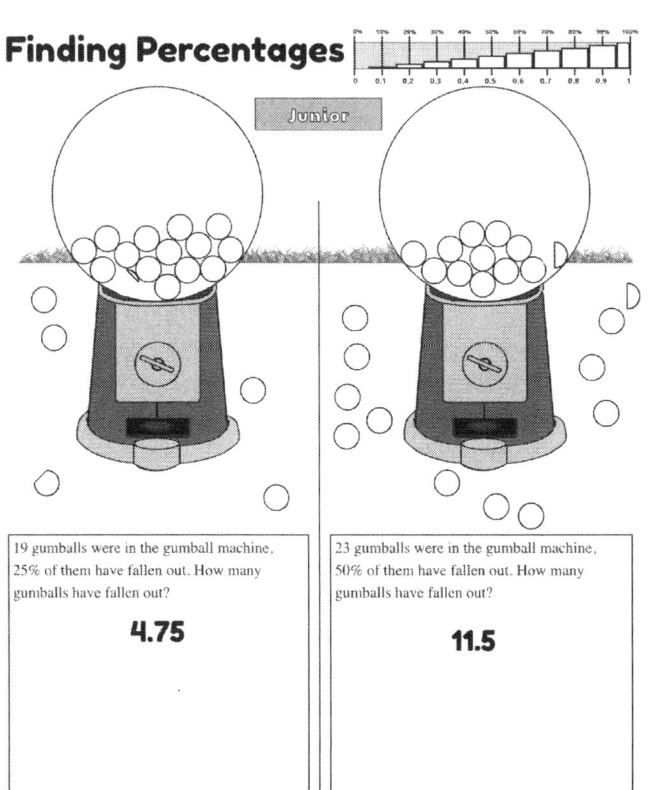

19 gumballs were in the gumball machine, 25% of them have fallen out. How many gumballs have fallen out?

4.75

23 gumballs were in the gumball machine, 50% of them have fallen out. How many gumballs have fallen out?

11.5

Gumball Puzzle 4

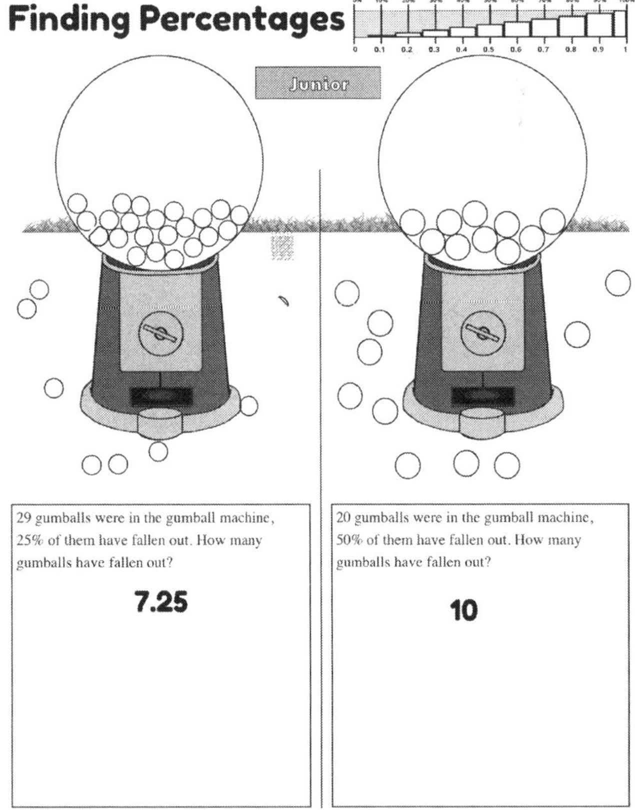

29 gumballs were in the gumball machine, 25% of them have fallen out. How many gumballs have fallen out?

7.25

20 gumballs were in the gumball machine, 50% of them have fallen out. How many gumballs have fallen out?

10

Gumball Puzzle 5

Finding Percentages

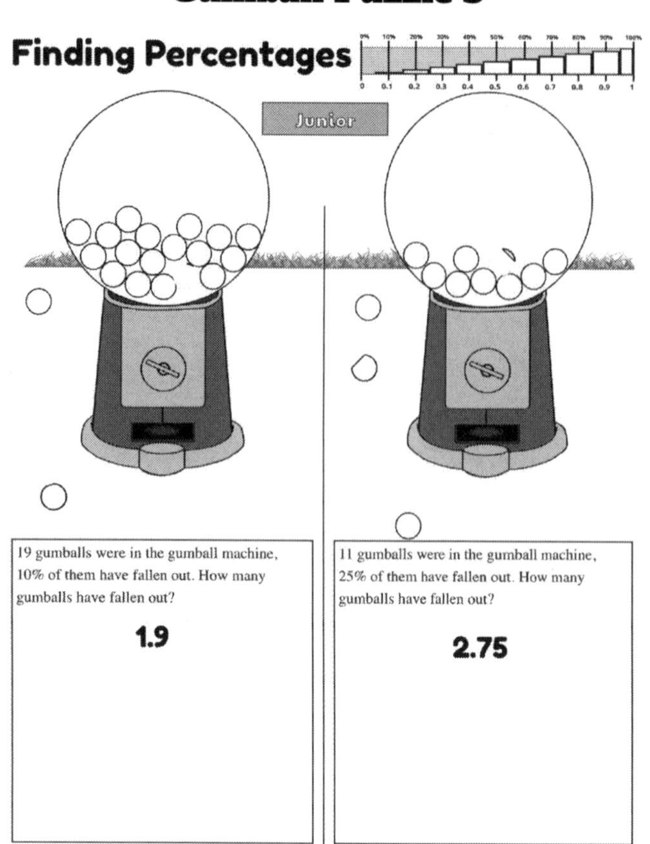

Junior

19 gumballs were in the gumball machine, 10% of them have fallen out. How many gumballs have fallen out?

1.9

11 gumballs were in the gumball machine, 25% of them have fallen out. How many gumballs have fallen out?

2.75

Gumball Puzzle 6

Finding Percentages

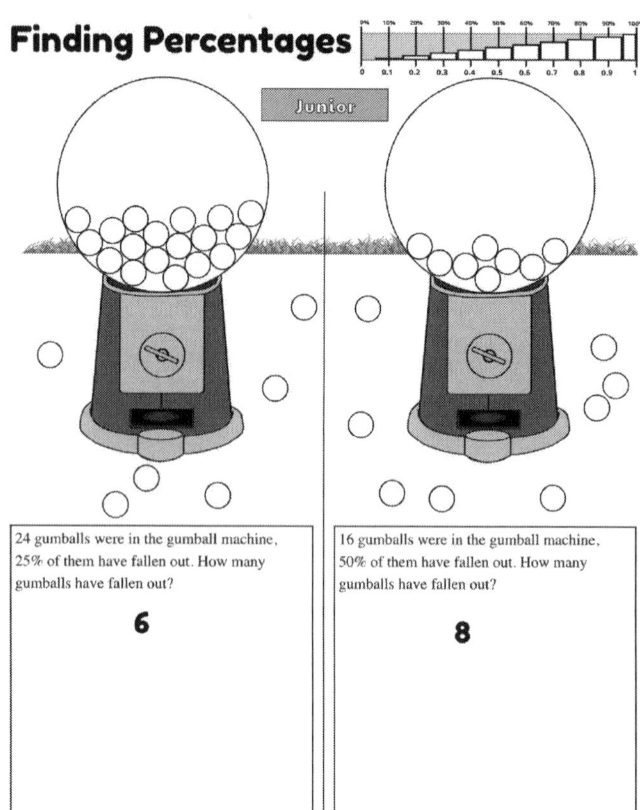

Junior

24 gumballs were in the gumball machine, 25% of them have fallen out. How many gumballs have fallen out?

6

16 gumballs were in the gumball machine, 50% of them have fallen out. How many gumballs have fallen out?

8

Gumball Puzzle 7

Finding Percentages

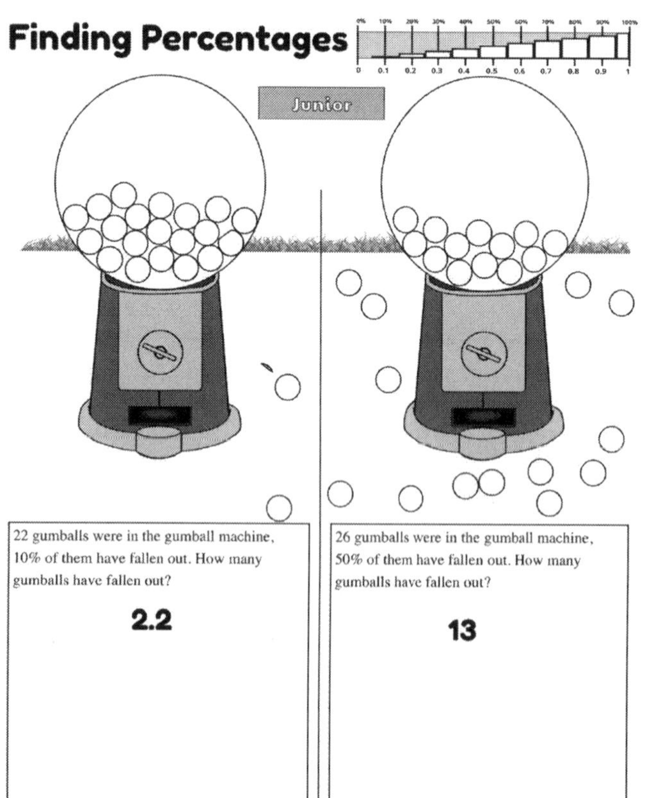

Junior

22 gumballs were in the gumball machine, 10% of them have fallen out. How many gumballs have fallen out?

2.2

26 gumballs were in the gumball machine, 50% of them have fallen out. How many gumballs have fallen out?

13

Gumball Puzzle 8

Finding Percentages

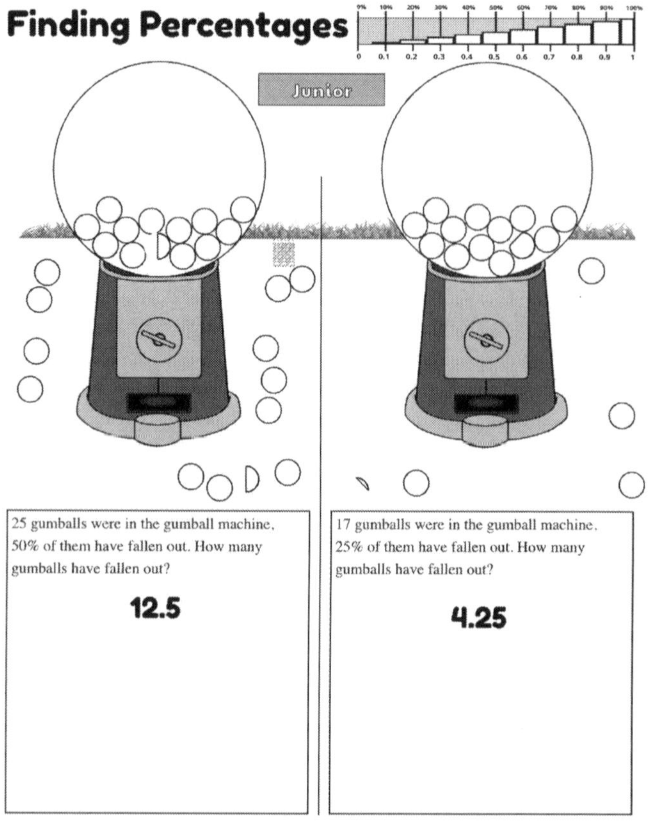

Junior

25 gumballs were in the gumball machine, 50% of them have fallen out. How many gumballs have fallen out?

12.5

17 gumballs were in the gumball machine, 25% of them have fallen out. How many gumballs have fallen out?

4.25

Gumball Puzzle 9

Finding Percentages

Medium

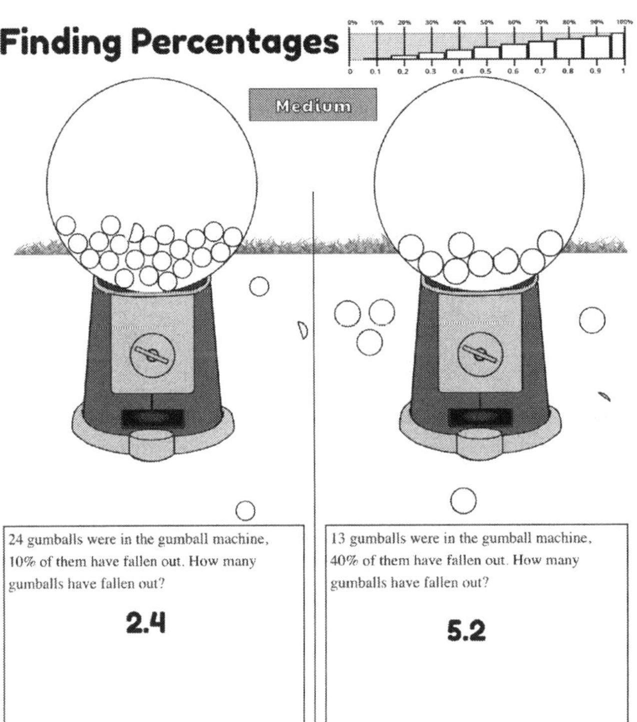

24 gumballs were in the gumball machine, 10% of them have fallen out. How many gumballs have fallen out?

2.4

13 gumballs were in the gumball machine, 40% of them have fallen out. How many gumballs have fallen out?

5.2

Gumball Puzzle 10

Finding Percentages

Medium

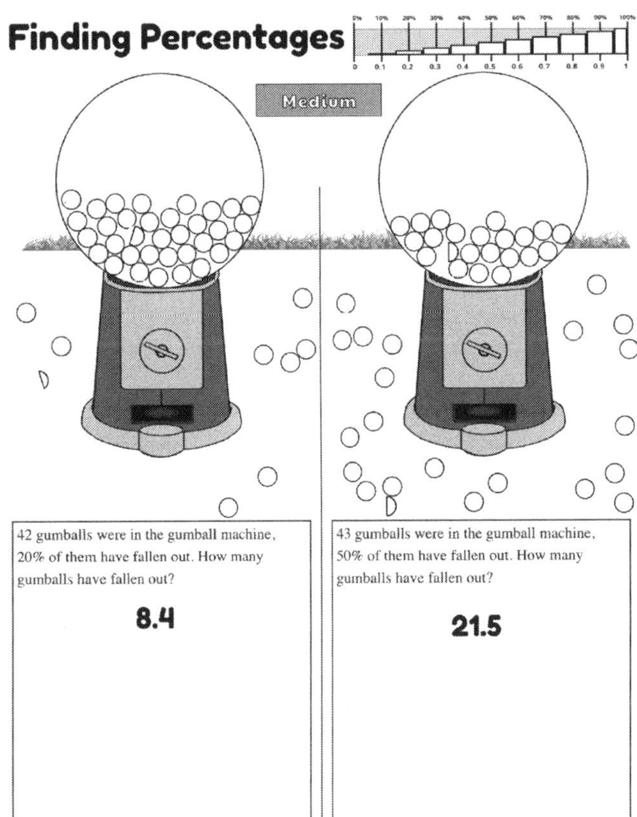

42 gumballs were in the gumball machine, 20% of them have fallen out. How many gumballs have fallen out?

8.4

43 gumballs were in the gumball machine, 50% of them have fallen out. How many gumballs have fallen out?

21.5

Gumball Puzzle 11

Finding Percentages

Medium

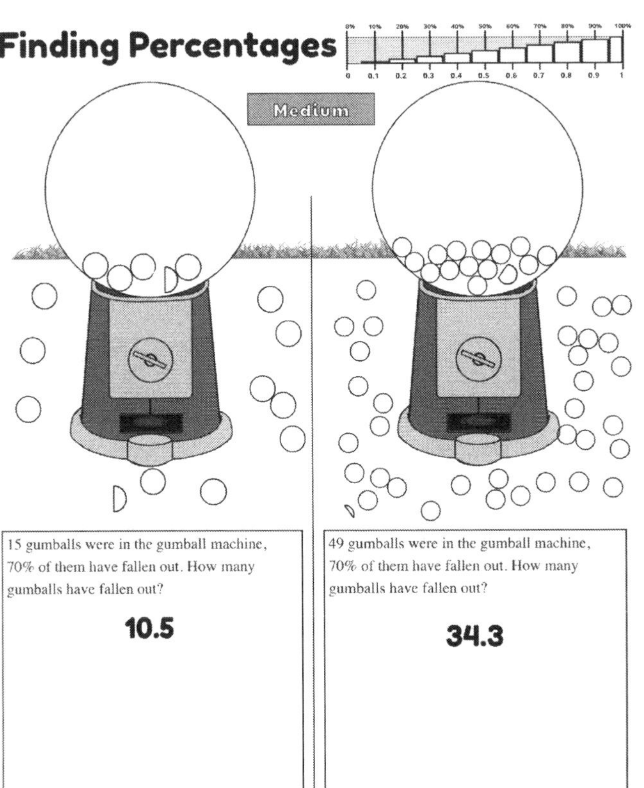

15 gumballs were in the gumball machine, 70% of them have fallen out. How many gumballs have fallen out?

10.5

49 gumballs were in the gumball machine, 70% of them have fallen out. How many gumballs have fallen out?

34.3

Gumball Puzzle 12

Finding Percentages

Medium

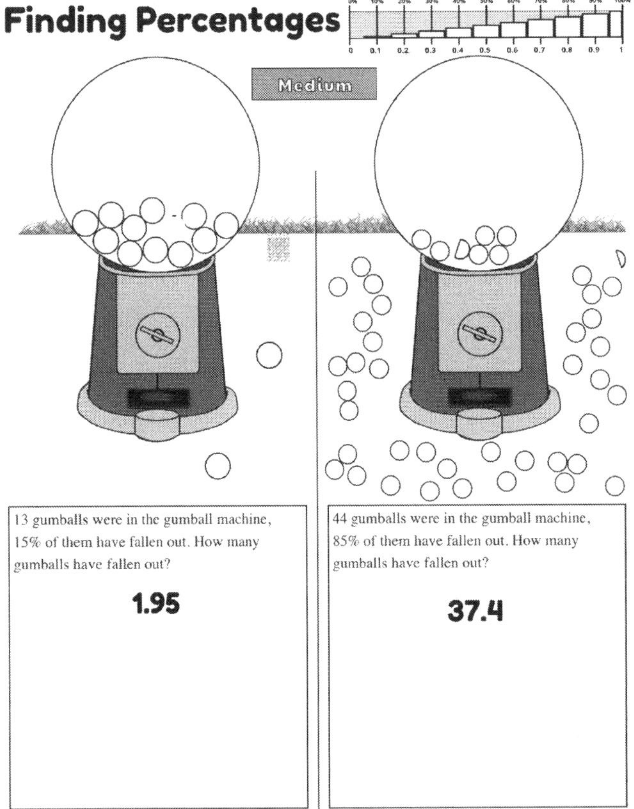

13 gumballs were in the gumball machine, 15% of them have fallen out. How many gumballs have fallen out?

1.95

44 gumballs were in the gumball machine, 85% of them have fallen out. How many gumballs have fallen out?

37.4

Gumball Puzzle 13

Finding Percentages

Medium

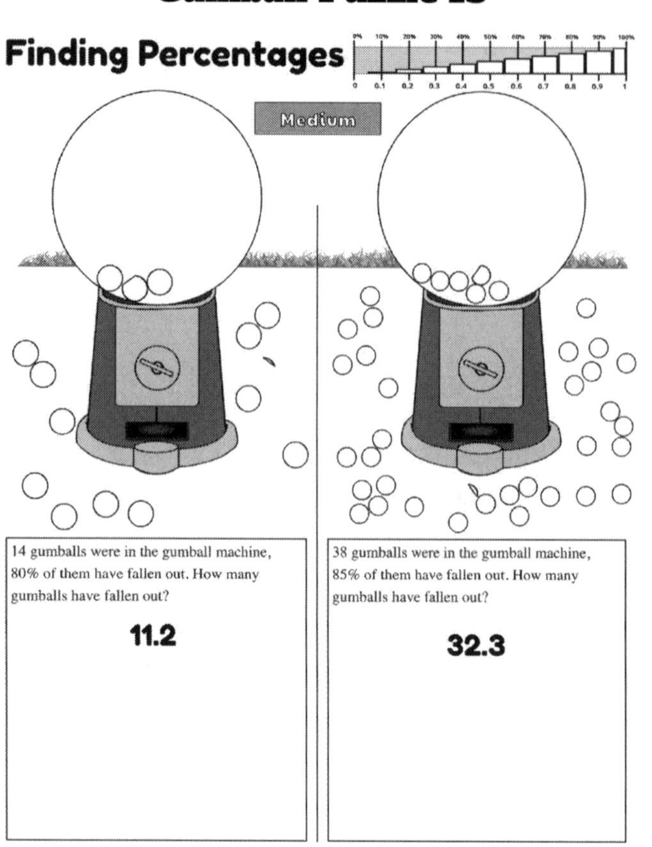

14 gumballs were in the gumball machine, 80% of them have fallen out. How many gumballs have fallen out?

11.2

38 gumballs were in the gumball machine, 85% of them have fallen out. How many gumballs have fallen out?

32.3

Gumball Puzzle 14

Finding Percentages

Medium

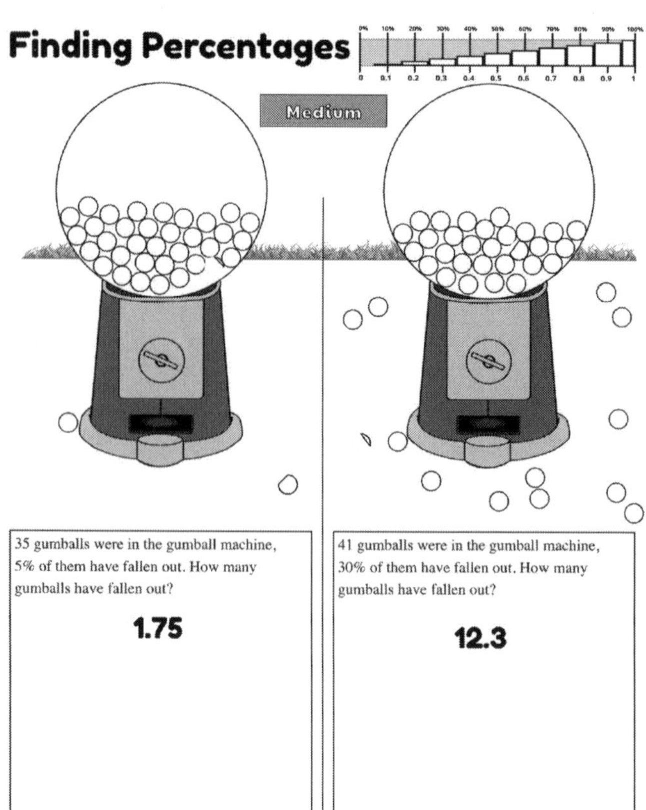

35 gumballs were in the gumball machine, 5% of them have fallen out. How many gumballs have fallen out?

1.75

41 gumballs were in the gumball machine, 30% of them have fallen out. How many gumballs have fallen out?

12.3

Gumball Puzzle 15

Finding Percentages

Medium

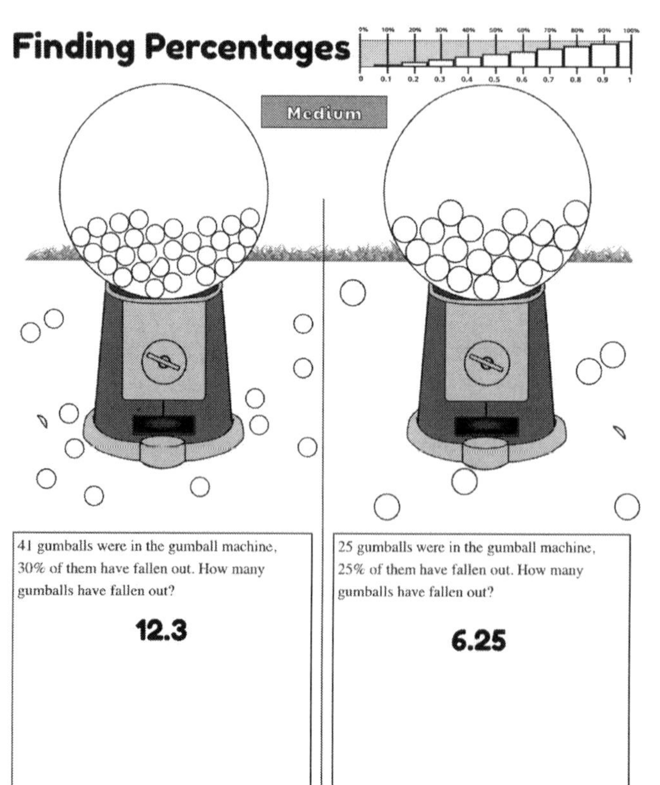

41 gumballs were in the gumball machine, 30% of them have fallen out. How many gumballs have fallen out?

12.3

25 gumballs were in the gumball machine, 25% of them have fallen out. How many gumballs have fallen out?

6.25

Gumball Puzzle 16

Finding Percentages

Medium

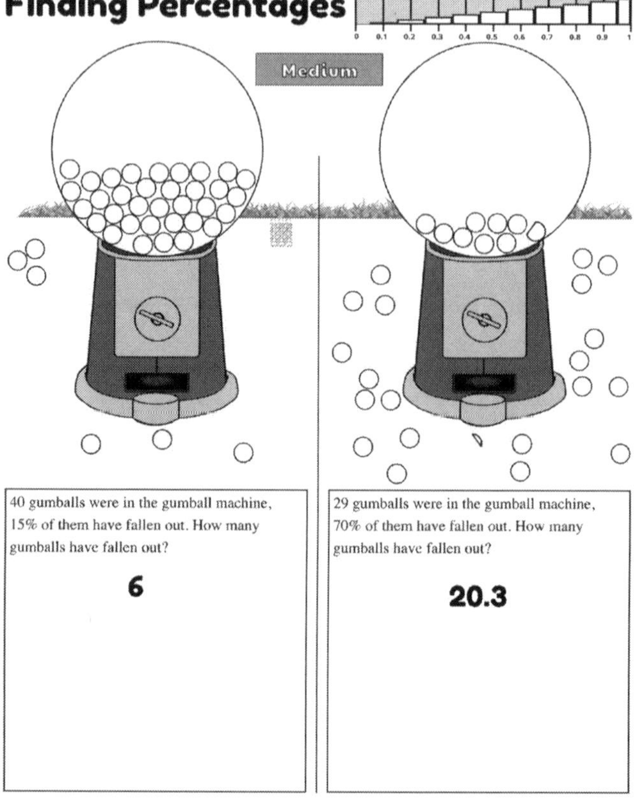

40 gumballs were in the gumball machine, 15% of them have fallen out. How many gumballs have fallen out?

6

29 gumballs were in the gumball machine, 70% of them have fallen out. How many gumballs have fallen out?

20.3

Gumball Puzzle 17

Finding Percentages

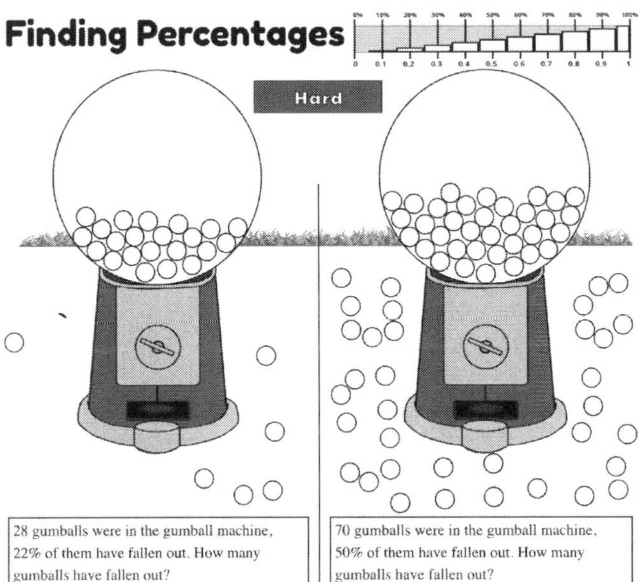

28 gumballs were in the gumball machine, 22% of them have fallen out. How many gumballs have fallen out?

6.16

Extra Challenge:
87% of the gumballs on the ground have been eaten by birds. How many were eaten?

5.36

70 gumballs were in the gumball machine, 50% of them have fallen out. How many gumballs have fallen out?

35

Extra Challenge:
96% of the gumballs on the ground have been eaten by birds. How many were eaten?

33.6

Gumball Puzzle 18

Finding Percentages

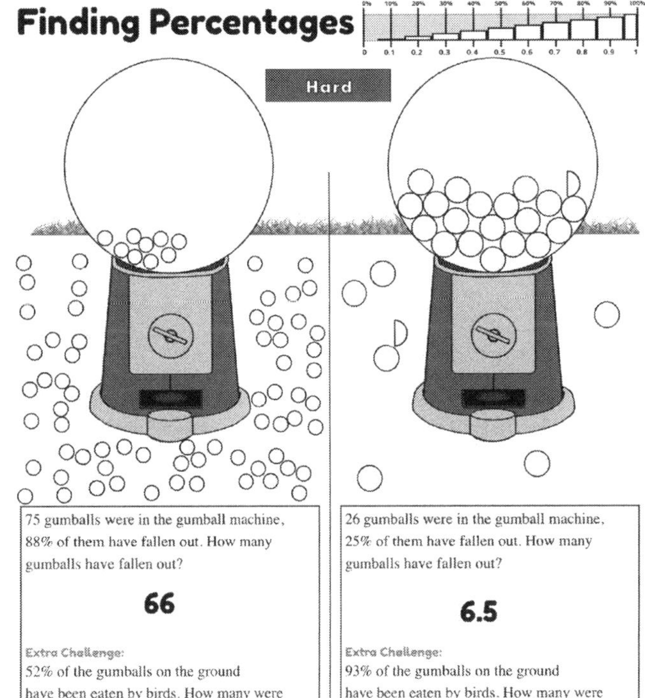

75 gumballs were in the gumball machine, 88% of them have fallen out. How many gumballs have fallen out?

66

Extra Challenge:
52% of the gumballs on the ground have been eaten by birds. How many were eaten?

34.32

26 gumballs were in the gumball machine, 25% of them have fallen out. How many gumballs have fallen out?

6.5

Extra Challenge:
93% of the gumballs on the ground have been eaten by birds. How many were eaten?

6.04

Gumball Puzzle 19

Finding Percentages

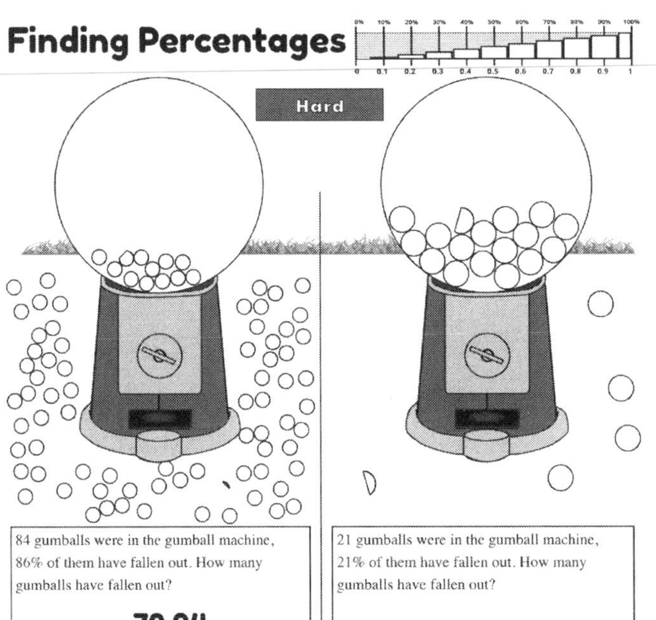

84 gumballs were in the gumball machine, 86% of them have fallen out. How many gumballs have fallen out?

72.24

Extra Challenge:
57% of the gumballs on the ground have been eaten by birds. How many were eaten?

41.18

21 gumballs were in the gumball machine, 21% of them have fallen out. How many gumballs have fallen out?

4.41

Extra Challenge:
85% of the gumballs on the ground have been eaten by birds. How many were eaten?

3.75

Gumball Puzzle 20

Finding Percentages

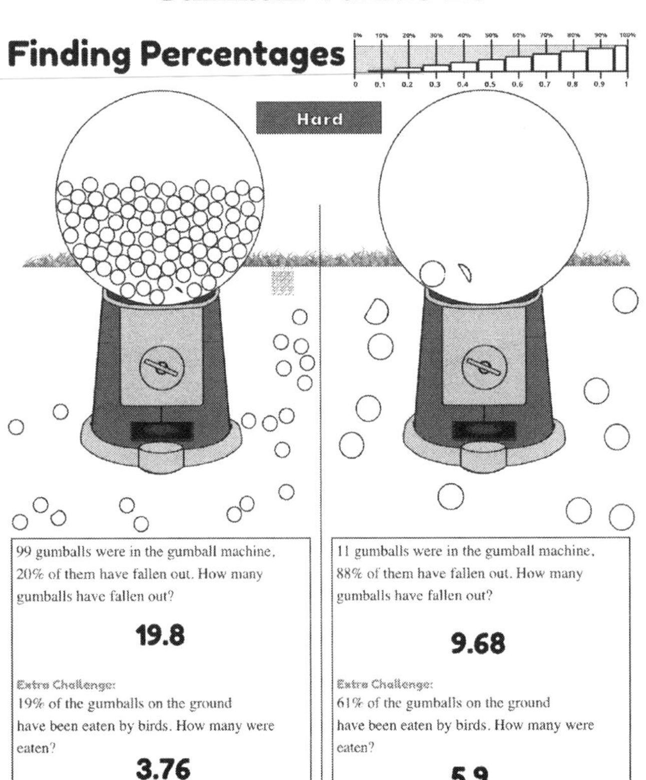

99 gumballs were in the gumball machine, 20% of them have fallen out. How many gumballs have fallen out?

19.8

Extra Challenge:
19% of the gumballs on the ground have been eaten by birds. How many were eaten?

3.76

11 gumballs were in the gumball machine, 88% of them have fallen out. How many gumballs have fallen out?

9.68

Extra Challenge:
61% of the gumballs on the ground have been eaten by birds. How many were eaten?

5.9

Gumball Puzzle 21

Finding Percentages

Hard

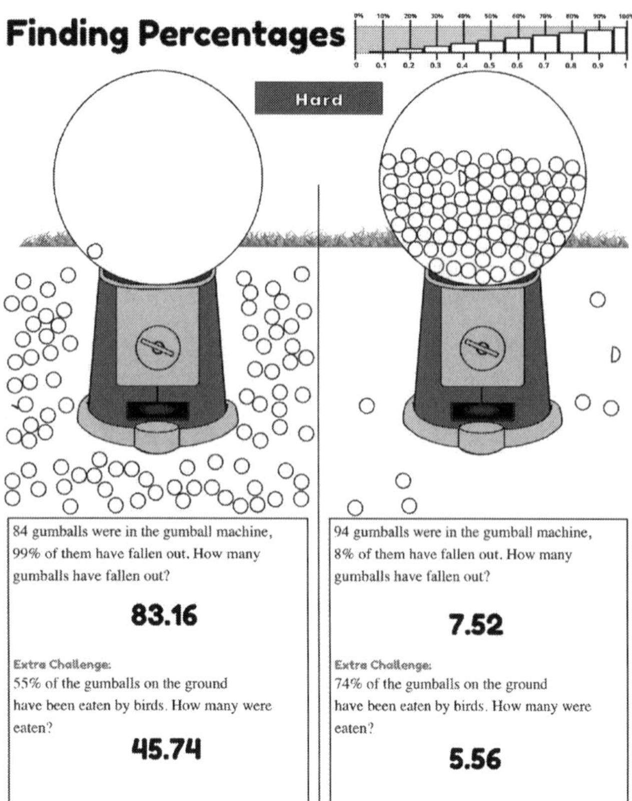

84 gumballs were in the gumball machine, 99% of them have fallen out. How many gumballs have fallen out?

83.16

Extra Challenge:
55% of the gumballs on the ground have been eaten by birds. How many were eaten?

45.74

94 gumballs were in the gumball machine, 8% of them have fallen out. How many gumballs have fallen out?

7.52

Extra Challenge:
74% of the gumballs on the ground have been eaten by birds. How many were eaten?

5.56

Gumball Puzzle 22

Finding Percentages

Hard

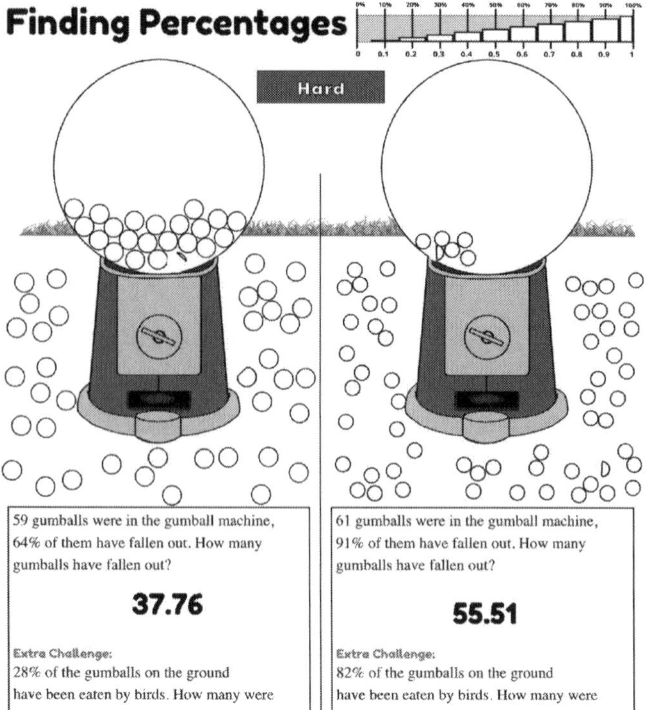

59 gumballs were in the gumball machine, 64% of them have fallen out. How many gumballs have fallen out?

37.76

Extra Challenge:
28% of the gumballs on the ground have been eaten by birds. How many were eaten?

10.57

61 gumballs were in the gumball machine, 91% of them have fallen out. How many gumballs have fallen out?

55.51

Extra Challenge:
82% of the gumballs on the ground have been eaten by birds. How many were eaten?

45.52

Gumball Puzzle 23

Finding Percentages

Hard

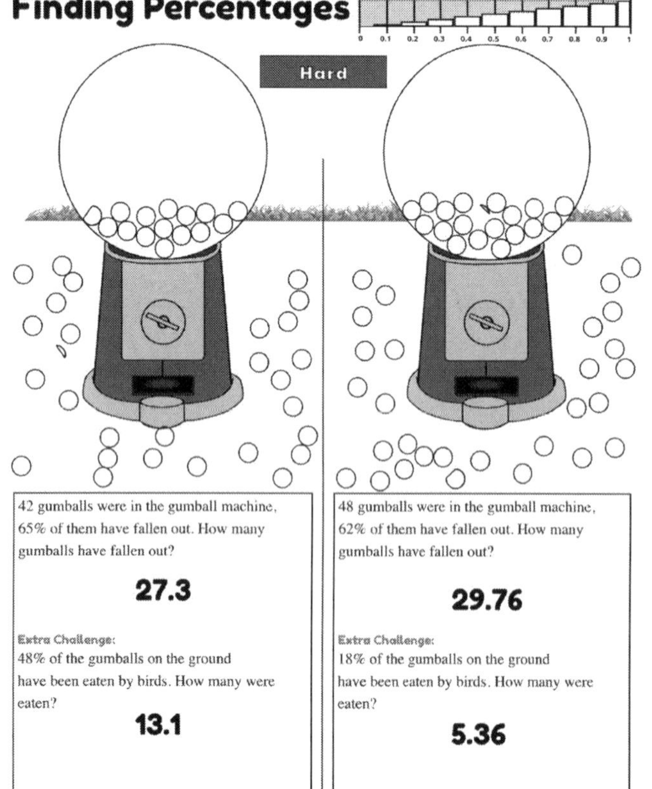

42 gumballs were in the gumball machine, 65% of them have fallen out. How many gumballs have fallen out?

27.3

Extra Challenge:
48% of the gumballs on the ground have been eaten by birds. How many were eaten?

13.1

48 gumballs were in the gumball machine, 62% of them have fallen out. How many gumballs have fallen out?

29.76

Extra Challenge:
18% of the gumballs on the ground have been eaten by birds. How many were eaten?

5.36

Gumball Puzzle 24

Finding Percentages

Hard

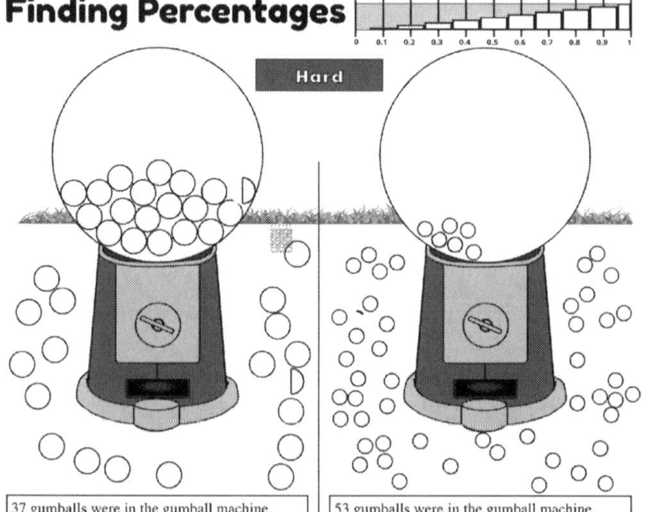

37 gumballs were in the gumball machine, 50% of them have fallen out. How many gumballs have fallen out?

18.5

Extra Challenge:
58% of the gumballs on the ground have been eaten by birds. How many were eaten?

10.73

53 gumballs were in the gumball machine, 89% of them have fallen out. How many gumballs have fallen out?

47.17

Extra Challenge:
66% of the gumballs on the ground have been eaten by birds. How many were eaten?

31.13

Roman Numerals Sheet 1

Roman Numerals

1	2	3	4	5	6	7	8	9	10
I	II	III	IV	V	VI	VII	VIII	IX	X

10	20	30	40	50	60	70	80	90	100
X	XX	XXX	XL	L	LX	LXX	LXXX	XC	C

500	1000
D	M

Junior

Write the correct number next to each Roman numeral:

1) XVIII = **18**
2) II = **2**
3) XXX = **30**
4) XIV = **14**
5) X = **10**
6) XVI = **16**
7) XXI = **21**
8) XXIV = **24**
9) II = **2**
10) I = **1**
11) XVIII = **18**
12) XXIII = **23**
13) XIV = **14**
14) XXVII = **27**
15) XXIV = **24**
16) XXVI = **26**
17) XIII = **13**
18) IV = **4**
19) XII = **12**
20) XII = **12**

Write the correct Roman numeral next to each number:

1) 4 = **IV**
2) 21 = **XXI**
3) 23 = **XXIII**
4) 9 = **IX**
5) 11 = **XI**
6) 23 = **XXIII**
7) 10 = **X**
8) 21 = **XXI**
9) 9 = **IX**
10) 18 = **XVIII**
11) 13 = **XIII**
12) 1 = **I**
13) 23 = **XXIII**
14) 15 = **XV**
15) 10 = **X**
16) 10 = **X**
17) 12 = **XII**
18) 13 = **XIII**
19) 13 = **XIII**
20) 7 = **VII**

Roman Numerals Sheet 2

Roman Numerals

1	2	3	4	5	6	7	8	9	10
I	II	III	IV	V	VI	VII	VIII	IX	X

10	20	30	40	50	60	70	80	90	100
X	XX	XXX	XL	L	LX	LXX	LXXX	XC	C

500	1000
D	M

Junior

Write the correct number next to each Roman numeral:

1) VIII = **8**
2) XXI = **21**
3) XVIII = **18**
4) XXII = **22**
5) XVII = **17**
6) XIX = **19**
7) XVIII = **18**
8) IX = **9**
9) XVIII = **18**
10) VII = **7**
11) XI = **11**
12) XII = **12**
13) XIII = **13**
14) XIII = **13**
15) XXX = **30**
16) XI = **11**
17) XXVI = **26**
18) IX = **9**
19) XVII = **17**
20) XXIX = **29**

Write the correct Roman numeral next to each number:

1) 13 = **XIII**
2) 14 = **XIV**
3) 8 = **VIII**
4) 10 = **X**
5) 29 = **XXIX**
6) 20 = **XX**
7) 9 = **IX**
8) 15 = **XV**
9) 12 = **XII**
10) 20 = **XX**
11) 24 = **XXIV**
12) 24 = **XXIV**
13) 24 = **XXIV**
14) 19 = **XIX**
15) 3 = **III**
16) 28 = **XXVIII**
17) 16 = **XVI**
18) 12 = **XII**
19) 13 = **XIII**
20) 5 = **V**

Roman Numerals Sheet 3

Roman Numerals

1	2	3	4	5	6	7	8	9	10
I	II	III	IV	V	VI	VII	VIII	IX	X

10	20	30	40	50	60	70	80	90	100
X	XX	XXX	XL	L	LX	LXX	LXXX	XC	C

500	1000
D	M

Medium

Write the correct number next to each Roman numeral:

1) XCVI = **96**
2) LXXXV = **85**
3) XCI = **91**
4) LXXIV = **74**
5) LXXXVI = **86**
6) LXXXVII = **87**
7) LXXX = **80**
8) LXIII = **63**
9) LVIII = **58**
10) XCIV = **94**
11) LI = **51**
12) LVIII = **58**
13) XCIV = **94**
14) XCII = **92**
15) XXXIX = **39**
16) LXXXIX = **89**
17) LVIII = **58**
18) LXVI = **66**
19) LXXXII = **82**
20) LIX = **59**

Write the correct Roman numeral next to each number:

1) 57 = **LVII**
2) 63 = **LXIII**
3) 79 = **LXXIX**
4) 44 = **XLIV**
5) 79 = **LXXIX**
6) 55 = **LV**
7) 52 = **LII**
8) 54 = **LIV**
9) 75 = **LXXV**
10) 64 = **LXIV**
11) 55 = **LV**
12) 39 = **XXXIX**
13) 35 = **XXXV**
14) 99 = **XCIX**
15) 95 = **XCV**
16) 49 = **XLIX**
17) 96 = **XCVI**
18) 92 = **XCII**
19) 91 = **XCI**
20) 54 = **LIV**

Roman Numerals Sheet 4

Roman Numerals

1	2	3	4	5	6	7	8	9	10
I	II	III	IV	V	VI	VII	VIII	IX	X

10	20	30	40	50	60	70	80	90	100
X	XX	XXX	XL	L	LX	LXX	LXXX	XC	C

500	1000
D	M

Medium

Write the correct number next to each Roman numeral:

1) XL = **40**
2) LXXXI = **81**
3) XLIII = **43**
4) LIV = **54**
5) LII = **52**
6) XL = **40**
7) L = **50**
8) XLVIII = **48**
9) LXXXIII = **83**
10) LXXXI = **81**
11) XC = **90**
12) LXXXVII = **87**
13) XLIV = **44**
14) XCVII = **97**
15) LXII = **62**
16) LXXXVIII = **88**
17) LXXXIX = **89**
18) XXXIX = **39**
19) LXXXVIII = **88**
20) LVI = **56**

Write the correct Roman numeral next to each number:

1) 94 = **XCIV**
2) 90 = **XC**
3) 64 = **LXIV**
4) 34 = **XXXIV**
5) 96 = **XCVI**
6) 87 = **LXXXVII**
7) 100 = **C**
8) 55 = **LV**
9) 99 = **XCIX**
10) 92 = **XCII**
11) 50 = **L**
12) 82 = **LXXXII**
13) 68 = **LXVIII**
14) 66 = **LXVI**
15) 100 = **C**
16) 92 = **XCII**
17) 91 = **XCI**
18) 33 = **XXXIII**
19) 70 = **LXX**
20) 97 = **XCVII**

Roman Numerals Sheet 5

Roman Numerals

1	2	3	4	5	6	7	8	9	10
I	II	III	IV	V	VI	VII	VIII	IX	X

10	20	30	40	50	60	70	80	90	100
X	XX	XXX	XL	L	LX	LXX	LXXX	XC	C

500	1000
D	M

Hard

Write the correct number next to each Roman numeral:

1)	DCCXI	=	**711**	11)	DLXXVI	=	**576**
2)	DCCXV	=	**715**	12)	CMXCI	=	**991**
3)	CMXXXI	=	**931**	13)	CMXLVII	=	**947**
4)	DCCLXIV	=	**764**	14)	CDXCVII	=	**497**
5)	DXXXII	=	**532**	15)	DCCCXCI	=	**891**
6)	CDXCVIII	=	**498**	16)	MIII	=	**1003**
7)	DCCXLIII	=	**743**	17)	DCCLXXXVII	=	**787**
8)	DCXCV	=	**695**	18)	DCCCIV	=	**804**
9)	DCCLXXV	=	**775**	19)	DCXXXIV	=	**634**
10)	DCCXCIX	=	**799**	20)	DCCXLIX	=	**749**

Write the correct Roman numeral next to each number:

1)	789	=	**DCCLXXXIX**	11)	1000	=	**M**
2)	519	=	**DXIX**	12)	877	=	**DCCCLXXVII**
3)	488	=	**CDLXXXVIII**	13)	906	=	**CMVI**
4)	628	=	**DCXXVIII**	14)	623	=	**DCXXIII**
5)	719	=	**DCCXIX**	15)	826	=	**DCCCXXVI**
6)	584	=	**DLXXXIV**	16)	982	=	**CMLXXXII**
7)	968	=	**CMLXVIII**	17)	824	=	**DCCCXXIV**
8)	580	=	**DLXXX**	18)	526	=	**DXXVI**
9)	884	=	**DCCCLXXXIV**	19)	956	=	**CMLVI**
10)	812	=	**DCCCXII**	20)	713	=	**DCCXIII**

Roman Numerals Sheet 6

Roman Numerals

1	2	3	4	5	6	7	8	9	10
I	II	III	IV	V	VI	VII	VIII	IX	X

10	20	30	40	50	60	70	80	90	100
X	XX	XXX	XL	L	LX	LXX	LXXX	XC	C

500	1000
D	M

Hard

Write the correct number next to each Roman numeral:

1)	DCXCVII	=	**697**	11)	DLXXXIII	=	**583**
2)	DCCXXVIII	=	**728**	12)	MX	=	**1010**
3)	CDXCVIII	=	**498**	13)	DLXXXVIII	=	**588**
4)	DCCLXXVII	=	**777**	14)	DCCCLXXVII	=	**877**
5)	DCCCLXXVI	=	**876**	15)	DCCCLXXVIII	=	**878**
6)	DXXVI	=	**526**	16)	CMXXIV	=	**924**
7)	DCCLIX	=	**759**	17)	DCLXXXVI	=	**686**
8)	DLVII	=	**557**	18)	DCCXXXVI	=	**736**
9)	CMXLVII	=	**947**	19)	CDXCIII	=	**493**
10)	DCCLVII	=	**757**	20)	DXCV	=	**595**

Write the correct Roman numeral next to each number:

1)	877	=	**DCCCLXXVII**	11)	839	=	**DCCCXXXIX**
2)	631	=	**DCXXXI**	12)	923	=	**CMXXIII**
3)	548	=	**DXLVIII**	13)	691	=	**DCXCI**
4)	524	=	**DXXIV**	14)	972	=	**CMLXXII**
5)	720	=	**DCCXX**	15)	754	=	**DCCLIV**
6)	677	=	**DCLXXVII**	16)	882	=	**DCCCLXXXII**
7)	704	=	**DCCIV**	17)	712	=	**DCCXII**
8)	530	=	**DXXX**	18)	514	=	**DXIV**
9)	765	=	**DCCLXV**	19)	538	=	**DXXXVIII**
10)	879	=	**DCCCLXXIX**	20)	828	=	**DCCCXXVIII**

Roman Numerals Sheet 7

Roman Numerals Market

1	2	3	4	5	6	7	8	9	10
I	II	III	IV	V	VI	VII	VIII	IX	X

10	20	30	40	50	60	70	80	90	100
X	XX	XXX	XL	L	LX	LXX	LXXX	XC	C

500	1000
D	M

Junior

There is a sale on at the Roman markets! Convert the Roman numeral price tags to Arabic numerals and calculate the final sale price of each item (after reductions). Round answer to 2 decimal places

25% OFF Item: Eggs Original Price: VIII	**£ 6.00** Sale Price = £ 6.00
10% OFF Item: Fish Original Price: VII	**£ 6.30** Sale Price = £ 6.30
50% OFF Item: Vase Original Price: XIV	**£ 7.00** Sale Price = £ 7.00
50% OFF Item: Fruit Original Price: VII	**£ 3.50** Sale Price = £ 3.50
10% OFF Item: Arrow Heads Original Price: I	**£ 0.90** Sale Price = £ 0.90

Roman Numerals Sheet 8

Roman Numerals Market

1	2	3	4	5	6	7	8	9	10
I	II	III	IV	V	VI	VII	VIII	IX	X

10	20	30	40	50	60	70	80	90	100
X	XX	XXX	XL	L	LX	LXX	LXXX	XC	C

500	1000
D	M

Junior

There is a sale on at the Roman markets! Convert the Roman numeral price tags to Arabic numerals and calculate the final sale price of each item (after reductions). Round answer to 2 decimal places

10% OFF Item: Vase Original Price: XIV	**£ 12.60** Sale Price = £ 12.60
25% OFF Item: Eggs Original Price: II	**£ 1.50** Sale Price = £ 1.50
50% OFF Item: Chicken Original Price: IX	**£ 4.50** Sale Price = £ 4.50
25% OFF Item: Books Original Price: X	**£ 7.50** Sale Price = £ 7.50
10% OFF Item: Fruit Original Price: II	**£ 1.80** Sale Price = £ 1.80

Roman Numerals Sheet 9

Roman Numerals Market

1	2	3	4	5	6	7	8	9	10
I	II	III	IV	V	VI	VII	VIII	IX	X

10	20	30	40	50	60	70	80	90	100
X	XX	XXX	XL	L	LX	LXX	LXXX	XC	C

500	1000
D	M

Junior

There is a sale on at the Roman markets! Convert the Roman numeral price tags to Arabic numerals and calculate the final sale price of each item (after reductions). Round answer to 2 decimal places

50% OFF Item: Sword Original Price: V	£ 2.50 Sale Price = £ 2.50
10% OFF Item: Jewellery Original Price: VI	£ 5.40 Sale Price = £ 5.40
50% OFF Item: Meat Original Price: III	£ 1.50 Sale Price = £ 1.50
50% OFF Item: Arrow Heads Original Price: IX	£ 4.50 Sale Price = £ 4.50
50% OFF Item: Vase Original Price: XIV	£ 7.00 Sale Price = £ 7.00

Roman Numerals Sheet 10

Roman Numerals Market

1	2	3	4	5	6	7	8	9	10
I	II	III	IV	V	VI	VII	VIII	IX	X

10	20	30	40	50	60	70	80	90	100
X	XX	XXX	XL	L	LX	LXX	LXXX	XC	C

500	1000
D	M

Junior

There is a sale on at the Roman markets! Convert the Roman numeral price tags to Arabic numerals and calculate the final sale price of each item (after reductions). Round answer to 2 decimal places

50% OFF Item: Beans Original Price: XI	£ 5.50 Sale Price = £ 5.50
10% OFF Item: Chicken Original Price: X	£ 9.00 Sale Price = £ 9.00
25% OFF Item: Eggs Original Price: XI	£ 8.25 Sale Price = £ 8.25
25% OFF Item: Books Original Price: IX	£ 6.75 Sale Price = £ 6.75
10% OFF Item: Bread Original Price: V	£ 4.50 Sale Price = £ 4.50

Roman Numerals Sheet 11

Roman Numerals Market

1	2	3	4	5	6	7	8	9	10
I	II	III	IV	V	VI	VII	VIII	IX	X

10	20	30	40	50	60	70	80	90	100
X	XX	XXX	XL	L	LX	LXX	LXXX	XC	C

500	1000
D	M

Junior

There is a sale on at the Roman markets! Convert the Roman numeral price tags to Arabic numerals and calculate the final sale price of each item (after reductions). Round answer to 2 decimal places

25% OFF Item: Arrow Heads Original Price: VIII	£ 6.00 Sale Price = £ 6.00
25% OFF Item: Fruit Original Price: I	£ 0.75 Sale Price = £ 0.75
25% OFF Item: Sword Original Price: XIV	£ 10.50 Sale Price = £ 10.50
10% OFF Item: Flour Original Price: II	£ 1.80 Sale Price = £ 1.80
25% OFF Item: Eggs Original Price: XI	£ 8.25 Sale Price = £ 8.25

Roman Numerals Sheet 12

Roman Numerals Market

1	2	3	4	5	6	7	8	9	10
I	II	III	IV	V	VI	VII	VIII	IX	X

10	20	30	40	50	60	70	80	90	100
X	XX	XXX	XL	L	LX	LXX	LXXX	XC	C

500	1000
D	M

Junior

There is a sale on at the Roman markets! Convert the Roman numeral price tags to Arabic numerals and calculate the final sale price of each item (after reductions). Round answer to 2 decimal places

10% OFF Item: Beans Original Price: VI	£ 5.40 Sale Price = £ 5.40
25% OFF Item: Arrow Heads Original Price: XII	£ 9.00 Sale Price = £ 9.00
50% OFF Item: Goblet Original Price: IV	£ 2.00 Sale Price = £ 2.00
50% OFF Item: Vase Original Price: XIV	£ 7.00 Sale Price = £ 7.00
10% OFF Item: Sword Original Price: XI	£ 9.90 Sale Price = £ 9.90

Roman Numerals Sheet 13

Roman Numerals Market

1	2	3	4	5	6	7	8	9	10
I	II	III	IV	V	VI	VII	VIII	IX	X

10	20	30	40	50	60	70	80	90	100
X	XX	XXX	XL	L	LX	LXX	LXXX	XC	C

500	1000
D	M

Junior

There is a sale on at the Roman markets! Convert the Roman numeral price tags to Arabic numerals and calculate the final sale price of each item (after reductions). Round answer to 2 decimal places

25% OFF
Item: Books
Original Price: II
£ 1.50
Sale Price = £ 1.50

25% OFF
Item: Fish
Original Price: VII
£ 5.25
Sale Price = £ 5.25

10% OFF
Item: Beans
Original Price: I
£ 0.90
Sale Price = £ 0.90

10% OFF
Item: Arrow Heads
Original Price: IV
£ 3.60
Sale Price = £ 3.60

50% OFF
Item: Jewellery
Original Price: X
£ 5.00
Sale Price = £ 5.00

Roman Numerals Sheet 14

Roman Numerals Market

1	2	3	4	5	6	7	8	9	10
I	II	III	IV	V	VI	VII	VIII	IX	X

10	20	30	40	50	60	70	80	90	100
X	XX	XXX	XL	L	LX	LXX	LXXX	XC	C

500	1000
D	M

Junior

There is a sale on at the Roman markets! Convert the Roman numeral price tags to Arabic numerals and calculate the final sale price of each item (after reductions). Round answer to 2 decimal places

50% OFF
Item: Vase
Original Price: XI
£ 5.50
Sale Price = £ 5.50

25% OFF
Item: Meat
Original Price: XII
£ 9.00
Sale Price = £ 9.00

50% OFF
Item: Beans
Original Price: VIII
£ 4.00
Sale Price = £ 4.00

50% OFF
Item: Vase
Original Price: VII
£ 3.50
Sale Price = £ 3.50

10% OFF
Item: Eggs
Original Price: I
£ 0.90
Sale Price = £ 0.90

Roman Numerals Sheet 15

Roman Numerals Market

1	2	3	4	5	6	7	8	9	10
I	II	III	IV	V	VI	VII	VIII	IX	X

10	20	30	40	50	60	70	80	90	100
X	XX	XXX	XL	L	LX	LXX	LXXX	XC	C

500	1000
D	M

Medium

There is a sale on at the Roman markets! Convert the Roman numeral price tags to Arabic numerals and calculate the final sale price of each item (after reductions). Round answer to 2 decimal places

70% OFF
Item: Vase
Original Price: CXIII
£ 33.90
Sale Price = £ 33.90

80% OFF
Item: Bread
Original Price: XCV
£ 19.00
Sale Price = £ 19.00

80% OFF
Item: Meat
Original Price: LII
£ 10.40
Sale Price = £ 10.40

65% OFF
Item: Arrow Heads
Original Price: LXXXV
£ 29.75
Sale Price = £ 29.75

5% OFF
Item: Eggs
Original Price: LXXV
£ 71.25
Sale Price = £ 71.25

Roman Numerals Sheet 16

Roman Numerals Market

1	2	3	4	5	6	7	8	9	10
I	II	III	IV	V	VI	VII	VIII	IX	X

10	20	30	40	50	60	70	80	90	100
X	XX	XXX	XL	L	LX	LXX	LXXX	XC	C

500	1000
D	M

Medium

There is a sale on at the Roman markets! Convert the Roman numeral price tags to Arabic numerals and calculate the final sale price of each item (after reductions). Round answer to 2 decimal places

15% OFF
Item: Fish
Original Price: LXII
£ 52.70
Sale Price = £ 52.70

10% OFF
Item: Chicken
Original Price: XCVIII
£ 88.20
Sale Price = £ 88.20

90% OFF
Item: Goblet
Original Price: CXI
£ 11.10
Sale Price = £ 11.10

85% OFF
Item: Vase
Original Price: CXXVI
£ 18.90
Sale Price = £ 18.90

75% OFF
Item: Jewellery
Original Price: CXLV
£ 36.25
Sale Price = £ 36.25

Roman Numerals Sheet 17

Roman Numerals Market

1	2	3	4	5	6	7	8	9	10
I	II	III	IV	V	VI	VII	VIII	IX	X

10	20	30	40	50	60	70	80	90	100
X	XX	XXX	XL	L	LX	LXX	LXXX	XC	C

500	1000
D	M

Medium

There is a sale on at the Roman markets! Convert the Roman numeral price tags to Arabic numerals and calculate the final sale price of each item (after reductions). Round answer to 2 decimal places

Discount	Item	Original Price	Answer	Sale Price
10% OFF	Beans	LXIX	£ 62.10	Sale Price = £ 62.10
30% OFF	Jewellery	CL	£ 105.00	Sale Price = £ 105.00
25% OFF	Fruit	XXXVIII	£ 28.50	Sale Price = £ 28.50
35% OFF	Vase	XCV	£ 61.75	Sale Price = £ 61.75
5% OFF	Meat	LXXXI	£ 76.95	Sale Price = £ 76.95

Roman Numerals Sheet 18

Roman Numerals Market

1	2	3	4	5	6	7	8	9	10
I	II	III	IV	V	VI	VII	VIII	IX	X

10	20	30	40	50	60	70	80	90	100
X	XX	XXX	XL	L	LX	LXX	LXXX	XC	C

500	1000
D	M

Medium

There is a sale on at the Roman markets! Convert the Roman numeral price tags to Arabic numerals and calculate the final sale price of each item (after reductions). Round answer to 2 decimal places

Discount	Item	Original Price	Answer	Sale Price
35% OFF	Goblet	CXXXV	£ 87.75	Sale Price = £ 87.75
35% OFF	Arrow Heads	XLIX	£ 31.85	Sale Price = £ 31.85
10% OFF	Chicken	CXVII	£ 105.30	Sale Price = £ 105.30
20% OFF	Sword	LXX	£ 56.00	Sale Price = £ 56.00
65% OFF	Bread	XXXIX	£ 13.65	Sale Price = £ 13.65

Roman Numerals Sheet 19

Roman Numerals Market

1	2	3	4	5	6	7	8	9	10
I	II	III	IV	V	VI	VII	VIII	IX	X

10	20	30	40	50	60	70	80	90	100
X	XX	XXX	XL	L	LX	LXX	LXXX	XC	C

500	1000
D	M

Medium

There is a sale on at the Roman markets! Convert the Roman numeral price tags to Arabic numerals and calculate the final sale price of each item (after reductions). Round answer to 2 decimal places

Discount	Item	Original Price	Answer	Sale Price
30% OFF	Eggs	CVIII	£ 75.60	Sale Price = £ 75.60
40% OFF	Bread	XCII	£ 55.20	Sale Price = £ 55.20
50% OFF	Arrow Heads	LXXXV	£ 42.50	Sale Price = £ 42.50
15% OFF	Beans	LXXXVIII	£ 74.80	Sale Price = £ 74.80
20% OFF	Fish	CXII	£ 89.60	Sale Price = £ 89.60

Roman Numerals Sheet 20

Roman Numerals Market

1	2	3	4	5	6	7	8	9	10
I	II	III	IV	V	VI	VII	VIII	IX	X

10	20	30	40	50	60	70	80	90	100
X	XX	XXX	XL	L	LX	LXX	LXXX	XC	C

500	1000
D	M

Medium

There is a sale on at the Roman markets! Convert the Roman numeral price tags to Arabic numerals and calculate the final sale price of each item (after reductions). Round answer to 2 decimal places

Discount	Item	Original Price	Answer	Sale Price
55% OFF	Beans	CVIII	£ 48.60	Sale Price = £ 48.60
5% OFF	Sword	CX	£ 104.50	Sale Price = £ 104.50
25% OFF	Fruit	CV	£ 78.75	Sale Price = £ 78.75
45% OFF	Bread	XXXVIII	£ 20.90	Sale Price = £ 20.90
10% OFF	Arrow Heads	LX	£ 54.00	Sale Price = £ 54.00

Roman Numerals Sheet 21

Roman Numerals Market

1	2	3	4	5	6	7	8	9	10
I	II	III	IV	V	VI	VII	VIII	IX	X

10	20	30	40	50	60	70	80	90	100
X	XX	XXX	XL	L	LX	LXX	LXXX	XC	C

500	1000
D	M

Medium

There is a sale on at the Roman markets! Convert the Roman numeral price tags to Arabic numerals and calculate the final sale price of each item (after reductions). Round answer to 2 decimal places

10% OFF
Item: Beans
Original Price: XC
£ 81.00
Sale Price = £ 81.00

85% OFF
Item: Vase
Original Price: LXI
£ 9.15
Sale Price = £ 9.15

55% OFF
Item: Books
Original Price: XLII
£ 18.90
Sale Price = £ 18.90

35% OFF
Item: Flour
Original Price: LXXXVI
£ 55.90
Sale Price = £ 55.90

60% OFF
Item: Fruit
Original Price: LXX
£ 28.00
Sale Price = £ 28.00

Roman Numerals Sheet 22

Roman Numerals Market

1	2	3	4	5	6	7	8	9	10
I	II	III	IV	V	VI	VII	VIII	IX	X

10	20	30	40	50	60	70	80	90	100
X	XX	XXX	XL	L	LX	LXX	LXXX	XC	C

500	1000
D	M

Medium

There is a sale on at the Roman markets! Convert the Roman numeral price tags to Arabic numerals and calculate the final sale price of each item (after reductions). Round answer to 2 decimal places

50% OFF
Item: Fruit
Original Price: XC
£ 45.00
Sale Price = £ 45.00

85% OFF
Item: Flour
Original Price: LXXX
£ 12.00
Sale Price = £ 12.00

55% OFF
Item: Bread
Original Price: CI
£ 45.45
Sale Price = £ 45.45

25% OFF
Item: Arrow Heads
Original Price: CXII
£ 84.00
Sale Price = £ 84.00

85% OFF
Item: Goblet
Original Price: XLVIII
£ 7.20
Sale Price = £ 7.20

Roman Numerals Sheet 23

Roman Numerals Market

1	2	3	4	5	6	7	8	9	10
I	II	III	IV	V	VI	VII	VIII	IX	X

10	20	30	40	50	60	70	80	90	100
X	XX	XXX	XL	L	LX	LXX	LXXX	XC	C

500	1000
D	M

Hard

There is a sale on at the Roman markets! Convert the Roman numeral price tags to Arabic numerals and calculate the final sale price of each item (after reductions). Round answer to 2 decimal places

1% OFF
Item: Arrow Heads
Original Price: DCXXXI
£ 624.69
Sale Price = £ 624.69

1% OFF
Item: Vase
Original Price: DCCIV
£ 696.96
Sale Price = £ 696.96

6% OFF
Item: Flour
Original Price: DCI
£ 564.94
Sale Price = £ 564.94

4% OFF
Item: Bread
Original Price: DCIII
£ 578.88
Sale Price = £ 578.88

82% OFF
Item: Meat
Original Price: DCCVIII
£ 127.44
Sale Price = £ 127.44

Roman Numerals Sheet 24

Roman Numerals Market

1	2	3	4	5	6	7	8	9	10
I	II	III	IV	V	VI	VII	VIII	IX	X

10	20	30	40	50	60	70	80	90	100
X	XX	XXX	XL	L	LX	LXX	LXXX	XC	C

500	1000
D	M

Hard

There is a sale on at the Roman markets! Convert the Roman numeral price tags to Arabic numerals and calculate the final sale price of each item (after reductions). Round answer to 2 decimal places

76% OFF
Item: Arrow Heads
Original Price: DCXVIII
£ 148.32
Sale Price = £ 148.32

76% OFF
Item: Chicken
Original Price: DCLXX
£ 160.80
Sale Price = £ 160.80

64% OFF
Item: Eggs
Original Price: DXXXVII
£ 193.32
Sale Price = £ 193.32

93% OFF
Item: Vase
Original Price: DCCLVI
£ 52.92
Sale Price = £ 52.92

58% OFF
Item: Jewellery
Original Price: DCCLXXX
£ 327.60
Sale Price = £ 327.60

Roman Numerals Sheet 25

Roman Numerals Market

1	2	3	4	5	6	7	8	9	10
I	II	III	IV	V	VI	VII	VIII	IX	X

10	20	30	40	50	60	70	80	90	100
X	XX	XXX	XL	L	LX	LXX	LXXX	XC	C

500	1000
D	M

Hard

There is a sale on at the Roman markets! Convert the Roman numeral price tags to Arabic numerals and calculate the final sale price of each item (after reductions). Round answer to 2 decimal places

82% OFF Item: Vase Original Price: DCCLVI	£ 136.08 Sale Price = £ 136.08
23% OFF Item: Beans Original Price: DXLII	£ 417.34 Sale Price = £ 417.34
5% OFF Item: Jewellery Original Price: CMXXXIV	£ 887.30 Sale Price = £ 887.30
84% OFF Item: Chicken Original Price: DCLXXXVI	£ 109.76 Sale Price = £ 109.76
73% OFF Item: Flour Original Price: DCXCIV	£ 187.38 Sale Price = £ 187.38

Roman Numerals Sheet 26

Roman Numerals Market

1	2	3	4	5	6	7	8	9	10
I	II	III	IV	V	VI	VII	VIII	IX	X

10	20	30	40	50	60	70	80	90	100
X	XX	XXX	XL	L	LX	LXX	LXXX	XC	C

500	1000
D	M

Hard

There is a sale on at the Roman markets! Convert the Roman numeral price tags to Arabic numerals and calculate the final sale price of each item (after reductions). Round answer to 2 decimal places

92% OFF Item: Jewellery Original Price: DCCCLXIV	£ 69.12 Sale Price = £ 69.12
83% OFF Item: Books Original Price: DCXXXVIII	£ 108.46 Sale Price = £ 108.46
83% OFF Item: Goblet Original Price: DCCLIX	£ 129.03 Sale Price = £ 129.03
77% OFF Item: Fruit Original Price: DCXXVI	£ 143.98 Sale Price = £ 143.98
43% OFF Item: Eggs Original Price: DCXLIV	£ 367.08 Sale Price = £ 367.08

Roman Numerals Sheet 27

Roman Numerals Market

1	2	3	4	5	6	7	8	9	10
I	II	III	IV	V	VI	VII	VIII	IX	X

10	20	30	40	50	60	70	80	90	100
X	XX	XXX	XL	L	LX	LXX	LXXX	XC	C

500	1000
D	M

Hard

There is a sale on at the Roman markets! Convert the Roman numeral price tags to Arabic numerals and calculate the final sale price of each item (after reductions). Round answer to 2 decimal places

73% OFF Item: Eggs Original Price: DLVII	£ 150.39 Sale Price = £ 150.39
47% OFF Item: Meat Original Price: DCLXXXV	£ 363.05 Sale Price = £ 363.05
95% OFF Item: Beans Original Price: DCCX	£ 35.50 Sale Price = £ 35.50
19% OFF Item: Vase Original Price: DCCXV	£ 579.15 Sale Price = £ 579.15
46% OFF Item: Goblet Original Price: DCCCXXXII	£ 449.28 Sale Price = £ 449.28

Roman Numerals Sheet 28

Roman Numerals Market

1	2	3	4	5	6	7	8	9	10
I	II	III	IV	V	VI	VII	VIII	IX	X

10	20	30	40	50	60	70	80	90	100
X	XX	XXX	XL	L	LX	LXX	LXXX	XC	C

500	1000
D	M

Hard

There is a sale on at the Roman markets! Convert the Roman numeral price tags to Arabic numerals and calculate the final sale price of each item (after reductions). Round answer to 2 decimal places

86% OFF Item: Meat Original Price: DCI	£ 84.14 Sale Price = £ 84.14
3% OFF Item: Sword Original Price: DCXCIV	£ 673.18 Sale Price = £ 673.18
10% OFF Item: Beans Original Price: DLXXIV	£ 516.60 Sale Price = £ 516.60
14% OFF Item: Bread Original Price: DLXXXI	£ 499.66 Sale Price = £ 499.66
83% OFF Item: Chicken Original Price: DCCLXXI	£ 131.07 Sale Price = £ 131.07

Roman Numerals Sheet 29

Roman Numerals Market

1	2	3	4	5	6	7	8	9	10
I	II	III	IV	V	VI	VII	VIII	IX	X

10	20	30	40	50	60	70	80	90	100
X	XX	XXX	XL	L	LX	LXX	LXXX	XC	C

500	1000
D	M

Hard

There is a sale on at the Roman markets! Convert the Roman numeral price tags to Arabic numerals and calculate the final sale price of each item (after reductions). Round answer to 2 decimal places

Discount	Item	Original Price	Answer	Sale Price
90% OFF	Fish	DCXXIV	£ 62.40	Sale Price = £ 62.40
9% OFF	Jewellery	DCCXXIV	£ 658.84	Sale Price = £ 658.84
26% OFF	Arrow Heads	DCCXVIII	£ 531.32	Sale Price = £ 531.32
52% OFF	Goblet	DCCCL	£ 408.00	Sale Price = £ 408.00
55% OFF	Books	DCXCIV	£ 312.30	Sale Price = £ 312.30

Roman Numerals Sheet 30

Roman Numerals Market

1	2	3	4	5	6	7	8	9	10
I	II	III	IV	V	VI	VII	VIII	IX	X

10	20	30	40	50	60	70	80	90	100
X	XX	XXX	XL	L	LX	LXX	LXXX	XC	C

500	1000
D	M

Hard

There is a sale on at the Roman markets! Convert the Roman numeral price tags to Arabic numerals and calculate the final sale price of each item (after reductions). Round answer to 2 decimal places

Discount	Item	Original Price	Answer	Sale Price
61% OFF	Chicken	DCXCVII	£ 271.83	Sale Price = £ 271.83
12% OFF	Vase	DCCXLIV	£ 654.72	Sale Price = £ 654.72
91% OFF	Eggs	DXLIII	£ 48.87	Sale Price = £ 48.87
31% OFF	Fish	DLXXXIX	£ 406.41	Sale Price = £ 406.41
31% OFF	Arrow Heads	DCLXXX	£ 469.20	Sale Price = £ 469.20

Sudoku Sheet 1 (Single)

8	7	9	5	2	3	6	4	1
4	3	6	8	7	1	9	5	2
5	1	2	6	4	9	3	7	8
7	8	3	2	1	6	5	9	4
9	4	1	7	8	5	2	6	3
6	2	5	9	3	4	1	8	7
3	6	7	4	9	2	8	1	5
2	9	4	1	5	8	7	3	6
1	5	8	3	6	7	4	2	9

Sudoku Sheet 2 (Single)

8	7	3	6	5	4	2	1	9
5	2	6	7	1	9	3	4	8
9	4	1	2	3	8	5	6	7
3	8	4	1	9	7	6	5	2
7	6	5	3	4	2	8	9	1
2	1	9	5	8	6	4	7	3
4	5	7	8	2	1	9	3	6
6	3	8	9	7	5	1	2	4
1	9	2	4	6	3	7	8	5

Sudoku Sheet 3
(Double)

9	6	2	5	4	8	7	3	1						
5	8	3	6	1	7	2	9	4						
4	7	1	3	2	9	5	8	6						
8	2	6	9	3	5	1	4	7						
7	3	5	4	8	1	9	6	2						
1	4	9	7	6	2	3	5	8						
6	5	4	1	7	3	8	2	9	1	5	3	7	4	6
2	9	7	8	5	6	4	1	3	6	7	8	2	5	9
3	1	8	2	9	4	6	7	5	2	9	4	1	8	3
						5	3	7	8	2	9	6	1	4
						9	6	1	3	4	7	8	2	5
						2	8	4	5	1	6	9	3	7
						7	5	2	9	3	1	4	6	8
						1	9	8	4	6	5	3	7	2
						3	4	6	7	8	2	5	9	1

Sudoku Sheet 4
(Double)

						9	1	4	5	8	2	3	7	6
						7	2	5	9	6	3	8	4	1
						6	8	3	7	4	1	9	5	2
						1	7	8	2	5	9	4	6	3
						5	3	9	4	1	6	2	8	7
						2	4	6	3	7	8	1	9	5
4	9	8	1	6	2	3	5	7	8	2	4	6	1	9
2	3	6	4	7	5	8	9	1	6	3	5	7	2	4
7	1	5	3	8	9	4	6	2	1	9	7	5	3	8
5	8	9	2	3	4	7	1	6						
6	2	3	5	1	7	9	4	8						
1	4	7	8	9	6	2	3	5						
8	6	1	7	4	3	5	2	9						
3	7	2	9	5	1	6	8	4						
9	5	4	6	2	8	1	7	3						

Sudoku Sheet 5
(Triple)

						5	6	1	4	3	2	9	7	8						
						9	2	7	5	1	8	3	6	4						
						8	4	3	6	7	9	5	2	1						
						4	7	9	1	8	5	6	3	2						
						6	8	5	3	2	7	4	1	9						
						1	3	2	9	6	4	7	8	5						
8	7	1	5	3	4	2	9	6	8	5	3	1	4	7	9	3	8	6	2	5
2	4	9	7	1	6	3	5	8	7	4	1	2	9	6	5	1	4	8	7	3
6	5	3	2	9	8	7	1	4	2	9	6	8	5	3	7	2	6	1	4	9
3	9	5	8	7	1	4	6	2				5	7	1	8	4	2	3	9	6
7	1	6	4	2	3	5	8	9				4	6	2	3	9	5	7	8	1
4	8	2	6	5	9	1	7	3				3	8	9	6	7	1	2	5	4
1	6	8	3	4	7	9	2	5				7	2	5	4	6	3	9	1	8
9	2	4	1	6	5	8	3	7				6	1	8	2	5	9	4	3	7
5	3	7	9	8	2	6	4	1				9	3	4	1	8	7	5	6	2

Sudoku Sheet 6
(Triple)

						2	1	3	4	8	7	9	5	6						
						4	6	9	2	1	5	8	3	7						
						5	8	7	9	6	3	2	4	1						
						8	4	5	1	2	6	3	7	9						
						7	2	6	3	4	9	5	1	8						
						3	9	1	5	7	8	6	2	4						
7	9	8	6	5	4	1	3	2	6	9	4	7	8	5	3	2	6	9	4	1
5	6	3	8	1	2	9	7	4	8	5	2	1	6	3	4	9	7	2	8	5
4	2	1	9	3	7	6	5	8	7	3	1	4	9	2	5	8	1	6	3	7
8	5	4	7	9	1	3	2	6				2	5	8	1	6	9	4	7	3
1	3	9	2	6	5	4	8	7				6	3	4	7	5	8	1	9	2
6	7	2	4	8	3	5	9	1				9	7	1	2	4	3	5	6	8
3	4	6	5	7	8	2	1	9				3	1	9	6	7	2	8	5	4
2	8	5	1	4	9	7	6	3				8	4	7	9	1	5	3	2	6
9	1	7	3	2	6	8	4	5				5	2	6	8	3	4	7	1	9

Sudoku Sheet 7 (Hard)

6	2	3	7	4	5	9	8	1				3	6	9	7	4	2	8	1	5
5	8	1	9	3	6	7	4	2				8	2	5	6	3	1	4	7	9
7	9	4	2	8	1	3	6	5				1	7	4	9	8	5	3	6	2
4	3	5	6	1	9	2	7	8				5	8	2	3	6	4	7	9	1
2	1	6	4	7	8	5	9	3				7	4	1	8	5	9	2	3	6
8	7	9	3	5	2	6	1	4				6	9	3	1	2	7	5	4	8
1	6	8	5	2	7	4	3	9	7	6	5	2	1	8	4	9	3	6	5	7
9	4	2	8	6	3	1	5	7	4	2	8	9	3	6	5	7	8	1	2	4
3	5	7	1	9	4	8	2	6	1	9	3	4	5	7	2	1	6	9	8	3
						3	9	5	8	4	2	6	7	1						
						6	4	8	3	1	7	5	2	9						
						2	7	1	6	5	9	8	4	3						
4	7	9	2	6	8	5	1	3	2	8	6	7	9	4	3	6	1	5	2	8
3	6	5	9	4	1	7	8	2	9	3	4	1	6	5	8	2	7	4	3	9
8	2	1	3	5	7	9	6	4	5	7	1	3	8	2	9	4	5	1	7	6
7	5	6	1	9	3	2	4	8				2	4	9	6	1	3	8	5	7
1	9	8	7	2	4	3	5	6				8	5	3	7	9	2	6	4	1
2	3	4	5	8	6	1	9	7				6	1	7	5	8	4	2	9	3
9	8	7	4	3	5	6	2	1				5	2	6	1	3	9	7	8	4
5	4	3	6	1	2	8	7	9				4	3	1	2	7	8	9	6	5
6	1	2	8	7	9	4	3	5				9	7	8	4	5	6	3	1	2

Sudoku Sheet 8 (Hard)

2	5	1	7	6	4	9	3	8				5	6	9	8	4	3	1	2	7
7	4	9	2	3	8	5	1	6				1	8	2	6	5	7	9	3	4
3	8	6	5	1	9	4	7	2				3	7	4	9	1	2	5	6	8
8	9	2	3	5	7	6	4	1				2	1	6	7	3	4	8	9	5
4	3	5	6	8	1	2	9	7				7	9	5	1	2	8	3	4	6
6	1	7	9	4	2	3	8	5				8	4	3	5	6	9	7	1	2
1	2	4	8	9	6	7	5	3	4	8	9	6	2	1	3	7	5	4	8	9
9	7	3	1	2	5	8	6	4	1	2	5	9	3	7	4	8	6	2	5	1
5	6	8	4	7	3	1	2	9	3	7	6	4	5	8	2	9	1	6	7	3
						9	7	5	6	3	1	8	4	2						
						4	3	1	2	5	8	7	6	9						
						6	8	2	7	9	4	3	1	5						
9	3	4	8	6	2	5	1	7	8	6	3	2	9	4	3	5	6	1	8	7
6	2	1	4	5	7	3	9	8	5	4	2	1	7	6	8	9	4	3	2	5
7	5	8	9	1	3	2	4	6	9	1	7	5	8	3	2	1	7	4	6	9
3	1	5	7	4	8	9	6	2				8	4	9	1	6	5	7	3	2
2	6	7	3	9	5	1	8	4				6	2	7	4	3	9	5	1	8
8	4	9	1	2	6	7	5	3				3	1	5	7	8	2	6	9	4
1	8	2	5	7	4	6	3	9				4	5	1	6	2	8	9	7	3
4	9	6	2	3	1	8	7	5				9	3	8	5	7	1	2	4	6
5	7	3	6	8	9	4	2	1				7	6	2	9	4	3	8	5	1

Maze Puzzle 1 (Square)

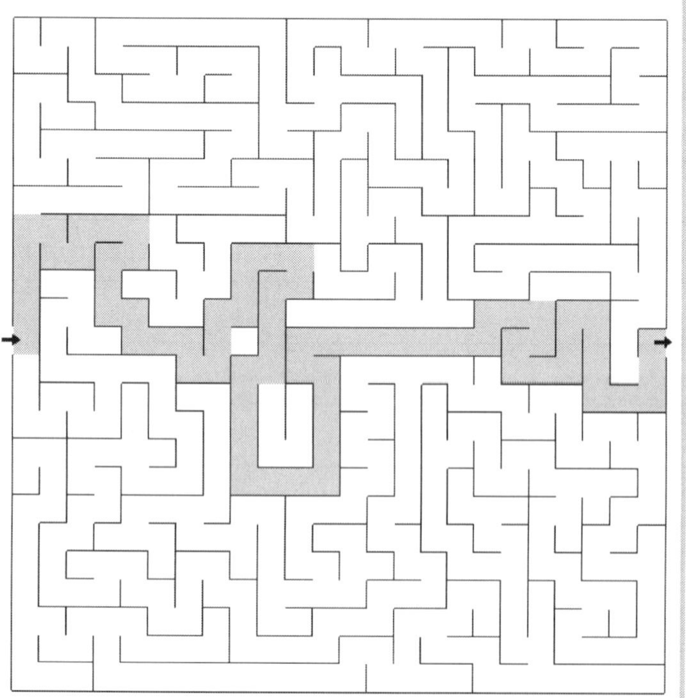

Maze Puzzle 2 (Square)

Maze Puzzle 3
(Spiral)

Maze Puzzle 4
(Spiral)

Maze Puzzle 5
(Diamond)

Maze Puzzle 6
(Diamond)

Maze Puzzle 7 (Medium)

Maze Puzzle 8 (Medium)

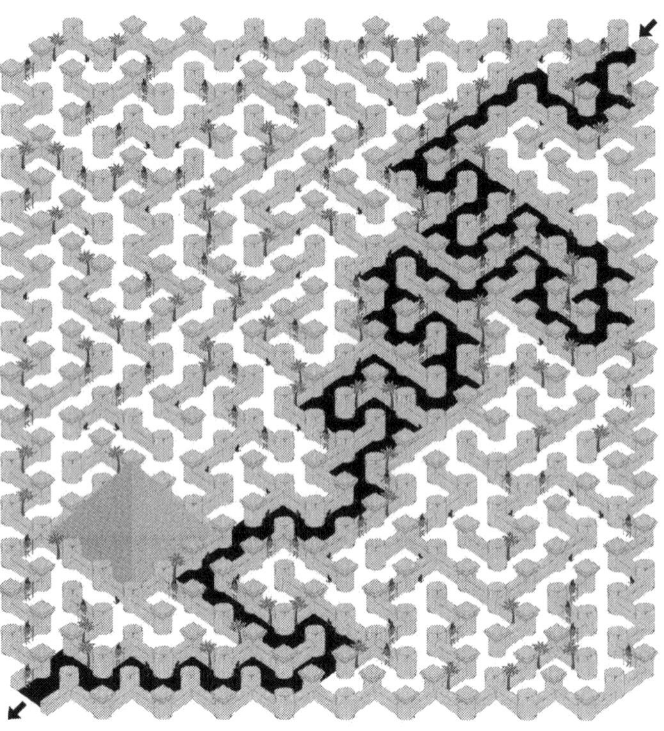

Maze Puzzle 9 (Medium)

Maze Puzzle 10 (Medium)

Maze Puzzle 11
(Medium)

Maze Puzzle 12
(Medium)

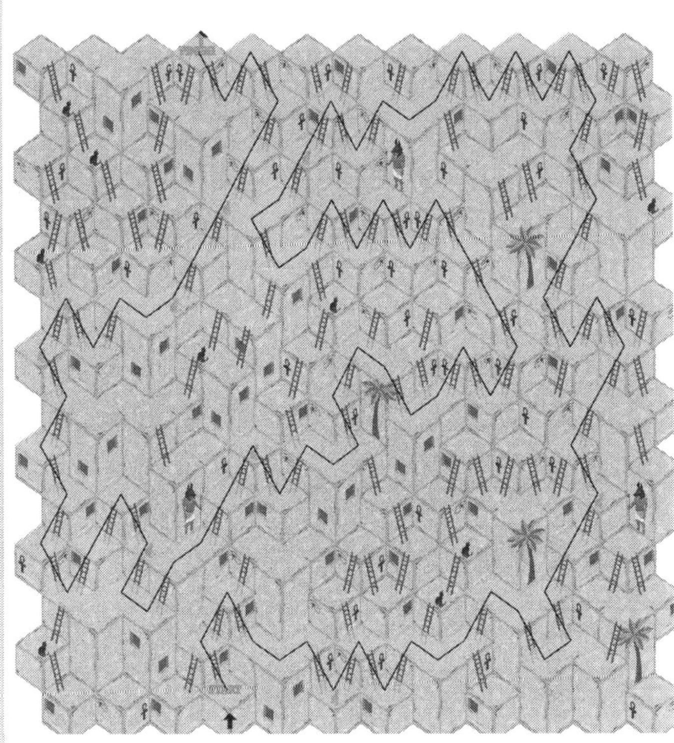

Maze Puzzle 13
(Medium)

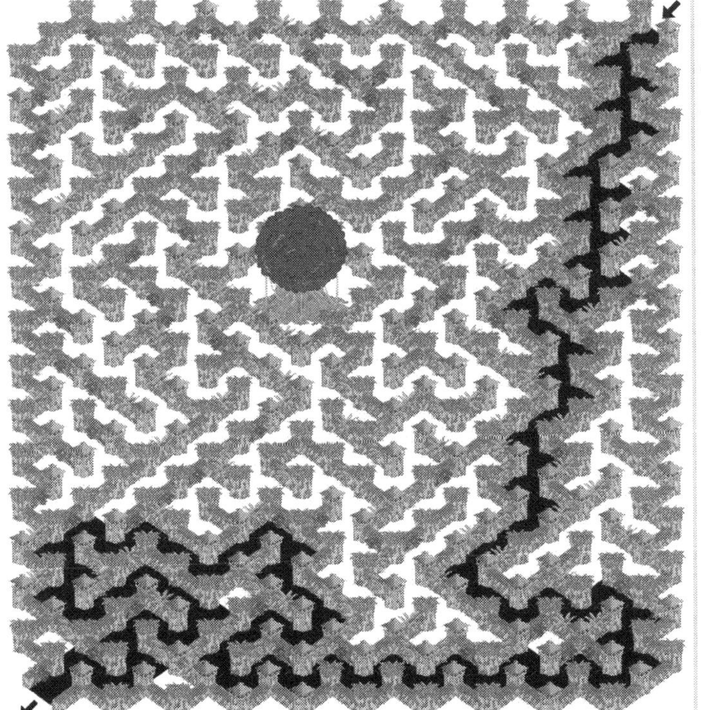

Maze Puzzle 14
(Medium)

Maze Puzzle 15 (Medium)

Maze Puzzle 16 (Hard)

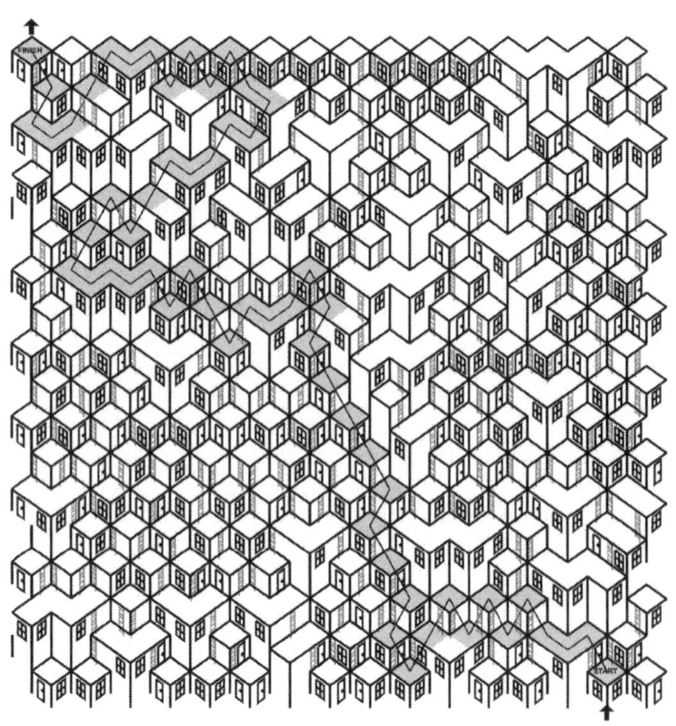

Maze Puzzle 17 (Hard)

Maze Puzzle 18 (Hard)

Maze Puzzle 19 (Hard)

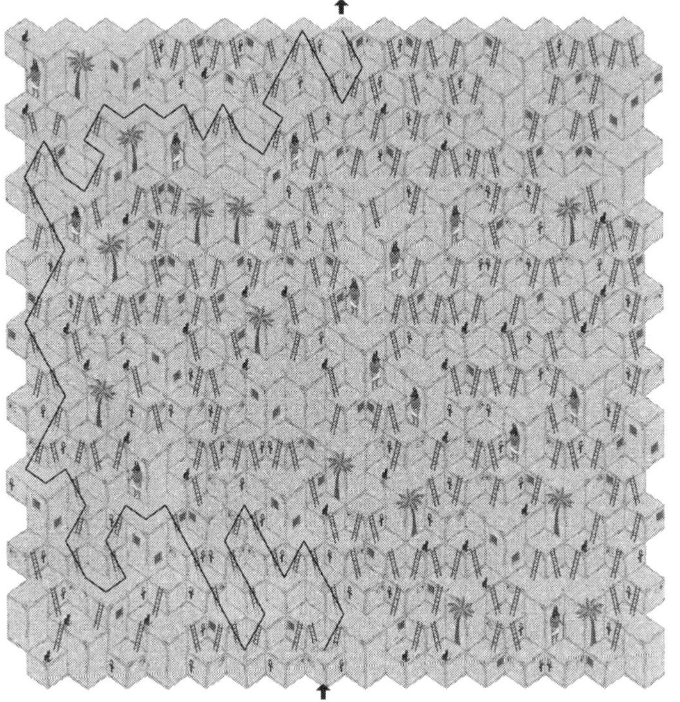

Maze Puzzle 20 (Hard)

We hope you loved the puzzles! If you did, would you consider posting an online review?

This helps us to continue providing great products, and helps potential buyers to make confident decisions.

For more KS2 puzzles, find our similar titles

Printed in Great Britain
by Amazon

62052852R00145